Perfecting Human Actions

Perfecting
Human Actions

ST. THOMAS AQUINAS ON HUMAN
PARTICIPATION IN ETERNAL LAW

John Rziha

THE CATHOLIC UNIVERSITY
OF AMERICA PRESS

Washington, D.C.

LIBRARY OF CONGRESS CATALOGING-IN-PUBLICATION DATA
Rziha, John (John Michael)
Perfecting human actions : St. Thomas Aquinas on human participation in
eternal law / John Rziha.
p. cm.
Includes bibliographical references (p.   ) and index.
ISBN 978-0-8132-1672-0 (pbk. : alk. paper)   1. Thomas, Aquinas, Saint, 1225?–1274.
2. Natural law—Religious aspects—Catholic Church.   3. Christian ethics—
Catholic authors.   4. Participation.   I. Title.
BJ255.T5R95 2009
171'.2092—dc22   2009007307

CONTENTS

ACKNOWLEDGMENTS

I would especially like to thank Dr. Michael Hoonhout for his many helpful comments and criticisms. His expertise on providence in God proved to be exceptionally valuable. I would also like to thank Dr. John Grabowski and Dr. Kevin White of the Catholic University of America for their helpful comments. I am also grateful to Dr. Ed Macierowski of Benedictine College for his many helpful suggestions. His language skills, especially in Latin and Italian, were a great resource.

I am most grateful to my wife who has been a constant source of support and encouragement throughout the writing process. I am also grateful to my six boys who have waited a long time for the day that this project would be completed and I could spend more time playing with them.

Last of all I am thankful to God who has allowed me to participate in a small way in His infinite knowledge of how humans are perfected.

ABBREVIATIONS OF
THOMAS'S WORKS

Compendium Theologiae	CP
De Substantiis Separatis	SS
Expositio libri De Hebdomadibus	DH
Expositio libri Posteriorum Analyticorum	PA
Quaestiones de Quolibet	QQ
Quaestiones disputatae de Anima	QD De Anima
Quaestiones disputatae de Malo	DM
Quaestiones disputatae de Potentia	DP
Quaestiones disputatae de Spiritualibus Creaturis	DSC
Quaestiones disputatae de Veritate	DV
Quaestiones disputatae de Virtutibus	De Virtut
Scriptum super Sententiis	Sent
Sentencia libri De anima	DA
Sententia libri Ethicorum	Ethic
Sententia libri Metaphysicae	Metaph
Sententia libri Physicae	Physic
Summa Contra Gentiles	SCG
Summa Theologiae	ST
Super De divinis nominibus	DN
Super De Trinitate	DT
Super Ioannem	Ioan
Super librum De causis	LC

TRANSLATIONS

Translations of excerpts from the Latin texts of Thomas into English are generally based on the English translations listed in the bibliography. If no English text was available, then the translation was my own. For the sake of a better literal sense, most of the available English translations were altered and these revisions were entirely my own. All translations that neither are from these works nor are my own are specifically referenced in a footnote.

Perfecting Human Actions

Introduction

Roughly 2,400 years ago, Plato raised the dilemma of the relation between morality and God in his work the *Euthyphro*. In this work, Plato questions whether or not actions are pious because they are already pious and on account of this piousness they are loved by the gods or are they pious because the gods' love for them makes them pious.[1] In other words, is there a higher standard beyond the gods that makes actions pious, or do the gods determine whether or not something is pious? If the first option is accepted, then the gods have no necessary relation to morality—for certain acts are moral whether or not the gods agree with them. If the second option is accepted, then morality appears to become arbitrarily determined by the love of the gods. In either case, these options have disastrous effects when applied to the Judeo-Christian God. If the first option is true, then God is not the all-powerful God who is the fullness of truth and hence need not be considered in moral decisions. If the second option is true, then God is arbitrary, and He is free to change the moral rules. Throughout history philosophers and theologians have gone astray because they have attributed one of these two views to God.[2]

---

1. Plato, *Euthyphro*, trans. G. M. A. Grube, in *Five Dialogues* (Indianapolis: Hackett, 2002), 8–13.

2. E.g., William Ockham in his understanding of the absolute power of God ultimately makes all morality arbitrarily legislated by the divine will (See Ockham, *Quodlibetal Question: Volumes 1 and 2, Quadlibets 1–7* [New Haven: Yale University Press, 1998], question 6.1). Many Protestant Reformers and later Enlightenment scholars were influenced by this view of God and freedom. In modern times, Craig Boyd shows how some scholars follow one of the two options suggested by Plato. On the one hand, some scholars believe that in

There is however a third option: God by nature is true and good, and all other things are true and good by participation in God. In this view, God is the source of all moral truth but not an arbitrary source. Through His wisdom, God has created a universe where each creature is fulfilled by performing its own proper action. When God legislates morality, this legislation is in accord with His divine wisdom, and when humans know moral truth, their knowledge participates in divine knowledge. The divine wisdom that orders all creatures to perform their proper actions is called the eternal law. By developing the notion of participation in eternal law, this work is meant to show the proper relation of human actions to God.[3]

The eternal law is the *ratio* of the divine governor directing all humans to act in accord with their end. It is the first exemplary cause of all human actions.[4] For Thomas Aquinas, the relation between creation and

---

a Divine Command theory, God's commands have no conformity to human reason; on the other hand, some scholars in their Natural Law moralities make God completely superfluous. He then explains how a proper understanding of participation solves both of these problems. See "Participation Metaphysics in Aquinas's Theory of Natural Law," *American Catholic Philosophical Quarterly* 79, no. 3 (2005): 431–45.

3. Other scholars have noted the pressing need of a study devoted to the notion of participation in eternal law. For example, Romanus Cessario states, "Due consideration of the *lex aeterna* would contribute much towards easing the repeated controversies, especially since the Enlightenment, over the role that natural law plays in Christian morality." (*The Moral Virtues and Theological Ethics* (South Bend: University of Notre Dame Press, 1991), 51. See also Cessario, *Introduction to Moral Theology* (Washington, D.C.: The Catholic University of America Press, 2001), xx–xxi.) Cessario believes that a variety of understandings of the natural law and its relation to human freedom have emerged in the last century, and that a study of the relation between the natural law and the eternal law would help to clarify the role of the natural law in the moral life (ibid.). See also Craig A. Boyd, "Participation Metaphysics in Aquinas's Theory of Natural Law," *American Catholic Philosophical Quarterly* 79 (2005): 431–45; Boyd argues in this article that any proper understanding of the natural law must take into consideration the reality that the natural law participates in the eternal law since God is the final, formal, and efficient cause of human actions). Another scholar, Martin Rhonheimer notes that in addition to a study of the natural participation of humans in the eternal law by the natural law, moral theology would be significantly enriched by a study of how humans supernaturally participate in the eternal law (i.e., how they participate in the eternal law by participating in the life of Christ through the power of the Holy Spirit); see Martin Rhonheimer, *Natural Law and Practical Reason,* trans. Gerald Malsbary (New York: Fordham University Press, 2000), 65, 226, 546–547.

4. Thomas also refers to God as the efficient and final cause of human actions (cf. *ST* I.105). However, when speaking of God as the first cause of human actions, he primarily focuses on humans participating in the eternal law (the exemplary cause). It is fitting to focus on the exemplary cause for two reasons: First, because although the final cause comes first in the order of the agent, it is the exemplary cause that gives form to things that are made and governed. For example, the exemplary cause determines the species of an action. Hence, to understand human actions, it is fitting to primarily focus on the exemplary cause.

God is that of an effect participating in its cause. In other words, all of creation is caused by God and is what it is because it participates in God. Because human actions are part of creation, they likewise are related to God as an effect participating in its cause, the eternal law. Consequently, in order to have a more perfect knowledge of human actions, the understanding of human participation in the eternal law is essential.

This notion of participation in the eternal law acts as a crucial foundation of moral theology by identifying the relation between the human agent and God within the human act. Because human agents participate in God's wisdom, they remain genuinely responsible for their own actions as the true cause of these actions. Yet at the same time their genuine responsibility does not place them in opposition to God's universal causality, but rather they share in it.[5] This work will show how the Thomistic notion of participation in the eternal law gives a foundation for moral theology where from the beginning our freedom and our actions are ordered to a particular end fittingly established by divine wisdom. By performing actions in accord with this end, humans are perfected.

In order to show how an understanding of Thomas's notion of participation provides a key insight into his moral theology, the first chapter will trace the recovery of the notion of participation by philosophers within the last century. A brief analysis of the work of Cornelio Fabro, L. B. Geiger, John Wippel, and Rudi Te Velde will show how the notion of participation is at the heart of Thomistic metaphysics insofar as it explains the relation between all creation and its Creator.

The second chapter seeks to specifically explain Thomas's notion of participation in the eternal law. It begins by looking at Thomas's theological understanding of the notion of participation. It shows how all creatures participate in God who is the efficient, exemplary, and final

---

Second, because an understanding of the exemplary cause includes an understanding of the other two types of causality. The exemplary cause orders the movements of things (efficiently caused) to their end (final cause). Hence, the concept of eternal law always includes an understanding of God as the end of creation and God as divine mover.

5. The notion of participation in eternal law acts as a foundation for moral theology in opposition to the notions of autonomy and deistic deontology upon which many contemporaries base their moral systems. In contrast to an autonomy that emphasizes the "free" causality of the human subject but at the expense of separating the individual from divine causality and guidance, the Thomistic notion of participation allows the individual to be a true cause of his or her actions by sharing in divine causality and guidance. In contrast to a deistic deontology where God gives the law but does not intervene in creation, the notion of participation emphasizes God's perpetual role in wisely moving and guiding humans to actions in accord with their proper end.

cause of their being and actions. After showing how the first act of the creature (the act of being) participates in God, this chapter shows how the second act of the creature (operation) participates in God. In reference to this second act, the creature participates in God's governing wisdom: the eternal law. All creatures, including humans, participate in the eternal law as moved and governed by it, but humans also participate in the eternal law in a special way: cognitively, as having a limited but genuine knowledge of it. This chapter explains this distinction between participation in the eternal law as being moved and governed by it and cognitive participation. By showing how these two types of participation fit into Thomas's theology of participation as a whole, this section of chapter two sets the foundation for chapters three and four, which will explain each type in detail.

The second part of chapter two seeks to explain what Thomas means by the eternal law and how it is related to all other aspects of his moral teaching. A brief analysis of the *Prima Secundae* of the *Summa Theologiae* shows that the eternal law orders humans to their ultimate end of happiness by causing them to perform actions in accord with this end. The eternal law directs humans to these actions by means of the natural and divine law (especially the new law of grace which is the primary element of the divine law). Both of these laws receive their content and authority from the eternal law and are determined to a particular society by human law. These laws cause humans to perform good actions which when repeated become the acquired virtues. Furthermore, the new law of grace causes the infused virtues within humans. These virtues then dispose humans to perform actions in accord with the end to which they are ordered by the eternal law.

The third chapter explains how humans participate in the eternal law as moved and governed by it. The eternal law moves and governs humans by means of their natural inclinations to their proper end. These inclinations are perfected by the acquired virtues, the infused virtues, and the gifts of the Holy Spirit. Hence, by means of the virtues and gifts humans are more perfectly moved and governed by the eternal law.

The fourth chapter explains how humans participate in the eternal law cognitively. Humans are able to participate in the divine intellect as sharing in God's knowledge through the natural light of the intellect and the infused light of grace. In reference to the eternal law, humans have a certain knowledge of the eternal law through natural reason and grace. This participation is increased by the acquired intellectual virtues, the infused intellectual virtues, and the gifts of the Holy Spirit that perfect the intellect. Through these virtues and gifts humans know more perfectly which acts are in accord with the eternal law and therefore their ultimate end.

The fifth chapter seeks to incorporate a few of the insights gleaned from the recovery of the notion of participation in the eternal law and apply them to contemporary misunderstandings of moral theory. This chapter shows how the notion of participation in the eternal law is a better foundation for a moral system than one that depends upon the contemporary notion of autonomy. This chapter also shows how the eternal law should guide humans in the political arena and how an understanding of human participation in the eternal law unites all of the various aspects of morality into one comprehensive system.

The goal of this work is to show how the Thomistic notion of participation in eternal law acts as a foundation for moral theology allowing the moral theologian to place the notions of happiness, law, and virtue in their proper context in the relation between the moral agent and God. God is the source and end of the moral life and a full understanding of happiness, law, and virtue cannot be obtained without understanding how the moral agent participates in eternal law. Furthermore, this work is meant to help moral theologians have a greater understanding of the theological vision of Thomas Aquinas so that they more perfectly understand the actual texts of Thomas. Thomas's moral thought cannot be separated from his metaphysics, his theology of God, and his anthropology. The notion of participation in eternal law in some way touches on all of these subjects, helping the moral theologian to have a more complete understanding of what Thomas presumed and intended in his theology of the human moral agent.

CHAPTER I

The Recovery of the
Notion of Participation

IN THE MIDDLE OF THE nineteenth century Catholic scholars began to look to the theology of the Scholastics, and in particular Aquinas, in order to defend the faith. These scholars believed that Scholastic philosophy was better equipped than the modern philosophical systems (e.g. Kantian idealism) to expound and defend the faith in the post-Enlightenment milieu.[1] This movement began a revival in Thomistic thought, which, although primarily composed of philosophers in its beginning, eventually also included theologians.[2] These scholars recovered many Thomistic insights that had been lost or neglected over the centuries.

Perhaps the area of Thomistic thought that most benefited from this revival was that of metaphysics.[3] John Wippel notes that in the late nineteenth and early twentieth centuries, various scholars offered different suggestions as to what they believed was the most important aspect in

---

1. Romanus Cessario, *A Short History of Thomism* (Washington, D.C.: The Catholic University of America Press, 2005), 86–87. See also Gerard McCool, *Neo-Thomists* (Milwaukee: Marquette University Press, 1994), 31–32.

2. Examples of philosophers within this revival are Josef Kleutgen, Cornelio Fabro, and Etienne Gilson. Examples of theologians are Garrigou-Lagrange, M. D. Chenu, and Yves Congar.

3. Some of the more famous Thomistic metaphysicians in this time period were Désiré-Joseph Cardinal Mercier, Cornelio Fabro, Etienne Gilson, Jacques Maritain, and Yves Simon.

Thomistic metaphysics.[4] Each of these scholars analyzed important metaphysical concepts such as the real distinction between essence and existence, the metaphysics of act and potency, and the primacy of the act of existing. To these important concepts Cornelio Fabro and L. B. Geiger during the late 1930s and early 1940s added another important aspect: the notion of participation.[5] In highlighting the indispensable role of participation in Thomistic metaphysics, Fabro stressed, in opposition to most other Thomists of the time, the Neoplatonic influence on Thomistic thought. In other words, Thomas's metaphysics was not simply built upon the insights of Aristotle, but it was also built upon the Neoplatonic thought of Proclus, Augustine, and Pseudo-Dionysius.[6] These studies by Fabro and Geiger deeply enriched later Thomistic scholarship in metaphysics by showing how the Neoplatonic notion of participation further advances the insights of Aristotle in explaining the real distinction between essence and existence, the limitation of act by potency, and the primacy of the act of being.[7]

To provide a solid foundation for the theological notion of participation in eternal law which will be examined later, in this chapter I will introduce and examine the thought of a few of the major scholars who helped retrieve the Thomistic philosophical notion of participation. I will begin with Fabro and Geiger, who initiated the retrieval, and then I will treat two recent works of Rudi Te Velde and John Wippel as examples of the continuing philosophical scholarship on participation. I will examine each author's basic explanation of participation, and then I will show how

---

4. John Wippel, "Thomas Aquinas and Participation," in *Studies in Medieval Philosophy*, 117–58, ed. John Wippel (Washington, D.C.: The Catholic University of America Press, 1987), 117.

5. Ibid., 117. See Cornelio Fabro, *La nozione metafisica di partecipazione secondo S. Tommaso d'Aquino* (Milan: Vita e Pensiero, 1939), and L. B. Geiger, *La Participation dans la philosphie de s. Thomas d'Aquin* (Paris: Librairie Philosophique J. Vrin, 1952).

6. See W. J. Hankey, "Dionysian Hierarchy in Thomas Aquinas: Tradition and Transformation," in *Denys l'Aréopagite et sa postérité en Orient et en Occident, Actes du Colloque International Paris, 21–24 Septembre 1994* (Paris: Institut d'Études Augustiniennes, 1997), 405–38.

7. For a greater explanation of the real distinction between act and existence by means of the notion of participation, see Rudi Te Velde, *Participation and Substantiality in Thomas Aquinas* (New York: Brill, 1995), 66–87. For the use of the notion of participation in elucidating act and potency, see W. Norris Clarke, "The Limitation of Act by Potency: Aristotelianism or Neo-Platonism," *The New Scholasticism* 26 (1952): 167–94. For an example of how the notion of participation illuminates the concept of being as the primary act, see Fabro, "The Intensive Hermeneutics of Thomistic Philosophy: The Notion of Participation," *Review of Metaphysics* 27 (1974): 449–87.

his recovery of the notion of participation has contributed to a greater understanding of metaphysics and related issues in Thomas.

CORNELIO FABRO

In an article published in 1974, Cornelio Fabro summarized his forty years of extensive study on the topic of participation.[8] He notes that what led him to this groundbreaking interpretation of Thomas was the debate in the first decades of the twentieth century over the principle of causality. Fabro sought to find a new way of understanding causality in Thomas that was both in opposition to those who thought the principle of causality could be directly reduced to the principle of noncontradiction and also in opposition to others who took an openly Kantian view of this principle.[9] In seeking a new explanation of causality by looking at the relation between creatures and God, Fabro realized that Thomas had placed the Platonic notion of participation at the very foundation of the Aristotelian couplet of act and potency (449–50).[10] This discovery allowed Fabro to argue that *ens* and its emerging act *esse* were based on the notion of participation,[11] which Fabro explains in his first book, *La nozione metafisica di partecipazione secondo S. Tommaso d' Aquino.*[12]

8. "The Intensive Hermeneutics of Thomistic Philosophy: The Notion of Participation," *Review of Metaphysics* 27 (1974): 449–87. Page numbers of references from this article will be given in parentheses in the text. This article functions as a very dense summary of Fabro's first book, *La nozione metafisica di partecipazione secondo S. Tommaso d'Aquino* (Milan: Vita e Pensiero, 1939).

9. Fabro explains that his initial research on participation came in response to the theme of a contest held by the Pontifical Academy of St. Thomas in 1934. The theme was "The principle of causality: its psychological origin, its philosophical formulation, and its necessary and universal value" (450).

10. Fabro realized that Thomas had used the notion of participation to found such concepts as the dependence of creation on divine motion, the composition in creatures of *esse* and essence, and the analogy between creation and God.

11. *Ens* (often translated as being) is the composite of *essence* and *esse*. *Esse* is also usually translated as "being" but can be translated as "existence" as well. Fabro does not refer to *esse* as existence because he feels that "to be" is much more than to "exist." See Fabro, "The Transcendentality of *Ens-Esse* and the Ground to Metaphysics," *International Philosophical Quarterly* 6 (1966): 389–427, and "Platonism, Neo-Platonism, and Thomism: Convergences and Divergences," *New Scholasticism* 44 (1970): 87.

12. Originally published in Milan: Vita e Pensiero, 1939. I had access to the third edition (Torino: Società Editrice Internazionale, 1963). In this book Fabro sought to give the historical background to the Thomistic notion of participation, beginning with Plato, extending through Aristotle, the Neoplatonists, and Christian sources that were influenced by Neoplatonism (Part 1). Then Fabro treats the Thomistic notion of participation and argues that there are two types of participation in Thomas: predicamental participation and tran-

Fabro states that the term *participation* in Latin literally means to "take part" *(partem capere)* or to "have part" *(partem habere)*. He then quotes Thomas: "To participate is like taking a part; thus when something receives a part of what belongs to another fully, it is said to participate in it."[13] For example, water is not hot by nature (it can be cold), but is only hot by receiving heat from something that is hot by nature (e.g., fire). The water is hot by participation. Fabro further explains that the act of participating can be looked at either from the perspective of the one participating or from the perspective of that in which one participates. In the former case, the one participating can be said to share or take part in something. In the latter case, that in which one participates is said to give and communicate something. For example, God gives his being, goodness, and truth to creatures that are said to participate in His being, goodness, and truth (453).

Fabro notes that most of the Thomistic metaphysical tradition primarily focused on the Aristotelian roots of Thomistic philosophy in response to the anti-Thomists who denied the legitimate use of Aristotle within Christian thought (451–52). Yet Fabro realized that there was no simple way to categorize Thomas's thought since he had thoroughly synthesized the best elements of many different traditions.[14] Consequently, in order to make his pioneering claim that the notion of participation was at the heart of Thomistic metaphysics, Fabro historically traced the notion of participation from Plato to Thomas (454–62).[15]

Fabro notes that Plato introduced the notion of participation into philosophy in order to explain the relation between sensible things (the many) and the Idea (the One) (454–56). Plato believed that sensible things participate in separate Ideas (or forms). For example, something can be called a circle only to the extent that it participates in the form of circularity. However, Aristotle rejects Plato's theory of separated forms and in doing so removes the possibility of participation in these separated

---

scendental participation (Part 2). In Part 3 Fabro notes some implications of predicamental participation and concludes by showing that Thomas's metaphysics is not strictly Aristotelian, but a synthesis of Platonic and Aristotelian thought.

13. *DH* I.2. As cited in Fabro, "Intensive Hermeneutics," 454.

14. E.g., Fabro notes that Thomas credits Plato, Aristotle, Augustine, the author of *De Causis*, Boethius, and Avicenna all with the view that possible being requires *necesse esse,* and God alone is per se *necesse esse;* see *La nozione metafisica di partecipazione secondo S. Tommaso d'Aquino,* 120–21.

15. *La nozione metafisica* . . . treats the notion of participation of Plato (46–53), Aristotle (54–74), Augustine (79–85), Pseudo-Dionysius (86–97), Boethius (98–106), the author of *De Causis* (107–112), and Avicenna (113–17).

forms.[16] In response to the Platonic explanation of participation in transcendent forms, Aristotle counters that forms inhere in matter and that individual beings possess in themselves the principles of their being and action (457).[17] At this point, Fabro notes that Greek thought was at an impasse where Platonic participation was contrasted to the immanence of forms in matter in Aristotle (457). It was the Neoplatonists who broke the impasse in their effort to reconcile Plato and Aristotle by clarifying the notion of participation by means of the Aristotelian notion of causality (457). For example, Plotinus sought to overcome the difficulty of the lack of causality in the Ideas through his doctrine of participation by means of emanation (459).[18] St. Thomas received this Neoplatonic view of participation through the writings of Augustine, Boethius, Dionysius, Proclus, and others (461–63).

Thomas develops his own original notion of participation based on the notion of *esse* as *actus essendi*. He does this by taking the general definition of participation, which is sharing in or taking part *(partem capere)* in something in a partial manner that belongs to another fully (453) and placing it within an Aristotelian framework that emphasizes that act is a perfection. For example, humans are perfected by the act of *esse* that takes part in the *esse* of God. Yet even here Thomas goes beyond Aristotle by seeing potency as the capacity to receive perfection and seeing act as the perfection of *esse* (462–64). Thus, in Thomistic thought, participation is a sharing in the essential act of another, which is limited by the potency of the participating subject. For example, God is the act of *esse* by nature, but humans have *esse* by sharing in God's *esse*. The degree to which humans participate in divine being is limited by the potency of the human nature, so that humans only share in divine *esse* in the mode suitable to humans (not as angels, etc.). Fabro calls this first or primary act of a substance (i.e., that of *esse*) "the immanent act of the substance

16. Cf. M. Annice, CSC, "A Historical Sketch of the Theory of Participation," *New Scholasticism* 26 (1952): 54.

17. Although Aristotle rejects Plato's use of participation, Fabro argues that traces of the doctrine of participation can still be found in Aristotle when he discusses the logical relation of individuals to a species and a species to a genus. He states that from this Aristotelian idea will come the Thomistic notion of predicamental participation (456).

18. See W. Norris Clarke, "The Meaning of Participation in St. Thomas," *Proceedings of the American Catholic Philosophical Association* 26 (1952): 149. Clark explains that Plotinus perfected the notion of participation by his theory of emanation. In this perfected theory, perfections are limited by the reception of the participant. For example, God is essentially good and thus unlimited goodness. However, the goodness of all other things is limited by the mode of their reception of the goodness of God.

or *esse substantiale*" (in contrast to the secondary acts of a substance: its operations).[19]

Thomas took the Platonic notion of participation and merged it with the Aristotelian notion of act and potency in order to show the dependence of the creature on the Creator, while still safeguarding the transcendence of God. In other words, creatures are in potency to a divine perfection, and through their actions they are able to share in an essential perfection of God without that perfection being part of the essence of the creature. The degree to which the creature participates in the act is limited by the particular capacity of the participant. For example, all creatures have *esse* not by their nature, but by participation in the *esse* of God. The manner in which something "is" (its *actus essendi*) is determined by the particular essence of a creature, which only has the capacity "to be" in a certain limited mode (unlike God who is the full perfection of being). Fabro emphasizes that the Thomistic notion of participation takes from Platonism the ideas "of exemplar relationship and absolute distinction between participating being and *Esse Subsistens,* and from Aristotelianism the principle of real composition and real causality at every level of participated, finite being" (469).

Within this Thomistic framework of participation, Fabro recognizes that there are two main types of participation: transcendental and predicamental. Transcendental participation refers to participation in *esse* and the pure perfections that are grounded in it (e.g., goodness and truth). In this type of participation, that which is participated in (e.g., goodness) exists apart from the participating subjects, which only have a likeness of the participated perfection. For example, the divine goodness transcends the goodness found in all creatures that are good by participation in it.

---

19. Fabro refers to *QQ* XII.5.5. In this article Thomas argues that everything that is in potency is rendered in act by means of participation in a superior act. Hence, every form is completed (caused to perform its act of being) by participation in the *esse* of the first and pure act (God). Thomas calls this initial act of the substance participating in the *esse* of God the *esse substantiale.* This "*esse substantiale* of a thing is not an accident, but the actuality of any existing form" (esse substantiale rei non est accidens, sed actualitas cuiuslibet formae existentis . . .). Thus, Thomas notes that although properly speaking *esse* is not an accident, nonetheless, when accident is taken in the broad sense meaning all that is not part of the essence, *esse* can be called an accident since in God alone "is *esse* His essence" (esse est eius essentia) (468).

Helen John James notes that the term "immanent act" which Fabro uses here refers to the immanent forms of Aristotle, the indwelling forms by which individual beings possess in themselves the principles of their being and action. See *The Thomist Spectrum* (New York: Fordham University Press, 1966), 102.

Predicamental participation refers to participation where the characteristics participated in do not exist apart from the participating subjects, so all participate univocally in the characteristic. Examples of this type of participation are that of an individual in a species, a species in a genus, matter in form, and a substance in accidents (471–74).[20]

The importance of Fabro's recovery of participation for understanding Thomas's writings can hardly be overestimated. Fabro draws out many implications of the notion of participation. I will mention four that are centered on the relation between creatures and their Creator.

The first implication is that Thomistic participation shows the total dependence of creation on God for all of its perfections, including its first perfection: its act of being. God alone is subsisting *esse,* and every other substance participates in *esse.* Now every substance that participates in a perfection is related to that which is participated in as potency to act. Hence, all created substances are in potency to their act of *esse* that they receive by participation in God who is essentially *esse.* Fabro states, "God as *Esse per essentiam* is the principle and actuating cause of *esse per participationem,* which is the proper actuating of every real essence" (484). In other words, all substances come to be and continue to remain in existence by participation in God (474).

Furthermore, there is a multiplicity of degrees of participation in the being of God corresponding to the multiplicity of natural forms within creation. This multiplicity is caused by God's wisdom. In other words, not only do things exist by sharing in God's *esse,* but their particular mode of being is wisely determined by God who orders the entire universe. The greater the mode of participation, the closer the essence is to God, resulting in a hierarchy of being within the universe. Thus, the exemplary causality of God is also elucidated by the notion of participation because the mode of something's *esse* is dependent upon the degree of participation it has in God's *esse* (476).

Consequently, the Thomistic notion of participation solves the problem in Plato's *Parmenides* that if many things exist, they must be both similar and dissimilar, one and many, at rest and in motion. Creatures are one in that they all share in being. However, they are many in that their

---

20. Fabro uses an extraordinary diversity of texts throughout the Thomistic corpus to support his distinction. Some of those cited include: In support of transcendental participation: *ST* I.45.4.3; 61.1; 104.1; *DV* XXI.5.6; *Ethic* X.1.2 (2110). In support of predicamental participation: *QQ* II.2.3; II.3.6; *Metaph* X.4 (1055 b 25); *DH* I.2, n. 24; *SCG* I.32; *ST* I.45.5.1.

forms have a variety of different potencies to their act of being. Hence all participate in being in different degrees causing a diversity of acts of being (482, 484).

The second implication of Fabro's work is that Thomistic participation affirms the real distinction between essence and the act of being *(esse)*. Fabro notes that in Thomas's early writings this distinction is dependent upon Avicenna's metaphysics, but in Thomas's more mature works "this distinction is a result of a better understanding of the primacy of act through the notion of participation" (467). Fabro argues that since God alone is *esse* by His essence, "all creatures are beings by participation, inasmuch as their essence participates in the *esse* which is the ultimate act of all reality; hence the essence of creatures is related to *esse* as potency to act" (467). In other words, a real distinction must exist between essence and *esse* in creatures because something can have *esse* either by essence or by participation. Since God alone is *esse* by His essence, all creatures must have *esse* by participation.[21] Because in transcendental participation what is held by participation is distinct from that which is by essence, in all creatures there is a real distinction between essence and *esse*.

Fabro notes that a consequence of this distinction is that Thomas can affirm (in opposition to the Augustinians) that the soul and created intelligences (angels), although simple in essence, are still composite beings of essence and *esse* and not simple beings like God. Hence, angels, although subsisting intelligences, are still dependent upon God for their creation and conservation (467).

A third implication of Fabro's work is that "participation provides the formula for the analogy between creatures and God" (468). Fabro quotes Thomas to make this point: "Creatures resemble God not by sharing a form of the same specific or generic type, but only analogically, inasmuch as God is being by His very essence, and other things [are only beings] by participation."[22] In other words, the notion of participation allows us to say that all created things are like God analogously because creatures are not of the same species or genus as God, but are only like God by participation. Participation allows for an analogical likeness, but excludes a univocal sameness because perfections are limited, composite,

---

21. If a creature's essence was its *esse*, it would be the cause of its own existence, which is impossible.

22. Fabro quotes *ST* I, 4.3.3. See also *La nozione metafisica*, 189.

and many in creatures but unlimited, simple, and unique in God (484).

The final implication that Fabro notes is that Thomas uses the notion of participation not only to explain the first act of a creature—substantial *esse*—but also to explain further acts that are superadded to this first act. Fabro explains that being embraces every aspect of everything.[23] He continues by noting that something has *esse* either substantially or relatively.[24] Substantial *esse* refers to the first act of the essence. It refers to all those participated perfections that a creature has naturally to the extent that its natural form participates in *esse*. However, in addition to these substantial perfections that something has to the extent it has *esse,* a creature has additional superadded perfections that it also has by participation (e.g., humans have wisdom or love). These additional perfections do not change a creature's mode of being substantially but only relatively (humans both with and without love are still both humans). In other words, the species of a creature does not change, but it does possess superadded acts that perfect its mode of being (the mode of being of the human that loves is more perfect).[25]

Fabro explains that every act that a creature has is added to its fundamental act of *esse,* and hence causes a distinct participation in God. The mode of the creature's participation changes because these superadded acts participate in the *esse* of God through the *esse* of the creature, to which they are united (the mode of being for someone who loves is that of a loving human).[26] Consequently, Fabro is able to speak of the participation of all human perfections in God. He specifically analyzes the participation of the intellect in God's knowledge and the supernatural participation of humans in God's nature by grace (478–81).[27]

As these four examples demonstrate, Fabro's recovery of participation shows how Thomas was able to transform Aristotelian metaphysics in light of the doctrine of creation by means of the Neoplatonic notion

23. "The Transcendentality of *Ens-Esse* and the Ground of Metaphysics," 409.

24. Fabro is referring to *DV* 21.5; *ST* I.5.1.1.

25. Ibid., 422.

26. See George Lindbeck, "Participation and Existence in the Interpretation of St. Thomas Aquinas," *Franciscan Studies* 17 (1957): 15, where he argues that only whole substances exist by their act of existence, and accidents exist only in a substance. He later refers to *DV* 2.3.16 to show that the more a creature approaches God [i.e., the greater its mode of participation], the more it has of *esse,* and the more it recedes, the more it has of non-*esse* [i.e., the more it lacks *esse*] (115).

27. See esp. *La nozione metafisica,* 299–314, where the highest mode of supernatural participation in God is the participation of Christ.

of participation. This recovery has significantly helped scholars to properly understand Thomas's metaphysics. In making this recovery, Fabro rightly avoids exaggerated claims about how the notion of participation is the key to all Thomistic metaphysics, while at the same time showing that it is a very important element of his thought. Thus, Fabro emphasizes that it is the combination of act/potency with *participatum/participans* that founds the new Thomistic notion of *esse,* which is the heart of Thomistic metaphysics (469–70), and this same combination allows us to understand how all moral acts participate in eternal law.

L. B. GEIGER

Shortly after Fabro's seminal work on participation was published, L. B. Geiger published his study *La Participation dans la philosophie de s. Thomas d'Aquin.*[28] Unlike Fabro's historical study, Geiger sought to define Thomas's notion of participation primarily by looking within the texts of the Thomistic corpus. He felt that the notion of participation was a key element in many Thomistic teachings such as certain proofs of God as perfect, good, one, and simple; the thesis on divine exemplarity; and the analogy between creatures and God. Geiger concluded that participation is the essential element of "all that ought to found and enrich our knowledge of God."[29] Thus, he believed that a proper understanding of the notion of participation is essential in order to comprehend Thomas's understanding of creation, God, and theological predication, since God is by essence what creatures are by participation (16).

Geiger claimed that because most scholars of his time were confused as to the meaning of the terms related to participation and because the notion of participation incorporates several diverse philosophical traditions, a misunderstanding of this Thomistic notion was common. Hence, many scholars missed key elements of Thomistic thought (19). In response to this phenomenon, Geiger sought to study the texts for a precise definition of the terms (26). Based on his research, Geiger believed that there are two different "systems" of participation in Thomas's works and

---

28. Louis Geiger, *La Participation dans la philosphie de s. Thomas d'Aquin* (Paris: Librairie Philosophique J. Vrin, 1952). Page references to this work will be in the text. Although Geiger was able to incorporate Fabro's *La nozione metafisica di partecipazione secondo S. Tommaso d' Aquino* in the footnotes, Geiger notes that his own work was already substantially finished before he had access to Fabro's work (8).

29. ". . . tout ce qui doit fonder et enricher notre connaissance de Dieu" (15).

that although Thomas does not specifically define them, Thomas knew
of both systems and used them in the appropriate circumstances (26).
Geiger defined the two systems as participation by composition and participation by similitude or formal hierarchy.[30] Geiger then spends the rest
of the book explaining these two systems and how each system applies to
the different ways Thomas uses the notion of participation.

Participation by composition refers to cases in which something is a
composition of two different elements where the first element (the subject) receives in a limited manner the second element. For example, when
a human participates by composition in the wisdom of God, it receives
this wisdom and possesses it in a limited manner in accordance with its
mode: human nature (27). The key emphasis in this type of participation
is that the subject's form *limits* the amount of a perfection it can *receive*
(27). Geiger gives the examples of matter participating in form and substance participating in an accident (49). When this notion of participation
is applied to the participation of essence in *esse,* the degree of *esse* a being
receives from God is limited by the essence, which can only exist in a
particular mode.[31] The key difference between this type of participation
and that of similitude is that in this mode limitation is a consequence of
composition. Geiger believes that St. Thomas attributes this form of participation to Plato and his followers (299).

In participation by similitude or formal hierarchy, rather than having
a subject that receives something superadded, the subject itself is limited
by the participation. In this case participation explains the diminished
and particular state of an essence in reference to the absolute plenitude
of God (29). The key point is that to participate in this manner means
to limit something, causing a hierarchy of beings based on how similar
they are to the First Cause. Geiger believes that this type of participation
is prior to participation by composition (394). Thus, when this system of
participation is applied to being, the essence itself is limited by participation, and because of this limitation it exists in its particular mode.[32] Unlike participation by composition where the created essence determines

30. Geiger finds support for his theory of these two types of participation in *DH* 3; *SS*
8; *ST* I.12.11.2; 27.2.3; 49.3; and *DP* 7.7.2.

31. As will be seen, Geiger does not believe participation by composition is the primary
type of participation of essence in *esse.*

32. Geiger does believe participation of similitude is the primary type of participation
of essence in *esse.*

the mode of participation, in participation by similitude the participation determines the mode of the essence.

Whereas Geiger believes that Thomas took the idea of participation by composition from the Platonists, the notion of participation by similitude is a result of Thomas's ingenious use of Aristotle. Geiger states that in the *Commentary on Boethius's "De Hebdomadibus"* Thomas solves the dilemma of whether goodness is attributed to something essentially or accidentally by introducing a new type of participation: participation by similitude. Geiger notes that Thomas says that a predicate can be attributed to a subject in two manners: either substantially or by participation.[33] Thomas goes on to state that in cases of matter and form and substance and accident, the forms and accidents that are participated in are apart from *(praeter)* the participating matter and subject. However, in the case of a species participating in a genus, Geiger notes that Thomas follows Aristotle and says that the genus does not exist apart from the species that participates in it. In this second type of participation the genus is predicated substantially of the species even though it is predicated by participation (40–46). Geiger then concludes that Thomas takes this form of participation and applies it to the participation of a created being in goodness. This allows Thomas to say that something is substantially good by participation in the goodness of God (47). Geiger believes Thomas came up with participation by similitude by applying the concept of this second type of participation to a creature's participation in the goodness of God.

Geiger also believes that Thomas applied participation by similitude to the creature's participation in *esse*. In participation by similitude, the act of participation causes the mode of the essence; hence Geiger concludes that it is by participation in the *esse* of God that all things receive their substantial predicates. Geiger argues that Thomas must have had participation by similitude in mind when speaking of participation in *esse* (rather than participation by composition), because when God produces a creature, the creature cannot receive *esse* before it exists because it is caused by receiving *esse* (52).

Although Geiger notes that Thomas uses both types of participation, he believes that Thomas considers participation by similitude to be the more fundamental of the two. Geiger argues that the composition of es-

33. *DH* 3.

sence and existence can only explain the internal structure of being, not its production or relation to the First Cause. Hence, although Geiger admits that participation of composition is present in already existing beings, prior to this form of participation is participation by similitude, which causes created existence as a participated likeness to the First and Perfect Being (396).

Although some scholars believe that Geiger's application of participation by similitude to Thomas's writings is somewhat problematic and forced upon the text,[34] there are points that can be gleaned from Geiger that show the importance of the notion of participation for Thomistic thought. However, in order to avoid duplication of the important points made by Fabro,[35] I will only focus on one point: Geiger's emphasis on the relation between the divine Perfection and the diversity in creation based on participation. Geiger notes that God in His simplicity is all possible perfection; hence Thomas is able to say that God contains within Himself the perfections of His creatures in an absolute mode.[36] Perfections that exist in creatures in a limited and dispersed way are found in God in an infinite degree (223–24). The essential perfections we distinguish in God are diffused to creatures by means of participation. The creature realizes a similitude of the *"Perfection Première,"* which is the nature or essence of the creature in its own particular mode of existence

34. E.g., several scholars have noted that Geiger's stress on the importance of participation by similitude results in the denial of the real distinction between essence and *esse* in creatures. Among these scholars are Helen John James, *The Thomist Spectrum* (New York: Fordham University Press, 1966), 116–17, and Fabro, *Participation et causalité* (Louvain: Universitaries De Louvain, 1961), 63–73. Fabro elsewhere notes that Geiger breaks the Thomistic synthesis of act/potency and *participatum/participans,* thus removing the emergence of the new Thomistic concept of *esse;* see "The Intensive Hermeneutics of Thomistic Philosophy: The Notion of Participation," 469. I agree with these scholars that Geiger is incorrect in the way that he makes this distinction between the two types of participation. Geiger makes this mistake because he fails to properly apply the principles of primary and secondary causality to the act of being. A primary cause produces an effect by working through a secondary cause, which is also a true cause of the effect. God is the primary cause of a creature's act of being, but the creature's essence is a true secondary cause of this action. Hence, there is no contradiction in saying that God creates a creature by causing a particular mode of participation in Divine Being (see *ST* I.44) and saying that the creature's essence causes a particular mode of being. See *LC* 25 and Te Velde, 217.

35. E.g., Fabro and Geiger both see the importance of the notion of participation to explain analogical knowledge of God and the dependence of creation upon the Creator. A difference is that Geiger believes that the role of composition of essence/*esse* is minimal in Thomas, while Fabro considers it to be very important. See Geiger, *La Participation . . . ,* 395–96.

36. Geiger refers to I *Sent* 43.1.2.1.

(226–29). Hence, by means of varying degrees of participation in the divine perfection, God has created a hierarchically ordered universe, where certain creatures are more perfect than other creatures.

Geiger stresses that the metaphor of God as an artist creating a beautiful work is not sufficient by itself to explain the "likeness of nature between the artisan and its work."[37] Therefore, by means of the notion of participation, the likeness of creation to its Creator can be affirmed (as a true sharing in the perfections of God) without neglecting the transcendence of God who is perfection by His essence rather than having perfections by participation.[38]

Apart from whether or not Geiger's two distinct systems of participation are a faithful interpretation of Thomas, Geiger certainly shows the value of looking at the universe by means of a metaphysics of participation. If the universe is looked at in this way, its unity and diversity are explained by its relation to God as the supreme principle (298). God is the cause of the unity in the universe because creatures are beings by participation in the One Being, yet diverse since all participate in that Being in various degrees (396). This diversity is caused by God's wisdom, which determines the mode in which each creature participates in His Being. Hence the notion of participation makes God the measure of the whole universe.

JOHN WIPPEL

In his recent book on metaphysics, John Wippel[39] extensively treats the theme of participation since he considers it to be a significant theme in

37. This idea of "similitude of nature" is not meant to undermine the fact that creation only has an analogical likeness to God.

38. Geiger elsewhere notes that the diversity in creation based on inequality of degrees of perfection is the starting point for a proof for God's existence (the fourth way—cf. *ST* I.2.3). If there are different degrees of perfection that can be measured, they must be measured in reference to a maximum. Hence, there must be something that is the uttermost perfection, and this is the cause of all other perfections (282–89). Consequently, Geiger, by illuminating the role of participation in the proof for God's existence based on degrees of perfection, is able to illuminate the meaning of this proof that demonstrates that God is absolute perfection as the measure of all perfections.

39. Although Wippel's most recent work on participation, which appears as a chapter in *The Metaphysical Thought of Thomas Aquinas: From Finite Being to Uncreated Being* (Washington, D.C.: The Catholic University of America Press, 2000), 94–131, is chronologically later than the work that will be examined below by Rudi Te Velde, the substance of Wippel's chapter on participation is found in an earlier article, "Thomas Aquinas and Participation," in *Studies in Medieval Philosophy*, ed. John Wippel (Washington, D.C.: The Catholic

Aquinas's metaphysics.[40] In this analysis of the Thomistic understanding of participation, Wippel follows Thomas's texts very closely, making only distinctions that are specifically mentioned by Thomas. Hence, although he is certainly indebted to the work of both Fabro and Geiger, he is somewhat critical of their distinctions, which he believes are not explicitly in the Thomistic texts.[41] In explicating his own view of participation, he goes directly to lecture 2 of Thomas's commentary on *De Hebdomadibus* and notes that participation is when "something receives in a particular fashion that which belongs to another in a universal (or total) fashion, the former is said to participate in the latter."[42] The text then immediately shows that participation can take place in different orders and in different ways. Thus, Wippel notes that Thomas says there are three major types of participation: (1) a species participates in a genus and an individual participates in a species, (2) a substance participates in an accident and matter in form, and (3) an effect participates in a cause (96–97). Participation of an essence in *esse* belongs to the third type, where the essence of individual creatures (the effects) participates in the *esse* of God (the cause).[43] Thus, Wippel sees the participation of creatures in God to be the participation of an effect in its cause with the effect being less perfect than the cause but yet possessing a likeness to the cause (116–17).

Wippel then identifies many important implications for metaphysics based on this view of participation. I will present the three implications that will be most pertinent for a better understanding of participation in eternal law. First, Wippel corrects Geiger's view that *esse* can be predicated substantially by means of participation. Wippel notes that in reference to the first type of participation (species in genus, etc.) there is no opposition between predication by participation and predication by substance. However, in the case of the second type of participation (subject in accident and matter in form), to be something by participation is opposed

University of America Press, 1987), 117–58, which Te Velde read before writing his work on participation. Consequently, I am treating Wippel's work before that of Te Velde.

40. *The Metaphysical Thought of Thomas Aquinas* (94–95). References to this work will be given parenthetically in the text.

41. Fabro's distinction is between predicamental and transcendental participation, while Geiger's is between participation by composition and by similitude.

42. Et ideo quando aliquid particulariter recipit id quod ad alterum pertinet universaliter, dicitur participare illud . . . . ; Wippel, 96–97.

43. This way of determining the main types of participation is very similar to that of Thomas Fay, "Participation: Transformation or Platonic and Neo-Platonic Thought in Metaphysics of Thomas Aquinas," *Divus Thomas* 76 (1973): 50–64.

to being something by essence, since an accident is not included in the
nature of a substance, and form is not included in the nature of matter.
Now, in the case of participation in *esse* (the third type: effect in cause),
the essence is distinct from the *esse* that it participates in, and therefore
esse also cannot be predicated substantially. God alone is His *esse*. In fact,
Thomas goes so far as to call *esse* an accident.[44]

Nonetheless, Wippel is quick to point out that *esse* is not a predicamental accident, but a special kind of accident since Thomas is only
trying to show that *esse* is not part of the essence, and nothing can be
predicated univocally of God and anything else (106–7). Hence, Wippel
seems to be correcting Geiger's claim that *esse* is predicated substantially
by means of participation while at the same time noting that *esse* is more
fundamental than any other accident since it alone accounts for the fact
that a particular entity exists.

The second implication from Wippel's reading of Aquinas is closely
related to the first implication on how *esse* is predicated. We have already
seen how Fabro shows that Thomas considers essence to be potency and
esse to be act. Wippel concurs with Fabro on this point and goes on to say
that the importance of this principle can hardly be overestimated since
the "intrinsic" and "essential" unity of a participating subject with what
it participates in depends on this principle (107).[45] He goes on to note
that since the participated perfection *(esse)* unites to the subject (essence)

44. Wippel, 106, refers to *QQ* 2.2.1: Secundum ergo hoc dicendum est quod ens prae-
dicatur de solo Deo essentialiter, eo quod esse divinum est esse subsistens et absolutum
. . . . Uno modo quasi existens de substantia participantis sicut genus participatur a specie;
hoc autem modo esse non participatur a creatura: id enim est de substantia rei quod ca-
dit in eius definitione, ens autem non ponitur in definitione creaturae, quia nec est genus
neque est differentia. Unde participatur sicut aliquid non existens de essentia rei, et ideo
alia quaestio est 'an est' et 'quid est'; unde, cum omne quod est praeter essentiam rei dicatur accidens, esse, quod pertinet ad quaestionem 'an est.' . . . accidens. (Therefore, we must
say that *ens* is predicated in the manner of an essence of God alone, inasmuch as divine *esse*
is subsistent and absolute being. . . . In one way it is participated in as though belonging
to the substance of the thing participating, as a genus is participated in by a species of it.
However, a creature does not participate in being this way for that belongs to the substance
of a thing which enters into its definition, but *ens* is not included in the definition of a creature because it is neither a genus nor a difference. So it is participated in as something not
belonging to the thing's essence. And therefore, the question 'Is it?' is different from the
question 'What is it?' So since all that is outside a thing's essence may be called an accident,
the being which pertains to the question 'Is it?' [is] an accident.) Translation is based on
Saint Thomas Aquinas, Quodlibetal Questions 1 and 2, trans. S. Edwards (Toronto: Pontifical
Institute of Mediaeval Studies, 1983).

45. W. Norris Clarke makes this same point in "The Limitation of Act by Potency: Aristotelianism or NeoPlatonism," *The New Scholasticism* 26 (1952): 167–94.

as act with potency, the result is a being that is not merely accidentally one but essentially one, *unum per se* (109). Hence, Wippel shows that although you cannot say that *esse* is predicated substantially (as Geiger does), you can say that it is united substantially with the essence.[46]

The last implication from Wippel's exposition is that the notion of participation allows Thomas to say that creatures share in the *esse* of God without falling into pantheism. Wippel notes that Thomas makes a distinction between three modes of *esse* that every creature participates in: *actus essendi* (the creature's own act of *esse*), *esse commune* (*esse* in general, that in which all creatures participate), and *esse Subsistens* (God). *Esse commune* signifies the *actus essendi* of all creatures that exist, but it does not exist apart from individual existent things except in the order of thought. Wippel notes that Thomas makes a distinction between both of these modes of *esse (commune* and *actus essendi)* and *esse Subsistens,* for the *esse* of God can never be identified with the *actus essendi* of any particular creature nor with all of the acts of being in common *(esse commune)*. Nonetheless, since every creature participates in *esse commune*, which participates in God, every creature truly participates in *esse Subsistens* through its own act of *esse* (110–16). By distinguishing between *esse commune* and *esse Subsistens* Thomas shows that God is beyond even the *esse* of all existing things, for He is pure *esse*. Consequently, the divine *esse* itself is not communicated to creatures, but only a likeness is communicated through participation (120). Hence, the notion of participation allows creatures to share in the attributes of God without implying a pantheistic universe.

While clearly persuaded by the arguments of Fabro and Geiger on the value of participation, Wippel uses a thorough study of the works of Thomas to show that Geiger is mistaken in believing that participated being is predicated substantially. Nonetheless, Wippel does affirm that *esse* is substantially united to the essence, which results in its being the fundamental accident of the essence without which the *ens* would not exist. Wippel also goes a step further than the essence/*esse* distinction to show that the *esse* of any particular creature, while in the likeness of God, is not God Himself.

---

46. This appears to be the point that Geiger is actually trying to make, since he does not believe that something can be predicated univocally of God and a creature.

Rudi Te Velde, a Dutch philosopher, recently devoted a full-length book to the subject of participation within Thomas Aquinas's treatment of creation called *Participation and Substantiality*.[47] Te Velde notes that although scholars accept Fabro and Geiger's insight that participation is a key concept in Thomas's metaphysics, nonetheless within Thomas's doctrine of creation this notion is still undeveloped (ix–x).[48] Te Velde believes that within Thomas's metaphysical account of creation, the term participation is "an intelligible and unified concept which is systematically integrated," and hence he goes against the current trend among scholars by arguing that there is no need to distinguish between different types of participation.[49] Although rejecting the need to distinguish between different types of participation as Fabro and Geiger did, Te Velde is highly influenced by both of them in his choice of Thomistic texts and in the implications that he draws from these texts. Consequently, I will only briefly mention his concept of participation and will quickly move to his more original contribution: his specific application of participation to creation and divine governance showing the importance of the notion of participation in Thomas's cosmology.

Te Velde notes that the title of his book *(Participation and Substantiality)* comes from the two terms used to describe how something exists in the two main traditions inherited by Thomas: Platonism and Aristotelianism (x). On the one hand, Plato used the notion of participation *(methexis)* in order to show the causal relationship between the one idea and the many particular instances of it. On the other hand, Aristotle used the idea of substance *(ousia)* to state how things exist in themselves as self-sufficient, apart from separated forms (xi–xii). Aquinas takes these two theories of reality believed by Aristotle to be mutually exclusive and reconciles them by means of a new kind of participation on the level of the substantial being of things (xiii, 15, 34, 66–83).

Te Velde argues that in the commentary on the *De Hebdomadibus*

47. New York: Brill, 1995. This book was a revised version of his dissertation written under the guidance of the Thomistic philosopher Jan Aertsen. References to this book will be parenthetically in the text.

48. Te Velde refers to John Wippel's "Aquinas and Participation," 117–58. Te Velde argues that Wippel's efforts to reconcile the approaches of Fabro and Geiger is evidence of the lack of consensus on the issue.

49. I have already shown how Fabro distinguishes between predicamental and transcendental, and how Geiger distinguishes between composition and similitude.

Thomas distinguishes between the three modes of participation in order
to show that participation does not imply opposition to what belongs to
the substance of a thing (15).[50] Although Te Velde believes that Thomas makes a real distinction between essence and the act of *esse*, Thomas
nonetheless grounds the being and goodness of a subject in the act of
the substance. Unlike most accidents, which are acts of the being *(ens)*
composed of both essence and *esse*, *esse* is the substantial act of the essence.[51]

Te Velde believes that Aquinas merged the Aristotelian concept of
substance with the Platonic concept of participation so that one can say
that something has being and goodness both in the substantial act of the
substance and by means of participation. Hence something can be said
to exist or to be good through its form even though its being and goodness are a participation in God. This is possible because the form of a
creature truly gives being[52] (or goodness) as the formal principle whereby
a thing is *(est)* and is called a being.[53] Yet the particular form only gives
being as the means through which God gives being to a particular subject
since "each thing participates in being according to its relation to the first
principle of being" and this participation is by means of its form (217).[54]
In other words, God grants being to each thing through the mediation
of the form that participates in *esse* (226). Consequently, since both the

50. *DH* 3. The three modes of participation is that of a species in a genus and an individual in a species, a substance in an accident and matter in form, and an effect in its cause.

51. Te Velde, 11–15, 34–44, 72. Although Te Velde is highly influenced by Geiger, he
accepts Wippel's point that Thomas calls *esse* an accident in *QQ* II.2.1 (see Wippel above).
Hence Te Velde is much more careful with his terminology and does not say as Geiger does
that something can be predicated substantially by means of participation. Instead he notes
that although the young Thomas accepts the Avicennian essence/*esse* distinction where *esse*
is an accident, Thomas will later develop his view by means of the notion of participation to
say that *esse* is the substantial act of the essence (66–83).

52. Te Velde points to *QD De Anima*, 10: *"forma dat esse et speciem"* (form gives *esse*
and species). Cf. *SS* 8; *DH* 2; *DP*, 3.16.22.

53. Te Velde refers to *SCG* II, 68: "forma sit principium essendi substantialiter ei cuius
est forma: principium autem dico non effectivum sed formale, quo aliquid est et denomi-
natur ens" (the form must be the principle of the substantial being of the thing whose form
it is; I speak not of the productive but the formal principle whereby a thing exists and is
called a being).

54. Te Velde (on 217) quotes *LC* 25: "unumquodque participat esse secundum habitudinem quam habet ad primum essendi principium. Res autem composita ex materia et
forma non habet esse nisi per consecutionem suae formae; unde per suam formam habet
habitudinem ad primum essendi principium." (Each thing participates in being according
to its relation to the first principle of being. Now what is composed of matter and form has
being in virtue of its form; therefore it is related through its form to the first principle of
being.—translation by Te Velde.)

particular form and God can be said to give *esse*, *esse* and those things convertible with it (e.g., goodness) can be said to be predicated both by virtue of the substance and by participation.

Te Velde shows the importance of the Thomistic notion of participation by showing its role in Thomas's theory of creation and divine governance. He believes that Thomas uses both the Neoplatonic notion of emanation and the concept of God as an artist to explain the relation of creation to God (102). To confirm this claim he directly quotes *De Potencia* 3.4.9, where Thomas states that there are two ways that creatures have an analogous likeness to God:

First, insofar as created things imitate in their own manner the idea of the divine mind, as artifacts imitate the form which is in the mind of the artificer. And secondly, insofar as created things imitate somehow the divine nature itself, in the sense that from the First Being, other beings proceed, and from the Good, good things, and the like for others.[55]

Te Velde then states, "The first sense of likeness concerns the exemplarity of the divine idea and fits in the *art* model of creation. All created things preexist according to the proper notion in the divine mind. . . . The second sense of likeness fits in the emanation model: all created things are to some extent similar to God in what they have of being and goodness."[56] Hence, all creatures have a likeness to both the divine ideas and the nature of God.

Although Te Velde speaks of creation by emanation, he contrasts this view of emanation with the strict Neoplatonic emanationism, which states that since nature properly produces something of like nature, diverse effects falling short of their cause are from a defect in nature, an "ontological fall." In contrast to this view of emanation, for Thomas, it is by knowledge that something produces ordered diverse effects, in-

---

55. Uno modo in quantum res creatae imitantur suo modo ideam divinae mentis, sicut artificiata formam quae est in mente artificis. Alio modo secundum quod res creatae ipsi naturae divinae quodammodo similantur, prout a primo ente alia sunt entia, et a bono bona, et sic de aliis; translation by Te Velde, 110–11. For the distinction between the production of something by a natural form and the production of something by an intelligible form, Te Velde refers to *De Potencia* 7.1.8 where Thomas explains that there are two ways that an agent can be a formal cause of something: by art and by nature. Natural generation is an example of formal causality by nature—e.g., a son has the same nature as his father (for like produces like). In the case of art, the effects do not have the same nature as the cause, but they do have a likeness to the concept that exists in the mind of the maker (103).

56. Emphasis in the original. Te Velde also refers to *DP* 7.7.6 and I *Sent* 1.2 for other examples of the "double exemplarity of God."

cluding some that are intentionally less than their cause. Because God's knowledge is His divine nature, He can produce diverse and limited effects by his nature (105–6). Hence, Te Velde notes that God does create by means of emanation, but that this notion for Thomas implies the idea of God as an artist who causes a planned limitation of *esse* in diverse ways based on His divine Wisdom (106–110). This entire notion of creation as a planned limitation of diverse beings is based on the notion of participation since it is by participation in the *esse* of God that something has a likeness of God, and God's wisdom determines the diverse ways that each creature participates in God's *esse* (118). Hence Te Velde notes that the notion of participation expresses at the same time "the intrinsic value and meaning of a creature which is a *being* as well as its essential imperfection inasmuch as it has only a part of being."[57]

Just as the notion of participation shows the relation of created beings to God, Te Velde also shows how Thomas considers the acts of creatures to be participations in the operation of God in divine government. Te Velde notes that Thomas argues that God as primary cause works in the world through true secondary causes in bringing creation to its proper end. Yet, although God works through creation by means of the natural powers of creatures, God as the primary cause of all actions exercises a greater responsibility for these actions than does any secondary cause (166).[58] Te Velde explains that to be a cause is to be responsible for the being of something else (177). However, only God, the primary cause, can give being by Himself since He alone is being by His essence.[59] Since acts also have being, all secondary causes in acting cause being to the extent that they participate in the primary cause. Therefore, the active power of every secondary agent is constituted (is what it is) by participation in the universal power of God. For God gives *esse* to all effects of these secondary agents by causing these agents to give *esse* in accord with their particular mode (176–77). For example, God causes human actions by moving humans to perform actions in accord with their mode: as free and rational agents.

The notion of participation helps to explain how the first cause infuses its effect more powerfully than do secondary causes, since it is only by participation in this cause that all secondary causes are able to give *esse* (168). Te Velde notes that it is necessary to posit participation in the

---

57. Emphasis in original.
58. Te Velde refers to *Liber de Causis* I and *De Potencia* 3.7.
59. *DP* 3.1; 3.7 and *ST* I.105.5.

universal cause since no particular cause can account for the being of its effect apart from God (182). Therefore, Te Velde shows that not only is the *esse* of creation a participation in the *esse* of God, but also that every action is a participation in the operation of God as establishing something that must have a particular mode of *esse*.

Consequently, like the other three authors studied, Te Velde considers the notion of participation to be very important to Thomistic metaphysics. However, the value of Te Velde's exposition is that he shows how the notion of participation applies to creation and divine government. In reference to creation, Te Velde shows that God creates beings with a likeness both to His nature and the ideas in His mind. God creates all things by causing a limited, wisely planned, participation in divine nature, which is *esse* and goodness essentially. In reference to divine government, Te Velde shows that the *esse* of every action is a participation in the operation of God.

By analyzing the work of these four Thomistic scholars, it is clear that the notion of participation lies at the foundation of Thomas's metaphysical thought. These scholars have shown how the notion of participation illuminates many of Thomas's brilliant principles, including the relation of creation to God, the unity amid diversity in creation because of its relation to God, and the analogy between creatures and God as effects made in the likeness of their cause.

The key point is that an understanding of the Thomistic notion of participation allows one to grasp that all things are (have *esse* in their own particular mode) in relation to God. Their mode of participation includes both their substantial act of *esse* which is in accord with their nature and all of their additional acts. Since something is perfect to the extent that it is in act, God is the focal point determining all perfections, both in reference to the substances of creatures and to their additional actions. Hence, the notion of participation is at the foundation of all that Thomas has to say about the perfections of created reality.

As Te Velde noted, creatures not only participate in God as created, but also as moved back to God by means of divine government.[60] Hence, the notion of participation is at the foundation of the understanding of the relation of the acts of all creatures to God. Since Thomistic moral theory is concerned with the rational creature's return to God by means

---

60. Te Velde, 160–83. See also 281 where Te Velde notes that an understanding of the role of participation illuminates two key concepts in Aquinas's moral teaching: natural law (as a participation in eternal law) and grace (as a participation in the divine nature).

of acts ordered to God, the notion of participation is also at the foundation of his moral thought.[61] Consequently, the following chapters will apply this philosophical recovery of the notion to participation to Thomas's theology of participation in eternal law.

61. Romanus Cessario argues that the notion of participation in eternal law is key to moral theology because it provides the foundational structure for human knowledge of moral truth. See *Introduction to Moral Theology* (Washington, D.C.: The Catholic University of America Press, 2001), 80.

CHAPTER 2

Participation in Eternal Law

CHAPTER ONE SHOWED that within the realm of metaphysics, the notion of participation is considered by four Thomistic scholars to be an indispensable aid to understanding Thomas's philosophy. All four of these scholars noted in various ways that the notion of participation explains the ordered diversity of creation by means of the degree of participation of each creature in God. Within this conceptual framework all things are what they are based on their relation to God, who is the cause of all being. Both the first perfection of a creature (the first act of the essence: *esse*) and all subsequent perfections (secondary acts) participate in God and hence have their source and reference point in God. Since moral theology is primarily interested in the return of rational creatures to God by means of becoming like God through their secondary acts, this second chapter will especially analyze how humans participate in God through their secondary acts. More specifically, this chapter will analyze the notion of human participation in eternal law since the eternal law as the governing wisdom of God is the source and reference point of all human acts. In order to study this form of participation, this chapter will first build upon the insights gleaned from the scholars in chapter one by showing Thomas's theological understanding of participation. Then in order to further explain the notion of eternal law and how it fits into Thomas's moral theory, the second part of this chapter will show the context in which Thomas speaks of the eternal law within the *Summa Theologiae*.

PART I: THOMAS'S THEOLOGICAL
UNDERSTANDING OF PARTICIPATION

Thomas notes that while both the philosopher and the theologian consider causes and judge according to them, the philosopher considers and judges according to caused causes, and the theologian judges according to divine causes.[1] Thus, whereas in the first chapter the philosophers Fabro, Geiger, and Wippel spoke of various different types of participation,[2] this chapter will examine with a more theological focus the notion of participation as it relates to God as the efficient, exemplary, and final cause of creation and created acts (*ST* I.44). Consequently, of the various types of participation mentioned in chapter one, this chapter is going to focus primarily on the third type of participation mentioned by Thomas in the second chapter of his commentary on the *De Hebdomadibus:* the participation of an effect in a cause.[3] Since God causes creatures to act in accord with their forms, at times the second type of participation, the participation of matter in form and subject in accident, will also be addressed.

Because the theologian judges things by considering creatures as effects participating in the divine cause, it is necessary to study certain aspects of God before studying the different ways a creature participates in God. After all, the wise man judges creatures by considering God (*ST*

---

1. *DP* 1.4. See Olivia Blanchette, *The Perfection of the Universe According to Aquinas* (University Park: Pennsylvania State University Press, 1992), chapter 4, on how the various types of causes discussed by Aquinas lead to the order within the universe.

2. Fabro distinguished predicamental participation from transcendental participation ("Intensive Hermeneutics of Thomistic Philosophy: The Notion of Participation," 471–74). Geiger distinguished participation by similitude from participation by constitution (*La Participation dans la Philosphie de s. Thomas d'Aquin*, 26), and Wippel, following the commentary on the *De Hebdomadibus*, distinguished participation of an individual in a species and a species in a genus from participation of matter in form and subject in accident from participation of an effect in its cause (*Metaphysical Thought of Thomas Aquinas: From Finite Being to Uncreated Being*, 96–97). The fourth scholar, Te Velde, argued that there was no need to distinguish between the different types of participation since Thomas uses the term as "an intelligible and unified concept which is systematically integrated"; see *Participation and Substantiality*, x.

3. The three types described in the commentary are the participation of an individual in a species and a species in a genus; matter in form and a subject in an accident; and an effect in its cause. See the section in chapter one on Wippel. I have chosen to follow the distinctions made by Wippel since they are taken directly from the Thomistic text. As Wippel notes, the distinctions made by Fabro and Geiger are not directly in the Thomistic texts (*Metaphysical Thought of Thomas Aquinas: From Finite Being to Uncreated Being*, 127–28), and hence I will not analyze them.

I.1.6 and preface of *LC*). Thus, this study of the theological notion of participation will begin with an examination of relevant aspects of Thomas's theology of God. Then it will investigate how the substantial perfections of creatures (the first act of the creature) participate in God who is their efficient, exemplary, and formal cause. Next it will investigate how the accidental perfections of creatures (secondary acts of the creature) participate in God who is their efficient, exemplary, and formal cause as well. Finally it will focus specifically on how humans as rational creatures participate in God in both by their substantial perfections and their accidental perfections. Within this section it will explain the distinction that Thomas makes between human participation in God as moved and governed by eternal law and cognitive participation in eternal law (*ST* I-II.93.5 & 6). This analysis of this dual participation leads to the final section of this chapter where I show specifically how a human participates in eternal law by showing the relation of the eternal law to other elements of Thomistic moral theory within the *Summa Theologiae*.

God as the Source of All Perfections

Because all perfections that are participated in must be caused by something that has these perfections essentially, all perfections found in anything must be originally and superabundantly in God (*CP* 21). Thus, in order to properly understand the participated perfections of creatures, it is necessary to first look at these perfections in God.[4] More specifically, a better understanding of the relation of the creature to God can be found by looking at God as the efficient, exemplary, and final cause of all created perfections.[5] By looking at participation in God as efficient cause, a better understanding of how a creature is created and sustained is ascer-

---

4. Cf. *DP* 3.5.1 where within in the context of explaining how it is necessary to understand God as essentially *esse* in order to understand *esse* in creatures, Thomas notes that to properly understand the effect, it is necessary to understand the cause.

5. Whenever a person creates a work of art, the notions of efficient, exemplary, and final causality can be used to properly understand the work of art. The person first has a goal or end that is the reason for which the artwork is made (the final cause). Then the person determines the form of the artwork within his mind (the exemplary cause). Finally the person creates the artwork in accord with the form (efficient causality). For example, a cathedral may be made for the purpose of praising God (final causality). Blueprints are then drawn that organize the cathedral for the purpose of praising God (exemplary causality). Finally the workers actually make the cathedral (efficient causality). Analogously, God's goodness is the final cause of all creation, his divine ideas are the exemplary cause, and his power is the efficient cause.

tained; as exemplary cause—its mode of being is illuminated; and as final cause—its role in creation (order to end) is clarified. Consequently, this section will treat a few attributes in God that pertain to Him in reference to this threefold causality.

Although on account of divine simplicity these various divine perfections and kinds of causality are one and identical to the divine essence itself, it is helpful to distinguish and correlate them individually for the sake of aiding human understanding. In reference to God as efficient cause, this study will briefly present Thomas's description of God as pure act and some implications that stem from this, such as that God's *esse* is His essence, and that God's power is infinite. In reference to God as exemplary cause, it will review the operation of the divine intellect: God's knowledge and, in particular, the divine ideas. In reference to God as final cause, it will analyze the goodness of God and the operation of the divine will: God's love.[6] Finally, it will discuss divine providence, which is related to both the divine intellect and the divine will, because the concept of divine providence is the foundation for the concept of the eternal law.

God is the efficient cause of all creation because He is essentially self-subsisting being (*ST* I.44.1). In question two of the *Summa Theologiae* Thomas proves the existence of God as the first being *(ens)*. From this truth Thomas is able to move to the conclusion that God is essentially *esse* (*ST* I.3). Thomas first shows that God is pure act. He states that the first being must of necessity be completely in act and in no way in potentiality. The reason God must be pure act is that although in any perfectible thing potency comes before act, "absolutely speaking, act is prior to potency; for whatever is in potency can be reduced into act only by some being in act."[7] Given this metaphysical necessity, that which is the first

---

6. See *DV* I.4.*sed contra* where Thomas states that God is the efficient, exemplary, and final cause of all things. "Consequently, the being of things is referred to God as efficient cause, their truth to Him as an exemplary cause, their goodness to Him as a final cause . . ." (et per quamdam appropriationem entitas rerum refertur ad deum ut ad causam efficientem, veritas ut ad causam exemplarem, bonitas ut ad causam finalem). Thomas goes on to note that properly speaking all three of these attributes of things could be referred to any single cause. For example, being, truth, and goodness in things can all be referred to God as efficient cause.

7. *ST* I.3.1: . . . simpliciter tamen actus prior est potentia, quia quod est in potentia, non reducitur in actum nisi per ens actu. Cf. *ST* I.3.8, I.4.1; *DSC* I; and *DP* 6.6. For Thomas created things only act because something else already in act causes them to act. For example, a piece of wood is in potency to the act of heating something (when it is chemically altered by fire), but in order to actually begin heating something, it must be lit on fire by something that is already performing the act of heating.

cause of all movement must be pure act without any potency, for if it had potency, it would have to be moved by something else, in which case it would not be the first cause. Consequently, Thomas argues that God is purely act and not in potency in regard to anything.

Thomas then shows that if God is pure act, God cannot have any matter in Him because matter stands in potency to form (*ST* I.3.2). Since God has no matter within Him, he must be pure form, and pure forms are subsisting *supposita*,[8] where *suppositum* and nature are identical (*ST* I.3.3). Therefore, Thomas is able to say that God is His own divinity, His own life, and whatever else that is predicated of Him (*ST* I.3.3). In other words, God is simple. There is no composition or division in God.[9] From this it follows that God is pure act by His essence.[10] If God is pure act by His essence, His essence is pure *esse:*

esse is the actuality of every form or nature, for goodness or humanity is spoken of as actual, only because they are spoken of as *esse*. Therefore, *esse* itself must be compared to essence, if the essence is distinct from it, as actuality to potentiality. Therefore, since in God there is nothing potential, as shown above, it follows that in Him, essence does not differ from His *esse*. Therefore, His essence is his *esse*.[11]

Thomas proves that because God is pure act, then He must be *esse* essentially.

From the truths that God is pure act and *esse* essentially, Thomas concludes that God is universally perfect.[12] As pure act, God must be perfect because a thing is perfect to the extent that it is in act and imper-

---

8. Deferrari defines suppositum as "that which underlies all the accidents of a things, i.e. the individual substance of a certain kind which is the subject of existence and all accidental modifications which constitute the individual"; see Roy Deferrari, *A Lexicon of St. Thomas Aquinas* (Washington, D.C.: The Catholic University of America Press, 1948), 1079–80.

9. Since God is simple, it is proper to say that God is all perfections, while creatures have perfections by participation.

10. See *SCG* I.16.5 where Thomas notes that only the first agent acts by its whole self, all others act by participation of something and not by essence. Therefore, only God is pure act. Cf. *SCG* I.38.

11. *ST* I.3.4: quia esse est actualitas omnis formae vel naturae, non enim bonitas vel humanitas significatur in actu, nisi prout significamus eam esse. Oportet igitur quod ipsum esse comparetur ad essentiam quae est aliud ab ipso, sicut actus ad potentiam. Cum igitur in deo nihil sit potentiale, ut ostensum est supra, sequitur quod non sit aliud in eo essentia quam suum esse. Sua igitur essentia est suum esse. Thomas also argues that since God is first being, He cannot have *esse* by participation and hence must be *esse* essentially. Cf. *SCG* I.22; *DP* 6.6; *DSC* I.

12. Where by "universally perfect" Thomas means that the excellence of no genus is lacking (*SCG* I.28).

fect to the extent it is in potency. For example, a creature is perfect when its proper potencies have been completely reduced to act. However, unlike creatures, God as pure act is completely perfect.[13] The perfection of God can also be deduced by the fact that God is *esse* essentially. Thomas explains that God is universally perfect by arguing that something is excellent according to how a thing has *esse:*

> For a thing is said to be more or less excellent according as its *esse* is limited to a certain greater or lesser mode of excellence. Therefore, if there is something to which the whole power of *essendi* belongs, it can lack no excellence that is proper to some thing. But for a thing that is its own *esse,* it is proper to be according to the whole power of *esse.*[14]

Since God's *esse* is His essence, God is every possible perfection of being. From this argument Thomas concludes that God is universally perfect, having the excellence of every genus.[15] If something is perfect to the extent it has a particular act of *esse,* God is the fullness of every perfection because He is *esse.*[16] Because God is the self-subsisting act of *esse,* all perfections of every genus must be predicated of Him essentially.[17]

As exemplary cause God causes things by His knowledge (*ST* I.14.8). Just as a human architect has the exemplary form of the house in his intellect before it is built, so also God has the exemplary form of all created beings within His mind. However, unlike the intellects of humans that

---

13. *SCG* 1:28; Cf. *ST* I.4.1: "a thing is perfect in proportion to its state of actuality" (aliquid esse perfectum, secundum quod est actu). In the case of a human being, for example, the human is perfected to the extent that he performs the acts proper to human nature. Thus, to the extent humans perform the acts of knowing and loving, they are more perfect. God, on the other hand, as pure act, has no potency to reduce to act but is all perfections, since perfections are acts. Hence, God as fully in act is perfect knowledge, love, and any other attribute that can be analogously applied to Him (*ST* I.3.3).

14. *SCG* I.28: nam res secundum quod suum esse contrahitur ad aliquem specialem modum nobilitatis maiorem vel minorem, dicitur esse secundum hoc nobilior vel minus nobilis. Igitur si aliquid est cui competit tota virtus essendi, ei nulla nobilitatum deesse potest quae alicui rei conveniat. Sed rei quae est suum esse, competit esse secundum totam essendi potestatem.

15. *SCG* I.28; Cf. *ST* I.4.2; *SS* 14. For example, in *SC* 13(14) Thomas argues that God knows all things because His *esse* is his essence and the knowledge of any knower is according to the mode of the substance.

16. In contrast to God who is every perfection, creatures have perfections in a limited manner. Thomas explains that just as a perfection is found in a thing according to how it *is,* defects are according to how a thing lacks being (*SCG* I.28).

17. Not only can one conclude that God contains all perfections since His essence is His *esse,* one can also conclude that there are no accidents in God. Unlike creatures which in addition to their essence have *esse* through additional participated forms, God acts only through His essential *esse* (*LC* 20; *SCG* 1.23).

are in potency to the act of knowing, God is his own act of understanding and the object understood:

Since His essence itself is also His intelligible species, it necessarily follows that His act of understanding must be His essence and His *esse*. Thus it follows from all the foregoing that in God, intellect, and the object understood and the intelligible species, and His act of understanding are entirely one and the same.[18]

God as the act of understanding understands Himself by means of Himself. God is essentially the intellectual power, the object understood, and the act of understanding (cf. *SCG* I.60). Thomas in the next article (14.5) concludes that because God's *esse* is His act of understanding, then He must understand Himself perfectly, which includes a perfect understanding of all that He causes, which is everything. Thus, God knows all other things by knowing Himself inasmuch as all His effects are in His essence in an intelligible mode, for all things are in God *virtually* (i.e., in respect to His power) as effects in their cause.[19] Consequently, although God is completely simple, distinctions between the act of understanding, the object understood, and the power to understand are helpful in showing how God is the cause of all things.

A few articles later (14.8) Thomas asks whether God's knowledge is the cause of all things.[20] Thomas states that the knowledge of God is to all creatures what the knowledge of the artist is to the art he makes. The knowledge of the artist is the cause of the art because the artist works by his intellect. God's knowledge is the exemplary cause of all created things insofar as His will is joined to it.[21] Specifically, He is the exemplary cause

18. *ST* I.14.4: Unde, cum ipsa sua essentia sit etiam species intelligibilis, ut dictum est, ex necessitate sequitur quod ipsum eius intelligere sit eius essentia et eius esse. Et sic patet ex omnibus praemissis quod in deo intellectus, et id quod intelligitur, et species intelligibilis, et ipsum intelligere, sunt omnino unum et idem. Cf. *ST* I.14.2, which states that since the intelligible species itself is the divine intellect, God understands Himself through Himself.

19. See also *SS* 14 where Thomas argues that because God's *esse* is His essence, in knowing His essence, God knows all possible forms of *esse* and therefore knows all that exists and could possibly exist.

20. See *ST* I.14.16 where Thomas notes that inasmuch as God knows Himself, He has only speculative knowledge, since knowledge of Himself cannot be ordered to operation. However, in reference to those things that He makes, God has both speculative and practical knowledge. He has speculative knowledge as knowing His works in themselves, and He has practical knowledge since as governor and creator His knowledge is ordered to operation.

21. God as final cause wills all other things as ordered to His goodness as an end (*ST* I-II.19.2). The intellect must be joined to the will since in the order of causality, the final cause is the cause of all causes; see *Metaph* V.2; n. 775; *ST* I.5.4. Also see Blanchette, chapter 4, on the four causes and the order of the universe.

of all things through His divine ideas which are the intelligible forms of all created things preexisting in the divine intellect.[22] Thomas states:

Whereas in other agents [the form of the thing to be made preexists] according to intelligible being, as in those that act by the intellect; and thus the likeness of a house preexists in the mind of the builder. And this may be called the idea of the house, since the builder intends to build his house like the form conceived in his mind. As then the world was not made by chance, but by God acting by His intellect, . . . there must exist in the divine mind a form to the likeness of which the world was made.[23]

Within God's practical knowledge are intelligible forms that are likenesses of all created things. Even though there are many ideas in God, the divine simplicity is maintained since in knowing His divine essence, God also knows each of the parts of the universe and their order to each other and to Him.[24] Thus, Thomas can say, "God is the likeness of all things according to His essence; therefore an idea in God is nothing other than His essence."[25]

As final cause of the universe, God as essentially good is the end to which all of creation is ordered. In order to show the goodness of God, Thomas argues that although humans make a distinction between goodness and being in their knowledge, they are the same in reality. He states that something is good as desirable and things are desirable as perfect. Since things are perfect insofar as they have being, then goodness and being are really the same (*ST* I.5.1). Since God is being by His essence,

---

22. *ST* I.15.1, 44.3; *DV* 3.1. Thomas notes that the equivalent of the Greek word *idea* is the Latin word *forma,* where form refers to the intellectual species within the speculative or practical intellect. Inasmuch as it is in the practical intellect, it is the exemplar cause of things. For more explanation on why divine ideas in Aquinas have both the function of cognitive principles (speculative knowledge) and exemplars (practical knowledge), see Wippel, *Thomas Aquinas on the Divine Ideas* (Toronto: Pontifical Institute of Mediaeval Studies, 1993).

23. *ST* I.15.1: In quibusdam vero secundum esse intelligibile, ut in his quae agunt per intellectum; sicut similitudo domus praeexistit in mente aedificatoris. Et haec potest dici idea domus, quia artifex intendit donum assimilare formae quam mente concepit. Quia igitur mundus non est casu factus, sed est factus a Deo per intellectum agente, . . . necesse est quod in mente divina sit forma, ad similitudinem cuius mundus est factus.

24. *ST* 15.1. Cf. *SCG* I.54 which states that God can know what is proper to each and everything through His knowledge of His essence by understanding both that whereby each given thing imitates His essence and that whereby the thing falls short of His essence. See Wippel, *Thomas Aquinas on the Divine Ideas,* 27.

25. *ST* I.15.1.3: Deus secundum essentiam suam est similitudo omnium rerum. Unde idea in deo nihil est aliud quam dei essentia. Cf. I.44.3 where Thomas notes that likeness to the divine essence can be shared diversely by different things (44.3).

He must also be goodness by His essence.[26] Hence, whereas all creatures are good by participation, God is goodness essentially (*ST* I.6.4).

The object of the will is the end that has the aspect of goodness (*ST* I.19.1.1). Thomas explains that the will of an intellectual creature is moved by some good that is outside of themselves. However, the intentional object of the divine will is God's own goodness that is His essence (*ST* I.19.1.3). In other words, whereas humans act in order to attain an end that is outside of themselves, God's end is His essence because He is goodness essentially. Furthermore, in willing His own essence, God wills all things that are apart from Him.[27] When a human agent wills something on account of an end, that which was willed is ordered to the end. For example, if a human wills to eat something on account of the end of health, the action of eating is ordered to health. Likewise, when God wills creatures apart from Himself, these creatures are ordered to the divine goodness that is God's end. Thomas explains:

Thus, then, He wills both Himself to be, and other things to be; but Himself as the end, and other things as ordained to that end; inasmuch as it befits the divine goodness that other things should participate in it.[28]

The first act of the will is to love. In humans, the will is moved to love by the goodness of an object. However, in God who is the cause of all, divine love causes the goodness of the created object (*ST* I.20.2). That God does not love all things equally is the reason that some things are better than others. Hence, God loves things that participate in His goodness in a greater degree more than those that participate in His goodness in a lesser degree (*SCG* III.95.5; *ST* I.20.4; *ST* I-II.110.1).

After treating the divine intellect in reference to God as exemplary cause and the divine will in reference to God as final cause, it is fitting to treat divine providence which pertains to both the intellect and the will (*ST* I.22.prologue). As just seen, God as final cause orders all things to His divine goodness by His love, but as exemplary cause He also orders them to the end of His goodness by the *ratio* (type) of His intellect. Di-

26. *ST* I.6.3: Thomas argues that things are good by their being, accidents, and end. However, in God alone are all three of these perfections by essence since God is being, has no accidents, and is the last end of all things.

27. *ST* I.19.2.3. Just as by knowing His own essence, He also knows all things, including knowledge of those things apart from His essence, so also by willing His goodness, He wills all things including those that are apart from His essence.

28. *ST* I.19.2: Sic igitur vult et se esse, et alia. Sed se ut finem, alia vero ut ad finem, inquantum condecet divinam bonitatem etiam alia ipsam participare. See also 19.1.1.

vine providence is the *ratio* within the divine intellect ordering all things to the divine goodness. Thomas explains that goodness within creatures is not only in regard to their substance, but also in regard to their order to their end. God creates this order to the end. Since God causes all by His intellect, it is necessary that the *ratio* of the order of all things toward their end preexists in the divine mind. This *ratio* in the divine mind ordering things to their end is called providence.[29]

The term providence *(providentia)* is the same term that is often translated as foresight when speaking of morals.[30] It is the chief part of the virtue of prudence, which perfects the intellect to find the proper means to an end. The person with foresight is able to see what leads to a particular end so as to order well his acts to achieve it, or if the person is a ruler, to order well his subjects to their common good.[31] Thomas analogously applies this perfection to God. However, since God is His own last end, nothing within Him can be ordered to another end, so only one type of prudence can be applied to God: sovereign prudence, the providence of a ruler. For God as ruler of all creation does order all things to Himself as end. In this sense providence can be suitably attributed to God (*ST* I.22.1; cf. *LC* 24).

Because all of creation is ordered to the divine goodness, everything is subject to divine providence. Thomas shows the comprehensiveness of God's plan by arguing that to the extent that something participates in *esse*, it must also be providentially ordered to a particular end. He argues:

For since every agent acts for an end, the ordering of effects toward that end extends as far as the causality of the first agent extends. . . . But the causality of God, Who is the first agent, extends to all being . . . Hence all things that have *esse* in whatsoever manner are necessarily directed by God toward some end . . . it necessarily follows that all things, inasmuch as they participate in *esse,* must likewise be subject to divine providence.[32]

---

29. I.22.1. Cf. I-II.79.1. See also *SCG* III.75 which states that the participation of divine goodness is accomplished through divine providence since it orders them to their ultimate end: divine goodness. Cf. *SCG* III.77.

30. For example, the Fathers of the English Dominican Province translate *providentia* as foresight in *ST* II-II.49.6: "Whether foresight *(providentia)* should be accounted a part of prudence?" See *Summa Theologica* (New York: Benzinger Brothers, 1948).

31. Cf. *ST* II-II.49.6.

32. *ST* I.22.2: Cum enim omne agens agat propter finem, tantum se extendit ordinatio effectum in finem, quantum extendit causalitas prima agentis. . . . Causalitas autem dei, qui est primum agens, se extendit usque ad omnia entia . . . Unde necesse est omnia quae habent quocumque modo esse, ordinata esse a deo in finem . . . necesse est omnia, inquantum participant esse, intantum subdi divinae providentiae. Cf. *ST* I.103.5; *SCG* III.64.

Since the end that God acts for in causing being is His own goodness, all creatures inasmuch as they participate in *esse* are also ordered to the divine goodness by divine providence. Thomas affirms this point by arguing that nothing hinders a particular cause except another particular cause. However, since all particular causes are under the universal cause, nothing takes place outside the range of the universal cause of being.[33] Since God is the universal cause of being, all things that exist in any way are subject to Him, even privations found in individual subjects, which He allows for the greater good of the whole of creation (I.22.2.2).

Thomas makes a distinction within providence between the *ratio* in the mind of God and the execution of this *ratio* (22.3), which is called divine government.[34] An analogy with the providence of a ruler is helpful to understand this distinction. There is a difference between the *ratio* of the law of the king, which is in his mind, and his execution of the law's *ratio* done through his directing his subjects to act for the greater good of the kingdom. Just as subjects through their lawful acts participate in the *ratio* of the king's law, which is the exemplary cause of their acts, so also all creatures participate in God's *ratio* by acting in accord with their created nature to bring all creation to its ordained end.[35] In other words, God as divine governor rules the world through secondary causes that act in accord with their created nature.[36] Thomas states, "God's immediate provision over everything does not exclude the action of secondary causes; which are the executors of His order."[37] Hence, the universality

33. *ST* I.22.2.1. The universality of providence is possible because being is the *proper* effect of God since He is being itself. Unintended effects can arise from a cause only if such effects are accidental by not being the proper effect of that cause. Because being is the proper effect of God, all things—substances, accidents, necessities, contingencies, etc. are included within providence. Only pure "nothing" would fall outside of his proper causality.

34. *ST* I.22.3; 22.1.2. See also *SS* 15 where Thomas states that providence in disposition (vs. execution) is more perfect as extending to more things, while execution is more perfect in the sense that God's providence is carried out by means of intermediaries and instruments by participation.

35. *ST.* III.72.8. Cf. *SCG* III.78.2 where Thomas states that every creature that carries out the order of divine providence does so by participation in the power of the first providential being, as an instrument of an agent. Cf. *SCG* III.113: Omnis enim res propter suam operationem esse videtur: operatio enim est ultima perfectio rei: Sic igitur unumquodque a deo ad suum actum ordinatur secundum quod divinae providentiae substat. (Each thing seems to exist for the sake of its operation; for, operation is the ultimate perfection of a thing. Therefore, each thing is ordered to its action by God according to the way in which it is subordinated to divine providence.)

36. See *ST* I.103.5 which states that God is the ruler of all as their cause, for God as the source of *esse* also gives perfection and the giving of perfection belongs to government.

37. *ST* I.22.3.2. . . . deus habet immediate providentiam de rebus omnibus, non ex-

of divine providence does not negate the true secondary causality of creatures but, on the contrary, is the cause of the secondary causality of the creatures.[38]

Governors implement that which they foresee by means of laws. Likewise, God as divine governor rules the universe through His eternal law which is His eternal *ratio* (*ST* I-II.91.1). Thus, after treating divine providence, it is proper to next treat eternal law, since when Thomas first speaks of the eternal law in the section on law, he immediately roots the eternal law in divine providence.[39] Thomas states:

> A law is nothing else but a dictate of practical reason in the ruler who governs a perfect community. Now it is evident, granted that the world is ruled by divine providence as was stated in the First Part, that the whole community of the universe is governed by divine reason. Wherefore the plan *(ratio)* itself of the government of things in God as existing in the ruler of the universe, has the nature of law. And since the divine reason's conception of things is not subject to time but is eternal, according to Proverbs 8, therefore, it is that this kind of law must be called eternal.[40]

Thomas compares divine providence with eternal law by noting that both are the *ratio* of a divine ruler. He notes that a law is nothing but a dictate of practical reason,[41] and thus inasmuch as God as provident ruler can be

---

cludunter causae secundae, quae sunt executrices huius ordinis. See also *SCG* III.70 which states that both God as higher agent and the creature as a lower agent are immediate causes, and see also *ST* III.19.3 which states that although God is the cause of all being, all can be called a cause by cooperating with God. Cf. *DV* 11.1; *SCG* III.67.

38. In reference to humans, the universal causality of divine providence does not negate free will but causes it, since God directs things to act in accord with their nature. Since by nature humans freely choose the means to achieve happiness, God moves them to act freely by divine government (*ST* I.22.2.4).

39. Since a law by its nature must be ordered to the common good as its end (I-II.90.2), and it is the role of providence (foresight) to order things in the present in order to obtain a future end (*ST* II-II.49.6), the background for law is the providence of the ruler. See also Oscar J. Brown, *Natural Rectitude and Divine Law in Aquinas* (Toronto: Pontifical Institute of Mediaeval Studies, 1981), 1–2, where Brown argues that when Thomas treats the subject of law, he at least implicitly always sets it within the context of providence. In relation to God, law is a continuation and perfection of creation moving creation back to its Author who is its beginning and end.

40. *ST* I-II.91.1: Nihil est aliud lex quam dictamen practicae rationis in principe qui gubernat aliquam communitatem perfectam. Manifestum est autem, supposito quod mundus divina providentia regatur, ut in Primo habitum est, quod tota communitas universi gubernatur ratione divina. Et ideo ipsa ratio gubernationis rerum in Deo sicut in principe universitatis existens legis habet rationem. Et quia divina ratio nihil concipit ex tempore, sed habet aeternum conceptum, ut dicitur Prov. VIII; inde est quod huiusmodi legem oportet dicere aeternam.

41. See *ST* I-II.90.1 where Thomas states that a law is the rule and measure of acts.

said to have a *ratio* that commands each creature to act for the common good of the universe, by definition He can also be said to have law.[42] Both the eternal law and divine providence are the eternal *ratio* of God and are universal in scope. Just as all of creation is subject to the created order of providence, all actions and movements are caused by eternal law (*ST* I-II.93.1; 93.5.3).

If divine providence and eternal law are both the *ratio* of God, why does Thomas make a distinction between them? In essence they are the same, but while the term providence emphasizes the wisdom ordering something to the end, the term law emphasizes the aspect of the command that moves something to its end.[43] To further understand the distinction between the two it is helpful to return to the analogy of sovereign prudence.[44]

In analyzing the virtue of prudence, Thomas makes a distinction between the three acts of the practical intellect that prudence perfects and the integral parts of prudence. The three acts of the intellect that prudence perfects are *consilium* (deliberation about the best means to an end), *iudicium* (judgment of the best means to an end), and *imperium* (commanding the act that was judged to be the best means).[45] Of these three, the third act, command, takes the form of law when made by a ruler to move his subjects to a particular end, for it is the *ratio* of the ruler directing his subjects to act in a particular manner (cf. *ST*

Since the rule and measure of human acts is reason, then law is a dictate of reason. Hence, law is in reason properly and in all other things by participation. See 90.4 for Thomas's complete definition of law: "a certain ordering of reason to the common good, by him who has care of the community and promulgated" (quaedam rationis ordinatio ad bonum commune, ab eo qui curam communitatis habet, promulgata).

42. See also *ST* I-II.93.1 where Thomas argues that just as in every artist there must pre-exist the *ratio* of the work of art, in every governor there must pre-exist the *ratio* of the order of things that are to be done by those who are subject to his government. This ratio of divine wisdom is the eternal law that directs all actions and movements. Cf. *SCG* III.64 and *ST* I-II.71.6.

43. See Michael Hoonhout who shows the relation between divine providence and eternal law in *The Systematic Understanding of Providence in the Summa Theologiae* (PhD. diss, Boston College, 1998), 233–45. Hoonhout states that the distinction between providence and eternal law is the same as the distinction between order and law. For a different view, see Cessario, *Introduction to Moral Theology*, 59. Cessario states that the eternal law stands in relation to providence as a theory of practice stands in relation to a conclusion for practical action. However, in the divine simplicity they are the same.

44. Sovereign prudence is the prudence of a ruler in governing. Thomas says that sovereign prudence is prudence in its special and most perfect sense (*ST* II-II.50.1).

45. *ST* II-II.47.8. See chapter four for a detailed explanation of the acts of the practical reason. Cf. *ST* I-II.11–17 on the different acts of the reason and will within a human act.

I-II.17.4 & 5). Unlike the three acts perfected by prudence, the integral parts of prudence are dispositions that must be present for prudence to exist. One of these dispositions is foresight *(providentia)*: the ordering of something in the present to reach a particular end.[46] Foresight is the most important integral part of prudence since it is absolutely necessary that the agent foresees the right action to reach a particular end *(ST* II-II.49.6.1). Included within a human act of *providentia* are the steps of counsel, judgment, and command, since it is necessary for us to take counsel and to judge in order to determine the proper form of the act to be commanded *(ST* II-II.49.6.3).

When the virtue of sovereign prudence is analogously applied to God, on the one hand, eternal law is the act of God's practical reason commanding all creation to act for its divinely appointed end *(ST* I-II.93.1). Thus, eternal law is God's command to order well the subjects of creation. On the other hand, divine *providentia* is God's foresight to order well all things to their final ends. Because *providentia* includes the acts of counsel,[47] judgment, and command, it is a broader concept than eternal law because it contains within itself the act of command that is central to any legislative act.[48] Thus, God's command of what He has foreseen in His providential wisdom is the eternal law.[49] Eternal law is God's wisdom directing all creatures to their proper end. Since it directs all things that have being, every action of every creature is caused by eternal law and participates in eternal law.

In summary, because all effects are like their cause, a better understanding of the cause leads to a better understanding of the effect. By analyzing these aspects of Thomas's theology of God, a greater understanding of the

---

46. *ST* II-II.48. Besides *providentia*, the other seven integral parts of human prudence are memory *(memoria)*, understanding *(intellectu)*, docility *(docilitate)*, shrewdness *(solertia)*, reason *(ratio)*, circumspection *(circumspectione)*, and caution *(cautione)*. Cf. I-II.56.5.3. Again, not all these elements apply to God, and of those that do, they apply only in an analogous sense.

47. It is essential to keep in mind that God does not take counsel as humans do but is essentially counsel (cf. *ST* I.22.1.1; II-II.52.3.3).

48. See also Walter Ferrell, *The Natural Moral Law According to Saint Thomas and Suarez* (Ditchling: St. Dominic's Press, 1930), 32–35, where he states that the relation between eternal law and providence is the relation between command and foresight in prudence. Ferrell than gives a commentary on God's act of creation and providence based on the parts of the human act given in *ST* I-II.7–17. Ferrell comes to the conclusion that the act of providence is the entire process of ordering creation, and eternal law is only the last step.

49. See also *SCG* III.115 which states that law is the rational plan of divine providence ordering creation to its end.

effect (creation as participating in God) can be obtained. God, who is pure act, *esse* by His essence, and all-powerful, is the efficient cause of all things. God, who contains within His essence the divine ideas of all beings, is the exemplar cause of all, and God, who is goodness itself and wills all things in willing His goodness, is the final cause of all beings. In addition to this, through His divine providence and eternal law, God orders all things to their proper end and directs them to this end.

The First Perfections of a Creature by Participation

Having treated the cause of all being, I will now move on to the effects that participate in this cause. Since divine providence has ordered all things to act in accord with their mode, before treating the operation of creatures (the secondary perfections), it is fitting to begin with the perfections of the substance (the first perfections).[50]

Thomas makes a distinction between the first perfection of a creature, which is the act of the substance bringing it into existence, and the secondary perfections, which are all acts that are superadded to the substance: accidental perfections.[51] Another way of saying this is that the first perfection refers to the substantial act of *esse,* and the secondary perfections refer to operation and superadded forms.[52] In other words, there are certain perfections that a creature has to the extent that it "is" (has

---

50. All things are perfect to the extent that they perform their proper act (*ST* I.4). For example, divine providence moves humans to perform actions (secondary perfections) in accord with their substance (the first perfection: human nature).

51. *QQ* 12.5.5; *QQ* 2.1.1; *CM* 5.9; *SCG* II.52 and 54. This distinction is not the same as the distinction between substantial predication of *esse* (which is only in God) and accidental predication of *esse* (which refers to all creatures) (*QQ* 2.2.1). Hence, when Thomas speaks of substantial *esse* in creatures, he does not mean that *esse* is predicated substantially of creatures (as part of their essence), but that *esse* is the initial act of the substance by which they are. Whereas the accidental act of *esse* is the further act by which an existing substance is further qualified (the *esse* of its accidents—*LC* 22; cf. *DP* 5.4.3). See also Wippel, *Metaphysical Thought of Thomas Aquinas,* 106–17; Fabro, *La Nozione,* 182–84 and "Intensive Hermeneutics . . . ," 468; and Joseph Owens, "The Accidental and Essential Character of Being," in *St. Thomas Aquinas on the Existence of God* (Albany: State University of New York, 1980), 65, 94–95.

52. *ST* I.42.1.1 which states that the first effect of form is being, for everything has being by its form. The second effect is operation, for every agent acts through its form. See also *ST* I.76.6 which states that the substantial act of *esse* makes everything actual and is hence called the "first of all acts" (Primum autem inter omnes actus est esse). See also Fabro, "The Transcendentality of Ens-Esse and the Ground of Metaphysics," *International Philosophical Quarterly* 6 (1966): 422–26.

esse), while other perfections have to be acquired by means of additional acts.[53] For example, all humans are good to the extent they have being, but only certain humans have acquired the additional perfections of wisdom. Thus, in this section I will analyze the perfections that a creature has to the extent that it has *esse*. In the next section I will examine secondary perfections since the type of secondary perfections that a creature can receive flow from their first mode of participation, because all act in accord with their form.[54] I will first show that all creatures participate in God as efficient cause inasmuch as their acts of *esse* participate in God who is essentially the act of *esse*. I will then show how the mode of this participation in the divine *esse* is caused by the divine ideas in God (as exemplary cause), which determine this mode of participation through the form of the creature. Finally, I will show how the creature is ordered to its particular end by participation in God who is the final cause. This diverse participation of the substance allows for the possibility of a variety of actions (secondary perfections) in which a subject is ordered to its proper end in accordance with its form.

As the efficient cause of creation, God moves all creatures to their act of *esse*. Since only in God can *esse* be identical to essence, *esse* must be a participated act for all other creatures.[55] Although the act of *esse* as

---

53. *ST* I.54.3.3; *ST* I.76.4; *ST* I.77.6; *DSC* I.9; *DV* 21.6.5; *SCG* II.68. Cf. *SCG* I.39 where Thomas notes that attributes that are "predicated essentially" have nothing extraneous mixed with them, but the subject of these predicates can have something besides being and goodness added to it by participation (cf. *DP* 7.4). In other words, if something extraneous was mixed with something that was predicated to the essence (e.g., *esse* and goodness), then the subject would become a different species. Hence, any secondary perfections are accidents received through participation in the *esse* of God (*ST* I.25.6).

54. Whatever is received into something is received according to the condition of the recipient (*ST* I.75.5; cf. I.89.1 & 4; *LC* 20). Hence, all secondary perfections are received according to the first perfection of the creature.

55. In Thomas's understanding of participation, whatever is predicated of something by participation, can always be reduced to something that has the perfection essentially. For example, Thomas will often speak of the participation of an iron bar in the heat of the fire. Thomas states, "For whatever is found in anything by participation, must be caused in it by that to which it belongs essentially, as iron becomes heated by fire." (Si enim aliquid invenitur in aliquo per participationem, necesse est quod causatur in ipso ab eo cui essentialiter convenit; sicut ferrum fit ignitum ab igne.—*ST* I.44.1; cf. *ST* I.3.8; I.4.2; I.61.1; I-II 5.6.2; *SCG* II.15; *DP* 3.5; *SS* 6.) The point of this example is that an iron bar does not have heat of its own essence but must receive it from something that is hot by its own essence. When this notion of participation is applied to the causality of God who is *esse* by essence, we can see that all creatures receive their *esse* from God (*QQ* 3.1.1, 12.5.5). See also *SCG* I.98: Omne autem quod est per participationem, reducitur ad id quod est per seipsum ("And all that is by participation is reduced to that which is through itself"). Cf. *ST* I.4.2 and *LC* 3. Even though Thomas will sometimes speak of participating in something that does not have

the primary act of a creature is unique, nonetheless, it is like secondary actions in that anytime that something is moved to act the agent moving the thing to act is the efficient cause of this action.[56] For example, if a person moves a saw to cut a board, the person is the efficient cause of the action of cutting. Since God moves all creatures to their acts (including the act of *esse*), God is the first efficient cause of all actions.[57] Thomas notes that all actions (including the first act of *esse*) participate in God who is act by His essence.[58]

Furthermore, all things act in accord with their form. For example, dogs perform dog actions, humans perform human actions. In relation to *esse*, dogs exist as dogs; humans exist as humans. Consequently, the mode of participation that each creature has in the *esse* of God is determined by the essence of the creature, for God causes it *to be* in accord with its natural form. God is the primary cause of the creature's being and the creature's essence is the secondary cause. Thomas explains that the relation between essence and *esse* in a creature is that between potency and act.[59] Unlike God who is pure act as pure being, in all creatures there is something that receives *esse* since all participate in the First Act

---

the perfection essentially, ultimately, the source of the participated perfection can be traced back to that which has the perfection essentially. For example, Thomas sometimes speaks of the passions participating in reason to the extent they are governed by reason (*ST* I-II.55.3.3, 56.4, 58.2). However, since reason is a participation in the knowledge of God who is truth by His essence, the reasonableness of the passions comes from God (*ST* I-II.19.4; II-II.52.2). Cf. *ST* I.45.5; *QQ* 12.5.5; and *ST* I.96.1: "All that is through participation is subject to what is essential and universal" (Omne autem quod est per participationem, subditur ei quod est per essentiam et universaliter).

56. *SCG* I.28.7. Thomas further states that all actions can be ultimately reduced to God who is the efficient cause of all. Cf. *DP* 7.2.9.

57. *ST* I-II 79.2: "Every action is caused by something existing in act, since nothing produces an action save insofar as it is in act; and every being in act is reduced to the first act, God, as to its cause, Who is act by His Essence." (Omnis autem actio causatur ab aliquo existente in actu, quia nihil agit nisi secundum quod est actu, omne autem ens actu reducitur in primum actum, scilicet deum, sicut in causam, qui est per suam essentiam actus. Unde relinquitur quod deus sit causa omnis actionis, inquantum est actio.)

58. *QQ* 3.1.1; 3.8.1. Since God alone is act itself, it is not possible that any creature be in act except inasmuch as it participates in the action of God. See also *QQ* 12.5.5: ". . . each and every thing that is in potency is made in act by the fact that it participates in a higher act. And something becomes most in act by participating in the first and pure act by likeness. And the first act is the subsisting *esse* through itself, from where everything receives completion through the fact it participates *esse*." (. . . quod unumquodque quod est in potentia fit actu per hoc quod participat actum superiorem. Per hoc autem aliquid maxime fit actu quod participat per similitudinem primum et purum actum. Primus autem actus est esse subsistens per se: unde completionem unumquodque recipit per hoc quod participat esse.)

59. See Clarke, "The Limitation of Act . . . ," 167–94.

to the extent that they have *esse*. Therefore, the nature that participates in *esse* is one thing and the participated *esse* cannot be identified with it. Consequently, the nature of all creatures is in potency to the participated *esse* that is act (*DSC* 1).[60] Whenever a primary cause works through a secondary cause, the action is only as perfect as the potency of the secondary cause allows.

Since something comes into being by performing its act of *esse*, God creates things by giving them their act of *esse* (*ST* I.41.1; *LC* 22). Thomas states, "for a subject to come to be is for the subject to participate in *esse* through the influence of a higher being."[61] Not only does it come into existence by participating in *esse*, it is through this same participation that the creature is sustained by God.[62] Thomas compares the way God creates and sustains creatures by causing their *esse* to the way the sun lights the air. Just as the air only retains light as long as it participates in the light of the sun, so also creatures have *esse* only as long as they participate in the *esse* of God (*ST* I.104.1). The key point here is that the air does not have the power to be lit up without the continuing action of the sun (for the air is not light by essence, but only by participation). When the sun goes down, the air grows dark. Likewise with *esse*, creatures are not *esse*

---

60. By nature, Thomas here means either an essence composed of form and matter or a subsistent form (an angel). Although form is an act in relation to either matter (if the substantial form) or a subject (if an accidental form), nonetheless as subjects participating in *esse*, they are in potency to *esse* (*DSC* 1.1). Cf. *Physic* VIII.21: "It is indeed necessary that every simple, subsisting substance be either its own *esse* or participate in *esse*. But a substance that is subsisting *esse* itself cannot be but one. Therefore, every substance that comes after the first simple substance participates in *esse*. But whatever participates is composed of that which participates and that which is participated in, and that which participates is in potency to that which is participated in. Hence every substance, no matter how simple it may be, if it comes after the first simple substance, is in potency to the act of being." (Necesse est enim quod omnis substantia simplex subsistens, vel ipsa sit suum esse, vel participet esse. Substantia autem simplex quae est ipsum esse subsistens, non potest esse nisi una, sicut nec albedo, si esset subsistens, posset esse nisi una. Omnis ergo substantia quae est post primam substantiam simplicem, participat esse. Omne autem participans componitur ex participante et participato, et participans est in potentia ad participatum. In omni ergo substantia quantumcumque simplici, post primam substantium simplicem, est Potentia essendi.) Cf. *ST* I.50.2.3, I.54.3; *DP* 7.2.9; *SCG* I.22, II.53; *SCG* III.66; *SS* 8; *DA* 1.6.

61. *SS* 9: Quia hoc ipsum est subiectum fieri secundum hunc factionis modum, quod est subiectum esse participare per influentiam superioris entis. This particular passage refers to all things that come to exist, including those which God causes by means of a secondary cause (influentiam superioris entis). All things, whether caused directly by God through creation or through a secondary cause, are moved from nonbeing to being by means of participation in *esse*. Cf. *ST* I.8.1, 45.5; *SCG* II.15; *CPT* 68; *QQ* 12.5.5.

62. Cf. *ST* I.8.1; cf. I.8.3.1, which states that God is essentially present in all things as the cause of their *esse*.

by essence, but only by participation, and hence if they are not sustained in *esse,* they cease to exist. Thus, God as efficient cause, creates and sustains all things by means of causing them to participate in Himself who is *esse* essentially.[63]

Whereas the existence of all things is explained by participation in God as efficient cause, the mode of being of each creature is explained by participation in God as exemplary cause. It is the exemplary *ratio* within the divine mind that causes the diversity of beings by causing a diversity of essences (*ST* I.14.6.3). The greater the potency of the essence, the greater the participated act of *esse.*[64] By causing a diversity of essences, God, as exemplary cause, causes a diversity of acts of *esse* and wisely orders the universe.[65] Thomas explains, "Things are not distinguished from one another in having *esse,* for in this they agree . . . things differ because they have diverse natures, to which *esse* is acquired in diverse modes."[66] Thomas shows that all creatures have *esse* by participation in the *esse* of God, but what makes each creature unique is its particular mode of participation in the *esse* of God based upon its diverse nature.[67]

Creatures that more fully participate in God are more like God by being closer to the divine likeness than others. Thomas explains:

The reason for the order of things is derived from the diversity of forms. Indeed, since it is in accord with its form that a thing has *esse,* and since anything, insofar as it has *esse,* approaches the likeness of God Who is His own simple *esse,* it must be that form is nothing else than a divine likeness that is participated in things. . . . But likeness that is viewed in relation to one simple thing cannot be diversified unless by virtue of the likeness being more or less close or remote. Now the nearer a thing comes to divine likeness the more perfect it is.[68]

---

63. *DP* 7.2.10; cf. *DP* 3.1.11.

64. See Owens, "The Accidental and Essential Character of Being," 92–95, on how although the efficient cause of being is God, the formal cause of being is the form of the creature. The form as potency to the act of being limits being to its own capacity.

65. See *ST* I.15.2 which states that the order of the universe is intended by God and created immediately by Him. Thomas explains that because there are many ideas in the divine mind, every creature has its own species according to which it participates in some degree in likeness to the divine essence. For God, by knowing His essence, knows all ways His essence is imitable. Since God's knowledge is the exemplar cause of all things, He intends and creates the order within the universe. Cf. *SCG* I.54; *DP* 3.16.

66. *SCG* I.26: Res ad invicem non distinguuntur secundum quod habent esse: quia in hoc omnia conveniunt . . . Relinquitur ergo quod res propter hoc different quod habent diversas naturas, quibus acquiritur esse diversimode. Cf. *DP* 7.2.9.

67. See *ST* III.3.8 which states that the divine Word is the exemplar likeness of all creatures. Creatures are established in their proper species by participation in this likeness.

68. *SCG* III.97: Ex diversitate autem formarum sumitur ratio ordinis rerum. Cum enim

Because there is a diversity of forms that vary in their degree of potency to their act of *esse,* creatures are more or less like God by participating to a greater or lesser degree in the *esse* of God.[69] Hence, although God creates the universe by causing created things to have *esse,* He causes it to have a particular mode of *esse* by causing a diversity of forms based on the divine ideas. Since some things are more like God than others based on their degree of participation in God's *esse,* God as exemplary cause creates an ordered universe.[70] From this diversity of forms comes a diversity of operation (*SCG* III.97), which will be treated below.

Because the final cause is the cause of all causes, the diversity and *esse* within creation can also ultimately be attributed to God as final cause. Another way of saying this is that the reason that God creates an ordered universe filled with diverse creatures is because of His goodness. The divine goodness is not fully manifested by any particular creature because created effects are not formally like God but only analogically like God.[71] In other words, no particular creature manifests the fullness of the divine goodness, but rather only the entire universe in its ordered diversity most fittingly manifests the breadth of divine goodness.[72] Therefore, because of His goodness, God has made an ordered universe where certain things are more like Him than others based on their mode of participation in *esse.*

Also, since all things are created on account of God's goodness and the end of the first agent is the end of all (*SCG* III.25), included in the natural inclination that each creature has to its particular act is an inclination to the one end that is common to all, the goodness of God (*SCG*

---

forma sit secundum quam res habet esse; res autem quaelibet secundum quod habet esse, accedat ad similitudinem dei, qui est ipsum suum esse simplex: necesse est quod forma nihil sit aliud quam divina similitudo participata in rebus . . . Similitudo autem ad unum simplex considerata diversificari non potest nisi secundum quod magis vel minus similitudo est propinqua vel remota. Quanto autem aliquid propinquius ad divinam similitudinem accedit, perfectius est. Cf. *SCG* I.32; *DV* 2.3.16; *ST* III.57.4; *LC* 19; 22.

69. *DP* 3.4.9 states that creatures are like God in two ways. First as imitating the divine ideas through their forms, and secondly by imitating the divine essence by having *esse* and goodness. Cf. Te Velde, *Participation,* 110–13; *DP* 3.6.25, 3.7.10, 7.1.8.

70. Because an effect is always like its cause, all things that participate in God as efficient, exemplary, and final cause are like God (*ST* I.6.4). Hence, likeness always accompanies the participation of an effect within its cause. See *SCG* I.29 which states that all creation is like God since whatever perfection is found in creation, is found in God essentially, and creatures have these perfections by a certain participation. Cf. *QQ* 12.5.5.

71. Cf. Blanchette, *The Perfection of the Universe,* 180–86. In Thomas, see *SCG* II.45.

72. *ST* I.47.1 & 2; *SCG* III.97. And even the whole universe only shows a small aspect of the glory of God.

III.97). Created reality must be ordered to an end because it arises from the intentional act of God's will. Although God necessarily wills His own goodness, He voluntarily wills things apart from Himself on account of His goodness. Since the ultimate end of all things is what the primary maker intends, God wills things as ordered to His goodness.[73] Therefore, because the end for which God creates is the divine goodness, creation by its nature has a divine end. However, all creatures achieve this common end by acting in accord with their mode. Thomas states that all things desire God in their proper mode: some through intellectual knowledge, some through sense knowledge, and others as having a natural desire without knowledge.[74] Hence, God as final cause has created a diverse world that is naturally inclined to His goodness and achieves this end by acting in accord with its particular mode.[75]

Thomas also explains that the divine goodness is the cause of creation by noting that goodness by its nature is diffusive (*SCG* III.24). Thomas notes that natural things have not only an inclination to goodness as to their end, but also an inclination to diffuse this goodness to others. He continues by noting that while the will of humans by nature communicates goodness, the divine will as goodness itself especially communicates its goodness as the source of all created perfections. It is fitting that all creation participates in the goodness of God who is the source of this goodness as the final cause of creation (*ST* I.19.2; I.5.4.2).

Because the mode of participation varies with the particular form, the more perfect the participation of a creature in goodness, the more extensively it can communicate its own goodness to creatures of lesser perfection.[76] Thomas states that a creature is most like God when it causes goodness in others: "Hence, a creature approaches more perfectly to God's likeness if it is not only good, but can also act for the good of other things. . . . But no creature would act for the benefit of another crea-

---

73. *ST* I.19.3. Cf. Joseph Owens, "Human Destiny in Aquinas," in *Human Destiny: Some Problems for Catholic Philosophy*, ed. Joseph Owens, 31–49 (Washington, D.C.: The Catholic University of America Press, 1985), 31–34.

74. *ST* I.6.1.2. See also *SCG* III.25 which states that although all creatures tend toward God who is their ultimate end, intellectual creatures attain this end by their proper operation of understanding God. Cf. I-II.109.3.

75. Thomas notes that the way a thing becomes most like God is its ultimate end (*SCG* III.25.8). This participation in the divine likeness through secondary perfections will be covered later.

76. *SCG* III.24. See also *Ethic* I.3 which states that there are two types of order: the relation of all things to their end and the relation of the particular parts to each other. The first type is the cause of the second.

ture unless plurality and inequality existed in created things."[77] In other words, because there is inequality in the universe, there is the possibility of one being acting for the good of another. By causing goodness in another creature, a creature is most like God. Therefore, in order for creatures to more properly manifest the goodness of God, it is necessary that there is a diversity of creatures and that this diversity includes inequality among creatures.[78] God as final cause creates an ordered universe where a diversity of forms results in a diversity of operations through which creatures can be more like God by causing goodness in others.

God as efficient, exemplary, and final cause has created an ordered universe by means of causing the participated acts of *esse* of all creatures. God through the divine ideas on account of His goodness has caused a diversity of forms; hence, a diversity of operations follow. The eternal law moves all things to their proper end through their substantial forms. Thus, in order to better understand the participation of the creature in eternal law through its operation, it is fitting to further analyze the first acts of the creature: the substantial perfections.[79] Substantial perfections can be divided into two categories, those convertible with *ens,* which all beings have to the extent that they have *esse* (such as goodness, truth, and oneness—i.e., anything that is is also in some sense one, intelligible, and good),[80] and those that refer to the specific manner of being *(entis).* This second category of perfections are not equally in all beings but only in those who participate in *esse* in a greater way (such as having life and

77. *SCG* II.45: Perfectus igitur accedit res creata ad dei similitudinem si non solum bona est sed etiam ad bonitatem aliorum agere potest . . . non autem posset creatura ad bonitatem alterius creaturae agere nisi esset in rebus creatis pluralitas et inaequalitas.

78. Human imperfections allow the more perfect to cause virtues to grow in the less perfect, for in causing this goodness in others, they are more like God. Thomistic morality is about more than an individual moral agent acquiring virtue, but includes a web of causality that is part of the order of providence. I owe this insight to Dr. Michael Hoonhout.

79. E.g., in humans the natural inclinations come from the substantial perfections that they have as living and understanding beings.

80. Since *ens* is the composition of *essentia* and *esse,* something is *ens* to the extent that it participates in *esse* (*Metaph* IV.1, XII.1; Cf. *DV* I.1.SC 4). See Fabro, who emphasizes that *ens* is both "content" *(essentia)* and "act" *(esse).* He continues, "Just as *loquens* is the one who speaks and *ambulans* is the one who walks, so, and primarily, the participle *ens* signifies the act of being: 'primarily,' because *esse* is what makes every act to be in act"; see "The Transcendentality of *Ens-Esse* and the Ground of Metaphysic," *International Philosophical Quarterly* 6 (1966): 411–12. Thus, since the participle *ens* refers to something to the extent it has *esse,* something also has those attributes that are convertible with *ens,* to the extent that it participates in *esse.* Cf. *SCG* II.15 which states that only God is *ens* by His essence, which is His [act of] *esse.* All other things are *ens* by participation.

understanding).[81] Both of these types of perfections are participations in God who is *esse* itself.

First, those perfections that are convertible with *ens* will be examined. There are certain perfections that are universal to all creatures because they are convertible with being. Thomas notes in *De Veritate* that being *(ens)* is what is first conceived by the intellect and there are certain other attributes that are common to all inasmuch as they have being. These attributes can be divided into two groups: those attributes that pertain to being considered absolutely: all beings can be said to be a thing *(res)* and one *(unum)*;[82] and those attributes that pertain to one being in relation to another. This latter group can again be divided into two: beings as divided from others are something *(aliquid)*, and beings as coming together from another *(convenientiam unius ab altero)*. These latter beings are either called good *(bonum)* in relation to the appetitive power of the soul,[83] and true *(verum)* in relation to the cognitive power.[84] The attributes of a thing—one, other (something), good, and true—are often referred to as the transcendentals since they transcend every genus and are attributable to all.[85] Hence, every creature to the extent it participates in *esse* also participates in these attributes.

Since these perfections are in something to the extent it has being, God as essential being also possesses these attributes essentially. Thomas speaks of God as essentially one (*ST* I.11), essentially good (*ST* I.6), and essentially truth (*ST* I.16.5). Likewise, all creatures are one, good, and true, to the extent that they participate in God.[86] Thus, Thomas often

81. For this distinction, see *DV* I.1 where Thomas distinguishes between two modes of being *(ens)*: one mode that refers to the special manner of existing and the other that refers to those attributes convertible with being.

82. See *ST* I.11.1: "One is convertible with being" (unum convertitur cum ente). The convertibility of oneness and being is a very common theme in Aquinas; see also *ST* I.11.3.2; *Metaph* IV.1; I *Sent.* 24.3; etc.

83. See *ST* I.5.1: "Goodness and being are the same and differ only in idea" (bonum et ens sunt idem secundem rem, sed differunt secundum rationem tantum). See also I-II.55.4.

84. *DV* I.1; Cf. *ST* I-II.55.4.1. Cf. *ST* I.16.3: "as good is convertible with being, so is the true. But as good adds to being the notion of desirable, so the true adds relation to the intellect" (sicut bonum convertitur cum ente, ita et verum. Sed tamen, sicut bonum addit rationem appetibilis supra ens, ita et verum comparationem ad intellectum). Cf. *ST* I.54.2; I-II.3.7.

85. Cf. *ST* I.30.3. See Joseph Owens, *An Elementary Christian Metaphysics* (Milwaukee: Bruce, 1980), chapter 8.

86. Although in theory, one could speak of a creature participating in the perfections of thingness and otherness to the extent that it participates in *esse,* I am not aware of Thomas ever making this kind of statement.

states that creatures are not good by essence but by participation (*DV* 21.5; *DH* 2–5; *SCG* I.38; I.40; III.20; *ST* I.106.4), and the greater the participation the higher the creature's place in nature (*ST* III.57.4).

Likewise, in speaking of a creature's participation in the oneness of God, Thomas states, "a thing has *esse* in the manner it possesses unity, for everything struggles as much as it can against any division of itself, lest it tend to non-*esse*."[87] The greater the participation of something in God as essentially one, the greater the unity existing within the creature, as higher creatures are more simple.[88]

Finally, just as good adds to *esse* a relation to the appetite, truth adds to *esse* a relation to the intellect (*ST* I.16.3). The truth that is substantially found in things is truth in the secondary sense, since truth is primarily in the intellect. This truth substantially found in things consists in its relation to the divine intellect and not in relation to ours (*ST* I.16.1.2; *DV* I.4). Thus, creatures are said to be true to the extent they express likeness to the form in the mind of God as exemplary cause.[89] The greater the creature's participation in truth the more it manifests God and hence the more God can be known by contemplating it (*ST* I.94.1). In conclusion, all creatures by their substantial act of being and apart from their operations possess goodness, oneness, and truth as convertible with their participated act of *esse*. The greater the participated act of *esse*, the greater the primary perfections of goodness, oneness, and truth. God causes these perfections by creating and sustaining every creature.[90]

Having treated those perfections that are convertible with being, it is now time to treat those perfections that are a special manner of being contained in the substantial act of *esse*. These perfections are not common to all creatures, but nonetheless are based on the particular form of a creature, and hence are in a creature to the extent it has *esse*. Thomas states that all grades of things reduce to three: being (as something is in

87. *SCG* I.42: Secundum hunc modum res habet esse quo possidet unitatem: unde unumquodque suae divisioni; pro posse repugnat ne per hoc in non esse tendat. Cf. *DH* 2; *ST* I.11.1.*sed contra;* III.2.9 which states in the first objection that what is united is by participation while what is one is by essence. (Although this is in the objection, Thomas affirms this as a correct principle.)

88. *LC* 10; Cf. *ST* I.11.4.3. For example, the greater the intellectual power, the less forms are needed to understand something (*ST* I.55.3).

89. *ST* I.16.1; cf. I.84.1. In the human speculative intellect something is truth in the primary sense if it corresponds to the truth in things (truth in the secondary sense—*ST* I.16.5).

90. As will be seen below, the goodness, unity, and truth of a creature are increased by operation and, in particular, by grace and glory.

itself), living (as tending to something else: capable of movement), and understanding (as having other things formally in itself—*LC* 18). In other words, all of creation can be placed in three different categories: All creatures have *esse*. Some have life and *esse*. And a few have understanding, life, and *esse* (*LC* 1, 3, 9; *DV* 10.1.5; Cf. *ST* I-II.2.5.3).

Since creatures that are alive and understand have these perfections inasmuch as they have *esse*, these perfections are contained in their substantial act of *esse*. Thus, in reference to life, Thomas states, "To live, is nothing more than having *esse* in this or that nature. . . . Hence, living is not an accidental, but an essential predicate."[91] Likewise in reference to understanding, to be a being that understands refers to a particular mode of having *esse*. Thomas explains that humans have life more perfectly than plants and animals by being able to order their movements intelligently. God who is understanding essentially has life most perfectly.[92] Thus, just as living is a form of *esse*, understanding is a form of living and therefore a form of *esse* (*ST* I.4.2.2; *LC* 12). Consequently, like goodness, humans have understanding to the extent they have *esse*, since it is natural for a human to understand.[93] Even though understanding and life are by means of participation, a creature has them to the extent that it has *esse* and hence they are modes of the substantial act of *esse* in a creature.

Among these three modes of the substantial act of being, there is a hierarchy of participation in God. Those with only being participate at the lowest level, while those with being, life, and understanding participate most perfectly.[94] The mode of the participation of the substance determines the type of secondary actions that a creature is naturally inclined to perform. For example, Thomas notes that humans are naturally inclined to be, to live, and to know the truth (*ST* I-II.10.1 and 94.2). From these substantial attributes also flow additional properties that a creature has to the extent it has *esse*. For example, since all humans have

91. *ST* I.18.2; cf. *ST* I.4.2.2; *LC* 12. Vivere nihil aliud est quam esse in tali natura . . . Unde vivum non est praedicatum accidentale, sed substantiale. In this passage Thomas is referring to living in the general sense of "being alive," not to particular operations of life, which are not predicated substantially.

92. *ST* I.18.3; *Ioan.* I.3. Note that in the *Summa Theologiae* Thomas treats the divine life (I.18) within the treatment of God's understanding (I.14–18) because to understand is a kind of life (prologue to I.14).

93. Here I am referring only to the active power of understanding and not to particular acts of understanding.

94. See *DV* 10.1.5 where Thomas states that only those that have being, life, and understanding are perfect enough to be said to be in the image of God. Creatures that only have being and life, like the plants and animals, fall short of this perfection.

an intellectual appetite by nature, they have a natural inclination to truth and the good inasmuch as they have *esse*.[95] Likewise, because freedom comes from a human's ability to know a variety of means to a particular end, humans have the capacity to be free inasmuch as they have *esse*.

In summary, God as efficient, exemplary, and final cause has established certain perfections within creatures that they have inasmuch as they participate in *esse*. Some of these perfections are convertible with *esse* and are in all creatures, while others are only in certain creatures because they are confined to a certain mode of being. The latter perfections are distinct modes of the first act of the creature, the act of *esse*. Both types of perfections participate in God as efficient cause inasmuch as He moves the essence to have *esse*. They participate in God as exemplary cause inasmuch as He causes them to have the act of *esse* in various modes based on how the form is a copy of a divine idea. They also participate in God as final cause as ordered to the divine goodness in accord with their particular mode.

The Second Perfections of a Creature by Participation

Because God creates things on account of an end, the whole of creation was made to be brought to this end. For all eternity God intended the end of a perfect universe. Because no creature fully manifests the divine goodness, a diverse abundance of creatures were created in order that creation as a whole would more perfectly participate in the divine goodness. However, because creatures are more like God when they act and cause being, God made all creatures in a state of potency to their particular type of action. Hence, by performing their particular type action, all creatures contribute to the perfection of the universe: the common good of all. Since God both creates and guides creatures to their proper perfection on account of the same end, each creature acts in accord with its particular mode. Hence, the variety of modes of substantial participation in God causes a variety of actions (secondary perfections) which are also participations in God who is all perfections essentially.[96]

The term secondary perfections refer to all acts that are in accord

95. In *ST* I-II.10.1 the good is naturally desired as the object of the will along with knowing the truth, living, and being.

96. Thomas notes in *SCG* III.97 that a form is a participation in the divine likeness. The nearer the form approaches the divine likeness, the more perfect it is, causing a diversity of perfections and a diversity of acts.

with the substantial form of the creature.[97] These acts include all accidental forms that perfect a substance with a special emphasis on operations.[98] It is through these secondary perfections that a creature reaches
its particular end, which is its greatest participation in the likeness of
God (*SCG* III.25). Since the eternal law directs creatures to their end,
it is especially in reference to these secondary perfections that a creature
participates in the eternal law, the governing *ratio* of God. Although the
eternal law as the *ratio* of God is primarily an exemplary cause, because it
directs things to an end by means of moving them to act, it is inherently
related to final and efficient causality. Hence, this section will once again
treat the participation of the creature in God as efficient, exemplary, and
final cause of all secondary perfections.

   This section will begin by explaining how creatures are ultimately
perfected by participating in the divine *esse* through their secondary perfections. Then, because creatures act as instrumental causes when they
cause secondary perfections, it will explain what Thomas means when
he calls creatures instrumental causes. In reference to God as efficient
cause it will show how although God alone can sufficiently cause *esse,*
creatures can be secondary causes of *esse* to the extent they participate in
the power of God. In reference to God as exemplary cause, it will show
how creatures as instrumental causes are moved by the *ratio* in the divine
mind. Whenever any creature is moved by this *ratio,* it participates in
eternal law. Finally, in reference to God as final cause it will show how
the secondary perfections cause the creatures to participate more perfectly in the goodness of God as achieving their predetermined end.

   God is the efficient, exemplary, and final cause of all secondary perfections by causing creatures not only to participate in His *esse* through
their substantial perfections but also through all of their accidental perfections. However, unlike the substantial perfections of a creature, accidental forms differ in the way that they have *esse* from the substantial
form. Thomas states that in contrast to what is apprehended as convertible with *esse* such as oneness and goodness, "accidents and nonsubsistent

---

97. Recall that all things are perfect to the extent that they are in act (*ST* I.4).

98. In reference to accidental forms (verses the substantial form) Thomas states that an
accident, inasmuch as it is a form, is a kind of act (*ST* I.66.1.3; cf. *SCG* I.23; *ST* I-II.110.4.3).
Among the different types of accidents, operation is especially important since it is through
operation that a creature achieves the particular end preordained by God (*ST* I.4.1). Hence,
when I speak of accidental perfections I am referring to those qualities and acts which are
the proper perfection of the creature as ordered by God to a particular end in accord with
the creature's nature.

forms are called beings, not as if they themselves had *esse,* but because by them something is, so also is it called good or one not by some distinct goodness or oneness, but because by them something is good or one."[99] In other words, only subsisting things are properly called beings. Accidents are only beings in a qualified sense because by them something exists in a certain mode but does not exist simply (*DP* 3.8; *DSC* 1.9). Thus, Thomas states that accidents are for the sake of the substance so that the substance can be perfected by them.[100]

Creatures can only be called good in the absolute sense through the secondary perfection of their proper operation.[101] Thomas states that goodness like being is accidental and substantial. If something has being substantially, this is called being in an absolute sense, but if something has being accidentally, this called being in a qualified sense.[102] The opposite is true of goodness. If something is good inasmuch as it has substantial being, it is good in a certain sense, but in order to be good without qualification, it must also have accidental goodness by means of operation.[103] In other words, unlike *esse* where the substantial act of *esse* alone can be called *esse* in an unqualified sense, something is not good without qualification unless it possesses accidental goodness.[104] For example, a human is not considered good unqualifiedly unless he possesses certain participated superadded activities such as knowledge and virtue.[105]

This notion that creatures are only good unqualifiedly through their proper operation leads to a very important distinction between the perfection of the universe in reference to its substantial forms, and its perfection in reference to its end that consists of either its operation or what

---

99. *ST* I-II.55.4.1: Quod sicut accidentia et formae non subsistentes dicuntur entia, non quia ipsa habeant esse, sed quia eis aliquid est, ita etiam dicuntur bona vel una, non quidem aliqua alia bonitate vel unitate, sed quia eis est aliquid bonum vel unum.

100. *SCG* III.75.10. Since something is perfect inasmuch as it is in act, Thomas elsewhere states that an accident ceases to be or comes to be inasmuch as a subject begins or ceases to be in act with a particular accident (*ST* I-II.110.2.3).

101. Thomas states that creatures attain their end by operation, which is the way that they are most like God, and therefore most perfect (*SCG* III.25.8).

102. Recall that accidents are only beings in a qualified sense because by them something exists in a certain mode but does not exist simply (*DP* 3.8; *DSC* 1.9). Cf. *SCG* III.75.10, which states that accidents exist on account of the substance so that substances can be perfected by them.

103. *DV* 21.5; *ST* I.5.1.1. By accidental goodness, Thomas means that it is not part of the substantial form but is nonetheless proper to the creature in that it naturally fulfills it.

104. There is the one exception of God who is good in the unqualified sense by His essence.

105. *ST* I-II.18.3; cf. I.5.1.3.

is attained by operation. In the first sense, the universe is already perfect from its creation as possessing the proper diversity of creatures to manifest God. In the second sense, the universe must be moved by divine government to its proper end, in particular to the beatitude of the saints (*ST* I.73.1). In other words, although created perfect in terms of its nature, each creature is created to be perfected by contributing to the perfection of the universe as a whole by means of its proper operation.

Because accidents perfect the substance, an accident changes the mode of participation that something has in the *esse* of God (although not the substantial mode). Thomas notes that God does not make a species better by a substantial difference or else it would become a different species, but He can give it a better manner of existence by adding things over and above the substance, such as virtue and wisdom (*ST* I.25.6). In other words, through its accidents a creature participates more perfectly in the *esse* of God. Thomas affirms this by noting that perfections are in a thing according to how a thing has *esse,* and defects according to how a thing lacks *esse* (*SCG* I.28; *ST* I-II.18.1).

Creatures receive these acts of *esse* by being moved by God to act.[106] Since God moves the creature to act, He is the primary cause of the action.[107] The creature is the secondary cause of the action by participating in the proper agency of God.[108] Whenever a creature is moved to perfection by means of operation, it causes *esse* as an instrumental cause. Thomas states that only God can cause *esse* absolutely. He argues, "the more universal effects must be reduced to the more universal and prior causes. Now among effects the most universal is *esse* itself: and hence it must be the proper effect of the first and most universal cause, that is God."[109] Thus after establishing that the proper act of God is to give *esse,*

---

106. God causes the actions of all creatures both by giving them the power to act and by moving them instrumentally to their particular action (*DP* 3.7).

107. Sometimes God will move creatures to act through other secondary causes (e.g., angels), but He is nonetheless always the primary cause of their movement.

108. *ST* I.105. See Gilson, *Christian Philosophy of St. Thomas Aquinas,* 179–86. Gilson notes that because God is the universal cause of being, all creatures, including humans, act as secondary and instrumental causes of operation. See also Bernard Lonergan, *Grace and Freedom* (New York: Herder & Herder, 1971), 21–137. Lonergan explains that Thomas's understanding of cooperating grace is based upon the notion of the human as an instrumental cause of supernatural acts. He states that man is always an instrument who is first governed and secondly governs (137).

109. *ST* I.45.5: Oportet enim universaliores effectus in universaliores et priores causas reducere. Inter omnes autem effectus, universalissimum est ipsum esse. Unde oportet quod sit proprius effectus primae et universalissimae causae, quae est deus. Cf. *ST* I.8.1 on how *esse* is the proper action of God alone. See also *SS* 10; *LC* 3; *DP* 3.7. See also Blanchette, *The*

he continues by stating that something participates in the proper action of another, not by its own power, but instrumentally, inasmuch as it acts by the power of another as air can heat other things by the power of fire.[110] Whenever any created agent causes anything, it causes being, and in this way it acts as an instrument of the first agent, God, whose proper effect is being.

Because the concept of instrumental causality is very helpful in explaining how creatures participate in divine causality through their secondary actions, it will be beneficial to analyze this concept more closely.[111] To explain instrumental causality, Thomas often uses the analogy of God compared to a craftsman and the creature compared to the in-

---

Perfection of the Universe, 163–68, who notes that universal causes are necessary to explain how more than one thing can participate in the same form. He then analogously applies this principle to show that God is the universal cause of being and creatures are only instrumental causes of being. He notes that just as the creature participates in being from God, so it also acts by God's power, where the power of God descends proportionally through beings (175).

110. *ST* I.45.5; *SCG* III.66. Since creatures can only cause being by participating in the power of God, Thomas notes that in every action they produce an effect greater than their power. See *SCG* III.103: "there proceeds from an instrument not merely an effect corresponding to the power of the instrument, but also an effect beyond its power, insofar as it acts through the power of the principal agent" (Ex instrumento autem procedit non solum suae virtuti correspondens effectus, sed etiam ultra propriam virtutem, inquantum agit in virtute principalis agentis). Cf. *SCG* I.43; *ST* I.75.5, I-II.55.2.1. Elsewhere Thomas states that the soul has a divine operation, since nothing gives *esse* except by participation in divine operation (*DP* 3.1).

111. Brian Shanley, "Divine Causation and Human Freedom in Aquinas," *American Catholic Philosophical Quarterly* 72 (1998), 106–8, while recognizing that Aquinas uses the term "instrumental" causality to explain the relation between creatures and God in causing *esse,* Shanley is reluctant to use the term because an instrument does not produce an effect by virtue of its own inherent causal power. Thus, use of the term "to categorize the activity of all created causes seems to run the risk of impugning their genuine causal capacity" (106). Furthermore, Shanley notes, "instrumental causes normally have their own proper activity that is independent of the principal cause and is precisely what is needed by the principal cause in order to accomplish the effect" (106). Because of the potential for misunderstanding, Shanley prefers to only use the terms primary and secondary causes rather than principal and instrumental causes. While I admit that using the term "instrumental" causality to refer to a creature's causation of being can be misunderstood, the term has several definite benefits. First, it emphasizes that all creatures cause being in accord with their form just as an instrument always acts in accord with its form. Second, an instrument also always acts according to how it is moved by the agent and thus always participates in the power, exemplar, and end of the agent. Third, a defect in an instrument causes an imperfect action even if the agent moved it perfectly. For example, sin is caused by a defect in a human (instrumental cause) not by a defect in God. Fourth, the term instrumental is less abstract than the term secondary.

strument. Thomas, in speaking of how the human nature of Christ is an instrument of His divine nature, says:

Wherever there are several mutually ordained agents, the inferior is moved by the superior . . . since what is moved by another has a twofold action, one which it has by its own form, the other, which it has inasmuch as it is moved by another; thus the operation of an axe according to its own form is to cut, but inasmuch as it is moved by the craftsman, its operation is to make benches. Hence the operation which belongs to a thing by its form is proper to it, nor does it belong to the mover, except insofar as he makes use of this kind of thing for his work: thus heating is the proper operation of fire, but not of a smith, except insofar as he makes use of fire for heating iron. But the operation which belongs to the thing, merely as moved by another, is not distinct from the operation of the mover; thus to make a bench is not the work of the axe independently of the work of workman. Hence, wherever the mover and the moved have different forms or operative powers, the proper operation of the mover and the proper operation of the moved must be distinct; although the moved participates in the operation of the mover and the mover uses the operation of the moved, and consequently, each acts in communion with the other.[112]

Since Thomas in this question is examining the proposition of faith that Christ has both a human and divine operation, he speaks of the relation between an instrument and its agent with extreme precision. He is careful to show, on the one hand, that both the agent and the instrument moved have their own proper effect, yet, on the other hand, to the extent the instrument is moved by the agent, the operation or use of the instrument is not distinct from that of the agent. Hence, as moved by the power of the agent, the instrument is said to participate in the act of the agent.

Thomas illustrates this point by the example of the ax and the crafts-

---

112. *ST* III.19.1: ubicumque sunt plura agentia ordinata, inferius movetur a superiori . . . Quia actio eius quod movetur ab altero, est duplex, una quidem quam habet secundum propriam formam; alia autem quam habet secundum quod movetur ab alio. Sicut securis operatio secundum propriam formam est incisio, secundum autem quod movetur ab artifice, operatio eius est facere scamnum. Operatio igitur quae est alicuius rei secundum suam formam, est propria eius; nec pertinet ad moventem, nisi secundum quod utitur huiusmodi re ad suam operationem, sicut calefacere est propria operatio ignis; non autem fabri, nisi quatenus utitur igne ad calefaciendum ferrum. Sed illa operatio quae est rei solum secundum quod movetur ab alio, non est alia praeter operationem moventis ipsum, sicut facere scamnum non est seorsum operatio securis ab operatione artificis. Et ideo, ubicumque movens et motum habent diversas formas seu virtutes operativas, ibi oportet quod sit alia propria operatio moventis, et alia propria operatio moti, licet motum participet operationem moventis, et movens utatur operatione moti, et sic utrumque agit cum communione alterius.

man. Both the craftsman and the ax have their own proper effect; the ax only acts in the manner befitting an ax, by cutting.[113] It can only act in a way befitting its particular mode because a participated act is limited by the particular form of the participant. Whereas pure act is infinite, participated act is limited by the capacity of the recipient (*DP* 1.2). Consequently, the degree that something participates in the infinite act of God is determined by the particular mode of the creature (*SCG* I.43; SS 8; *DV* 21.6.5).

Since the craftsman also acts by his proper effect, when the ax is moved by the craftsman, its operation becomes that of the craftsman in making a bench. For, "the bench is not like the ax, but is like the art which is in the craftsman's mind."[114] When the analogy is applied to the relation between creatures and God, all creatures act as instrumental causes of actions by participation in the power of God, the divine agent. Both the instrument and the agent act by their proper effect. In reference to the instrument (creation), this means that the action is in accord with the capacity of the form of the creature.[115] For example, God moves plants to perform plant actions (e.g., being and living) and humans to perform human actions (e.g., rational acts). In reference to the agent (God), the proper effect of God is to cause being, which He as primary cause does by moving creatures to act in accord with the *ratio* in the divine intellect.

The analogical application of the notion of instrumental causality to creation is also helpful in explaining defective actions: those that do not fulfill the nature of a creature (e.g., sin in humans). If a tool is defective, even if the craftsman moves it perfectly, the action will be defective as well. Thomas notes, "For unless an instrument is well-disposed, no matter how perfect the principle agent may be, a perfect action of the agent

---

113. Thomas notes in *ST* III.62.1.2 that the instrument as moved does not work apart from exercising its proper action. Cf. I.45.5; *LC* 23.

114. *ST* III.62.1: Unde effectus non assimilatur instrumento, sed principali agenti, sicut lectus non assimilatur securi, sed arti quae est in mente artificis.

115. Thomas states that God wishes to act by means of the natural forms wisely caused in creatures in order to preserve the order of things (*DP* 3.7.16). In this way, creatures are not just recipients of divine action, but actors as well. This requires that creatures have a natural form that gives specificity to the effect. See II *Physic* 14, n. 268: "nature is nothing else than the *ratio* of a certain art, namely the divine art, instilled in things by which the things themselves are moved to a determinate end, as if the ship maker, in making a ship, bestowed on the planks the power to be moved of themselves to bring about the form of the ship" (natura nihil est aliud quam ratio cuiusdam artis, scilicet divinae, indita rebus, qua ipsae res moventur ad finem determinatum: sicut si artifex factor navis posset lignis tribuere, quod ex se ipsios moverentur ad navis formam inducendam).

does not come about through the instrument."[116] Hence in reference to creation, even though God's action of moving each creature is perfect, due to defects in the creatures as instrumental causes, they do not always succeed in performing their proper actions.[117] These defects and corresponding actions are permitted by God because all things are created in view of the collective end of the whole universe. God permits individual corruption/loss of form because although a particular individual creature may fail in attaining the end for which it was created, this failure contributes to the perfection of the universe as a whole.[118] However, the defect is only attributed to the instrumental cause, while the goodness of the act (both as having being and contributing to end) is attributed to both God and the instrumental cause.

Because these defects are caused only by the instrumental cause, God does not cause evil, but nonetheless moves and directs the creature to the action inasmuch as the action is good and has being. Hence, divine providence only causes the action to the extent that it contributes to the goodness of the universe as a whole. This truth explains Romans 8:28: "We know that all things work for good for those who love God. . . ." In other words, when creatures (both humans and others) inflict trials, temptations, and afflictions upon the Christian, these actions are directed by the divine *ratio* only to the extent that they are able to cause

116. *ST* I-II.58.3.2: Sicut non sequitur perfecta actio alicuius agentis per instrumentum, si instrumentum non sit bene dispositum, quantumcumque principale agens sit perfectum. Cf. *ST* I-II.58.3.2, 65.3.1.

117. Thomas notes that inasmuch as the act has being and is an act, it is from God; inasmuch as it is deficient, it is caused by a deficient secondary cause. Thomas gives the analogy of a man who limps. Although the moving power causes a proper walking motion, on account of the curvature of the leg a man limps (*ST* I.49.2.2). Cf. *DP* 1.6.5 and especially *DP* 3.6.20 where Thomas notes that even a sinful act is caused by God as first cause to the extent it has *esse* and is an action, but the deformity in the act is referred only to the human will, the secondary cause.

118. Thomas notes in *ST* I.22.2.2, "to his [God's] providence it pertains to permit certain defects in particular effects, that the perfect good of the universe may not be hindered, for if all evil were prevented, much good would be absent from the universe" (ad ipsius providentiam pertinetut permittat quosdam defectus esse in aliquibus particularibus rebus, ne impediatur bonum universi perfectum. Si enim omnia mala impedirentur, multa bona deessent universo). Thomas further quotes Augustine who notes that God permits evil to exist in His works that He may produce good even from evil. In reference to humans, Thomas in I.23.3 notes that some men are permitted to fall away from the end of eternal life because providence permits defects for the good of the whole. However, providence is not the cause of sin (only the free human is the cause of it), but it is the cause of eternal punishment (I.23.3.2).

goodness for the Christian and the universe as a whole (*ST* I.22.2.2). The defect in the action is completely on the part of the secondary cause. Thus, although all things have a particular end (secondary perfections in accord with their nature), not all things attain this end on account of the greater good of the universe.

When an instrument is moved to perform its proper action, the instrument is given the power to move by the agent (efficient cause); it is moved in accord with the exemplar in the agent's mind (exemplary cause), and the end of its action is the end of the agent (final cause). For example, the cutting tool is moved by the physical strength of the craftsman; it is moved in accord with the form of the bench in his mind, and the end of this action is having a bench to sell. Likewise, all creatures are given the power to act by God who moves them in accord with the exemplar in His mind to the end He created them to fulfill.

Because God created a variety of creatures in order to attain the ultimate end through their proper operation, God as efficient cause moves all creatures to their particular effect by causing them to act in accord with their form. By being moved in this way, creatures become instrumental causes of *esse* by participating in the power of God who is *esse* essentially. Thus, although God alone has the power to sufficiently cause *esse*, creatures can be secondary causes of *esse* to the extent that they participate in His power.[119]

Now just as the craftsman moves the instrument in accord with the form in his mind, God as exemplary cause of all secondary perfections moves all creation in accord with the form in His mind. In other words, just as the bench produced by the craftsman is not like the ax, but is like the form in the craftsman's mind (*ST* III.62.1), the actions of all creation are not like the substance of the creature, but they are like the form in the mind of God. Hence the forms in the divine mind are the exemplary cause of all things, including secondary perfections.[120] Thomas makes a distinction between the divine ideas that are the *ratio* of divine wisdom

119. Thomas states that although God is the cause of all being, all can be called a cause of being as cooperating with God (*ST* III.19.3; *SCG* III.67).

120. God's practical knowledge is the cause of all things by knowing the divine essence in every way that it can be participated in according to likeness (*ST* I.15.2). Since all things, including secondary perfections, are a participation in the divine essence which is all perfections essentially, then secondary perfections are also caused by the *ratio* in the divine intellect. Cf. *QQ* 4.1.1 which states that the divine essence itself is the exemplar of all things, and one can only speak of a plurality of divine ideas because different things imitate the divine ideas in diverse modes. See also *SCG* I.66.9 which states that God's essence is the exemplary cause of the effects of all secondary causes by knowing the effects that preexist in them.

inasmuch as by it all things are created and the eternal law that is the *ratio* of divine wisdom inasmuch as by it all things are moved to their proper actions. Thomas states:

Wherefore as the *ratio* of the divine wisdom, inasmuch as by it all things are created, has the character of art, exemplar, or idea; so the *ratio* of divine wisdom, as moving all things to their due end, bears the character of law. Accordingly the eternal law is nothing else than the *ratio* of divine wisdom.[121]

Because a practical *ratio* is an exemplary cause of something, both the divine ideas and the eternal law are the *ratio* of divine wisdom. However, the first is more properly said to be the exemplary cause of the first act of the substance (being), and the second is more properly said to be the exemplary cause of the second act (operation).[122]

Just as the mode of the first act of *esse* is determined by participation in God as exemplary cause, the mode of all secondary acts are determined by participation in the eternal law. In other words, God moves creatures to cause acts of a particular type that are like the *ratio* in the divine mind. Likewise, just as God causes the mode of the first act of *esse* through the substantial form of the substance, God as the divine agent causes the secondary acts through the form of the creature inasmuch as all instruments act in accord with their form.

Thomas notes that just as the law of a human ruler acts as a principle of action moving his subjects to a particular end, the eternal law moves all of creation to its proper end by impressing upon each creature an interior principle of action to its particular end. Thomas states:

Now just as man, by such pronouncement, impresses a kind of inward principle of actions on the man that is subject to him, so God imprints on the whole of

121. *ST* I-II.93.1: Unde sicut ratio divinae sapientiae inquantum per eam cuncta sunt creata, rationem habet artis vel exemplaris vel ideae; ita ratio divinae sapientiae moventis omnia ad debitum finem, obtinet rationem legis. Et secundum hoc, lex aeterna nihil aliud est quam ratio divinae sapientiae, secundum quod est directiva omnium actuum et motionum. Cf. R. J. Henle, *The Treatise on Law: Introduction and Commentary* (South Bend: University of Notre Dame Press, 1993), 47.

122. See *ST* I-II.93.5 where Thomas notes that the eternal law imprints on the whole of nature the principle of its proper actions. Elsewhere Thomas argues that the eternal law as the *ratio* of the divine intellect is truth itself in the same fashion as the *ratio* in the mind of God as divine artist is also truth. Thomas argues that unlike in the human mind where the truth of the intellectual form is measured by the thing it is like, the divine intellect is the measure of all things in reference both to creation and to divine governance (*ST* I-II.93.1.3; cf. I.16.1, 84.1). Hence, just as things can be said to be true in the secondary sense by participation in the likeness of God, actions can be said to be true by participation in eternal law.

nature the principle of its proper actions. . . . [T]hus all actions and movements of the whole of nature are subject to the eternal law.[123]

The interior principles of action that each creature has by eternal law are its internal faculties and these faculties' corresponding natural inclinations. Thomas notes that an inclination follows every form (*ST* I.80.1). Hence, both natural forms and intellectual forms are followed by inclinations, and the inclination that follows the natural form of a creature is called the natural inclination (*ST* I.80.1; 19.1; *SCG* IV.19).

These natural inclinations directly flow from the nature of the creature and are the means through which God guides all creatures to their appropriate ends.[124] Thomas states, "it is evident that all things participate somewhat in the eternal law, insofar as, namely, from its being imprinted on them, they derive their respective inclinations to their proper acts and ends."[125] For example, humans are naturally inclined to be, to live, and to understand.[126] Hence, the eternal law moves them to perform these types of actions. Consequently, all creatures participate in the eternal law as governed and moved by it to the extent their actions are determined by their natural inclinations which come from their natural forms.[127] Thus, all of creation is directed to the end by being moved in accord with the exemplar in the divine mind.

Agents form exemplars of actions within their mind on account of their end (the final cause). In reference to God, as divine agent he wills the intellectual forms of the actions of all creatures on account of the ultimate end: the divine goodness.[128] Hence, the eternal law, the *ratio* of

123. *ST* I-II.93.5: Sicut autem homo imprimit, denuntiando, quoddam interius principium actuum homini sibi subiecto, ita etiam deus imprimit toti naturae principia proprium actuum. . . . Et per hanc etiam rationem onmes motus et actiones totius naturae legi aeternae subduntur.

124. *ST* I.103.1. See also *ST* I.5.5 where Thomas states that following upon the form of something is an inclination to an end or an action since everything, insofar as it is in act, acts and tends toward that which is in accordance with its form.

125. *ST* I-II.91.2: Manifestum est quod omnia participant aliqualiter legem aeternam, inquantum scilicet ex impressione eius habent inclinationes in proprios actus et fines. Cf. 93.6.

126. This is not a complete list of human natural inclinations. Other natural inclinations will be covered in chapter 3 such as the natural inclination to acquire or receive additional forms (e.g., habits) which act as additional interior principles of motion. Hence, the eternal law also moves humans in accord with these additional forms.

127. *ST* I.5.5, 29.1.4, 73.1; *SCG* IV.19. See also *ST* I-II.13.2.3 which states that even in irrational animals we notice certain marks of wisdom because they have a natural inclination to act in an orderly manner as ordained by God. Cf. *ST* I.60.5.

128. Thomas notes in *ST* I.19.4 that the divine intellect is the cause of things only as

God, is commanded on account of the divine goodness, and because the end of the first agent is the end of all, the eternal law orders all secondary agents to the divine goodness as their end.[129] Thomas uses the analogy of a leader of an army to explain how the ends of all secondary causes are ordered to the end of the first agent: the commander of the army intends the end of victory, while the right ordering of a particular regiment is intended by one of the lower officers in order to achieve the same end of victory (*ST* I-II.18.7; 1.2; 9.1). Likewise, all of creation by seeking its particular end tends toward God (*SCG* III.19; *ST* I.6.1.2). The way that creatures attain their particular end is by performing their proper operation to which they are inclined by eternal law (cf. *SCG* III.64.11).

Because the end of the agent is also the end of the instrument, God's proper end is the final cause of all secondary perfections. By willing His own goodness, God wills that each creature attains its own end.[130] By achieving this particular end through operation, the creature participates in God's goodness in such a way as to be called good in an absolute sense (cf. *ST* I.103.2). Because God is pure act, it is fitting that the highest form of participation of creatures in God's goodness is by means of operation.

God as the first agent is the efficient, exemplary, and final cause of the acts of all secondary agents (creatures). The analogy of the craftsman and the tool helps to explain this threefold participation in God. In reference to God as efficient cause, the instrument participates in the power of the agent. In reference to God as exemplary cause, the instrument participates in the *ratio* of the agent as directed to its particular operation. And in reference to God as final cause, the instrument is moved to achieve the end of the agent. By calling all created causes instruments of the providence of God, Thomas can affirm the universal efficacy of divine providence, yet at the same time affirm the integrity of the created subject that truly causes every act and hence truly possesses every perfection that it has. Thomas uses the analogy of the craftsman and the cutting tool by noting that if the tool does not operate by means of its

---

conjoined with the divine will because "His [God's] inclination to put in act what His intellect has conceived appertains to the will" (inclinatio eius ad agendum quod intellectu conceptum est, pertinet ad voluntatem). Cf. 14.8.

129. *ST* I-II.93.1; cf. 93.4.1; *SCG* III.17. Cf. *ST* I.60.5.3 which states, "Everything has a natural inclination toward what is the absolutely universal good" (Habet naturalem unumquodque in id quod est bonum universale simpliciter).

130. Not withstanding cases where God allows a creature to not attain its end on account of the good of all.

own form in producing the bench, then there is no need for the tool at all. For the tool cuts the wood by its own form in producing the bench which is the proper effect of the craftsman (*ST* I.45.5). Likewise with every created operation, the created agent, while acting by means of its own form, is able to cause an effect beyond its power by bringing about *esse* which is the proper action of God (*SCG* III.103; *DP* 7.2).

Natural Human Participation in God

Having seen how all creatures participate in God who is the first cause of their actions, it is now fitting to move on to an analysis of how humans specifically participate in God who is the first cause of all of our actions. For humans, like all of creation, the participation of the first act in God causes the mode of participation of the second act since all act in accord with their form. Hence, this section will briefly show specifically how humans participate in God in reference to their first acts. Then it will show how humans participate in God in reference to their secondary acts. While treating this mode of participation, a distinction will be made between human participation in eternal law as moved and governed by it (found in all of creation) and human cognitive participation (found only in rational creatures). Finally, this section will end with a distinction between natural human participation in eternal law and supernatural participation by grace.

Human Participation by Means of the First Act

Humans, like all creatures, participate in God who is the efficient, exemplary, and final cause of their being. Although by participation in God as efficient cause humans perform their act of being, what makes the human act specific is the mode of participation. This mode is determined by the *ratio* of God through the substantial form of the creature since the relationship between the substantial form and the act of *esse* is that of potency to act. Because God causes this particular act of being on account of His goodness, the creature is ordered to the divine goodness in accord with its form. The form of a human is that of a living, understanding being (*ST* I.4.2.2; I-II.2.5.3; *LC* I; 3; 9; 12). Thomas notes that humans are said to be in the image and likeness of God, because unlike animals and other lower creatures which only have the primary perfections of living and being, humans have living, understanding, and being (*DV* 10.1.5; cf. *ST* I.45.7).

Because humans, like all creatures, are ordered to the goodness of God that is attained through operation, these primary human perfections contain natural principles of action. These natural principles of action are its powers that dictate the type of actions humans can perform. In the case of humans, as both living and understanding beings, humans have the vegetative power (to maintain health), the sensitive power (to acquire sense knowledge), the power of locomotion (to move), and the intellectual power (to understand truth). In addition, an appetitive power accompanies the sensitive power (the sense appetites or passions—to seek the bodily good) and the intellectual power (the will—to love the rational good).[131] Each power has an inclination whereby it naturally tends toward its proper object.[132] For example, Thomas notes that the intellect is naturally ordered to the true, the will to the universal good, the irascible appetite to the arduous good, and the concupiscible appetite to the moderation of the delectable.[133] Because humans are bodies with souls, they have natural inclinations that cause both the body and the soul to perform their proper actions (e.g., health is the proper action of the body and attaining God through knowledge and love is a proper action of the soul).

Among these interior principles of action, the power that distinguishes humans from all of the other animals is the intellectual power and its

---

131. In describing the powers of the soul, Thomas distinguishes powers based on degrees of living where some creatures have a vegetative power, others a sensitive power, others the power of locomotion, and still others have the intellectual power. The appetitive power is in both those with a sensitive power and an intellectual power (*ST* I-II.78.1). He then breaks each of these powers down into more specific powers such as the vegetative into the nutritive, augmentative, and generative; the sensitive into the interior and exterior senses; the intellective into the active and the passive; the appetitive into the rational (will) and the sensitive (irascible and concupiscible passions—*ST* I.77–83).

132. *ST* I.80.1. See also the reply to the third objection which states: "Each and every power of the soul is a form or nature, and has a natural inclination to something. Wherefore each and every power desires by the natural appetite that object which is suitable to itself" (Unaquaeque potentia animae est quaedam forma seu natura, et habet naturalem inclinationem in aliquid. Unde unaquaeque appetit obiectum sibi conveniens naturali appetitu). Cf. *ST* I-II.10.1 and 94.2: which state that since every form is followed by a particular inclination, humans have a natural inclination to be, to live, and to understand. Cf. I.60.1. See also Anthony Lisska, *Aquinas's Theory of Natural Law* (Oxford: Clarendon Press, 1996), 100, who notes the link between the manifold inclinations to ends and the natural law. For more on natural inclinations, see Pinckaers, *Sources of Christian Ethics,* 400–456, and *Morality,* 97–111.

133. *ST* I-II.85.3; Cf. I.81.2; I.63.4.2 and 3. See also *ST* I.82.2 and I-II.17.6 where Thomas notes that a consequence of these natural inclinations is that the intellect necessarily adheres to first principles and the will necessarily adheres to the last end and anything necessarily connected to it.

corresponding appetite. Just as there are different modes of being based on a creature's degree of participation in God, there are different modes of the living.[134] Thomas notes that the soul as the form of the body determines the mode of living for humans. He continues:

> For the soul is the primary principle of our nourishment, sensation, and local movement; and likewise of our understanding. Therefore, this principle by which we primarily understand, whether it be called the intellect or the intellectual soul, is the form of the body. . . . [T]he proper operation of man as man is to understand; because he thereby surpasses all other animals. Whence Aristotle concludes in the *Ethics* [X.7] that the ultimate happiness of man must consist in this operation as properly belonging to him.[135]

Although the animals share with humans the powers of nourishment, sensation, and local movement, the power that distinguishes humans from all the animals is the power to understand.[136] Since all creatures are ordered to the goodness of God by means of their proper act, the act by which humans are naturally ordered to God is the act of understanding.

Because understanding and the corresponding act of the will (loving) are the highest powers of a human, in performing these actions, humans are perfected. Since God created all creatures to be happy when they perform their proper actions, the acts of understanding the truth of a being and loving its goodness is an act of happiness (*ST* I.76.1). However, although the understanding and loving of any good can potentially bring some happiness, humans are ultimately inclined to the understanding and loving of that which is truth and goodness by essence: God.[137] In

---

134. See also Eleonore Stump and Norman Kretzman who argue that the form specific to humans is that of the cognitive and appetitive rational powers. Consequently, human nature is fulfilled when these powers are moved to act. "Being and Goodness," in *Divine and Human Action,* ed. Thomas Morris (Ithaca, N.Y.: Cornell University Press, 1988), 285–87. Cf. *ST* I-II.18.1.

135. *ST* I.76.1: Anima enim est primum quo nutrimur, et sentimus, et movemur secundum locum; et similiter quo primo intelligimus. Hoc ergo principium quo primo intelligimus, sive dicatur intellectus sive anima intellectiva, est forma corporis. . . . Propria autem operatio hominis, inquantum est homo, est intelligere, per hanc enim omnia animalia transcendit. Unde et Aristoteles, in libro ethic., in hac operatione, sicut in propria hominis, ultimam felicitatem constituit.

136. Cf. *ST* I.18.3 where Thomas notes that there are different degrees of life based on how perfectly a creature moves itself. Humans have life more perfectly than do the plants and animals as they are able to move themselves intelligently. Cf. *ST* I.76.1; *DV* 10.1.5.

137. Thomas notes that the object to which the intellect is naturally inclined is the universal true and the object to which the will is naturally inclined is the universal good. The intellect is not perfected until it is filled with that which is truth by essence (God) and not

knowing and loving God a human attains the end of happiness to which God as final cause orders him.[138] Consequently, just as humans have a natural inclination to know and love, they have a natural inclination for this knowing and loving to be perfected in the act of happiness.

To say that humans are naturally inclined to happiness means that every human by nature seeks happiness (*ST* I-II.2.4). However, as rational creatures, humans can know and choose a variety of means to achieve their end of happiness.[139] This ability of the intellect to determine a variety of means to the end and of the will to choose the means to the end is called free choice *(liberum arbitrium)*. Through the power of free choice humans are naturally able to freely choose the proper means to achieve happiness (*ST* I.83; *QQ* 1.4.2.2).

It is this natural constitution as ordered self-movers that God as first agent perfects when He moves human agents to act freely. Thomas states, "God moves all creatures according to their mode. So divine motion is imparted to some things with necessity; however, it is imparted to the rational nature with liberty."[140] Not only is there no contradiction between the free actions of humans and the universal causality of divine providence, divine providence is the cause of freedom through which it orders humans to their ultimate end (*ST* I.22.2.4).

In freely determining the means to happiness, humans are inclined by God to act in accord with their form. Since the form of the human is the rational soul, humans are naturally inclined to act in accord with reason.[141] Thomas notes that the good action is one that is in accord with reason.[142] For an act to be in accord with reason, a human chooses what

---

by participation. Likewise, a good by participation can never completely satisfy the will, but only that which is good by essence, God, who is the universal good (*ST* I-II.2.8 and 3.7; cf. 1.5, 3.4). See also *SCG* III.19–21, 25.

138. See *ST* I-II.1–5 and the section on happiness later in this chapter.

139. *ST* I-II.13.6, I.83; cf. I-II.10.2, 14.3. It is also the case that although a human by necessity seeks happiness, he may not completely understand what happiness is and hence may seek a false end (*ST* I-II.5.8).

140. *QQ* 1.4.2.2: Quod deus movet omnia secundum modum eorum. Et ideo divina motio a quibusdam participatur cum necessitate, a natura autem rationali cum libertate. Cf. *ST* I.22.2.4.

141. *ST* I-II.18.5, 55.2, 85.2.

142. See *ST* II-II.47.6 where Thomas states that the end of the moral virtues is the human good, and the good of the human soul is to be in accord with reason. Therefore, the ends of the moral virtues must preexist in reason as the naturally known principles (synderesis). See also *ST* I-II.54.3 where Thomas notes that a good habit disposes an agent to an act suitable to the agent's nature. Human acts of virtue are suitable to human nature since they are according to reason. Cf. *ST* I.19.1.

reason has determined to be in accord with the end to which humans are naturally inclined.

However, because the reason is capable of being determined to several things and in different modes, habits are necessary for a human to always act in accord with reason.[143] In other words, because humans are capable of choosing a variety of perceived goods, including perceived goods that are not ordered to their ultimate end, they need a disposition to always incline them to act in accord with reason. Just as nature inclines humans to their proper end, habits act as a "second nature" inclining humans to always choose the same type of act (*ST* I.18.2.2; I-II.108.1.2). Habits that dispose humans to act in accord with their rational nature are called virtues (*ST* I-II.54.3). Since virtues are necessary so that humans consistently choose acts ordered to their ultimate end, Thomas notes that humans have a natural inclination to virtue.[144] This natural inclination is essential because virtues, like the powers of the soul, act as interior principles of action by moving humans to their proper end (*ST* I-II.49. prologue).

Humans, like all of creation, have principles of action imprinted upon them by the exemplary *ratio* of God. Through these principles God guides them to perform actions ordered to the ultimate end. Since the ultimate end of a creature is the greatest operation of its highest power, the proper end of humans is the act of knowing and loving that which is true and good by essence. This is the act of happiness. However, although humans are naturally inclined to the end of happiness, the means of achieving this end as well as the conception of what happiness is can be freely determined. Hence, the additional principles of the virtues are needed to dispose humans to consistently choose actions in accord with reason. Furthermore, because humans have bodies, they also have natural inclinations that they share with other creatures (such as to life and existence). Thus, the mode to which humans participate in the *esse* of God is

---

143. See *ST* I-II.55.1 where Thomas explains the necessity of virtue for a rational nature. He notes that there are some powers that are determinate to their acts and these natural powers are themselves called virtue. But the rational powers, which are not determinate to one particular action but are inclined indifferently to many, are in need of good habits to perfect them. Cf. *ST* I-II.58.4.3, 85.2.1; *DV* 22.5. Cf. John Bowlin, *Contingency and Fortune in Aquinas's Ethics* (Cambridge: Cambridge University Press, 1999), 58–60.

144. *ST* I-II.60.1, 63.1, and 2.93.6. Cf. *ST* I-II.85.1 where Thomas states that since this inclination to virtue is rooted in human nature, like all natural inclinations, it can never be wholly destroyed. However, it can be diminished, since sin causes an inclination to perform similar sinful acts, forming vices that are contrary to this natural inclination to virtue.

that of a bodily, rational, free creature ordered to the act of knowing and loving God.

Human Participation through Their Second Acts

Humans, like all creatures, act as instrumental causes of action, whereas God acts as the first or agent cause of the action (*ST* I-II.68.3.2; *SCG* III.20). In all cases of instrumental causality, inasmuch as the instrument acts, it participates in the power of the agent who is the efficient cause of the movement. Since the instrument is moved in accord with the *ratio* in the agent's mind, the agent is also the exemplary cause of the movement. Finally, since the end of the agent is the end of the instrument, the final cause of the instrument is found in the intention of the agent. However, the agent is this threefold cause by moving the instrument in accord with the instrument's own form. Thus, humans are moved as free rational beings who know and freely choose the action to which they are moved (*ST* I-II.1.1).

Because humans know the form of the action to be performed, humans have a certain knowledge of the *ratio* in the First Agent. Hence, Thomas notes that humans participate in eternal law in two ways. First, they are governed and moved by eternal law like all other creatures. Second, they cognitively participate in eternal law inasmuch as they govern themselves and others (*SCG* 113 & 114). Thomas explains:

There are two ways in which a thing is subject to eternal law, as explained above: first, by participating in the eternal law by way of knowledge; secondly by way of action and passion, i.e., by participating in the eternal law by way of a principle of motion: and in this second way, irrational creatures are subject to the eternal law, as stated above. But since the rational nature, together with that which it has in common with all creatures, has something proper to itself inasmuch as it is rational, consequently it is subject to the eternal law in both ways; because while each rational creature has some knowledge of eternal law, as stated above, it also has a natural inclination to that which is in harmony with the eternal law; for we are naturally adapted to be the recipients of virtue as stated in *Ethics* II.[145]

145. *ST* I-II.93.6: Respondeo dicendum quod duplex est modus quo aliquid subditur legi aeternae, ut ex supradictis patet, uno modo, inquantum participatur lex aeterna per modum cognitionis; alio modo, per modum actionis et passionis, inquantum participatur per modum principii motivi. Et hoc secundo modo subduntur legi aeternae irrationales creaturae, ut dictum est. Sed quia rationalis natura, cum eo quod est commune omnibus creaturis, habet aliquid sibi proprium inquantum est rationalis, ideo secundum utrumque modum legi aeternae subditur, quia et notionem legis aeternae aliquo modo habet, ut supra dictum est; et iterum unicuique rationali creaturae inest naturalis inclinatio ad id quod est

Thomas notes that, like all creatures, humans participate in eternal law as inclined or moved to their proper end; however, unlike all creatures, humans are also able to know something of the eternal law and therefore knowingly participate in God's providence. Thus, this section will first briefly show how humans participate in eternal law through their operation as moved and governed by it (by way of a principle of motion). Then it will briefly show how humans participate in the eternal law cognitively.

Natural Human Participation in Eternal Law as Moved and Governed by It   Like all of creation, humans are moved and directed by the eternal law to their operation in accord with their form. Although every power of the soul is inclined to its proper action, what makes human action distinct from that of irrational creatures is that it flows from a rationally formed will. Thomas notes:

Of actions done by man those alone are properly called human, which are proper to man as man. Now man differs from irrational animals in this, that he is master of his actions. . . . Now man is master of his actions through his reason and will; wherefore also free choice is defined as the faculty of will and reason. Therefore, those actions are properly called human which proceed from a deliberate will.[146]

Thomas goes on to note that because the object of the will is the good as end, all human actions are done for an end (*ST* I-II.1.1). Like all of creation, humans are naturally inclined to that which is *esse* essentially; however, because the powers specific to rational creatures alone are those of the intellect and will, humans are inclined to God as the universal truth and the universal good.[147]

This action of knowing and loving the universal good is the act of happiness. Although humans may disagree on what the object of the act of happiness is, they nonetheless implicitly seek the universal good

---

consonum legi aeternae; sumus enim innati ad habendum virtutes, ut dicitur in II ethic. . . . Cf. I-II.91.2, I.103.1.3; *DN* 2.5.

146. *ST* I-II.1.1: Actionum quae ab homine aguntur, illae solae proprie dicuntur humanae, quae sunt propriae hominis inquantum est homo. Differt autem homo ab aliis irrationalibus creaturis in hoc, quod est suorum actuum dominus. Est autem homo dominus suorum actuum per rationem et voluntatem, unde et liberum arbitrium esse dicitur facultas voluntatis et rationis. Illae ergo actiones proprie humanae dicuntur, quae ex voluntate deliberata procedunt. Thomas continues by noting that although other actions can be found in a human, they are not called human actions unless they proceed from the reason and will.

147. *ST* I-II.2.8 and 3.7. Recall that beings are called true *(verum)* in relation to the cognitive power and good *(bonum)* in relation to the appetitive power.

inasmuch as they desire any good as their ultimate end.[148] Consequently, although the end, happiness, is determined by nature, humans are free to choose what they think will make them happy and the means to this end. It is the job of the reason to determine this means, which the will chooses (*ST* I-II.13.1). Hence, for Thomas, the eternal law directs humans to human actions when the will freely chooses the action the intellect has judged to be a means to happiness.[149]

Because human actions differ from those of the rest of creation, humans participate in God as efficient, exemplary, and final cause in a unique way when they act. As efficient cause, God gives both the intellect and the will the power to act (*ST* I.105). As exemplary cause, God gives the intellect the intellectual forms by which it understands and causes things (*ST* I.105.3). As final cause, God is the source of all goodness that moves the will since He is universal good from which all other things are good by participation (*ST* I.105.4; I-II.9.6). In other words, like all creatures, humans are moved to their acts instrumentally by the power, *ratio,* and goodness of God.[150] However, unlike irrational creatures, humans are moved and guided to act intellectually by means of a certain knowledge of the *ratio* in the mind of God and appetively by means of a desire for the good that is found essentially in God alone.[151] Hence, humans as rational beings are governed by the eternal law so that they freely determine the actions they perform.[152]

148. See *ST* I.44.4.3: "All things desire God as their end, when they desire some good thing, whether this desire be intellectual or sensible or natural (without knowledge); because nothing is good and desirable except inasmuch as it participates in the likeness of God" (Omnia appetunt deum ut finem, appetendo quodcumque bonum, sive appetitu intelligibili, sive sensibili, sive naturali, qui est sine cognitione, quia nihil habet rationem boni et appetibilis, nisi secundum quod participat dei similitudinem). This passage comes from the treatment of God as the final cause of all creation, for the end of the first agent is the end of the instrument.

149. The understanding of the roles of the intellect and the will within a human action will be treated in much greater detail in chapters 3 and 4.

150. Although God is the first cause of all human actions, often he causes human actions through many intermediary causes (i.e., created exterior principles of action). Thus, God directs and guides how humans act in part by being the first cause and provident overseer of all the conditions we live under: politics, economics, culture, neighborhood, etc.

151. *DP* 3.7; *ST* I.45.5. See Joseph Owens, "Human Destiny in Aquinas," 36. Owens notes that humans are instrumental causes with free choice, which Owens refers to as a "highly refined instance of being."

152. *ST* I-II.21.4.2: Quod homo sic movetur a deo ut instrumentum, quod tamen non excluditur quin moveat seipsum per liberum arbitrium ("Man is moved by God as an instrument in such a manner that at the same time he himself he moves by his free-will"). Cf. *ST* I.22.2.4. See also *ST* I.112.1 where angels are called intelligent instruments and especially

However, because the rational powers within humans are inclined to many possible actions (*ST* I-II.55.1), humans need good habits to perfect them so that they always choose the action in accord with right reason.[153] Habits as superadded perfections act as additional interior principles of actions.[154] If the habit is in accord with human nature (a virtue), then these habits perfect the natural inclination to good human acts. However, if the habit is against human nature (a vice), then the natural inclination to good human acts is diminished.[155] Because the eternal law directs humans to their operation through their natural inclinations, if the inclinations are perfected by virtue, then the participation in eternal law is increased; if the inclinations are diminished by vice, then the participation is decreased.[156] Just as sharpness and dullness affect the way that a craftsman moves an ax to the end of making a bench (for all are moved in accord with their form, including superadded forms), virtue and vice make humans more or less properly disposed to their ultimate end.[157]

ST III.19.1 where the human nature of Christ acts as an instrument of the divine nature. Although it is moved immediately by the divine nature, it has its own proper form whereby it acts.

153. *ST* I-II.55.2 & 3; cf. *DH* 2 where Thomas notes that creatures seek their own completion which causes them to be good. Since the goodness of the creature is proportional to the form, all have a natural inclination to that which completes it either from nature or by an acquired habit. See also *ST* I.5.5, 19.1; I-II.18.3, 56.3, 58.4.1, 71.2, 99.2.

154. Thomas notes that a habit is an act in respect to the powers of the soul and is in potency in respect to operation (*ST* I-II.49.3.1). Because something is most like God when it is in act, it is fitting that God created humans with a natural inclination to virtue, since through the additional forms of the virtues the human soul acquires an additional perfection, making it more like God. Recall that secondary perfections are for the sake of the substance, so that the substance can be perfected by them (*SCG* III.75).

155. *ST* I-II.85.1. Thomas notes in the second response that although nature precedes a voluntary action, it has an inclination to a certain voluntary action. Nature is not changed by performing a particular action, but the inclination can be changed insofar as it is favorably directed to its proper end (Cf. I-II.85.4). In other words, although actions can never change nature, they can diminish or enhance natural inclinations. Nonetheless, the natural inclination always exists even if it is not in act (I-II.85.2.3), just as the faculty of sight still exists even if one's eyes are closed. Cf. Vernon Bourke, "The Role of Habitus in the Thomistic Metaphysics of Potency and Act," in *Essays in Thomism*, ed. Robert E. Brennan, 103–9 (New York: Sheed & Ward, 1942). Bourke states that virtues represent a metaphysical perfectant increasing the potency of the powers of the soul to perform good acts (105–7).

156. *ST* I-II.93.6. Cf. *ST* I.49.3.4: "No being is called evil by participation, but by privation of participation" (nullum ens dicitur malum per participationem, sed per privationem participationis). Cf. *DP* 3.6.14 which states something is good as participating in goodness and evil as lacking this participation, and *DP* 3.6.2 which states that something is evil as in potency and deprived of its proper and due act.

157. Thomas notes in *SCG* III.20, "things are ordered to God as an end, not merely according to their substantial act of *esse*, but also according to those accidents which are added as pertinent to perfection, and even according to the proper operation which also

The Natural Cognitive Participation of a Human Act in God The eternal law moves and governs humans as rational creatures capable of self-direction.[158] Unlike irrational creatures, humans have a certain knowledge of the eternal law and are not only moved and governed by the eternal law but also govern themselves and others in accord with the eternal law.[159] By knowing and agreeing with the *ratio* of the governor they participate at a higher level in the eternal law than creatures that are simply moved by that *ratio*.[160]

Cognitive participation involves the participation of the human intellect in the divine intellect. Since God is understanding essentially, humans partake in the perfection of understanding by participating in the knowledge of God (*ST* I.79.4; *DSC* 10; cf. *LC* 18). When humans understand, God is the cause of the human act of understanding by giving humans the intellectual power to understand and the intelligible forms by which they understand.[161] Since all effects participate in their cause, in humans the power to understand, the object known, and the act of

---

belongs to the thing's perfection" (Quod res ordinantur in deum sicut finem non solum secundum esse substantiale, sed etiam secundum ea quae ei accidunt pertinentia ad perfectionem; et etiam secundum propriam operationem, quae etiam pertinet ad perfectionem rei). In other words, things are ordered to the goodness of God substantially by means of their natural inclinations, through acquired virtues, and through their operation. Cf. *SCG* III.21; *DV* 21.5; *SS* 12; *DH* 4.

158. *ST* I-II.91.6; *SCG* III.25. Thomas makes a distinction between movement from a natural inclination and from a rational inclination in *ST* I.80.1. He states that the inclination that follows the substantial form is the natural inclination, whereas the inclination that follows the apprehended form is a sensitive or rational inclination (Cf. *ST* I-II.8.1, I-II.35.1). The sensitive inclination is the sensitive appetite while the rational inclination is the intellectual appetite of the will (*ST* I-II.1.2, 6.5.2).

159. In distinguishing between the two types of participation (by inclination and cognitively) Thomas states in *SCG* III.113, "the rational creature participates not only by being governed, but also as governing, for he governs himself in his personal acts and even others" (Participat igitur rationalis creatura divinam providentiam non solum secundum gubernari, sed etiam secundum gubernare: gubernat enim se in suis actibus propriis, et etiam alia). Cf. *ST* I-II.91.2.

160. *SCG* III.147. Cf. Fabro, *La Nozione Metafisica di Partecipazione Secondo S. Tommaso d'Aquino* (Turin: Società Editrice Internazionale, 1950), 299–302, where Fabro notes that every creature is limited and hence must participate according to its mode. However, cognitive participation in a certain fashion makes up for that limitation since the rational creature can be said to be infinite because it can have the whole universe within itself in its form and can therefore approach the infinity of God as made in His likeness.

161. *ST* I.105.3; cf. *ST* I-II.93.2. See also Fabro, *La Nozione Metafisica di Partecipazione Secondo S. Tommaso d'Aquino,* 280–85, where Fabro notes that the agent intellect in knowing something both participates in the intellectual light of God and participates in the intelligible species (the act and form of the thing known) which is reducible to the first form (God).

understanding all participate in the divine intellect (*ST* I.14.8.3; 84.5). More specifically, the light (power) of the human intellect participates in God who is the divine light (the intellectual power—*ST* I.89.1); the intelligible species, through which humans understand, participates in God who is the object of divine understanding, the divine *ratio,* from which all intelligible forms flow; and the human act of understanding participates in God who is the act of understanding.[162]

In reference to the natural light of reason participating in the divine light, Thomas will often state that the created light of the intellect participates in the divine light. For example, he states:

We say all things are seen in God and all things are judged in Him, because by the participation of His light we know and judge all things; for the light of natural reason itself is a participation of the divine light; as likewise we are said to see and judge of sensible things in the sun, that is, by the sun's light.[163]

Just as the light of the sun gives us the ability to see sensible things, God's intellectual light gives the human intellect the power to "see" (understand) intelligible things.

In reference to the human intellectual forms participating in the exemplars in the divine mind, because all things are copies of a divine exemplar, to the extent that we know anything we participate in divine knowledge. However, this participation is not by directly knowing the eternal *ratio* (except in heaven) but is through knowledge of sensible things.[164] Thomas states, "The intelligible species which are participated in by our intellect are reduced as to their first cause, to a first principle which is by its essence intelligible: God. But they proceed from that prin-

---

162. *ST* I.84.5. Recall that in God, the divine essence, the object understood, the intelligible species, and His act of understanding are entirely one and the same (*ST* I.14.4).

163. *ST* I.12.11.3: Omnia dicimur in Deo videre, et secundum ipsum de omnibus iudicare, inquantum per participationem sui luminis omnia cognoscimus et diiudicamus, nam et ipsum lumen naturale rationis participatio quaedam est divini luminis; sicut etiam omnia sensibilia dicimus videre et iudicare in sole, idest per lumen solis. Cf. *SCG* III.53, 58; *ST* I.89.1; I-II.91.2; III.9.2.1, 10.4; *LC* 9; QD *De Anima* 5.6; etc.

164. Thomas notes that Plato explained human knowledge as the direct participation in separate forms. However, since direct participation does not account for the role of the body, Thomas held that although the ultimate cause of the intelligible species which our intellect participates in is that which is by essence intelligible (God), they proceed from that principle by means of sensible forms and material things (*ST* I.84.4 & I.84.4.1; I-II.5.6.2). See also John Jenkins, *Knowledge and Faith in Thomas Aquinas* (Cambridge: Cambridge University Press, 1991), 59–60. Jenkins states that since humans move from sense perception of particulars to abstraction of intelligible forms to universal principles to *scientia,* natural things are the medium between God's *scientia* and human *scientia.*

ciple by means of the forms of sensible and material things, from which we gather knowledge . . . ."[165]

Not only can the intellect be said to participate in God's knowledge in the above two ways, it can be said to participate in the eternal law which is God's knowledge as commanding all creation to act. Thus, every act of the intellect participates in the eternal law. The acts of the speculative intellect participate in the eternal law because knowing truth for its own sake is a participation in the eternal contemplation of God which is the end to which the eternal law orders humans. And the acts of the practical intellect participate in the eternal law because all human actions are formally caused by the practical intellect and the exemplary cause of these practical forms in the human mind is the eternal law. Thomas notes that the rule and measure of human action is twofold: human reason and divine reason.[166] The divine reason as the first cause perfects and rules the human reason which as the second cause participates both in the intellectual power and the *ratio* of the first cause (*ST* II-II.52.2). Because the eternal law is not known directly, humans are able to determine the proper action by means of the intellect discerning the order within nature (for all things are ordered to their particular end).[167] To the extent humans determine the action properly ordered to their ultimate end, they have a certain knowledge of the eternal law.[168]

165. *ST* I.84.4.1: Species intelligibiles quas participat noster intellectus, reducuntur sicut in primam causam in aliquod principium per suam essentiam intelligibile, scilicet in deum. Sed ab illo principio procedunt mediantibus formis rerum sensibilium et materialium, a quibus scientiam colligimus. . . . Cf. *ST* I.14.8.3, I-II.3.6; *DT* I.1; *DV* II.3. See also E. Gilson, *The Philosophy of St. Thomas Aquinas,* trans. E. Bullough (New York: Barnes & Noble, 1993), 242–50, for a description of how St. Thomas borrows from both Aristotle and St. Augustine to state that the intellectual soul knows all things by participation in the divine light which contains the eternal essences of all things. Yet this participation takes place by means of sensible things from which the intellect abstracts their intelligible species.

166. *ST* I-II.63.2, I-II.19.4; II-II 17.1.

167. When the human intellect naturally understands an ordinance of reason, this participated knowledge is called natural law (*ST* I-II.91.2). Just like all participation in knowledge, the truths of natural law are not a direct knowledge of divine reason but are by means of intelligible forms, which are abstracted from things that man knows naturally. See *ST* I-II.74.7 where Thomas states, "human acts can be regulated by the rule of human reason, which rule is derived from the created things that man knows naturally; and further still from the rule of the divine law" (actus humani regulari possunt ex regula rationis humanae, quae sumitur ex rebus creatis, quas naturaliter homo cognoscit; et ulterius ex regula legis divinae . . .).

168. Because human knowing and natural truth are true participations in God, the human intellect can naturally know God, yet not by knowing His essence. Thomas notes that there are three ways that something can be known: by essence in the knower, by the presence of likeness in a power that knows, and by the image of an object taken from something

In summary, humans naturally participate in God both in terms of their first act (that of *esse*) and their secondary acts (operation). In reference to the first act, humans participate in God who is the efficient cause of their act of *esse*, the exemplary cause of their mode of *esse*, and the final cause of their being naturally ordered to their particular end. In reference to secondary actions, humans participate in God who is the efficient cause by giving them the power to act, the exemplary cause by giving the species of the acts, and the final cause in that all acts are ordered to an end. Because God moves humans to rational actions, they participate in God through their actions in two ways: first, as moved and governed by the eternal law, and second, by actually having a certain knowledge of the eternal law. In both cases, their mode of participation is limited by their natural form, which determines their potency to act.[169]

Supernatural Human Participation in God

Although the natural form of humans limits them to a certain type of act, still the rational character of that act enables them to apprehend universal notions of being and goodness and to naturally desire to see and love God. Thomas notes that man is in potency to divine beatitude, "which consists in the vision of God, and to this he is ordered as to an end: since the rational creature is capable of that knowledge insofar as he is made to the image of God."[170] However, although created with a natural desire to know and love God as He is, humans cannot by their natural abilities fulfill this desire (ST III.9.2.3). Human reason by its own power can only know created things, which can never give knowledge of God's essence as it is. Therefore, in order for this natural desire to be fulfilled, God pro-

---

else reflecting the object. No creatures naturally know God in the first way, angels naturally know God in the second way, and humans on earth naturally know God in the third way (*ST* I.56.3, I.6.1.2). Since eternal law is God, humans only know eternal law naturally by means of the image of God reflected in the order discernable in nature.

169. Even though the acquisition of the virtues perfects the natural inclinations and thus increases their mode of participation, nonetheless, they are still limited by their natural form.

170. *ST* III.9.2: ad scientiam beatorum, quae in visione Dei consistit, et ad eam ordinatur sicut ad finem, est enim creatura rationalis capax illius beatae cognitionis, inquantum est ad imaginem Dei. In the third response Thomas notes that beatific knowledge is in one way above the nature of the human soul inasmuch as it cannot reach it by its own power, but in another way it is in accordance with its nature as made in God's image. See also *ST* I-II.113.10; III.11.1, 23.1.

vides humans with a supernatural principle for action to give humans the ability to supernaturally know God on earth and to know the essence of God in heaven.[171] By means of this supernatural principle, the will is also able to love God as He is (*SCG* III.51.1; III.147; *ST* I-II.109.3; II-II.2.3; cf. *ST* I.62.2).

This supernatural principle is the grace of the Holy Spirit, who inclines humans to act in a way that surpasses their nature. Thomas states, "There is a twofold good of man, one which is proportioned to his nature; the other which exceeds the faculty of his nature."[172] He continues by noting that in reference to the natural good of humans, humans cannot receive forms and perfections beyond their natural potency. However, in reference to the good exceeding human nature, humans attain it by receiving forms and perfections that exceed the capacity of their nature since these perfections have God as their principle.[173]

Thomas continues by noting that just as the first perfection of man, his soul (i.e., his substantial form), forms matter in a way beyond the capacity of material nature, so also man's ultimate perfection, the happiness of eternal life, also exceeds the capacity of human nature. Since the actions ordered to an end must be proportional to that end, humans must have supernatural principles to perform actions ordered to their ultimate end. Thomas states:

And because everything is ordered to its end by some activity, and those things which are for the sake of an end must be proportioned to the end, it is necessary that there should be some perfections of man whereby he is ordered to the supernatural end which exceeds the capacity of man's natural principles. But this

---

171. Keep in mind that although grace as a supernatural principle for action allows humans to fulfill a natural desire, it is *utterly gratuitous* even if it does perfect nature.

172. *De Virtut* I.10: Quod est duplex hominis bonum; unum quidem quod est proportionatum suae naturae; aliud autem suae naturae facultatem excedit. See also *ST* I.23.1 which states that providence directs things toward an end. The end is twofold, one beyond nature (eternal life and seeing God—predestination) and one proportionate to nature. Cf. *ST* I-II.62.1; II-II.26.3).

173. *De Virtut* I.10: Unde videmus quod perfectiones et formae quae causantur ex actione naturalis agentis, non excedunt naturalem facultatem recipientis: potentiae enim passivae naturalis proportionatur virtus activa naturalis. Sed perfectiones et formae quae proveniunt ab agente supernaturali infinitae virtutis, quod deus est, excedunt facultatem naturae recipientis (Hence, we see that the perfections and forms which are caused by the actions of the natural agent do not exceed the natural capacity of the recipient, for the natural passive power is proportioned to the natural active power. But the perfections and forms which come from a supernatural agent of infinite power, that is from God, exceed the capacity of the receiving nature).

can only be if over and above the natural principles there are supernatural principles of actions infused in man by God.[174]

Thomas then identifies the natural principles of operation in man as the intellect and the will and the supernatural principles as grace and the theological virtues, which are principles of knowledge and love of supernatural truth and goodness (*De Virtut* 1.10; Cf. I-II.63.3). Through these supernatural principles humans are able to exceed their natural limitations in being moved by God to meritorious acts.

In all cases of participation, the relation of the participant to that participated in is that of potency to act. In natural participation, the participated act is limited to the natural potency of the form. Since grace allows humans to exceed their natural potency, Thomas makes a distinction between participation by nature and participation by grace (often participation by glory is also included).[175] In the case of participation by nature, the natural potency of the subject is the principle for all of the acts of the human. In the mode of participation by grace, the supplemental form of grace acts as a supernatural principle allowing the human to act in a way that surpasses his natural ability to be moved. This supernatural participation receives its consummation in the beatific vision, where the human perfectly acts by means of the additional principle of glory.[176] Through supernatural participation in God, humans are able to achieve the supernatural end to which they are ordered by God.

174. *De Virtut* 1.10: Et quia unumquodque ordinatur ad finem per operationem aliquam; et ea quae sunt ad finem, oportet esse aliqualiter fini proportionate; necessarium est esse aliquas hominis perfectiones quibus ordinetur ad finem supernaturalem, quae excedant facultatem principiorum naturalium hominis. Hoc autem esse non posset, nisi supra principia naturalia aliqua supernaturalia operationum principia homini infundantur a deo.

175. Thomas will often speak of three modes of participation: by nature, grace, and glory. For example, he speaks of participation in divine sonship by nature, grace, and glory (*ST* I.33.3; cf. *ST* III.23.1.1, III.45.4); three degrees of participated knowledge: by nature, grace, and glory (*ST* I.12.2, 106.1; cf. *DSC* 10); three degrees of virtue: social virtues (in the sense the community is the end) are by nature, perfecting virtues are by grace, and perfect virtues are by glory (I-II.61.5); three degrees of participating in the image of God (*ST* I.93.4); and the knowledge of the angels is also divided into these three categories (*ST* I.61–62, I.89.2.2; cf. I.109.1; II-II.1.8). Although humans are less than the angels by nature, by grace and glory they are equals (*ST* I.20.4.2, I.108.8). Also Thomas notes that in the order of nature, grace comes midway between nature and glory, where glory is the end of the operation of nature helped by grace (*ST* I.63.3).

176. Although Thomas, following the biblical terminology, often makes a distinction between participation by grace (the principle of supernatural acts in general) and glory (the principle of supernatural acts in heaven), both are of the same genus (*ST* II-II.24.3.2), and I will treat them together.

When analyzing natural participation in God, a distinction was made between participation through the first act of the soul and participation through secondary acts; now, in this section on supernatural participation, an analogous distinction will be made between how the soul participates in the divine nature through habitual grace and how supernatural acts participate in God. In reference to these supernatural actions, the further distinction between participation by means of a principle of motion (by grace and the infused virtues) and cognitive participation (by the light of grace) also applies.[177]

Grace as Participation in Divine Nature

Strictly speaking, habitual grace is a nonsubstantial participated perfection since it does not cause a human to become a different species.[178] Nonetheless, unlike any other accidental perfection, grace perfects the essence of the soul itself, rather than a specific power as in the case of the virtues.[179] Consequently, it has the same relation to supernatural acts as human nature has to natural acts.[180] Because of this relation between grace and supernatural acts, it is fitting to view human participation in God through grace as being analogous to the way humans participate in God through

177. For just as natural principles (the powers of the soul and virtues) cause acts by participating in God, supernatural principles (grace and the infused virtues) cause actions by means of supernatural participation. Furthermore, just as the natural principles yield cognitive participation by means of the natural light, so also the supernatural principles yield cognitive participation by the means of the light of grace and glory (*ST* I.62.2; *SCG* III.147).

178. Thomas makes a distinction between habitual or sanctifying grace, which is a supernatural form perfecting the soul, and cooperative grace as the movement of the Holy Spirit. Thomas notes that God gratuitously aids humans in two ways: first, by giving them habitual grace and secondly, by moving them to act in a manner beyond their nature (*ST* I-II.110.2).

179. Cf. Bourke, "The Role of Habitus . . . ," 107–8. Bourke states that whereas virtues perfect the powers, the soul is a complete form and cannot be in a state of habit by nature. However, by grace it can be raised to a supernatural level of existence. See also Jordan Aumann, "Mystical Experience, the Infused Virtues and the Gifts," *Angelicum* 58 (1981): 35–36, who states that there are three modes of supernatural perfection: perfection of substance by grace, perfection of operation by the infused virtues, and perfection of the end by the beatific vision.

180. Just as the various powers of the soul make human acts possible through the natural inclinations of the powers, grace makes supernatural acts possible through its supernatural inclinations: the theological virtues. See *ST* I-II.62.3, "The theological virtues direct man to supernatural happiness in the same way as by the natural inclination man is directed to his connatural end" (Virtutes theologicae hoc modo ordinant hominem ad beatitudinem supernaturalem, sicut per naturalem inclinationem ordinatur homo in finem sibi connaturalem). Cf. II-II.26.6; *De Virtut* I.10.

their first act. Thomas confirms this by making a distinction between the participation of the soul in divine nature through grace and the participation of the individual powers in a specific divine attribute:

> . . . grace, as it is prior to virtue, has a subject prior to the powers of the soul, so that it is in the essence of the soul. For as man through his intellective power participates in the divine knowledge through the virtue of faith, and with respect to the power of the will participates in the divine love through the virtue of charity, so also in the nature of the soul does he participate in the divine nature, after the manner of likeness, through a certain regeneration or re-creation.[181]

Grace perfects the soul itself by making it like God so that it can perform actions beyond its natural ability.[182] Thus, although both grace and the infused virtues are supernatural principles of action, habitual grace is more fundamental as perfecting the soul itself to be endowed with the faculty to cooperate with God in causing supernatural acts.

Just as the soul in natural participation is like God, since an effect is always like its cause, so also the soul through the supernatural participation of habitual grace becomes more like its divine cause (*ST* I-II.110.4, 112.1; cf. *ST* I.6.1; SS 14). However, there is a substantial difference between natural participation and supernatural participation. Whenever there is participation in something, there are degrees of participation in it. For example, a virtuous act participates in the eternal law to a greater degree than does a nonvirtuous act. However, the difference of degree can be either accidental or substantial (*ST* I.75.7). For example, that one bar is hotter than another by its participation in fire is a case of an accidental difference of degree; but that an angel participates in the *esse* of God in a higher degree than that of a human is a case of a substantial

---

181. *ST* I-II.110.4: . . . gratia, sicut est prius virtute, ita habeat subjectum prius potentiis animae, ita scilicet quod sit in essentia animae. Sicut enim per potentiam intellectivam homo participat cognitionem divinam per virtutem fidei; et secundum potentiam voluntatis amorem divinum, per virtutem caritatis; ita etiam per naturam animae participat, secundum quandam similitudinem, naturam divinam, per quandam regenerationem sive recreationem. As a scriptural authority for the idea that grace is a participation in divine nature, Thomas, in his later works, often refers to 2 Peter 1:4, "He hath given us most great and most precious promises; that by these you may be made partakers of the Divine Nature" (maxima et pretiosa nobis promissa donavit, ut per haec efficiamini divinae consortes naturae—the English translation is from the Latin of the *Summa Theologiae,* not the Greek of the original 2 Peter). For places where Thomas refers to 2 Peter 1:4 see *SCG* IV.4.3; *ST* I-II.50.2, I-II.62.1, I-II.110.3, III.3.4.3, III.62.1.

182. Thomas compares the superadded form of habitual grace as perfecting the soul to heat in reference to water. Water by its own power cannot heat anything, but with the superadded form of heat it can heat things (*ST* I-II.109.1).

difference of degree (*ST* I.75.5). Because grace is an accidental perfection, it does not substantially change the *esse* of the soul (it remains a human soul). However, grace is a substantially different accidental perfection than any natural accidental perfection, and it causes substantially different actions than do these perfections. For example, an act of charity coming from a soul perfected by grace is supernatural whereas an act coming from a soul perfected by the acquired virtues remains natural.[183]

All things are like their cause. In reference to God as efficient cause, grace gives the soul a higher mode of being, and hence goodness, making it more like God who is essentially being and goodness.[184] Through this higher mode of being humans are able to transcend their nature through a supernatural participation in divine nature. Thomas notes that through grace, a human is not only a living and understanding being but is ultimately a living, understanding, and supernaturally happy being.[185]

While the being is caused by God as efficient cause, the particular higher mode of being is caused by God as exemplary cause. Thomas states that the divine wisdom diffuses its likeness to all things and higher things participate in it to a greater degree than do lower things.[186] Through grace humans are more like the exemplary wisdom in the divine mind.[187] Specifically, grace perfects the entire soul to perform ac-

183. Through grace Thomas will speak of humans as gods by participation (*ST* I-II.112.1, I.13.10; *CP* 215; cf. *SCG* III.147). However, humans do not substantially become God, but they do become divine by operation since their acts of knowing and loving God are divine acts (Cf. *ST* III.2.10, III.4.1)

184. *SCG* II.35; *ST* I.4.3, II-II.26.2.2. Recall that the greater the mode of being of something the more it is like God and hence the more perfect that it is (*SCG* III.97).

185. See *ST* I-II.2.5.3 where Thomas notes that some desire the likeness of God "according to being only, some as to living being, and some as to being which is living, intelligent and happy" (secundum esse tantum, quaedam secundum esse vivens, quaedam secundum esse vivens et intelligens et beatum).

186. *ST* I.9.1.2: Nihil enim esse potest, quod non procedat a divina sapientia per quandam imitationem, sicut a primo principio effectivo et formali; prout etiam artificiata procedunt a sapientia artificis. Sic igitur inquantum similitude divinae sapientiae gradatim procedit a supremis, quae magis participant de eius similitude, usque ad infima rerum, quae minus participant dicitur esse quidam processus et motus divinae sapientiae in res . . . (For nothing can exist which does not proceed from the divine wisdom by way of some kind of imitation, as from the first effective and formal principle; as also the works of art proceed from the wisdom of the artist. And so in the same way, inasmuch as the likeness of the divine wisdom proceeds in degrees from the highest things, which participate more fully of its likeness, to the lowest things which participate of it in a lesser degree, there is said to be a kind of procession and movement of divine wisdom to things). Cf. I.44.3.

187. Cf. *ST* III.23.2 which states that the whole Trinity adopts us as sons through grace: the Father as the author, the Son as exemplar, and the Holy Spirit as imprinting on us the likeness of the exemplar.

tions of knowing the universal truth and loving the universal good in a way exceeding the soul's created limitations.[188]

In reference to God as final cause, God's goodness is the end of creation. However, each thing is inclined to the end of divine goodness in accord with its particular form. Since humans are rational creatures, by nature they are inclined to actions of naturally knowing God as the cause of created things and naturally loving Him above all things (*ST* I-II.109.1 & 3). However, grace orders humans to their ultimate end of knowing and loving God as He is (cf. *SCG* III.20, 21, 25) and thus attaining the divine goodness itself (*ST* I-II.5.2). Hence, through grace, humans have a greater participation in the end of the divine goodness.[189]

As seen above, the nature of a participant limits its degree of participation. However, through grace humans are able to participate in God as efficient, exemplary, and final cause in a way that exceeds their natural potency.[190] Thomas explains that humans have an obediential potency to grace which then acts as an additional form perfecting a human's mode of being. He states:

In every creature there is an obediential potency, insofar as every creature obeys God in receiving whatever God wills. So too then there is in the soul something in potency which is naturally reduced to act by a connatural agent, and in this way it is in potency to acquired virtues. In another way there is a potency in the soul which is not naturally led to act, but only by the divine power, and in this way the infused virtues are potentially in the soul.[191]

---

188. *ST* I-II.4. From the happiness of the soul there will be an overflow to the body after the resurrection of the dead (*ST* I-II.4.6). Hence, grace in its consummation (participation by glory) perfects the entirety of the human being.

189. God wills the existing of things on account of His goodness. Therefore, grace, like all things, is caused by God's provident love. Unlike human love that is attracted to a preexisting good, the love of God causes something to be good. To the extent God loves something, it has *esse* and is hence good. However, for rational creatures God has a special love causing them to participate in the divine good in a way above their nature. (*ST* I-II.110.1).

190. Thomas notes that man is perfected in two ways: one according to the capacity of his nature and the other according to supernatural perfection. It is by the latter that man is perfect simply speaking and by the former he is only perfect in a certain respect (*De Virtut* I.10.1).

191. *De Virtut* I.10.3: Quod in tota creatura est quaedam obedientialis potentia, prout tota creatura obedit deo ad suscipiendum in se quidquid deus voluerit. Sic igitur et in anima est aliquid in potentia, quod natum est reduci in actum ab agente connaturali; et hoc modo sunt in potentia in ipsa virtutes acquisitae. Alio modo aliquid est in potentia in anima quod non est natum educi in actum nisi per virtutem divinam; et sic sunt in potentia in anima virtutes infusae. See also *ST* III.11.1, which states that humans, like all creatures, have a double passive potency. One is proportionate to the natural agent, and the other is proportionate to the first agent and is called obediential potency. This potency can reduce any agent to a

Insofar as humans are governed by God, they have a natural potency to receive natural perfections and forms (e.g., acquired virtues and natural operation).[192] However, because God has predestined humans to a supernatural end, they have an additional potency in the soul that can only be moved to act by the divine power (cf. *ST* III.24.2.2). In other words, because God has ordained humans to the supernatural end of knowing and loving Him as He is, they have a certain "potency" to grace that supernaturally perfects the soul to know and love God, allowing it to participate in God in a way beyond its natural capacity.[193]

Just as human nature is naturally inclined to cause good actions through virtues, habitual grace analogously causes supernatural good actions through virtues. From the superadded form of grace flows the supernatural inclinations of the theological virtues which act as principles of good actions through the infused moral and intellectual virtues.[194] Just as natural actions are good if determined by reason to be in accord with human nature, so also supernatural actions are good if in accord with divine nature of which humans participate through grace.[195] Since

---

higher act than the natural potency can. Cf. *DV* 8.12.4 and *DP* 6.1.18. Because this potency is beyond natural principles, there is no limit to a human's ability to participate in God. Thomas says that charity is not limited by the potency of the subject since as charity increases there is a corresponding increase in the ability to receive further increase (*ST* II-II.24.7). See also Steven Long, "Obediential Potency, Human Knowledge, and the Natural Desire for God," *International Philosophical Quarterly* 37 (1997): 45–63. Long shows the role of obediential potency in knowing and loving God as He is.

192. Although the natural potency of humans restricts their mode of participation in God, this potency is not opposed to supernatural perfections but rather requires it, analogous to the way that the limitedness of a power requires the perfection of a virtue. "The power is not taken away by the form, but the privation which is opposed to the form" (*ST* I.62.7: non tollitur potentia per formam, sed tollitur privatio, quae opponitur formae). Likewise, the natural inclination of the soul is not taken away by grace, but the privation opposed to grace is removed.

193. Because of this given potency, human freedom is preserved when God moves humans to act by means of a supernatural principle just as it is preserved when God moves humans by a natural principle. Thomas states that man freely acts when acting from a suitable habit that inclines as second nature, and since grace is like an interior habit, it makes us freely do those things becoming to grace (I-II.108.1.2; *SCG* III.148; cf. *ST* I.62.7, 105.6.1; I-II.113.3; *SCG* IV.22).

194. *ST* I-II.63.3; *DV* 27.2 which states that to naturally obtain an end something must possess three things: a nature proportionate to the end, an inclination to the end, and a movement toward the end. Hence, in reference to the supernatural end, grace is needed to make nature proportionate to end. The virtue of charity perfects inclination, and the other virtues perfect movement. It is by means of charity and the other virtues that the inclination toward God and the movement toward Him are perfected.

195. Thomas notes, a virtue is good as befitting a particular nature, either essential or participated (*ST* I-II.110.3.2 and 3).

the eternal law is the divine reason that dictates which actions are in accord with divine nature, these actions participate in the eternal law at a substantially higher degree than do only natural actions. Consequently, grace perfects human nature to participate in the eternal law in a supernatural way.

Supernatural Human Participation in God as Moved and Governed by Him

Through the superadded form of habitual grace, God is able to move and direct humans to more perfect actions. Just as God moves and directs humans as instrumental causes in natural causality, God also moves and directs humans as instrumental causes in supernatural causality. The way that an instrument can be moved and directed is always limited by its nature, since all things act in accord with their nature. However, habitual grace as a participation in divine nature allows humans to make divine nature the principle of their supernatural actions (*ST* I-II.110.3). By cooperating with habitual grace, humans are able to act in accord with divine nature and thus in a manner that substantially differs from acting in accord with human nature.[196]

Whenever there is an increase in the capacity of an instrument to act, the agent can move and direct the instrument to more perfect actions. For example, a craftsman making a bench moves and directs a hand saw differently than a power saw. Because the capacity for actions has changed in a human with grace, it is fitting that God as the divine agent moves and directs them to substantially more perfect actions.[197]

Although actions flowing from grace differ specifically from natural actions, Thomas notes that they are nonetheless free human actions. Thomas notes:

Man must reach his ultimate end through his own operations. Now, everything operates in accord with its own form. So in order that man may be brought to

196. Since habitual grace is a participation in divine nature that causes the human as a secondary cause to participate in God's moving power in a mode beyond human nature, Thomas, following the Greek Fathers, will on occasion speak of humans as gods by participation (*ST* I-II.112.1, I.13.10; *CP* 215; Cf. *SCG* III.147). However, keep in mind that since participation by its nature causes only a likeness between the participant and the thing participated in, humans do not become gods by nature but only by operation (Cf. *ST* III.2.10; III.4.1).

197. Thomas notes that the more perfect the principle, the more perfect the act, and since acts of grace depend on the Holy Spirit moving us, they are more perfect than acts from a natural principle because of their likeness to the higher nature of God (*ST* I-II.114.2.2; I-II.114.3; II-II.23.3.3).

his ultimate end through his own operations, a form must be superadded to him from which his operations may get a certain efficacy for meriting his ultimate end.[198]

Although grace is not an intensification of natural power but is a supernatural principle of actions (*SCG* III.53; 147; *ST* I-II.5.6), meritorious actions caused by it must be in accord with the form of the human agent. Since humans act as free rational beings, even supernatural actions are free actions because they proceed from a deliberate will (cf. ST I.62.7). Thus, Thomas notes that inasmuch as grace causes actions that are freely consented to, it is called cooperating grace since the human cooperates with God in performing the action.[199]

In reference to participation in God as efficient cause of human actions, humans with grace are now able to supernaturally participate in the power of God, which allows them to direct themselves to actions that are in accord with the end of knowing and loving God as He is. In reference to God as exemplary cause, humans with habitual grace are able to be directed more in accord with the *ratio* in the mind of God. In other words, in directing themselves to supernatural actions, they participate in the eternal law as governed by it at a higher level (*ST* I-II.93.6). Finally, since the end of the agent is the end of the instrument, through grace humans are able to perform actions that intend and merit the goodness of God Himself (Cf. *SCG* III.51.1; *SCG* III.147; *ST* I-II.109.3). Consequently, since the eternal law moves humans to their ultimate end, through the supernatural principle of grace humans are able to participate in eternal law as moved and governed by it in a supernatural manner.[200]

The Supernatural Cognitive Participation of a Human Act in God

Because even in their supernatural actions humans are directed to act by their reason, reason must also be supernaturally perfected by supernatu-

---

198. *SCG* III.150: Oportet quod homo ad ultimum finem per proprias operations perveniat. Unumquodque autem operatur secundum propriam formam. Oportet igitur, ad hoc quod homo perducatur in ultimum finem per proprias operations, quod superaddatur ei aliqua forma, ex qua eius operations efficaciam aliquam accipiant promerendi ultimum finem. Cf. *De Virtut* 1.10; *ST* I.62.6; I-II.68.1.

199. *ST* I-II.112.2. Cf. Bernard Lonergan, *Grace and Freedom*. The entire book explains operating and cooperating grace in the writings of Thomas.

200. *ST* I-II.62.3; I-II.91.4.1; I-II.98.1; III.57.4. The greatest participation in eternal law by a principle of motion is the participation in glory that takes place in heaven when the blessed know and love God as He is by means of His essence (*ST* I.109.1; III.10.4).

ral knowledge in order to direct humans to actions in accord with their supernatural end. Thomas notes that just as acquired virtues (through which humans achieve their natural end) are in accord with the natural light of reason, the infused virtues (through which humans achieve their supernatural end) are in accord with the light of grace (*ST* I-II.110.2). The light of grace allows humans to have a certain supernatural knowledge of the eternal law that orders them to their ultimate end.

As seen above, humans naturally participate in God's knowledge both by means of a participated intellectual power and by participated intelligible forms. In supernatural participation both modes are also perfected. Not only do humans have an intellectual light beyond nature, the light of grace or glory, but also the intelligible forms by which they understand are beyond natural apprehension as revealed by divine revelation on earth or, at the end, as seen directly in heaven. However, unlike on earth where all the forms are a participation in the *ratio* of God, in participation by the light of glory, the form known is not a participated form but the essence of God itself. Supernatural participation can be either imperfect (on earth) or perfect (in heaven). I will begin with imperfect supernatural participation on earth.

After showing that in this life God cannot be known in His essence but only through the images of His effects (*ST* I.12.12), Thomas goes on to show that, although on earth God cannot be fully known even by supernatural participation, a higher knowledge of Him beyond natural knowledge can be obtained. Thus, Thomas states:

The knowledge which we have by natural reason contains two things: images derived from the sensible objects; and the natural intelligible light, enabling us to abstract from them intelligible conceptions. Now in both of these, human knowledge is assisted by the revelation of grace. For the intellect's natural light is strengthened by the infusion of gratuitous light; and sometimes also the images in the human imagination are divinely formed, so as to express divine things better than those do which we receive from sensible objects, as appears in prophetic visions; while sometimes sensible things, or even voices, are divinely formed to express some divine meaning. . . .[201]

This participation is so great that although the angels are greater than humans by nature, Thomas notes that by grace and glory we are equals (*ST* I.20.4.2; I.108.8).

201. *ST* I.12.13: Cognitio enim quam per naturalem rationem habemus, duo requirit, scilicet, phantasmata ex sensibilibus accepta, et lumen naturale intelligibile, cuius virtute intelligibiles conceptiones ab eis abstrahimus. Et quantum ad utrumque, iuvatur humana cognitio per revelationem gratiae. Nam et lumen naturale intellectus confortatur per infusionem luminis gratuiti. Et interdum etiam phantasmata in imaginatione hominis formantur

Hence, on earth in order to have a higher understanding of God, images that more adequately represent God have been divinely revealed, and in order that these images can be understood, a higher power of understanding is given to humans by means of the light of grace (Cf. *ST* I.88.3.1). In other words, to aid our understanding of God while wayfarers, God has revealed Himself through sensible phantasms and then gives humans the grace to understand these intelligible forms.

This additional cognitive participation is necessary because the perfection of the rational creature consists not only in what belongs in respect to nature but also in respect to its supernatural end (*ST* II-II.2.3). Thomas states that it is necessary for man's salvation that God reveals knowledge beyond the natural knowledge of human reason since man is directed to God as his end. "But the end must first be known by men who are to direct their thoughts and actions to it."[202]

This knowledge of God as end is given to humans through faith and its corresponding gifts of the Holy Spirit. In other words, in order for humans to properly order their actions to their supernatural end, they must have a proper understanding of the end of attaining God. Since a greater understanding of the end changes the means that are chosen, the perfection of the speculative intellect through faith flows over into the practical intellect.[203] Thus, in this world a supernatural participation through faith is necessary both to perfect the speculative and the practical intellect in order that a human may be properly ordered to God. Both the perfection of the speculative and the practical intellect perfect participation in the eternal law. The speculative intellect participates in the eternal law through contemplation of God through faith because it is a participation in the ultimate end to which humans are ordered by

---

divinitus, magis exprimentia res divinas, quam ea quae naturaliter a sensibilibus accipimus; sicut apparet in visionibus prophetalibus. Et interdum etiam aliquae res sensibiles formantur divinitus, aut etiam voces, ad aliquid divinum exprimendum . . . . Cf. I.12.13.1–3. In reality, all the events of salvation history, especially the events of Christ's life and passion, give us new forms to contemplate in order to have a greater understanding of God.

202. *ST* I.1.1: Finem autem oportet esse praecognitum hominibus, qui suas intentiones et actiones debent ordinare in finem. Thomas continues in this passage to state that is fitting that God revealed not only truths pertaining to God that are beyond natural knowledge but also truths that can be known naturally, since these truths could only be discovered by a few, after a long period of time, and with an admixture of error.

203. Cf. *ST* II-II.8.3 and *ST* II-II.52.2 in regard to the necessity of the Holy Spirit to supernaturally counsel the mind to perfect prudence. In reference to the necessity of a supernatural perfection of the practical intellect in general, see *ST* I-II.63.2; I-II.71.6.5; I-II.74.7; II-II.17.1.

the eternal law. The practical intellect participates in the eternal law by supernaturally determining the actions that are most in accord with the ultimate end of humans.

However, faith by its nature, while perfecting the intellect, is nonetheless an imperfect participation in relation to the participation of glory (*DV* 14.1.5). Perfect participation is by glory, where God not only unites the form of His essence to the intellect but also gives the intellect the power to understand it. Thomas notes that since everything known is in the knower according to the mode of the knower, humans can only know God in His essence if God gratuitously unites Himself to the created intellect as an object made intelligible to it (*ST* I.12.4). Thomas explains:

Everything which is raised up to what exceeds its nature, must be prepared by some disposition above its nature. . . . But when any created intellect sees the essence of God, the essence of God itself become the intelligible form of the intellect. Hence, it is necessary that some supernatural disposition should be added to the intellect in order that it may be raised up to such a great and sublime height. Now since the natural power of the created intellect does not avail to enable it see the essence of God, as was shown in the preceding article, it is necessary that the power of understanding should be added by divine grace. Now the increase of the intellectual powers is called the illumination of the intellect. . . .[204]

Thus, in glory the intelligible form is God Himself (*ST* I.12.2), and the participated light is the highest human manner of participation in the divine intellect. By this participation humans see the divine essence in itself by a participation in the divine understanding.[205] This knowledge entails a direct knowledge of the eternal law.

204. *ST* I.12.5: Omne quod elevatur ad aliquid quod excedit suam naturam, oportet quod disponatur aliqua dispositione quae sit supra suam naturam. . . . Cum autem aliquis intellectus creatus videt deum per essentiam, ipsa essentia dei fit forma intelligibilis intellectus. Unde oportet quod aliqua dispositio supernaturalis ei superaddatur, ad hoc quod elevetur in tantam sublimitatem. Cum igitur virtus naturalis intellectus creati non sufficiat ad dei essentiam videndam, ut ostensum est, oportet quod ex divina gratia superaccrescat ei virtus intelligendi. Et hoc augmentum virtutis intellectivae illuminationem intellectus vocamus. . . .

205. Although by participation in the light of glory God will be seen as He is, nonetheless He cannot be understood as He understands Himself. Thomas argues in *ST* I.12.7 that everything is knowable according to its degree of *esse*, and God who is infinite *esse* is infinitely knowable. "Now no created intellect can know God infinitely. For the created intellect knows the divine essence more or less perfectly in proportion as it receives a greater or lesser light of glory." He continues by noting that since the light of glory is created, it cannot be infinite and thus cannot fully comprehend God (Nullus autem intellectus creatus potest deum infinite cognoscere. Intantum enim intellectus creatus divinam essentiam

Since to the extent to which the intellect understands God, it understands everything, not only is the speculative intellect perfected by knowing God but also the practical intellect. On earth even with the aid of grace humans are not always able to know the action that is most perfectly in conformity with the eternal law due to their inability to know all the possible circumstances (Cf. *ST* I-II.19.10.1) In glory, however, the connection between the universal and the particular good will always be seen, and the eternal law will also be followed perfectly (*ST* I-II.93.2).

In conclusion, all things participate in God as an effect participates in its cause. Since all created things are like the form in the mind of their artist, God's exemplary knowledge causes the way that each thing imitates the divine essence through participation in the divine *esse*. God's exemplary knowledge in reference to the created order is called the divine ideas and in reference to the order of operation is called the eternal law. The divine ideas, through the natural form of the creature, determine the mode that a creature participates in God by means of their first act of *esse*. Likewise, the eternal law determines the mode that a creature participates in God by means of their operation. Since all things participate in eternal law according to their form, humans, unlike other creatures, participate not only as moved by divine providence but also as rationally governing themselves and others. However, because the eternal law orders humans to a supernatural end, humans must be perfected by grace in order to achieve their ultimate end. Through habitual grace humans are made like God by participating in divine nature (*ST* II-II 23.3.3). This supernatural form acts as the principle of actions that are beyond human nature. In performing these actions humans are both moved and governed supernaturally by the eternal law and have a certain supernatural knowledge of the eternal law. By explaining operation in terms of participation, Thomas on the one hand safeguards the transcendence of God

---

perfectius vel minus perfecte cognoscit, inquantum maiori vel minori lumine gloriae perfunditur. Cum igitur lumen gloriae creatum, in quocumque intellectu creato receptum, non possit esse infinitum, impossibile est quod aliquis intellectus creatus deum infinite cognoscat). Since humans know God to the extent that they receive a greater or lesser light of glory, there can be different degrees of participation in God's light causing different levels of understanding of the divine essence (*SCG* III.58; cf. *ST* I-II.5.2.3). Thus, the mode of understanding is more perfect in some than in others due to increased charity, which results in a greater desire (*ST* I.12.6). Therefore, by grace some blessed souls are raised to the higher orders of angels and see God more clearly than do the lower orders (*ST* I-II.4.5.6). Thomas notes that among the angels and saints Mary has the highest participation in God's goodness (*ST* III.27.5). Cf. *SCG* III.51; 53.

who is pure act and thus all perfections essentially, and on the other hand respects the integrity of creatures who are true causes of their actions.[206]

PART II: THE ETERNAL LAW AS CAUSE OF HUMAN ACTIONS IN THE *PRIMA SECUNDAE*

As the final cause of all creation, God orders all that He creates to a particular end. It is by means of His divine providence that He directs these creatures to their end, since the ruler with foresight is able to see what leads to a particular end so as to order well those subject to him (*ST* I.22.2). For example, a general foresees what each regiment must do in order to attain victory and then commands the leaders of the regiments to do these things. Just as the ruler commands what is foreseen, eternal law is the command of divine providence. Although I have in general shown how eternal law moves humans to their proper end, in order to more fully show the role Thomas assigns to eternal law in human action, I will show its role within the *Prima Secundae* of the *Summa Theologiae*.

Within the *Prima Secundae* Thomas gives a detailed account of human actions and their causes (Cf. I-II.6.prologue). By showing the relation of the principles of human actions (e.g., happiness, virtue, law, grace) to the eternal law, the role of the eternal law in human actions will be seen. Likewise, by showing the relation of these moral principles to eternal law, the relation of all the moral principles to each other will be illuminated.[207]

The *Prima Secundae* is a part of the *Summa Theologiae* that was carefully structured by Thomas to teach about God, not only as He is in Himself, but also as He is as the beginning and end of all creatures.[208]

---

206. Using the philosophical notion of participation to explain all actions avoids various theological errors regarding the God-world relation. For example, the notion precludes deism because God is the first cause of all actions, occasionalism (the belief that God directly causes every action in such a way that the causality of the creature is only an illusion) because creatures are true causes by acting in accord with their mode, and pantheism because creatures are not God by essence when they participate in the *esse* of God but only by participation.

207. The interrelation among effects is caused by their relation to their cause. Hence, the relation of all the principles of moral actions to each other is caused by their relation to the eternal law. Hence, an understanding of their relation to the eternal law increases an understanding of their relation to each other (cf. *SCG* III.97; *ST* I.44.1).

208. See the prologue to the *Summa Theologiae* where Thomas states that one of the reasons for writing this work was to correct the poor pedagogical structure that was common to books within the science of sacred doctrine. This poor structure resulted in the

The *Prima Pars* treats God and creation inasmuch as it proceeds from God who is its beginning. The *Secunda Pars* treats the rational creature's return to God as its end, and the *Tertia Pars* treats Christ who is the way to God.[209] Thomas divides the *Secunda Pars* into two parts. In the first part (the *Prima Secundae*), Thomas begins with the last end of humans (1–5), then moves to human acts (6–48), followed by the intrinsic principles of human acts in general (49–89), and concludes with the extrinsic principles of human acts in general (90–114). In the second part (the *Secunda Secundae*), Thomas treats the virtues (intrinsic principles) and their corresponding laws and gifts (extrinsic principles) specifically. Therefore, following Thomas, I will begin by treating the proper end of humans, since all actions are done on account of this end. Then I will move to the interior causes of action (the virtues), and finally I will treat the exterior causes of action (law and grace), which is where Thomas specifically treats the eternal law.

The End of Human Acts: Happiness

Since all acts are for an ultimate end (*ST* I-II.1.4), Thomas begins his treatment of the rational creature's return to God by looking at the ultimate end of a human: the act of happiness.[210] Now, the end of all things is twofold: there is the object itself to which they are directed, and there is the attainment of this object (*ST* I-II.1.8). Hence, happiness is both an object and an act. As an act, it is the highest act of the highest power. In rational creatures, the highest act is that of knowing and loving that which is most knowable (essentially truth) and lovable (essentially

---

multiplication of arguments while at the same time causing confusion to the students because of the lack of proper order. Hence, Thomas sought to order the *Summa Theologiae* according to the order of the discipline (secundum ordinem disciplinae).

209. Cf. *ST* I.2.prologue. See J. P. Torrel, *Saint Thomas Aquinas,* translated by Robert Royal (Washington, D.C.: The Catholic University of America Press, 1996), 145–58. Torrel explains the format of the *Summa* and states that Thomas noted that the universe attains full perfection by returning to its beginning. Humans specifically return to God by knowing and loving Him as He is.

210. Aquinas, when describing his method in the prologue to question one of the *Prima Secundae,* states, "We shall first consider the ultimate end of human life; and then those things by means of which man is able to advance toward this end, or to stray from it: for the end is the rule of whatever is ordained to the end. And since the ultimate end of human life is stated to be happiness . . ." (Ubi prima considerandum occurit de ultimo fine humanae vitae; et deinde de his per quae homo ad hunc finem pervinire potest, vel ab eo deviare, ex fine enim oportet accipere rationes eorum quae ordinatur ad finem. Et quia ultimus finis humanae vitae ponitur esse beatitudo . . .).

good).[211] It through this act of knowing and loving God as truth and goodness that humans attain their ultimate end (God Himself). Thomas states that all creatures are directed to God as the ultimate object, but only rational creatures can properly be said to attain God by the action of knowing and loving Him.[212] In other words, the ultimate end can refer either to the object to which humans, like all things, are ordered (God), or it can refer to the act of the intellect and the will attaining this object (the act of happiness). Since the natural object of the intellect is the universal truth and the natural object of the will is the universal good, nothing can fully satisfy the intellect and the will except that which is true and good by essence and not by participation.[213]

Because humans, like all creatures, desire their own perfection, all humans by necessity desire to be happy.[214] However, because perfect happiness consists in knowing and loving the divine essence, and humans by natural power cannot know God in His essence, only imperfect happiness can be attained by natural powers (*ST* I-II.5.5). Thomas notes:

Perfect human happiness consists not in that which perfects the intellect by some participation, but in that which is so by its essence. . . . Therefore the contemplation of whatever has participated truth, does not perfect the intellect with its

---

211. *ST* I-II.1.8; II-II.19.12. Happiness occurs when a human performs the act to which God has ordered him. Since humans are rational creatures ordered to the universal true and good, the most perfect act is knowing the supreme good (God) and delighting in Him (*ST* I-II.3.8, I-II.5.1; cf. I.109.4; *LC* 24). Thomas affirms this in *ST* I-II.55.2.3: "Since God's substance is His act, the highest likeness of man to God is according to some operation. Wherefore, as was said above [I-I.3.2], happiness or bliss by which man is made most perfectly conformed to God, and which is the end of human life, consists in an operation" (Cum dei substantia sit eius actio, summa assimilatio hominis ad deum est secundum aliquam operationem. Unde, sicut supra dictum est, felicitas sive beatitudo, per quam homo maxime deo conformatur, quae est finis humanae vitae, in operatione consistit). Cf. *ST* I.26.1, which states that happiness is "the perfect good of the intellectual nature" (bonum perfectum intellectualis naturae) and hence belongs to God perfectly because God is happiness by His essence (see also *SCG* I.102).

212. *ST* I-II.1.8: All irrational creatures attain their final end by sharing in the divine likeness through their acts of being, living, or even knowing. Elsewhere Thomas notes that in regard to the object, happiness is the supreme good absolutely (as God), while on the part of the act, happiness is the supreme good of the creature as its highest operation/perfection (*ST* I.26.3.1). Cf. *SCG* III.116.

213. *ST* I-II.2.8; 3.7. The essence of happiness is an act of the intellect in knowing the good while the proper accident of happiness is the will delighting in the good apprehended (I-II.3.4; 4.1).

214. *ST* I.82.1 & 2. Thomas states that all humans have the same last end in respect to the end itself, since all desire their own perfection. However, people disagree as to what this last end consists of: some say riches, others pleasure, etc. (*ST* I-II.1.7).

final perfection. . . . God alone is truth by His essence, and that contemplation of Him makes man perfectly happy.[215]

Because only God is truth by His essence, no created beings can bring about perfect happiness; however, they can bring about a certain amount of imperfect happiness.

Since all beings participate in truth and goodness to the extent they have *esse,* all beings can bring happiness to humans to the extent the intellect knows them and the will delights in them, where the degree of happiness obtainable by knowing and delighting in them is in proportion to their participation in divine goodness (*ST* I-II.2.6). In other words, any good to the extent that it is known and delighted in brings about some happiness to humans when the intellect contemplates its goodness, but the greater the good, the greater the potential happiness. Hence, on earth, the greatest natural happiness comes from contemplating God as known through created effects and delighting in Him as loved more than any other good, and the greatest supernatural happiness on earth comes from contemplating and delighting in God as known through faith and loved through charity. The perfect happiness of knowing and loving God as essential truth and goodness only takes place in heaven through participation in the light of glory.[216] For although happiness in the present life is a participation of the happiness in God,[217] it is imperfect both on account of the lower degree of knowledge and love of God and the inconstancy of the act.[218]

215. *ST* I-II.3.7: Perfecta hominis beatitudo non consistit in eo quod est perfectio intellectus secundum alicuius participationem, sed in eo quod est per essentiam tale. . . . Quidquid ergo habet veritatem participatam, contemplatum non facit intellectum perfectum ultima perfectione. . . . relinquitur quod solus deus sit veritas per essentiam, et quod eius contemplatio faciat perfecte beatum. Cf. I-II.5.3.2, 66.5.2.

216. Just as there are three degrees of participation in God: by nature, by grace, and by glory, there are three degrees of happiness: natural happiness, supernatural happiness on earth, and perfect happiness in heaven.

217. Thomas states in *ST* I-II.3.1.1: "God is happiness by His essence: for He is happy not by acquisition or participation of something else, but by His Essence. On the other hand, men are happy as Boethius says, by participation; just as they are called gods by participation" (Deus est beatitudo per essentiam suam, non enim per adeptionem aut participationem alicuius alterius beatus est, sed per essentiam suam. Homines autem sunt beati, sicut ibidem dicit boetius, per participationem; sicut et dii per participationem dicuntur). Cf. *SCG* I.102; *ST* I.26.3.1.

218. In heaven, knowledge and love of God are perfect, causing perfect happiness. However, even in heaven there are degrees of happiness based upon the greatness of the love that a human or angel has for God. The greater the love, the greater the act of knowing God and therefore the greater the act of happiness. See *ST* I.12.6 where Thomas notes

God has created humans to be like Him by sharing in His acts of knowing and loving His divine goodness (Cf. *ST* I.93). Humans have a natural inclination to know and love the divine goodness and other things inasmuch as they participate in the divine goodness. In heaven, humans perfectly fulfill this natural inclination, but on earth humans are happy by knowing and loving God through natural means and especially through the supernatural means of faith and charity. Also, because all things participate in God's truth and goodness, happiness includes knowing and loving created things to the extent that they participate in God's *esse*. This knowledge and love of things causes human actions since the intellect is inclined to contemplate the good it attains and the will seeks to rest in that which it loves. The greater the good attained through human actions, the greater the happiness here on earth. Consequently, for Thomas, the good life consists first and foremost in contemplating God. Second, it consists in contemplating things as participating in divine truth and contemplating the goodness of the end attained through human actions. Accompanying this contemplation is delight in God and delight in other things in which the will can rest and hope.

Humans in this life are not capable of performing the perfect act of happiness but can only perform actions which are ordered to this ultimate end. Hence, Thomas notes that humans obtain the end of happiness by means of various actions (*ST* I-II.6.prologue). Since it is the nature of law to order acts to their proper end (*ST* I-II.93.3), the eternal law directs the actions of humans to their proper end of happiness: knowing and loving God.[219]

---

that there are different degrees of understanding God's essence by means of the light of glory. The greater the love of God, the greater the comprehension of God through a greater participation in the light of glory that illuminates the intellect. In other words, when humans and angels directly know God, the perfection of their understanding is proportional to the amount they love God, because then they have a greater desire to comprehend God, and this desire is fulfilled. In other words, charity gives them a greater disposition to be illuminated. Likewise, happiness in heaven is unchangeable since man participates in eternity (*ST* I-II.5.4.1, 67.4.2; cf. *ST* I.10.2–4). Thomas states in *ST* I-II.3.2.4 that in heaven, "man's mind will be united to God by one, continual, everlasting operation" (Quia una et continua et sempiterna operatione in illo beatitudinis statu mens hominis deo coniungitur). See also *ST* II-II.18.2.2 where Thomas states: "The happiness of the saints is called eternal life, because through delighting in God they participate as it were in God's eternity which surpasses all time so that the continuation of happiness does not differ in respect to present, past, and future" (Beatitudo sanctorum dicitur vita aeterna, quia per hoc quod deo fruuntur, efficiuntur quodammodo particeps aeternitatis divinae, quae excedit omne tempus. Et ita continuatio beatitudinis non diversificatur per praesens, praeteritum et futurum).

219. *ST* I-II.93.1. Cf. *ST* I-II.71.6.3 which states that eternal law first and foremost directs

The Intrinsic and Extrinsic Principles of Human Action

Although humans by nature are determined to the end of happiness in general, they are not determined to the means to this end, because the intellect is open to a variety of forms and can thus present to the will many things worthy of pursuit. Hence, humans need additional principles which dispose them to actions in accord with true happiness. These additional principles are both intrinsic *(intrinsecus)* and extrinsic *(extrinsecus)*.[220] The intrinsic principles are the powers of the soul and the virtues, and the extrinsic principles are law and grace as given by God who instructs us and aids us.[221]

The intrinsic powers give humans the ability to perform human actions. However, because of the limitations of the powers of the soul (both caused by its initial state of potency and its weakness), the intrinsic principles must be strengthened and assisted by extrinsic principles.[222] These extrinsic principles direct and move the intrinsic principles to cause good actions that are in accord with their ultimate end. In other words, human beings are not sufficient to perform good actions without the help of others. Humans must be guided, must be taught, and must gain wisdom from a variety of sources, even at the level of basic operative moral principles (e.g., the formation of our consciences).

Likewise, virtues are not in humans by nature but must be acquired by means of repeated good actions. The external principle of the law is

---

man to his end and in consequence makes man to be well disposed in regard to things that are directed to the end.

220. Thomas uses the terms *intrinsecus* and *extrinsecus* in the prologue of *ST* I-II.49 to distinguish between these two types of principles, but he often uses the terms *interior* and *exterior* instead (e.g. *SCG* III.88.5, 139.17; *ST* I. III.4, 117.1; I-II.68.1; 90.prologue). In this context, the key is that something is an intrinsic or interior principle if it flows from the nature of the agent, and something is an extrinsic or exterior agent if it helps the intrinsic principle by strengthening it or assisting it (cf. *ST* I.117.1 and *ST* I-II.68.1; 90.prologue).

221. *ST* I-II.49.prologue and I-II.90.prologue. In reference to the necessity of the virtues in performing actions ordered to happiness, see *ST* I-II.49.4, 62.1. As to the exterior principles, see I-II.91.4 for the necessity of divine law and I-II.109 for the necessity of grace. For more on the interior and exterior principles, see Bourke, *Ethics* (New York: Mcmillan Co., 1951), 153 and 162.

222. Thomas notes in *ST* I.117.1 that the exterior principle does not act as a principle agent (the interior principle) in causing an act, but "by strengthening it, and by furnishing it with instruments and assistance, of which [the interior principle] makes use in producing the effect" (confortando ipsum, et ministrando ei instrumenta et auxilia, quibus utatur ad effectum producendum). Thomas continues by noting that knowledge is obtained both from one's own resources (coming from interior principles) and from instruction (coming from an exterior principle).

necessary to direct and move humans to these good actions so that they perform like actions repetitively in order to form virtues.[223] Without the law, they will not know or do the good actions that cause the virtues.[224] These virtues then dispose humans to perform good actions. Because of the need of external principles, humans must be formed within a community where parents and others instruct them, direct them, and move them to good actions to perfect and assist their own interior principles of action. Not only are other humans necessary, but because supernatural actions must be done to achieve the ultimate end, God must act as an external principle of action assisting humans to perform supernatural actions. God instructs humans through divine revelation and guides and moves them to good human actions by means of the new law of grace.[225]

Because all good laws, both from nature and grace, are derived from the eternal law, the eternal law is the ultimate exterior principle of action. As already seen, it moves humans to action in both of the ways that it can be participated in (by a principle of motion and cognitively). Specifically, in reference to participation by a principle of motion, the eternal law moves humans to actions through the interior principles of the powers of the soul by means of their natural inclinations, including a natural inclination to virtue that perfects these inclinations. In reference

223. In reference to law ordering humans to action through virtue, see *ST* I-II.92.1 which states, "It is the proper effect of law to lead its subjects to their proper virtue: and since virtue is that which makes its subject good, it follows that the proper effect of law is to make those to whom it is given, good, either simply or in some particular respect" (Hoc sit proprium legis, inducere subjector ad propriam ipsorum virtutem. Cum igitur virtus sit quae bonum facit habentem, sequitur quod proprius effectus legis sit bonos facere eos quibus datur, vel simpliciter vel secundum quid). See also I-II.107.2, 93.6. See also Richard Berquist, *Human Dignity and Natural Law* (Santa Paula, Calif., Thomas Aquinas College Lecture Series, 2002), 7, who states that the precepts that determine which activities are virtuous are the natural law since it determines which activities achieve our natural end.

224. Law is an exterior principle. As an exterior principle it assists the interior principles of the natural inclinations to perform the proper actions that are necessary for the development of acquired virtue.

225. In reference to the new law of grace causing theological virtues that cause meritorious actions, see *ST* I-II.110.4.1 which states: "As from the essence of the soul flow its powers, which are the principles of deeds, so likewise the virtues, whereby the powers are moved to act, flow into the powers of the soul from grace. . . . For grace is the principle of meritorious works through the medium of the virtues, as the essence of the soul is the principle of vital deeds through the medium of the powers" (Sicut ab essentia animae effluunt eius potentiae, quae sunt operum principia; ita etiam ab ipsa gratia effluunt virtutes in potentias animae, per quas potentiae moventur ab actus. . . . Est enim gratia principium meritorii operis mediantibus virtutibus, sicut essentia animae est principium operum vitae mediantibus potentiis). Cf. *ST* I-II.108.2, 109.2, 110.3.2; *SCG* III.116.

to cognitive participation, the eternal law moves humans to actions by means of the natural and divine laws through which it is known. These exterior principles cause the interior principles of the virtues, which in turn perfect the powers of the soul to perform actions ordered to God. Having already shown how the eternal law moves humans through their natural principles, following Thomas, I will now show how the eternal law moves humans to their proper end by means of the virtues and laws derived from it.[226] I will begin by briefly explaining what a virtue is and then showing how laws, including the law of grace, are derived from the eternal law.

The Eternal Law and the Virtues

In order to understand how the eternal law orders humans to good actions through the virtues, it is helpful to understand that a virtue is a good habit that perfects the powers of the soul and is caused either by repeated like acts or by divine infusion.[227] In reference to a virtue being a good habit, Thomas notes that a habit is an accidental quality by which someone is disposed well or ill in accord with his nature (49.2). Now, since a habit is in relation to a creature's nature, and its nature is ordained to the end of operation (for humans, the act of happiness) or to the end that is attained by operation (for humans, this end is God), a habit is necessarily ordained to act.[228] If the habit disposes the creature to an act in accord with its nature, then the habit is good; if it disposes the

226. In the *Prima Secundae* Thomas likewise does not treat the powers of the soul under the interior principles because he has already treated them in the *Prima Pars;* however he does treat the virtues.

227. Cf. *ST* I-II.55.4 where Thomas defines a virtue as "a good habit of the mind by which we live righteously of which no one can make bad use, which God works in us, without us" (bona qualitas mentis, qua recte vivitur, qua nullus male utitur, quam deus in nobis sine nobis operatur). He notes that this definition covers all four causes of virtue: The formal cause is "a good habit," the material cause is "of the mind," the final cause is "by which we live righteously, of which no one can make bad use," and the efficient cause for the infused and theological virtues is "which God works in us, without us." The best definition of something is one that covers all four types of cause.

228. *ST* I-II.49.3. Thomas notes that a habit can be considered to be both an act and in potency to operation. In reference to the former, a habit is called the first act, and operation is called the second act (*ST* I-II.49.3.1, 55.2). See also Vernon Bourke, "The Role of Habitus in the Thomistic Metaphysics of Potency and Act," in *Essays in Thomism* (New York: Sheed & Ward, 1942), 103–9. Bourke argues that there are three types of operational potencies: that which is always active (e.g., the divine power, agent intellect, and physical strength), that which is always passive (the passions), and that which is both active and passive (a habit). Hence, virtue is both in potency to act and at the same time as a quality is already in act. Cf. *ST* I.87.2.

creature to act against the proper end of its nature, it is bad (54.3). Since a virtue is a good habit, it disposes humans to act in accord with their rational nature by performing actions that are ordered to their ultimate end of knowing and loving God (55.3).

The subject of virtues is the powers of the soul that they perfect.[229] Thomas explains that since a virtue is a habit ordered to operation, it must belong to the soul because all operation proceeds from the soul through its powers (56.1). Specifically, a virtue causes good acts by means of perfecting the powers of the soul (56.1). Thomas singles out four powers of the soul that are perfected by human virtues: the intellect which is perfected by the acquired intellectual virtues and faith; the will which is perfected by justice, hope, and charity; and the irascible and concupiscible powers which are perfected by fortitude and temperance, respectively.[230] These virtues act as interior principles of good actions by perfecting the powers of the soul.

The efficient cause of virtue is the repetition of like acts in reference to the acquired virtues and divine infusion in reference to the infused virtues.[231] Humans have a natural aptitude toward the acquired virtues. Thomas notes that the acquired virtues are within humans inchoatively (63.1) and are caused by habituation (63.2), which is the repeated performance of acts of a particular type and intensity within a human's natural ability.[232] These virtues can be strengthened by acts that are either in proportion to the intensity of the habit or exceed it, causing a greater natural participation in the divine perfection on which that virtue is

229. Although one could call a disposition of the body a virtue, strictly speaking a *human* virtue belongs only to the soul (55.2).

230. *ST* I-II.56–62. The intellectual virtues are virtues in a relative sense since they make a human good in reference to a particular aptness to act well. For example, science helps someone to act well but could also be used improperly. The subject of virtue in an absolute sense is the will because the will intends the end for which a human acts. A good will makes man good simply speaking (*ST* I-II.56.3).

231. *ST* I-II.56.4, 63.1, 63.3. The term "infused virtues" refers both to the theological virtues and the infused moral and intellectual virtues (*ST* I-II.63.3 and 65.3).

232. Thomas notes that habits are caused in passive powers by a multiplication of acts, since a passive principle is moved by an active principle (*ST* I-II.51.2). Many repeated acts are necessary for a habit to come into existence because the active principle must completely overcome the passive, and this cannot be done in a single act if the passive power is inclined to many things. Thus, in reference to the moral virtues, many acts are needed because reason (the active principle) cannot overcome the appetitive power (the passive power) at once since the appetitive power is inclined variously. However, a single self-evident proposition can cause the habit of science (51.3).

modeled (52.3). Hence, these virtues that stem from natural principles are efficiently caused by like acts of the proper intensity.

Unlike the acquired virtues, the infused virtues are produced within us by divine operation alone (63.2). Because humans are ordered to a supernatural end and the means to the end must be in accord with the end, humans must have these virtues in order to perform meritorious acts. These infused virtues act as supernatural principles, allowing humans to reach their end of knowing and loving God as He is (63.3.3).

The eternal law, by directing humans to rationally choose actions of a particular type, is the ultimate cause of the natural virtues and by means of the law of grace is the direct cause of the supernatural virtues. These virtues perfect the powers of the soul so that the eternal law can move humans more perfectly to actions that are ordered to their ultimate end of happiness.[233]

Eternal Law as the Ultimate Source of Law

As the rule and measure of all human actions, the eternal law is the cause of all other types of law. In order to understand how the eternal law causes all other types of law, it is necessary to understand Thomas' definition of a law, for it varies somewhat from most modern conceptions. Thomas in *ST* I-II.90 defines law as "a certain ordering of reason to the common good, by him who has care of the community and promulgated."[234] First, for Thomas, law is formally caused by the reason as directing those ruled to good actions. Thomas notes that a true law must be in accord with right reason, for it belongs to reason to rule and measure acts by directing things to an end (90.1). Although formally caused by the reason, as a promulgated command, law is efficiently caused by the will. Second, Thomas notes that the law must be ordered to the common good, which for humans is the happiness of the community (90.2). Finally, Thomas emphasizes that the law must come from a legitimate

233. See *SCG* III.116 which states that the end of law is to make man cling to God by means of love. Since man's goodness stems from virtue, law also intends to make men virtuous, and the precepts of the law intend acts of virtue. Cf. *ST* I-II.94.4, 108.2. See Paul Waddell, *The Primacy of Love* (New York: Paulist Press, 1992), 35–74, on the relation of the infused virtues, especially charity, to happiness.

234. *ST* I-II.90.4: *Quaedam rationis ordinatio ad bonum commune, ab eo qui curam communitatis habet, promulgata.* R. J. Henle, *The Treatise on Law: Introduction and Commentary* (South Bend: Univeristy of Notre Dame Press, 1993), 45, states that the dictate of reason is the formal cause of law, the one promulgating is the efficient cause, the common good is the final cause, and the act of promulgating is the material cause.

authority and must be promulgated (90.3 and 4). Any "law" that does not fit this definition violates human nature and is not really a law but rather "violence."[235]

Now, in moral actions, the law takes the form of the end of the action (*ST* I-II.90.2, 13.3). For example, the end of universal goodness becomes the precept: good is to be done and pursued and evil avoided (*ST* I-II.94.2). Because law takes the form of the end, the law directs the human agent to choose a means that is in conformity with the law.[236] In order for an action to be a human action, the end of the action must be known (*ST* I-II.1.1). Consequently, since law takes the form of the end, every human action in some way derives from a law. Since the eternal law is the divine *ratio* ordering humans to their end, the knowledge of these laws is a cognitive participation in eternal law.

However, humans are not able to know the eternal law directly, and hence there is the need for intermediary laws (human, natural, and divine) to guide humans in accord with it. Just as God cannot be known directly by a human on earth but only indirectly through His effects that never fully manifest Him, eternal law can also only be known in its effects. In reference to the practical intellect, this knowledge is obtained either by means of the intellect naturally understanding the ends to which humans are naturally inclined (I-II.92.4), or by means of the intellect supernaturally understanding divine revelation.[237] The eternal law is the ultimate rule of human reason; however, because it cannot be directly known on earth, immediately following his treatment of eternal law (I-II.93), Thomas covers the ways in which the eternal law is known: natural law, human law, and divine law.[238]

All of these laws are derived from and receive their authority from

235. Thomas notes that violence is done to the will when an extrinsic principle moves it in a way that is not in accord with nature (*ST* I-II.6.4).

236. Thomas states in *ST* I-II.90.2, "Now the first principle in practical matters, which are the object of the practical reason, is the last end" (Primum autem principium in operativis, quorum est ratio practica, est finis ultimus). For example, a practical syllogism might state: Giving alms is good. This is a case where one can give alms. Therefore, give alms. The statement that giving alms is good acts as both the end and the law.

237. *ST* I-II.19.4.3; *DM* 2.4. See also Rhonheimer, *Natural Law*, 257–59. Although no humans in this life have direct knowledge of the eternal law, nonetheless, all humans to the extent that they know the first indemonstrable principles of practical reason have some knowledge of the eternal law (Cf. *ST* I-II.93.2).

238. *ST* I-II.94–108. See also James P. Reilly, *St. Thomas on Law* (Toronto: Pontifical Institute of Medieval Studies, 1990), 12, who notes that Thomas presents a theology of eternal law, which culminates in divine law directing man to a supernatural end.

the eternal law. Since the eternal law is the *ratio* directing all humans to their end, all other laws that are in accord with reason directing humans to their end are derived from and receive their authority from the eternal law.[239] This includes not only human laws,[240] but also the natural and divine law that proceed from the divine mind (*ST* I-II.97.3). All three types of derived laws, as ordering humans to their proper ends, are participations in the eternal law or *ratio* of God. In this way the eternal law that is not known directly by humans in this life is nonetheless the source and authority of all laws on earth. Hence, now I will analyze natural, human, and divine law in order to show more fully how humans are able to know and be directed by the eternal law.

Natural, Human, and Divine Law as Derived from Eternal Law

After treating the eternal law, Thomas begins with the intellect's natural participation in the eternal law: natural law. In introducing natural law, Thomas makes the distinction between the mode of participation in eternal law universal to all creatures (as moved and governed) and the mode that is distinct to rational creatures: cognitive participation, where the divine light is impressed upon human reason. Thomas then states, "The light of natural reason by which we discern what is good and evil, which is the function of natural law, is nothing other than an impression of the divine light in us. It is therefore evident that the natural law is noth-

---

239. Keep in mind that although eternal things are known by means of temporal things, temporal things are then judged according to the laws of eternal things (*ST* I.79.9).

240. Thomas states in *ST* I-II.93.3, "Wherever there are movers ordained to one another, it is necessary that the power of the second mover be derived from the power of the first mover; since the second mover does not move except insofar as it is moved by the first. Wherefore we observe the same in all those who govern, so that the *ratio* of government is derived by secondary governors from the first governor, . . . Since the eternal law is the *ratio* of government in the supreme governor, all the *rationes* of government in the inferior governors must be derived from the eternal law. . . . Therefore, all laws, insofar as they participate in right reason, are derived from eternal law" (In omnibus autem moventibus ordinatis oportet quod virtus secundi moventis derivetur a virtute movenits primi, quia movens secundum non movet nisi inquantum movetur a primo. Unde et in omnibus gubernantibus idem videmus, quod ratio gubernationis a primo gubernante ad secundos derivatur, . . . Cum ergo lex aeterna sit ratio gubernationis in supreme gubernante, necesse est quod omne rationes gubernationis quae sunt in inferioribus gubernantibus, a lege aeterna deriventur. . . . Unde omnes leges, inquantum participant de ratione recta, intantum derivantur a lege aeterna). Because all true human laws are derived from the eternal law, human law that does not participate in right reason does not have the nature of law, but of violence.

ing else then the rational creature's participation in the eternal law."[241] Specifically, the natural law is the practical intellect's natural cognitive participation in eternal law. Because the natural law is this participation, it receives both its content and authority from the eternal law.

In reference to eternal law giving natural law its content: the eternal law has imprinted all of creation, including humans, with particular inclinations to an end (I-II.91.2; 93.5). Through their natural reason humans are able to recognize these inclinations and to determine that certain actions are in accord with these inclinations and others are not.[242] This ability to recognize the inclinations and determine the proper norms that flow from them is natural cognitive participation in the eternal law.

As seen above, the human intellect can only know something because the light by which it knows and the intelligible forms by which it comes to understand participate in the essence of God, who is both the act of understanding and the object understood. In morals, the intelligible forms by which humans understand participate in the eternal law. The way these intelligible forms participate in the eternal law is not through direct vision, but by humans coming to understand the ends to which they are naturally inclined.[243] God has ordered humans to a variety of goods that participate in His own goodness. Thus, by ordering humans to these natural ends, He has ordered them to Himself. Since the eternal law orders humans to God, the natural knowledge of the goods to which humans are naturally inclined is a participation in the eternal law. Thus, the content of natural law, the practical intelligible forms derived from natural knowledge of human inclinations, is a participation in the reason of God who, as the prudent legislator, created humans with natural inclinations.[244] For this reason, Thomas states that the natural law is

241. I-II.91.2: Lumen rationis naturalis, quo discernimus quid sit bonum et malum, quod pertinet ad naturalem legem, nihil aliud sit quam impressio divini luminis in nobis. Unde patet quod lex naturalis nihil aliud est quam participatio legis aeternae in rationali creatura.

242. Just as being is the first thing that falls under the speculative reason, good is the first thing that falls under the apprehension of the practical reason giving the first principle of practical reason. All other laws flow from the first principle of practical reason (good is to be done and pursued and evil avoided). The inclinations of other human powers are also apprehended by the practical reason giving other principles (I-II.94.2; cf.I-II.10.1).

243. See *ST* I-II.74.7 where Thomas states, "Human acts can be regulated by the rule of human reason, which rule is derived from the created things that man knows naturally; and further still from the rule of the divine law . . ." (actus humani regulari possunt ex regula rationis humanae, quae sumitur ex rebus creatis, quas naturaliter homo cognoscit; et ulterius ex regula legis divinae . . .).

244. See Clifford Kossel, "Natural Law and Human Law," 171–93, in *Ethics of Aquinas*

contained primarily in the eternal law and only secondarily in the natural code *(iudicatiorio)* of human reason (I-II.71.6.4). The natural power to understand these intelligible forms is the divine light operating in the practical intellect. Hence, the intellect that participates in God's eternal *ratio* receives both the ability to understand and the content of natural law from the eternal law.

Because the natural law receives its content from the eternal law, it also receives its authority from the eternal law. In turn, human reason, as it knows and commands the natural law, is morally binding because it participates in the eternal law.[245] Since laws by their nature are for the sake of moving someone to a particular proper end,[246] they must reflect this true teleological order to be genuine laws (as Thomas defines them). Otherwise, they are only the arbitrary commands of a ruler, are unjust, and have no binding authority upon the subject (93.3.2; cf. 96.4). Thus, Thomas often states that humans are to act in accord with their reason that determines how they are to attain their ultimate end.[247] Nonetheless, he confirms that human reason is only binding because it participates in the eternal law. Thomas states:

Wherever a number of causes are subordinate to one another, the effect depends more on the first than on the second cause: since the second cause acts only in virtue of the first cause. It is from eternal law, which is the divine reason, that human reason is the rule of the human will, from which the human will's goodness is measured. . . . It is evident that the goodness of the human will depends on the eternal law much more than on human reason: and when human reason fails, we must have recourse to eternal reason.[248]

(Washington, D.C.: Georgetown University Press, 2002), 171–76. Kossel notes that the natural law is caused by the eternal law. However, in the order of discovery, one begins with the effects and works back to the cause. Hence, natural law has its own intelligibility without explicit knowledge of the eternal law. Nonetheless, for perfect understanding of the natural law, the eternal law must be known.

245. See I-II.19.5 where Thomas states that one's conscience is binding because human reason participates in eternal law. Cf. I-II.19.4.1. See Rhonheimer, *Natural Law*, 64–66, 235, who argues it is necessary to show that the authority of natural law is derived from the eternal law in order to correct the misunderstandings of natural law such as those made by people who equate the natural law with human autonomy.

246. Recall that a law is a dictate of reason ordering humans to the common good (*ST* I-II.90.1 & 2).

247. For example, see *ST* I-II.19.3 where Thomas states that the goodness of will depends on reason which alone can apprehend the universal good.

248. I-II.19.4: In omnibus causis ordinatis, effectus plus dependet a causa prima quam a causa second, quia causa secunda non agit nisi in virtute primae causae. Quod autem ratio humana sit regula voluntatis humanae, ex qua eius bonitas mensuretur, habet ex lege

Natural law is the proximate rule of human acts, but the primary rule of human acts is eternal law. In sum, since the natural inclination of humans to their particular end has its source in eternal law, natural law, which moves humans to act in accord with these ends, is binding as a participation in the eternal law.

Although the natural law when coupled with prudence is sufficient for moving humans to their natural end, all the precepts of the natural law are not self-evident to everyone, for some are only known by the wise (*ST* I-II.100.1). Hence, humans need another law that is derived from the natural law but is explicitly dictated by a human authority: human law. Thomas notes that it is appropriate for there to be human laws because, although humans have a natural aptitude to virtue, some type of training is necessary in order to bring virtue to perfection. Hence, laws are established to move people to virtuous acts by restraining them from doing evil and moving them to do good (I-II.95.1). By moving humans to become virtuous, the law orders them to their ultimate end.

Since true human laws move humans to actions ordered to their ultimate end, human law must also be in accord with eternal law, which orders all things to their ultimate end. The way that human laws are derived from the eternal law is by means of natural and divine law.[249] Thomas explains that all precepts of human law are derived from either the natural law or the divine law (95.2 & 3). If human law is not derived from these two laws, it is no longer a law but a perversion of law (95.2 & 3). Thomas notes,

Human law has the nature of law insofar as it is according to right reason; and it is clear that in this respect, it is derived from eternal law. But insofar as it deviates from reason it is called an unjust law and has the nature not of law but of violence.[250]

Human law as derived from eternal law causes good acts that are in accord with eternal law. Because humans participate in divine providence

---

aeterna, quae est ratio divina. . . . Unde manifestum est quod multo magis dependet bonitas voluntatis humanae a lege aeterna, quam a ratione humana, et ubi deficit humana ratio, oportet ad rationem aeternam recurrere.

249. Thomas notes that everything ruled and measured must have a form proportionate to its rule and measure, and the higher rule and measure of human law is the divine and natural law (I-II.95.3). Divine law is covered in the section below.

250. Lex humana intantum habet rationem legis, inquantum, est secundum rationem rectam, et secundum hoc manifestum est quod a lege aeterna derivatur. Inquantum vero a ratione recedit, sic dicitur lex iniqua, et sic non habet rationem legis, sed magis violentiae cuiusdam. Cf. 96.4.

as self-directing, it is fitting that they exercise this self-direction by making laws which move themselves and other humans to their ultimate end of knowing and loving God.

If the ultimate end of humans were proportionate to the natural faculties of humans, natural law and human law would suffice in directing humans to natural happiness. However, since humans are ordained to the end of eternal happiness which is beyond natural human capacity, God has given humans a divine law.[251] This law that was divinely revealed can be divided into two states based upon its degrees of perfection: the imperfect state of the old law and the perfect state of the new law (91.5, 98.1).

The old law refers to the law given by God in the Old Testament. The new law is the law given by Christ and consists primarily of the grace of Holy Spirit (who is given by Christ), and secondarily of physical elements, which are necessary due to our bodily nature, such as the written texts of the Gospel, the sacraments, and so on.[252] In reference to its physical element, the new law contains the written laws of charity to God and neighbor along with the specific application of these ends as known through the New Testament and Church teaching. In reference to the spiritual element, as ordered by divine providence, it contains the *ratio* of every human action directed to the end of eternal life. Thomas notes that although the old law is good as being in accord with reason, it is imperfect since it is unable to move humans to the proper end of divine law: participation in everlasting happiness. Only the new law, which gives the grace of the Holy Spirit and causes charity which fulfills the law, is able to move humans to everlasting life. This grace could not have been given by the old law, since it was reserved for Christ (98.1).

Like the natural and human law, divine law also receives its content and authority from the eternal law. However, despite the fact that Thomas places divine law after natural and human law, divine law has the great-

251. I-II.91.4. God has also bestowed divine law to aid humans in making proper judgments, to direct humans interiorly as well as exteriorly, and to forbid all sins (I-II.91.4).

252. The new law, which surpasses human nature, is the law of grace. Thomas states, "The new law is principally the grace itself of the Holy Spirit" (principaliter lex nova est ipsa gratia spiritus sancti). Secondarily, the new law is a written law that disposes humans to that grace or pertains to the use of that grace (I-II.106.1). For secondary literature on the new law, see Pinckaers, *Sources*, 175–82, and "The Recovery of the New Law in Moral Theology," *Irish Theological Quarterly* 64 (1999): 3–15. See also Yves Congar, "Le Saint Esprit dans la théologie Thomiste de l'agir moral," in *Atti Del Congresso Internazionale: Tommaso D'Aquino Nel Suo Settimo Centenario* (Napoli: Edizioni Domenicane Italiane, 1974), 9–19.

est participation in the eternal law and the most extensive content.[253] Even in its imperfect form of the old law, the divine law "is distinct from natural law, not as being altogether different from it, but as something superadded to it. For just as grace presupposes nature, so must the divine law presuppose the natural law."[254] Just as grace perfects nature, the divine law perfects the natural law. Consequently, the divine law is a higher form of participation in eternal law than that of the natural law and the new law is the highest cognitive participation in the eternal law. Thomas notes, "Now no state of the present life can be more perfect than the state of the new law, since nothing can approach nearer to the last end than that which is the immediate cause of our being brought to the last end."[255] The new law, as the law of grace guiding humans to actions in accord with their supernatural end and helping them perform these actions,[256] is the immediate cause of our last end: eternal happiness (106.4). By giving the intellect knowledge of the eternal law in a way surpassing nature, the new law receives its content and authority from the divine wisdom Himself (II-II.19.7).

In summary, the eternal law is the *ratio* of God moving humans to

253. Instead of ordering the types of law from most universal to least universal (i.e., eternal law, divine law, natural law, and human law), Thomas begins with law as in God (93), then as directing humans to a natural end (94–97), and then as directing humans to a supernatural end (98–108). However, strictly speaking, human law (95–97) is also derived from divine law (95.3). See Dennis Billy, "The Theological Foundation of Thomas' Teaching on Law," *Divus Thomas Piacenza* 67–68 (1990–1991): 253.

254. I-II.99.2.1: . . . distinguitur a lege naturae non tanquam ab ea omnino aliena, sed tanquam aliquid ei superaddens. Sicut enim gratia praesupponit naturam, ita oportet quod lex divina praesupponat legem naturalem. See also I-II.91.4.1 which states that the eternal law is participated in proportionately to the capacity of human nature by means of the natural law. However, since humans are ordered to a supernatural end, they must be directed in a higher way. Divine law, as an additional law given by God, directs humans in this higher way by allowing humans to more perfectly participate in eternal law. See also 94.4.1 which states that the law and the gospel contain much beyond nature, but everything in natural law is in the law and the gospel. Cf. I-II.63.2, 71.6.5, 74.7; II-II.52.2; *SCG* III.116. See also Thomas Hibbs, "Divine Irony and the Natural Law," *International Philosophical Quarterly* 30 (1990): 419–29.

255. I-II.106.4: Nullus autem status praesentis vitae potest esse perfectior quam status novae legis. Nihil enim potest esse propinquius fini ultimo quam quod immediate in finem ultimum introducit.

256. See *ST* I-II.106.1 where Thomas notes that there are two ways that something can be instilled into man. First, by flowing from his nature (the natural law) and secondly, by being added to his nature by a gift of grace. "In this [second] way the new law is instilled into man, not only by indicating to him what he should do, but also by helping him to accomplish it" (Et hoc modo lex nova est indita homini, non solum indicans quid sit faciendum, sed etiam adiuvans ad implendum). Cf. I.64.1; I-II.19.4, 63.2, 74.7; II-II.8.3.

their proper end. Since humans are moved to this end not only by an interior principle of motion but also cognitively, humans must have knowledge of this *ratio*. Although direct knowledge of the eternal law is impossible on earth, true knowledge of it can be obtained by means of the natural law known by natural reason and the divine law known by revelation (and also the human law to the extent it is derived from the natural and the divine law). Since eternal law is the divine reason moving things to their proper end, a law has authority to the extent that it shares in this reason. Consequently, by means of natural, human, and divine law the intellect participates in the eternal law. These laws act as exterior principles moving humans to perform actions ordered to their ultimate end.

Grace as the Supernatural Principle of Happiness

Since the new law is primarily the law of grace, it is fitting that Thomas immediately follows the section on law (90–108) with the section on grace (109–114). The new law acts as a transition between the two ways that God as an exterior principle moves humans to Him.[257] Thomas has already introduced the role of grace as a principle moving persons to eternal happiness within the section on law. Consequently, in the questions devoted specifically to grace, Thomas expands on the role of grace as an exterior principle moving humans to their particular, ultimate end of eternal happiness.

When discussing the essence of grace, Thomas distinguishes between grace as someone's love of another and grace as a gift bestowed on the one loved. Hence, the term grace can be used to refer to God's eternal love, which is God Himself, or it can refer to a created gift that stems from His love (*ST* I-II.110.1). Since Thomas is treating grace within the context of exterior principles of good actions, Thomas will primarily focus on grace as a gift bestowed on rational creatures causing them to act in a manner beyond their nature. Thomas then makes a further distinction between habitual grace, which is a superadded form allowing humans to exceed their natural capacity in acting, and the supernatural

---

257. The new law also acts as a transition between law and the *Tertia Pars* since the new law is the law of Christ. This law moves humans to their end of eternal happiness as brought about by faith in Christ, who as both God and man reveals the new law and gives the grace to justify all humans (cf. I-II.106.2). On this point, see Dennis Billy, "The Theological Foundation of Thomas' Teaching on Law," *Divus Thomas Piacenza* 67–68 (1990–1991): 247–48. See also Thomas O'Meara, "Interpreting Thomas Aquinas: The Dominican School," in *Ethics of Aquinas,* ed. Stephen Pope (Washington, D.C.: Georgetown University Press, 2002), 355–73, on why the section on grace is placed where it is in the *Summa*.

movement of grace which moves humans to these actions (*ST* 110.2). Habitual grace perfects the soul as a whole (110.4) and allows humans to be supernaturally moved to acts that merit eternal life by means of charity and the other virtues as formed by charity (114.4).

In relation to eternal law, grace gives humans the ability to supernaturally participate in eternal law by both modes of participation (by a principle of motion and cognitively). In reference to the former mode, it causes the theological virtues and the infused moral virtues which serve as interior principles of supernatural actions. In reference to cognitive participation, grace is the principle of faith and of the Holy Spirit's gifts of knowledge, understanding, wisdom, and counsel that perfect the intellect and allow humans to act according to the wisdom of God. Through grace, humans are moved by the eternal law to perform meritorious actions, and since they are moved as rational creatures, their intellect is also supernaturally perfected, thereby allowing humans to cooperate in the performance of divine actions.

Examining the role that Thomas attributes to the eternal law within the *Prima Secundae* reveals its importance as the divine exemplary cause of all human actions. The eternal law as the governing *ratio* of God directs humans to act for the divinely intended end: participation in divine goodness by means of the act of happiness. The eternal law directs humans to this ultimate end by means of intrinsic and extrinsic principles. More specifically, the eternal law by means of law and grace (extrinsic principles) directs humans through the powers of the soul which are perfected by the virtues (intrinsic principles) to perform meritorious actions.

On the natural level, the eternal law moves humans to perform human actions by means of their natural inclinations. However, because these inclinations do not always cause actions in accord with the end of happiness, the exterior principle of law (especially human law derived from natural law) is needed to move and guide humans to perform *good* human actions. These good human actions when done repetitively form virtues that give humans the ability to perform even better human actions.[258] Finally, on account of the perfections of the powers of the soul, humans are able to contemplate and delight in the goodness that they

---

258. Once humans have attained virtue, they are able to determine good laws for themselves and others. They are now able to move and guide others to good actions which form virtues. . . .

attain through their actions: the act of natural happiness. Hence, law and virtue increase participation in eternal law, which results in greater happiness.

On the supernatural level, the eternal law likewise guides and moves humans to actions that attain eternal happiness. However, human nature is not a principle that is capable of causing actions that are in accord with eternal happiness. Because actions are in accord with the nature of the agent, grace, as a participation in divine nature, gives humans the ability to perform divine actions. The divine law guides the mind to perform these actions through supernatural cognitive participation in the eternal law. Likewise, the infused virtues perfect the powers of the soul to perform actions that are in accord with their supernatural end of eternal life.[259] Hence, grace and virtue cause a supernatural participation in eternal law that results in supernatural happiness here on earth and perfect happiness in heaven.

The eternal law as the *ratio* of God orders humans to their proper end by means of their principles of action. Hence, an understanding of the relation of the various principles of actions to the eternal law shows that Thomas has one cohesive moral theory where each principle has an essential role.

CONCLUSION

Since God as the divine legislator is the exemplary cause of every human action through His eternal law, humans are said to participate in the eternal law whenever they act. This notion of participation allows Thomas to proclaim God as the primary cause of all actions, while still declaring humans to be the true secondary causes in reaching their ultimate end. Because all secondary causes act in accord with their particular form, humans as rational and free agents are not only governed by the eternal law but also govern themselves and others. This results in two types of participation in the eternal law: as governed by it and as having a certain knowledge of it. In both of these ways, the human powers can be perfected to participate at a higher degree through the virtues, grace,

---

259. The infused virtues are caused by God alone. Nonetheless, supernatural acts that are caused by principles beyond our nature strengthen already existing infused habits since humans as rational creatures cooperate with grace as true causes of these actions (I-II.51.4.1; II-II.24.6; cf. I-II.19.10, 62.3).

and the gifts of the Holy Spirit. Since the eternal law orders humans to the attainment of God, greater participation in it results in humans being more like God through their actions, and they already begin to share in the gift of eternal life through the indwelling of the Holy Spirit. Hence, in chapter three I will show how humans can perfect their participation in eternal law by means of a principle of motion through grace and virtue, and in chapter four I will show how they can perfect their cognitive participation through faith and wisdom.

CHAPTER 3

Participation as Moved
and Governed

AS SEEN IN CHAPTER 2, humans participate in the eternal law in two ways: as moved and governed by it and as having a certain knowledge of it (cognitive participation). Whereas the first of these modes of participation refers to God's exemplary causality of the movement of the entire soul to act, the second mode of participation refers to the human intellect's knowledge of this divine exemplar. Participation as governed is the cause of cognitive participation. In other words, God governs all creatures to act in accord with their form. Hence, the human act of knowing the eternal law is determined by God's governing humans to know the eternal law. Thus, following the order of causality in this work, I will first analyze how humans perfect participation as governed in this chapter and analyze how humans perfect cognitive participation in the next.

Before showing how humans perfect their natural and supernatural participation in eternal law as moved and governed by it, I will explain a few foundational issues. First, because the ability to perfect one's participation implies that there can be different degrees of participation, I will explain in greater detail how there are different degrees of participation in eternal law. Second, I will explain why a greater participation in eternal law is essential for humans to reach their ultimate end of happiness.

Just as there can be different degrees of participation by a human subject in the reason of a human governor, there can be different degrees of participation in the eternal law. Analogous to the way that God orders all of creation to its end, a human governor orders his subjects to the state's end. Inasmuch as a particular subject acts in accord with the ordering reason of a human governor, the governor's reason is the exemplary cause of the action of the subject. However, inasmuch as the subject falls short of the reason of the governor in performing his action, the governor is not said to be the exemplary cause of the deficiency in the action; rather, the subject alone is the cause of this deficiency. Thus, a subject only participates in the reason of the governor to the extent that his action conforms to the reason of the governor. Since there can be various degrees of conformity between the reason of the governor and that of the action of the subject, there can be various degrees of participation.

For example, a general could have a detailed plan to take a fortress which includes his soldiers scaling the wall of a fortress by climbing ropes at midnight. A particular soldier may not understand this command and might instead scale the wall by means of a ladder. Inasmuch as the soldier is caused to scale the wall by the general, his act is caused by the general and therefore participates in the general's reason. Inasmuch the soldier did not follow the command, the deficiency in the action is attributed to him alone. Another soldier might be undisciplined and therefore does not arrive until 1:00 A.M. to scale the wall. In both of these cases the degree of participation of the soldier's actions in the reason of the general is imperfect and may prevent the soldiers from achieving the end of the general: taking the fortress. By precisely following the command of the general, the soldier's participation in the general's reason would be perfected.

In reference to the divine Governor, God orders humans, like all creatures, to the end of His goodness by means of His Wisdom. To the extent human actions are in accord with this wisdom, they are caused by the eternal law and are said to participate in it. However, to the extent that they are deficient, they are caused by the human alone.[1] Because there can be various degrees of conformity between the eternal law and a human action due to both a lack of knowledge of the eternal law and a

---

1. Thomas notes that inasmuch as the act has being and is an act, it is from God; inasmuch as it is deficient, it is caused by a deficient secondary cause (*ST* I.49.2.2; I-II.79.2; *DP* 1.6.5). Cf. *DP* 3.6.20 where Thomas notes that to the extent an act has *esse* and is an action, it is from God since the *esse* and action of a sinful act are caused by God as first cause, but the deformity in the act is referred only to the human will.

lack of rectitude of the rational and sense appetites, there can be various degrees of participation in eternal law. Thomas notes that whereas the participation of the wicked in eternal law is imperfect, the participation of the good is more perfect on account of the perfection of their natural inclinations by grace and virtue (*ST* I-II.93.6). Because eternal law is the exemplar moving humans to their proper end, greater participation results in a more perfect attainment of the end. This is analogous to human governance, where the greater the participation of the acts of subjects in the reason of the human governor, the more perfectly the end assigned by the governor is attained.

However, there are some dissimilarities between the eternal law and the reason of a human governor. Whereas a subject can completely cease to participate in the wisdom of a human governor and even cause the failure of the governor to reach the end that he intended, all humans (as well as all of creation) participate in the eternal law and therefore in some way have a role in bringing the universe to its end as intended by God (*ST* I.103.5–8). Because God's knowledge is the exemplary cause of every action inasmuch as it has being and is an act (*ST* I.49.2.2), even if humans are not performing actions ordered to their particular end of eternal happiness, they nonetheless participate in eternal law. The eternal law guides all creatures to their particular ends through their natural inclinations.[2] Since all human actions are caused by the natural inclinations of the intellect to the truth and the will to the good, all human actions participate in the eternal law (even if only minimally).[3] Even the wicked as subject to the eternal law participate in it.[4] Thus, the eternal

2. See chapter 2 on how God moves and directs all creatures to their operation by moving them in accord with their form, which contains natural inclinations to a particular end. Cf. *ST* I-II.93.5.

3. Because a human action by definition is an action that flows from a will that is determined by reason to a particular good (*ST* I-II.1), all human actions in some sense are in accord with reason and are ordered to a good. In other words, every human action is done on account of something perceived as good by the intellect. Another way of saying this is that all human actions are performed because the agent believes the act will make him happy. Cf. *ST* I.103.8.1; I-II.91.2.2; II.28.2.1; *DP* 3.7.15. See also John Bowlin, *Contingency and Fortune in Aquinas's Ethics* (Cambridge: Cambridge University Press, 1999), 125, where Bowlin states, "even sinful action is human action. It is done for the sake of one of the ends that we know and will by nature, which is equivalent to saying that it is rational in some minimal sense and thus dependent upon some minimal participation in eternal law."

4. Thomas notes in *ST* I-II.93.6: "Accordingly, the good are perfectly subject to the eternal law, as always acting according to it: whereas the wicked are subject to the eternal law, imperfectly as to their actions, indeed, since both their knowledge of good, and their inclination thereto, are imperfect; but this imperfection on the part of action is supplied on the

law moves all humans to all of their actions by imprinting upon them natural inclinations that act as the principles of their actions.[5] Inasmuch as humans participate in the eternal law they in some way help to bring the universe to its divinely intended end.

Although all humans by necessity participate in the eternal law, the more perfectly a human participates in the eternal law, the more perfectly he achieves the end to which he is naturally inclined. Just as a human governor orders each subject to an individual end for the sake of the common good, God orders humans (and all creatures) to a particular end by which they attain the divine goodness. In the case of humans, this particular end is the act of happiness by which they attain God.[6]

However, humans are not able to obtain perfect happiness immediately, but only through many human actions that are ordered to this ultimate end. The greater the conformity between the actions of the human and the eternal law, the closer the human is to the end of happiness. Likewise in human affairs, the greater the conformity between the acts of a subject and the reason of the governor, the closer the subject is to the end intended by the governor. For example, in order for a general to achieve the end of winning a battle, he must also intend a particular end for each of his officers. He then commands the officers to perform a certain action to achieve their particular end. To the extent the officers perform the action they were commanded to perform, they achieve their

---

part of passion, insofar as they suffer what the eternal law decrees concerning them . . ." (Sic igitur boni perfecte subsunt legi aeternae, tanquam semper secundum eam agentes. Mali autem subsunt quidem legi aeternae, imperfecte quidem quantum ad actiones ipsorum, prout imperfecte cognoscunt et imperfecte inclinantur ad bonum, sed quantum deficit ex parte actionis, suppletur ex parte passionis, prout scilicet intantum patiuntur quod lex aeterna dictat de eis . . .). Thomas then quotes a passage from Augustine who in speaking of divine foreknowledge and original sin states that even the actions of the fallen angels and sinners fall within God's divine plan. See St. Augustine, *The First Catechetical Instruction,* translated by Joseph Christopher (Westminster, Md.: The Newman Bookshop, 1946), chapter 18.

5. Thomas notes in I-II.93.5, "God imprints on the whole of nature the principle of the appropriate actions" (Deus imprimit toti naturae principia proprium actuum). Thomas explains that just as man in governing others impresses a certain inward principle of motion on the one subject to him, so God likewise rules by means of placing an inward principle of motion on creatures (I-II.93.5). However, unlike humans who can only imprint a principle of motion on rational creatures, God places a principle of motion on all creatures (I-II.93.5.2). See also I-II.91.2 where Thomas states that since all are subject to divine providence, all things participate in eternal law which is imprinted upon them as their rule and measure. For from the eternal law that is imprinted upon them they receive their respective inclinations to their proper acts and ends.

6. See *SCG* III.115 & 116 which notes that divine law principally orders man toward God who is achieved by a union of knowledge and love.

particular end and the battle is won (assuming perfect military prudence on the part of the general). Likewise, to the extent humans participate in the divine command of eternal law, they achieve their end of eternal happiness. Since God governs all humans to their proper end, a greater participation in eternal law causes a greater participation in happiness.[7] Inasmuch as humans are naturally inclined to their ultimate end, they are also naturally inclined to participate in the eternal law (*ST* I-II.93.6.2) and should therefore seek to increase their participation in it.[8]

Participation in eternal law as moved and governed by it can be increased by perfecting the natural inclinations. Although the degrees of participation in eternal law are in theory infinite, Thomas speaks of three levels of participation: that of the wicked whose natural inclinations are corrupted, that of the good who act according to their natural inclinations, and that of the good who act according to supernatural inclinations. After explaining the two modes of participation (by a principle of motion and cognitive), Thomas states:

Both modes [of participation in eternal law], however, are imperfect and to a certain extent destroyed in the wicked, because in them the natural inclination to virtue is corrupted by vicious habits, and, moreover, the natural knowledge of good is darkened by passions and habits of sin. But in the good both modes

---

7. Although the final cause precedes the exemplary cause in reference to the agent who is causing since all things are done on account of an end, in reference to the thing caused the form precedes the end (*ST* I.5.4). For example, the end for which the house is built precedes the exemplar of the house in the architect's mind since he designs the house to fulfill a particular function. However, in the actual building of the house, the form of the house precedes the actual house which achieves the end intended by the builder. In reference to humans and their final end, although God's eternal law as exemplar cause of human actions presupposes the end of divine goodness, human participation in the eternal law precedes participation in happiness.

8. Because the perfection that a substance has by participation is not the substantial form, but an accidental form, it can be increased. Thomas notes that although the substantial form of a subject cannot change, a subject can increase its participation in any form that is accidental (*ST* I-II.52.1, 112.4.3; III.7.2; *DSC* 8). In *ST* I-II.52.2 Thomas states: ". . . increase and decrease in forms which are capable of intensity and remissness, happen in one mode not on the part of the very form considered in itself, but from the diverse participation by the subject. Wherefore such increases of habits and other forms is not caused by an addition of form to form; but by the subject participating more or less perfectly, one and the same form" (. . . augmentum et diminutio in formis quae intenduntur et remittuntur, accidit uno modo non ex parte ipsius formae secundum se consideratae, sed ex diversa participatione subiecti. Et ideo huiusmodi augmentum habituum et aliarum formarum, non fit per additionem formae ad formam; sed fit per hoc quod subiectum magis vel minus perfecte participat unam et eandem formam). Therefore, humans can increase their participation in eternal law. Cf. *ST* I-II.53.2.1 which states that the intensity of the participation can also decrease.

[of participation] are found more perfect, because in them, besides the natural knowledge of good, there is the added knowledge of faith and wisdom; and again, besides the natural inclination to the good, there is the added movement of grace and virtue.[9]

The lowest level of participation is that of the wicked whose natural inclinations are corrupted by vicious habits.[10] The good, however, have two perfections of participation: the perfection of nature and also the superadded perfection of grace and virtue.[11] In other words, just as God by his grace both heals fallen human nature to perfect the natural powers of humans and elevates human nature so that human acts can be formed by charity (*ST* I-II.109.2, 109.4, 109.8), so also the good participate not only by perfected natural principles, but also by the supernatural principles of grace and virtue.

Hence, the proper way to interpret the statement, "But in the good both modes [of participation] are found more perfect, because in them, besides the natural knowledge of good, there is the added knowledge of faith and wisdom; and again, besides the natural inclination to the good, there is the added movement of grace and virtue," is that the natural knowledge of the good and natural inclination to the good refer to perfected natural participation in eternal law and that participation by the superadded forms of faith, wisdom, grace, and virtue refer to supernatural participation in eternal law.[12] Since a more perfect participation in

9. *ST* I-II.93.6: Uterque tamen modus imperfectus quidem est, et quodammodo corruptus, in malis; in quibus et inclinatio naturalis ad virtutem depravatur per habitum vitiosum; et iterum ipsa naturalis cognitio boni in eis obtenebratur per passiones et habitus peccatorum. In bonis autem uterque modus invenitur perfectior, quia et supra cognitionem naturalem boni, superadditur eis cognitio fidei et sapientiae; et supra naturalem inclinationem ad bonum, superadditur eis interius motivum gratiae et virtutis.

10. See I-II.85.2 where Thomas argues that the natural inclination to the good of nature (virtue) cannot be destroyed by sin but it can be diminished.

11. See chapter 2 for the distinction between participation by nature and participation by grace and glory.

12. Thomas has placed these superadded forms in the order of causality. Grace is placed before virtue as the external principle of the infused virtues (I-II.110.3.3) and faith is placed before wisdom as the cause of the gift of wisdom (*ST* II-II.19.7). For parallel passages where Thomas uses the same words and word order: grace and virtue (*gratiae et virtutis*), see especially the section on baptism where Thomas asks in *ST* III.69.4 whether baptism confers grace and virtue. Thomas answers, "Now the fullness of grace and virtue flows from Christ the Head to all His members" (A capite autem Christo in omnia membra eius gratiae et virtutis plenitudo derivatur). Thomas makes the same point in 69.6 in reference to children receiving the influx of grace and virtue from Christ the Head (recipiant influxem gratiae et virtutis). In the case of infant baptism it is clear that Thomas is referring to the infused virtues. Another good example is *ST* I.113.2 where Thomas notes that good actions require

eternal law results in a more perfect attainment of happiness, I will show that participation in the eternal law can be perfected by perfecting the natural inclination to the good and then I will show how the acquired virtues perfect this natural inclination. After treating the perfection of natural participation in eternal law I will treat supernatural participation by grace and virtue.

PERFECT NATURAL PARTICIPATION
IN ETERNAL LAW

Inasmuch as anything is moved by a command to a particular end, it participates in it (*ST* I-II.90.1.1). In reference to the eternal law, all things participate in it as an instrumental cause participates in the exemplary form in the mind of the agent.[13] In all cases of instrumental causality, the instrument is moved both in accord with its own form and in accord with the exemplary form in the agent's mind. For example, inasmuch as a cutting tool acts in accord with its own form it cuts, but inasmuch as it is moved by the form in the craftsman's mind, it makes benches.[14] Hence, there are two causes of every action, the divine agent who is the first cause and the created agent who acts by means of participation in the divine power (efficient cause), wisdom (exemplary cause), and good-

---

two things: good inclinations (from good habits of moral virtue) and that reason discovers the proper methods to make perfect the good of virtue (from prudence). God guards man in regard to the first by *infusing grace and virtue*. The distinction Thomas makes in this passage between inclination and reason corresponds to the two modes of participation. Hence, Thomas shows that participation by a principle of motion is perfected by *infused* grace and virtue. For other passages using grace and virtue the same way, see II-II.19.3.1; III.15.3, 79.1.2. See also I-II.85.4 where Thomas places the words in the opposite order and appears to mean natural virtue and grace. On the other hand, in other contexts Thomas contrasts the mode of virtue and grace from that of glory (see Rom 8.6). For passages on faith and wisdom, see I-II.113.4.2 and II-II.19.7.

13. *SCG* III.94.10. See chapter 2 on how all creatures act as instrumental causes, and they participate in the eternal law which is the exemplary cause of the action of the instrument. Cf. *De Trinitate* I.1.

14. Cf. *ST* III.19.1 which states, "Wherever there are several ordered agents, the inferior is moved by the superior . . . since what is moved by another has a twofold action, one which it has in accord with its own form, the other, which it has inasmuch as it is moved by another; thus the operation of an axe according to its own form is to cut, but inasmuch as it is moved by the craftsman, its operation is to make benches" (ubicumque sunt plura agentia ordinata, inferius movetur a superiori. . . . Quia actio eius quod movetur ab altero, est duplex, una quidem quam habet secundum propriam formam; alia autem quam habet secundum quod movetur ab alio. Sicut securis operatio secundum propriam formam est incisio, secundum autem quod movetur ab artifice, operatio eius est facere scamnum).

ness (final cause).[15] The eternal law as the exemplary form in God's mind determines how a creature is divinely moved to the ultimate end.

Because all instrumental causes are moved in accord with their form, the eternal law moves creatures to act in accord with their form. One way that Thomas explains this truth is by noting that the eternal law moves creation to its proper end by imprinting a principle of action on it. Thomas in comparing the divine lawgiver with a human lawgiver states:

> But he [man] can impose a law on rational beings subject to him, insofar as by his command or pronouncement of any kind, he imprints on their minds a rule which is the principle of action. Now just as man, by such pronouncement, impresses a kind of inward principle of actions on the man that is subject to him, so God imprints on the whole of nature the principle of its proper actions.[16]

The principle of action for the whole of nature refers to the form of each creature that is naturally inclined to a particular end. In humans, the powers of the soul act as these principles of actions. Because God has created all things as ordered to His divine goodness, these powers are naturally inclined to the divine goodness in their own particular way.[17] Hence, the eternal law moves humans to their appropriate actions by means of their natural inclinations. Inasmuch as these natural inclinations perfectly move humans to their end, they cause actions that are in accord with the eternal law, and there is a certain natural perfection of participation in the eternal law. These natural inclinations are perfected by virtues, but before showing how virtues perfect these inclinations, I will briefly cover the human natural inclinations that cause human actions.

Human Natural Inclinations

In chapter 2, I showed how humans have a natural inclination to happiness, a natural inclination to act in accord with reason in performing actions ordered to happiness, and a natural inclination to virtue. I will now

---

15. Thomas notes that both God and the human agent are immediate and complete causes (*DP* 3.7; *SCG* III.70; 94).

16. *ST* I-II.93.5: Rebus autem rationalibus sibi subiectus potest imponere legem, inquantum suo praecepto, vel denuntiatione quacumque, imprimit menti earum quandum regulam quae est principium agendi. Sicut autem homo imprimit, denuntiando, quoddam interius principium actuum homini sibi subiecto, ita etiam deus imprimit toti naturae principia proprium actuum.

17. See chapter 2 on different powers of the human soul and their inclinations. Cf. *ST* I.73.1, 80.1, 103.1; *SCG* IV.19.

further analyze these inclinations to further show how the human act participates in the eternal law. Because God creates humans for the sake of an end, the divine goodness, humans like all of creation are naturally inclined to the divine goodness.[18] However, each creature is inclined to the divine goodness in accord with its form. Hence, as intellectual beings, humans are inclined to the divine goodness by knowing and loving God.[19] This act of knowing and loving God is called happiness.

Although humans seek happiness by nature,[20] as rational creatures, humans can know and choose a variety of means to achieve their end of happiness. The principles of these human actions are the powers of the intellect, will, and sense appetites.[21] Because each of these powers has its own proper object to which it is inclined, each of these powers has a distinct role in the human act.[22] Thomas states that the intellect is naturally inclined to truth, the will to the universal good as apprehended by the intellect, the irascible appetite to the arduous good, and the concupiscible appetite to moderation of the delectable.[23] I will briefly show the role of each of these powers in a human act beginning with the intellect, following with the the will, and ending with the sense appetites.

Thomas makes a distinction between the speculative and the practical

18. Thomas notes that all creatures, including humans, are naturally inclined to God (*ST* I.6.1.2; *SCG* III.25).

19. *SCG* III.116. Cf. Pinckaers, *Morality,* 70–71, where Pinckaers notes that the natural inclination toward truth and goodness has its source and end in God. It causes man to participate in God's creative freedom by conforming man to his wisdom and goodness.

20. See *ST* I-II.5.8 where Thomas notes that all people desire happiness in general but not happiness in particular (many see different ends as the source of happiness). Cf. I-II.10.2. Since happiness consists in the attainment of the perfect good (*ST* I-II.3.4), humans like all creatures have a natural inclination to God as well. See *SCG* III.19 where Thomas notes that all desire to be and all are by participating in God. Therefore, all desire to be like God. Likewise, all participate in good as becoming like God. See also *SCG* III.20 which states that becoming like God is the ultimate end of all. Cf. *SCG* III.21, 25.

21. *ST* I-II.56. Cf. *ST* I.77.1 where Thomas states that the soul as act is not in potency toward another act according to its essence, but according to its power. Cf. *ST* I.54.1 and I.77.6.2 where Thomas states that the soul is the active cause of its powers and the end of them.

22. Thomas states in *ST* I.80.1.3: "Each and every power of the soul is a form or nature, and has a natural inclination to something. Wherefore each and every power desires by the natural appetite that object which is suitable to itself" (Unaquaeque potentia animae est quaedam forma seu natura, et habet naturalem inclinationem in aliquid. Unde unaquaeque appetit obiectum sibi conveniens naturali appetitu). Cf. I-II.10.1.

23. *ST* I-II.85.3; cf. I.81.2, 63.4.2 and 3; *De Virtutibus in communi* 8. See also *ST* I.82.2 and I-II.17.6 where Thomas notes that a consequence of these natural inclinations is that the intellect necessarily adheres to first principles and the will necessarily adheres to the last end and anything necessarily connected to it.

intellect. Whereas the things apprehended by the speculative intellect are directed toward consideration of the truth, the things apprehended by the practical intellect are directed toward operation.[24] Since the practical intellect is ordered to action, when speaking of the intellect as the principle of actions, we are primarily concerned with the practical intellect.

Just as the speculative intellect in order to understand something must first abstract the intellectual forms of things from phantasms and then compose and divide these forms into propositions, the practical intellect likewise forms propositions through the composition and division of abstracted intellectual forms (*ST* I-II.90.1.2). However, unlike the propositions of the speculative intellect, which are directed toward the consideration of truth, practical propositions are ordered to actions, which are determined by practical reasoning. In practical reasoning the intellect reasons from a universal proposition (a law) to particular actions by means of a singular proposition. Thomas gives this example in *ST* I-II.76.1: One should not kill his father (the universal proposition). This man is his father (the singular proposition). Therefore, he should not kill this man (the action to be chosen). This movement from an apprehended end (the universal proposition) to a particular action is called counsel or deliberation (*ST* I-II.14). It is followed by the intellectual act of judgment, in which the practical intellect judges the action to be in conformity with the first principles of action (II-II.48 & 51). Finally, the practical intellect commands that the action be performed (I-II.17). Consequently, the practical intellect is the principle of an action first by apprehending the end of the action (the universal principle) and then by determining the proper means of achieving this end by practical reasoning and finally commanding that the action be performed.[25]

The will is the rational appetite. It is inclined to the intellectual forms apprehended by the intellect.[26] In other words, it is the power of the soul to love the good as apprehended by the intellect. It is not only moved by that which is apprehended by the intellect, but it also moves the other powers of the soul to act.[27] Since the will is the primary mover of all the

---

24. *ST* I.79.11. See chapter 4 for a more detailed analysis of both the speculative and the practical intellect.

25. See chapter 4, the moral acts of practical intellect, for a detailed analysis of the role of reason in the moral act. Cf. *ST* I-II.12–17.

26. *ST* I.80.1. Cf. *De Virtutibus in communi* 4.2 where Thomas notes that the natural inclination of the will is to both the ultimate end and the good of reason. He goes on to say that therefore one can sin if the good of reason is clouded by the passions. See also *DT* 1.3.4.

27. *ST* I-II.80.2. Michael Sherwin in *By Knowledge and By Love: Charity and Knowledge*

FIGURE 1. Some Steps of the Human Action

INTELLECT	WILL
Judgment *(judicium)* of universal proposition (the end)	Intention *(intentio)* to attain end
Deliberation *(consilium)* of means (if necessary)	Consent *(consensus)*
Judgment *(judicium)* of means	Choice *(electio)* of means
Command *(imperare)*	Execution *(usus)*

powers of the soul, including the intellect, for every act of the intellect, there is a corresponding act of the will (*ST* I-II.16.1; 17.1). Once a good is apprehended by the intellect, the will may be attracted to it, and if it is, it intends it as an end to be pursued. It then moves the intellect to take counsel as to the best means of attaining this end. The will then consents to the deliberation of counsel (*ST* I-II.15) and chooses the action, which is judged by the intellect to be in conformity with the first principles (*ST* I-II.13). Finally, it executes the action by moving the other powers of the soul to perform the action (*ST* I-II.16). Last of all it delights in the good that has been attained (ST I-II.11). Consequently, the will is a principle of action by being attracted to the good, by choosing the means of attaining the good, and by moving the other powers of the soul.

To see how the intellect and will work together in causing an action, see the table above, which shows eight of the steps of an ideal action beginning with a universal proposition that is understood and ending with the execution by the will.[28] (See figure 1.)

---

in the Moral Theology of St. Thomas Aquinas (Washington, D.C.: The Catholic University of America Press, 2005) nicely shows the interaction of the intellect and the will. He states that the acts of the will presuppose the cognition of the intellect. He continues, "Willing presupposes cognition of something as simply good; intending presupposes cognition of a good understood as attainable through some means; choosing presupposes the cognitive judgment that a particular good is the best means to attaining an intended end." However, he then notes that although the intellect directs the will, the will is free to act or not act or in choosing to choose this or that (32).

28. See *ST* I-II.11–17, especially 17.3.1. Perhaps the most recent work on the steps of the moral act is by Michael Sherwin, *By Knowledge and by Love*. Sherwin also presents a table and explanation of the steps of the moral action (84–85). As he notes in his footnote (n 91), his figure is identical to that of Daniel Westberg's except that he adds the earlier step that Sherwin calls affirmation (see chapter 4 of this work on the first step of the practical intellect: simple apprehension for a detailed analysis of this step). Westberg, *Right Practical Reason* (Oxford: Clarendon Press, 1984), chapters 8–12, gives a detailed analysis of the process of the moral act. He explains the structure of *ST* I-II.11–17 by stating that there are three basic

Although not listed on the above table, the sense appetites (passions) are also principles of human actions inasmuch as they participate in reason. Just as an inclination from the will follows intellectual knowledge, an inclination from the sense appetites follows sense knowledge (*ST* I.80.2). In other words, unlike the will that is attracted to the good apprehended by the intellect, the sense appetites are attracted to the good apprehended by the senses. The sense appetites enter into the act as principles because every action is an application of an end (universal premise) to a particular situation (a singular premise). Since knowledge of singulars comes from the senses,[29] in every particular action, along with the intellectual knowledge of the good to which the will is attracted, there is also sense knowledge of goods to which the sense appetites are attracted. Thomas explains that the passions affect the intellect because although the sensitive powers have a natural aptitude to obey reason, the rational powers have an inborn aptitude to receive from the sensitive powers (*ST* I-II.50.3.1; cf. I-II.17.7). In other words, whenever intellectual forms are abstracted from sense knowledge within a human action, the sense appetites can influence the reason both positively or negatively and sometimes even blind the reason. For example, since counsel applies the universal end to a singular premise and knowledge of singulars always includes sense

---

parts to an act: intention (including the intellect's act of apprehension: I-II.12), choice (including judgment: I-II.13) and execution (including command: I-II.16–17). Because many actions can be determined without deliberation, deliberation and consent are treated after judgment and choice (I-II.14–15), even though in the moral act they precede them. Other earlier scholars posited twelve steps to a complete human act. For example, J. A. Oesterle, *Ethics: The Introduction to Moral Science* (Englewood Cliffs, N.J.: Prentice-Hall, 1958), 85, and Gilson, *The Philosophy of St. Thomas,* chapter 15. Although different scholars had slight variations on the steps, generally they had the same eight steps listed above plus two steps before judgment of the end (apprehension of good and volition of good apprehended) and two steps after execution by the will (passive use and delight). Here I only give the steps in moving from the end to the means. In chapter 4, I show the acts of the intellect both before judgment of the end and after execution of the means in a way that includes all twelve steps but varies slightly from the traditional twelve steps.

29. Thomas especially points to the cogitative sense as the sense by which the intellect knows the singular premise. It is also called the particular reason. For more on the cogitative sense, see *DV* 10.5; *ST* I.78.4. See John Naus, *The Nature of the Practical Intellect According to St. Thomas Aquinas* (Rome: Libreria Editrice Dell'Università Gregoriana, 1959), 192–97, who explains Thomas's understanding of how humans know singulars. Naus says that humans know singulars through the senses of memory, imagination, and the cogitative sense. However, in reference to practical knowledge, the cogitative sense provides the knowledge of the singular premise through which the operation is determined. He then states that not only do deliberating and judgment come into contact with the sensitive powers but also command since the intellect commands a singular action. Cf. George Klubertanz, "St. Thomas and the Knowledge of the Singular," *The New Scholasticism* 26 (1952): 135–66.

knowledge, the step of counsel is always accompanied by the sense appetites. These sense appetites can either aid the reason in finding the proper means or hinder the reason.

Not only do the passions affect the intellect because intellectual knowledge begins with sense knowledge, but they also affect the intellect because the intellect is only able to cause acts through the will and the will causes actions through the medium of the sense appetites (*ST* I.20.1.1). In other words, because humans have bodies, knowledge comes into the soul from the outside via the bodily senses. Likewise, the will causes actions ordered to goods that are outside of the soul via the bodily sense appetites. In both cases the sense appetites can be said to be a cause of human actions inasmuch as they are in conformity with reason.

The sensual good to which the passions are inclined may or may not be in conformity with the good apprehended by the intellect. If they are not in conformity with this good, they can cause the intellect to counsel and judge in accord with the sensual good rather than with the good of reason.[30] However, if the desired good is in conformity with the good of reason, the intensity of the goodness of an act is increased.[31] Thomas states:

> When a passion forestalls the judgment of reason, so as to prevail on the mind to give its consent, it hinders counsel and the judgment of reason. But when it follows that judgment, as through being commanded by reason, it helps toward the execution of reason's command.[32]

Although not morally good or evil in themselves, passions are morally good inasmuch as they are in accord with reason and morally evil as acting against reason.[33]

---

30. Thomas notes that if the passions (sense appetites) are antecedent to the reason, they can overcome reason by obscuring judgment and hindering counsel, causing the will to be moved by a particular good that is not in accord with right reason (*ST* I-II.24.3; I.95.2; cf. *ST* I-II.9.2, 10.3).

31. See I-II.24.3 where Thomas argues that a passion acting in conformity with reason increases the goodness of the act.

32. I-II.59.2.3: *Passio praeveniens iudicium rationis, si in animo praevaleat ut ei consentiatur, impedit consilium et iudicium rationis. Si vero sequatur, quasi ex ratione imperata, adiuvat ad exequendum imperium rationis.* Cf. *De Virtutibus in communi* art. 4.1 where Thomas notes that in virtuous actions the passions follow reason, while in sinful actions reason is drawn to follow the passions.

33. Thomas argues that the passions can cause a man to judge something as fitting and good that he would not judge as fitting and good if not affected by the passion. Sometimes a passion can fully bind the reason so that a man has no use of reason (*ST* I-II.10.3).

Because reason determines the means to the ultimate end of happiness, the appetitive powers are naturally inclined to act in accord with reason. Thomas affirms this by noting that because God moves all things in accord with their form and the substantial form in humans is the rational soul, humans are naturally inclined to act in accord with reason.[34] Hence, the intellect is inclined to know God and perfectly reason to the proper means to eternal happiness. The will is inclined to love God and choose the means determined by the reason. And the sense appetites are inclined to the sensual good as determined by reason.

Although the soul by necessity seeks happiness, the reason can determine many different ways of achieving this and seek many different goods as the ultimate end. Likewise, the appetitive powers are attracted to various goods in different ways (*ST* I-II.51.3). This ability to determine and choose many different ways to happiness causes humans to have free choice. However, this ability also requires that humans have habits to perfect the intellect, will, and sense appetites so that all the actions of the soul are ordered to true happiness.

Thomas states that habits are necessary for humans because humans exhibit the following three conditions:

In the first place, that that which is disposed should be distinct from that to which it is disposed; and so it should be related to it as potency to act. . . . Second, that that which is in potency to another be capable of being determined in many ways and to diverse things. For if something be in potency to another, and only to it, there is no place for disposition and habit . . . Third, that several things must come together to dispose the subject to one of those things to which it is in potency, which things capable of being adapted in various ways so as to be disposed well or ill to a form or to an operation.[35]

---

34. *ST* I-II.18.5, 55.2, 85.2. Cf. *ST* I-II.54.3 where Thomas notes that a good habit disposes an agent to an act suitable to the agent's nature. Thus human acts of virtue are suitable to human nature since they are according to reason. See also II-II.47.6 where Thomas states that the end of moral virtues is the human good, and the good of the human soul is to be in accord with reason. Therefore, the ends of moral virtues must preexist in reason as the naturally known principles (synderesis). Cf. *ST* I.19.1.

35. *ST* I-II.49.4: Primo quidem, ut id quod disponitur, sit alterum ab eo ad quod disponitur; et sic se habeat ad ipsum ut potentia ad actum. . . . Secundo requiritur quod id quod est in potentia ad alterum, possit pluribus modis determinari, et ad diversa. Unde si aliquid sit in potentia ad alterum, ita tamen quod non sit in potentia nisi ad ipsum, ibi dispositio et habitus locum non habet . . . Tertio requiritur quod plura concurrant ad disponendum subiectum ad unum eorum ad quae est in potentia, quae diversis modis commensurari possunt, ut sic disponatur bene vel male ad formam vel ad operationem. Cf. I-II.55.1. See also *De Virtutibus in communi* art. 1 where Thomas states that some powers only act, some are only moved, and others are both moved and act. Those which only

All created things fulfill the first condition, since all created things are in potency to their proper act. Only God who is pure act is exempt from this condition.[36] However, only rational creatures who move themselves by having knowledge of the end and knowledge of the means to the end fulfill the second condition, since only rational creatures are moved by God with liberty.[37] In other words, unlike irrational creatures, rational creatures are able to move themselves to their end as having dominion over their actions (*ST* I-II.1.2; 93.5), since the rational will is not determined to any particular participated good.[38] Humans meet the third condition since several powers of the soul must work together in order to act and these powers are perfected to perform good actions by many different movements.[39] In other words, a human does not acquire the disposition necessary to perform good actions with a single act, but it takes many acts and the perfection of various powers to cause good habits. Thus, humans are naturally inclined to habits because they are in potency to act, they need to be determined to a particular type of action, and several powers must be perfected by repetitive actions to perform actions ordered to the ultimate act of happiness.

Humans are naturally inclined to a particular type of habit: good habits, which are called virtues.[40] Whereas bad habits or vices also dispose the powers of the soul to a particular action, these actions are against nature inasmuch as they are not ordered to the natural end of humans. Thomas notes that since a habit is said to be a principle of an act in relation to nature (*ST* I-II.49.3), it can either be in accord with nature or

---

act, for example, God and the agent intellect, do not need virtues. Those both acting and moved need virtues that abide in the subject to determine it to its proper action (but not in a way that necessitates the power to its act). These virtues are necessary for uniformity in operation, for promptness in acting, and to make the accomplishment of the action pleasant. Cf. Vernon Bourke, "The Role of Habitus in the Thomistic Metaphysics of Potency and Act," in *Essays in Thomism* (New York: Sheed & Ward, 1942), 103–9.

36. Thomas only speaks of God as having good habits analogously. For example, he states that a habit is essentially in divine nature and by participation in a human soul (*ST* I-II.50.2).

37. *QQ* I.4.2.2. Cf. *ST* I-II.68.3.2 where Thomas states that humans need a habit because they are an instrument that works through free will. Cf. 50.1.

38. *ST* I.83.1; I-II.50.5.3; cf. I-II.10.1. See also *ST* I-II.13.6 where Thomas states that the will chooses freely since the will can tend to whatever the reason apprehends as good and the reason can apprehend as good to act or not act and also various particular goods. Only happiness is chosen by necessity. Cf. I-II.10.2, 14.3.

39. *ST* I.77.2. See also *ST* I-II.5.7 where Thomas notes that humans reach happiness in accord with divine wisdom by many motions of activity. Cf. *ST* I-II.6.prologue which states that happiness is obtained by means of certain acts.

40. See Bowlin, *Contingency*, 49.

contrary to nature. If it is in accord with nature, it is called a virtue (in the general sense of the word); if it is against nature, it is a vice. Since to act in accord with nature is to act according to reason, a virtue is a habit that causes actions that are in accord with reason. Thomas states:

Now man is constituted in his species through his rational soul: and consequently whatever is contrary to the order of reason is, properly speaking, contrary to the nature of man, as man; while whatever is in accord with reason, is in accord with the nature of man, as man. . . . Therefore, human virtue, which makes a man good, and his work good, is in accord with man's nature inasmuch as it accords with his reason. While vice is contrary to man's nature inasmuch as it is contrary to the order of reason.[41]

Virtues perfect the powers of the soul to perform actions that are ordered to the end of happiness. Hence, inasmuch as humans are naturally inclined to the end of happiness, they are also naturally inclined to virtue.

These natural inclinations cause good actions, which result in a natural perfection of the human. Because humans, like all creatures, are ordered to a particular act, they are perfect to the extent that they are in act.[42] Furthermore, inasmuch as they are in act, they have a certain likeness to God who is perfect act. In terms of the notion of participation, this likeness is explained because all things that participate in a particular perfection become like that which has the perfection essentially.[43] Since human actions are secondary perfections of humans, these perfections make humans like God who is perfect as pure act.

41. *ST* I-II.71.2: Homo autem in specie constituitur per animam rationalem. Et ideo id quod est contra ordinem rationis, proprie est contra naturam hominis inquantum est homo; quod autem est secundum rationem, est secundum naturam hominis inquantum est homo. . . . Unde virtus humana, quae hominem facit bonum, et opus ipsius bonum reddit, intantum est secundum naturam hominis, inquantum convenit rationi, vitium autem intantum est contra naturam hominis, inquantum est contra ordinem rationis. Cf. I-II.49.2.

42. *SCG* 1:28; cf. *ST* I.4.1: "a thing is perfect in proportion to its state of actuality" (aliquid esse perfectum, secundum quod est actu).

43. See *ST* I.6.4: "From the first being, essentially such, and good, everything can be called good and a being, inasmuch as it participates by way of a certain assimilation all be it in a remote and defective manner . . . everything is called good from the divine goodness as the first exemplary, effective, and final principle of the whole of goodness. Nevertheless, everything is called good by reason of the likeness to the divine goodness inhering in it, which is formally its own goodness, whereby it is denominated good" (A primo igitur per suam essentiam ente et bono, unumquodque potest dici bonum et ens, inquantum participat ipsum per modum cuiusdam assimilationis, licet remote et deficienter. . . . Sic ergo unumquodque dicitur bonum bonitate divina, sicut primo principio exemplari, effectivo et finali totius bonitatis. Nihilominus tamen unumquodque dicitur bonum similitudine divinae bonitatis sibi inhaerente, quae est formaliter sua bonitas denominans ipsum). Cf. *SCG* II.35; *ST* I.4.3, 9.1.2; II-II 26.2.2.

Because humans are instrumental causes of all their actions, and an instrumental cause participates in the exemplar in the divine mind, all humans participate in the eternal law. Since an instrumental cause is directed in accord with its form, humans are moved by the eternal law by means of the natural inclinations of the intellect, will, and passions. Furthermore, because these powers are undetermined in reference to determining the means to happiness, they must be perfected by good habits, which dispose them to cause actions that are in conformity with the end to which they are naturally inclined. To the extent humans perform these actions, they are perfected and they are like God who is all perfections by essence. Just as a good human general orders each of his troops to perform actions in their areas of expertise, God as divine governor orders every creature to act in accord with its form. And just as a human general would order his troops to repeat a particular procedure a number of times to perfect the procedure in order to more perfectly participate in his military wisdom, so also God inclines humans to more perfectly participate in eternal law by acquiring virtue. Thus, I will next show specifically how the acquired virtues perfect participation in eternal law.

The Perfection of Participation in Eternal Law by Acquired Virtue

Because the participation of an instrument is always limited by the mode of the participant (*SCG* I.43), by increasing their mode of being through superadded secondary perfections, humans are able to increase their participation.[44] These secondary perfections that increase their capacity to participate in God are good habits. In other words, because the mode of being of humans is increased by virtues, which give humans a greater potency to act,[45] God can direct them to perform more perfect actions. Just as a human general can govern his army to a greater end if his army is well trained, God moves humans to a greater end if they have superadded good habits.

A slight modification of the example Thomas nearly always uses when

---

44. This increased mode of participation does not change the substance of humans, or else they would become a different species, but it does gives them a better manner of being *(esse)* accidentally by adding secondary perfections such as virtue over and above the substance. See chapter 2 and *ST* I.25.6; *DP* 3.8; *DSC* 1.9.

45. Cf. *ST* I-II.49.3.1 which states that a habit is an act of the soul, but at the same time is in potency in respect to operation.

speaking of instrumental causality will be helpful to illustrate this point. Thomas uses the example of a craftsman using a cutting tool to make a bench (*ST* III.19.1; III.62.1; etc.). In the example, the cutting tool is the instrumental cause that is moved by the power of the craftsman in accord with the form in his mind. If the cutting tool is given the additional disposition of sharpness, then the craftsman can use it to make more intricate and beautiful benches (because carving with a dull cutting tool is very difficult). Hence, the cutting tool can more perfectly participate in the art in the craftsman's mind. Likewise, a human with good habits can be moved much more perfectly in accord with eternal law. Thomas affirms this by noting, "For unless an instrument is well disposed, no matter how perfect the principle agent may be, a perfect action of the agent does not come about through the instrument."[46] Thus, although the principle agent (God) is perfect, perfect human acts will not follow unless humans are perfected by good habits.[47] The good habits that perfect humans consist of both natural and supernatural good habits. However, since I am now only analyzing natural participation, I will now show specifically how the acquired virtues, which are natural good habits, perfect participation.

As seen above, humans need habits because they are distinct from that to which they are disposed, they need to be determined to a particular type of action, and several powers must be perfected by repetitive actions to perform actions ordered to the ultimate act of happiness. This section will show how virtues as good habits allow humans to attain that to which they are disposed, determine humans to good actions, and perfect the various powers to perform good actions.

The first condition to be covered is that humans are distinct from that to which they are disposed. Humans are ordained to the operation of happiness and the attainment of God by this operation (Cf. *SCG* III.113). Although humans are only inclined to perfect happiness by the super-

---

46. *ST* I-II.58.3.2: Sicut non sequitur perfecta actio alicuius agentis per instrumentum, si instrumentum non sit bene dispositum, quantumcumque principale agens sit perfectum. This follows from the principle that in order for an action that proceeds from two principles to be perfect, both principles must be perfected by a habit corresponding to the operation (*ST* I-II.58.3.2, 65.3.1).

47. Cf. *ST* I-II.68.3.2 where Thomas states that the good habits of the gifts of the Holy Spirit are necessary for a human to be perfectly moved by the Holy Spirit since humans as instrumental causes with a rational soul require habits to perfect them. See also *ST* III.7.1.3 where Thomas notes that Christ needed habitual grace because his human nature is an instrument with a rational soul. Cf. *DV* 29.1.9.

natural inclinations of the theological virtues, they are naturally inclined to the natural happiness of natural knowledge and love of God. Since humans by nature are not the act of knowing and loving God, but are only in potency to this act (*ST* I.79; Cf. *ST* I.77.1), they need superadded dispositions that allow them to perform natural acts of knowing and loving God.[48] These dispositions are the acquired virtues.[49] Thomas explains that a habit is a kind of medium between mere power and mere act.[50] Thus, since humans cannot perform the act of knowing and loving God by their essence, they need the intellectual virtues to perfect the intellect and the virtue of justice to perfect the will to naturally know and love God (*ST* I-II.50.4, 56.6). In addition they need virtues to perfect the sense appetites to keep them from seeking a sensual good over the natural good of God.

The second condition that makes virtues necessary is that humans are capable of determination in several modes and to diverse things. Although powers apart from reason are determined to one thing, reason is a power that compares several things, and thus the rational appetite (the will) may be moved by several apprehended goods (I.82.2.3). In other words, although the will by necessity adheres to the last end (happiness), the intellect can compare many goods that can be ordered to the end of happiness. Consequently, provided that these goods are not necessarily connected to happiness, the will does not adhere to any of them by necessity.[51] The acquired virtues are necessary to determine the powers of the soul to actions that are ordered to happiness.[52] Specifically, the practical intellect, will, and sense appetites are perfected to determine the powers of the soul to actions ordered to happiness, as is shown below.

The practical intellect must be perfected both to know the end (ac-

---

48. Thomas states in *ST* I-II.50.6 that the higher the form, the less potency something has and the more it is in act by its nature. To the extent it is in potency in regard to its proper act, it needs a habitual perfection in order to perform its act. Thus, the human intellect is in potency as regards all intellectual things and therefore for the understanding of all things needs a habit. However, angelic intellect is act, although not pure act (for only God is pure act), and so far as angels are in act through their own essence, they do not need a habit, but insofar as they are in potency, they need a habitual perfection. Cf. I.55.1 & 2.

49. Thus, Thomas states that a habit is a disposition of a subject which is in a state of potency either to form or operation (*ST* I-II.50.1). Cf. I-II.49.3.

50. *ST*.I.87.2. Elsewhere he notes that a habit is an act of the soul, but at the same time it is in potency in respect to operation (*ST* I-II.49.3.1; cf. I.77.6).

51. Since it is only when the intellect knows God as He is that the necessary connection between particular goods and happiness is shown, apart from participation in eternal law by glory, the will does not desire anything by necessity (*ST* I.82.2; I-II.10.2).

52. See Bowlin, *Contingency*, 58–84, 125.

tion) that is intended and to reason to the proper means to this end.[53] The end that is intended is the universal proposition of the practical syllogism.[54] The virtue that perfects the intellect to know this proposition is understanding. The virtue of understanding perfects the practical intellect to properly form universal propositions by means of apprehension and judgment. The type of understanding that pertains to the practical intellect's understanding of the first principles of natural law is called synderesis (*ST* I.79.12; II-II.47.6.1; *DV* 16.1–17.2). The human with synderesis is able to immediately grasp the first principles of practical reasoning with certainty.[55]

Once the end is understood, the intellect must be perfected to reason to the proper means. The virtue of prudence perfects the intellect to determine the proper means to this end. Thomas notes that in order for the intellect to determine the proper means, the intellectual actions of counsel and judgment must be perfected by virtues:

. . . [to be] suitably ordained to the due end man needs to be rightly disposed by a habit of his reason, because taking counsel and choosing [by a judgment in the intellect], which are about things ordained to the end, are acts of the reason. Consequently, an intellectual virtue is needed in the reason, through which the reason is perfected so that it may be suitably disposed toward things ordained to the end.[56]

Taking counsel and judging (which determine the object to be chosen) are essential steps in any human act, but in order for a subject to consistently choose good acts, the intellect must be perfected by *euboulia*

---

53. The intellect is the formal cause of an action by determining the form of the act. Hence, both the intellect and the will must be perfected in order for an act to be good (*DM* 6.6; cf. *ST* I-II.57.5). See also *ST* I-II.58.4.1 where Thomas states that the inclination of things devoid of reason is without choice, and hence does not require reason. But the inclination of moral virtue is with choice and hence requires reason that is perfected by an intellectual virtue.

54. See *Ethic* VI.9, n. 1247, which states that one type of understanding deals with unchangeables and another deals with the particular or minor proposition in practical reasoning. The latter is an understanding of the sensible and singular. Cf. *ST* I-II.76.1.

55. See chapter four, "Practical Understanding," for a more detailed analysis.

56. . . . convenienter in finem debitum ordinatur, oportet quod homo directe disponatur per habitum rationis, quia consiliari et eligere, quae sunt eorum quae sunt ad finem, sunt actus rationis. Et ideo necesse est in ratione esse aliquam virtutem intellectualem, per quam perficiatur ratio ad hoc quod convenienter se habeat ad ea quae sunt ad finem (*ST* I-II.57.5). Strictly speaking, choosing *(eligere)* is not an act of the intellect, but an act of the will. However, although it is materially an act of the will, it is formally an act of the intellect, since the intellect imposes the order upon the will (I-II.13.1). In order for the will to choose, the intellect must first judge the conclusion of a practical syllogism and this act of judging is followed by the act of choosing (*ST* I-II.13.1.2).

to properly take counsel and *synesis* and *gnome* to properly judge. These three virtues are treated by Thomas under the virtue of prudence. *Euboulia* (good counsel) is the virtue that perfects the intellect to properly inquire into the best means of achieving the end (*ST* I-II.51.1). This inquiry includes deriving a conclusion from the universal proposition by means of the practical syllogism. *Synesis* is the virtue that perfects the intellect to judge the conclusion by the universal principle under ordinary conditions, in other words, judging by common rules (51.3); and *gnome* is the virtue that perfects the intellect to judge well when special circumstances apply, in other words, when the common rules do not apply and judgment must be by higher principles.[57]

Once the suitable means has been determined by counsel and judgment, the intellect must be perfected by the virtue of prudence to command the action (II-II.47.8). The human with prudence is able to determine the proper action and command the other powers of the soul to perform the action. Understanding, prudence, and the intellectual virtues connected to it perfect the intellect's natural inclination to act in accord with reason, thereby allowing the intellect to participate more perfectly in the eternal law (*ST* I-II.65.1; cf. *ST* I-II.19.4, 21.2, 91.3.2).

The will is perfected by the virtue of justice to will the good in accord with reason. Thomas notes that because the will does not desire anything by necessity, habits are needed to will the true good in a stable and constant way. Thomas states:

The will from the very nature of the power is inclined to the good of the reason. But because this good is varied in many ways, the will needs to be inclined, by means of a habit, to some fixed good of the reason, in order that action may follow more promptly.[58]

The naturally acquired habit that perfects the will to intend and choose the good in accord with reason is the virtue of justice.[59] Acquired jus-

---

57. *ST* II-II.51.4. See chapter four for a more detailed analysis of all three of these intellectual virtues.

58. *ST* I-II.50.5.3: Voluntas ex ipsa natura potentiae inclinatur in bonum rationis. Sed quia hoc bonum multipliciter diversificatur, necessarium est ut ad aliquod determinatum bonum rationis voluntas per aliquem habitum inclinetur, ad hoc quod sequatur promptior operatio. See also David Gallagher, "The Will and Its Acts (Ia-IIae, qq. 6–17)," in *The Ethics of Aquinas,* ed. Stephen Pope (Washington, D.C.: Georgetown University Press, 2002), 67–89, esp. 67. Cf. Bowlin, 83, and Paul Waddel, *The Primacy of Love,* 79, who notes that humans are naturally lovers, but must learn to love the right things in the right way.

59. *ST* I-II.56.6. Cf. Livio Melina, *Sharing in Christ's Virtues* (Washington, D.C.: The Catholic University of America Press, 2001), 64–66.

tice perfects natural love so that the will is consistently inclined to the good of one's neighbor and God (as known naturally).[60] By means of the virtue of justice a human is able to perpetually and constantly give others their due (*ST* II-II.58.1). Justice perfects the natural inclination of the will to the good of others and in doing this allows the human to be moved more perfectly in accord with the eternal law.

Just as the will, because it is rational, can be moved by various goods, so also the sense appetites can be moved by various sensual goods. The sense appetites do not need a virtue to perfect them to be moved by sensual goods, but they do need a virtue to perfect them to be determined to the sensual good in accord with reason.[61] The virtues of temperance and fortitude determine the sense appetites to the sensual good in accord with reason (*ST* I-II.56.4). Temperance perfects the concupiscible appetite to seek the delectable good in accord with reason, and fortitude perfects the irascible appetite to seek the arduous good in accord with reason.[62]

The virtues of temperance and fortitude perfect the sense appetites so that rather than hindering the counsel and judgment of reason, they aid the reason in commanding the action. Thomas states:

When a passion forestalls the judgment of reason, so as to prevail on the mind to give its consent, it hinders counsel and the judgment of reason. But when it fol-

60. The virtue of religion, which is one of the virtues annexed to justice, is an acquired virtue, not a theological virtue. It is the virtue of giving God the honor that is due to Him inasmuch as he is known through natural reason (*ST* II-II.81).

61. *ST* I-II.50.3. See also *ST* I-II.56.4 which states, "The irascible and concupiscible powers can be considered in two ways. First in themselves, insofar as they are parts of the sensitive appetite: and in this way they are not fit to be the subject of virtue. Secondly, they can be considered as participating in the reason, from the fact that they have a natural aptitude to obey reason. And thus the irascible or concupiscible power can be the subject of human virtue: for, insofar as it participates in the reason, it is the principle of a human act. And to these powers it is necessary to assign virtues" (Irascibilis et concupiscibilis dupliciter considerari possunt. Uno modo secundum se, inquantum sunt partes appetitus sensitivi. Et hoc modo, non competit eis quod sint subiectum virtutis. Alio modo possunt considerari inquantum participant rationem, per hoc quod natae sunt rationi obedire. Et sic irascibilis vel concupiscibilis potest esse subiectum virtutis humanae, sic enim est principium humani actus, inquantum participat rationem. Et in his potentiis necesse est ponere virtutes). Thomas continues by noting that when one power is moved by another power, both powers must be well disposed to act. Thus, both the reason and the sense appetites must be perfected. The sense appetites are perfected by a habitual conformity to reason.

62. Thomas notes that the sense appetites are good to the extent they are in conformity with reason (*ST* I.81.3; I-II.24.3). He states that the natural inclination of the sense appetites to the good is like a blind horse if it not accompanied by right reason. The faster it runs, the more grievously it will be hurt (*ST* I-II.58.4.3). For example, someone with courage not accompanied by reason may risk his life in an unjust war.

lows that judgment, as through being commanded by reason, it helps toward the execution of reason's command.[63] (I-II.59.2.3)

Although the sense appetites can diminish the goodness of an action by hindering reason,[64] if the passions are ordered by reason, they enhance the goodness of an act.[65] For example, if anger precedes reason, it can diminish the rationality of an act or even completely remove it if it completely overcomes reason. However, if reason recognizes a true injustice and the soul becomes angry on account of this injustice, then the passion of anger can motivate the human to act to remove the injustice. Through the virtues of temperance and fortitude, the passions habitually act in accord with reason (I-II.59.5.1, 56.4.4; I-II.59.5). Inasmuch as the passions obey reason, the goodness of an act is increased, which causes a more perfect participation of the human agent in eternal law.

The acquired virtues determine the powers of the soul to their proper actions. Thomas states:

It is proper to a habit to incline a power to act, and this belongs to a habit, insofar as it makes whatever is fitting to it, to seem good, and whatever is repugnant to it, to seem evil. For even as the taste judges of flavors according to its disposition, even so does the human mind judge things to be done, according to its habitual disposition. Hence the philosopher says (*Ethic.* III.5) that such as a man is, so does the end appear to him.[66]

Virtues as good habits determine humans to actions that are fitting to the particular power. These habits form the mode of being of the human (in reference to secondary perfections) and cause the proper end to ap-

63. Passio praeveniens iudicium rationis, si in animo praevaleat ut ei consentiatur, impedit consilium et iudicium rationis. Si vero sequatur, quasi ex ratione imperata, adiuvat ad exequendum imperium rationis. Thomas here refers to the three acts of the intellect that are perfected by prudence: counsel *(consilium)*, judgment *(iudicium)*, and command *(imperium*—*ST* II-II.47.8). If the passions (sense appetites) are antecedent to the reason, they can overcome reason by obscuring judgment and hindering counsel, causing the will to be moved by a particular good that is not in accord with right reason (*ST* I-II.24.3; I.95.2; cf. *ST* I-II.9.2, 10.3).

64. Thomas argues that the passions can cause a man to judge something as fitting and good that he would not judge as fitting and good if not affected by the passion. Sometimes a passion can fully bind the reason so that a man has no use of reason. (*ST* I-II.10.3).

65. See I-II.24.3 where Thomas argues that a passion acting in conformity with reason increases the goodness of the act.

66. *ST* II-II.24.11: Habitui vero proprium est ut inclinet potentiam ad agendum quod convenit habitui inquantum facit id videri bonum quod ei convenit, malum autem quod ei repugnat. Sicut enim gustos diiudicat sapores secundum suam dispositionem, ita mens hominis diiudicat de aliquo faciendo secundum suam habitualem dispositionem, unde et

pear good.[67] The cardinal virtues of prudence, justice, temperance, and fortitude cause the soul to recognize the proper end and to act in accord with it. By determining the powers of the soul to the good to which they are naturally inclined, the virtues perfect the natural inclinations and likewise the participation in eternal law.[68]

The third condition that makes virtues necessary is that humans are disposed to their proper act by means of several powers being properly ordered through many acts. Because all the powers of the soul are principles of action, inasmuch as the intellect orders the will, which executes the action through the sense appetites, all these powers must be perfected by virtues (*ST* I.20.1.1; I-II.61.1 & 2; 62.3; II-II.47.15). Thomas notes that both the intellectual and the appetitive powers must be perfected: "Accordingly for a man to do a good deed, it is requisite not only that his reason be well disposed by means of a habit of intellectual virtue; but also that his appetite be well disposed by means of a habit of moral virtue."[69] As already seen, in order for the soul to be determined to actions in accord with its end, not only must the appetites be inclined to this end, but reason must be perfected by prudence to determine the proper means to this end. When all the powers of the soul are perfected, the intellect cognitively participates in the eternal law by knowing the proper action to be performed. The will participates in the reason of the intellect inasmuch as it chooses the action determined by the intellect and the sense appetites likewise participate in reason as being inclined to the sensual good in accord with reason.[70] In this way, the entire soul participates

philosophus dicit, in III ethic., quod qualis unusquisque est, talis finis videtur ei. Thomas makes the same point in *ST* I-II.9.2. See also Thomas Ryan, "Revisiting Affective Knowledge and Connaturality in Aquinas," *Theological Studies* 66 (2005): 50–56. Ryan argues that the "affective knowledge of the passions" (i.e., that they are attracted to certain goods and not others) comes from them being habitually disposed in accord with right reason.

67. See Livio Melina, *Sharing in Christ's Virtues,* who states that the grasp of the good depends on the disposition of the subject because emotion is a foretaste of the meaning that reason can bring to light. Virtues are needed to make what is truly good to appear good. For the virtuous human, good is the good *simpliciter* (44). See also Bowlin, *Contingency,* 138.

68. Because a habit causes the natural inclinations to be so perfectly inclined to the good, Thomas speaks of them as second nature. See *ST* I.18.2.2 where Thomas states that above the natural operations are superadded virtues inclining like a second nature. Cf. I-II.108.1.2 in regard to grace inclining like a second nature.

69. *ST* I-II.58.2: Sic igitur ad hoc quod home bene agat, requiritur quod non solum ratio sit bene disposita per habitum virtutis intellectualis; sed etiam quod vis appetitiva sit bene disposita per habitum virtutis moralis. Cf. 56.6, 58.4, 57.5, 60.1.

70. See *ST* I-II.58.2 where Thomas states, "Hence, just as the appetite is the principle of the human act, insofar as it participates in reason, so moral habit has the character of human virtue insofar as it is in conformity with reason" (Unde sicut appetitus est principi-

in eternal law as governed by it through the natural practical knowledge of the intellect. Thus, several powers must be perfected by virtues in order to perform actions in accord with the natural end of humans.[71]

Not only must all of the powers of the soul be perfected, it takes many actions for them to be perfected. Thomas notes that whenever an active power moves a passive power, the passive power is disposed by the action of the active power. In being moved to act, the passive power becomes like the active power.[72] If similar acts are multiplied, a certain quality is formed in the power that is passive and moved. The quality is a habit (*ST* I-II.51.2). It is through many actions that the acquired virtues are developed in the practical intellect, will, and sense appetites.

---

um humani actus secundum quod participat aliqualiter rationem, ita habitus moralis habet rationem virtutis humanae, inquantum rationi conformatur). Cf. I-II.56.4 where Thomas states that the irascible and concupiscible appetites are considered virtuous as participating in reason where they are principles of acts by obeying reason. See also *ST* I-II.26.2 56.4 and 61.2 and also *ST* I.95.1 where Thomas notes that in the state of innocence man's rectitude to God consisted in the fact that reason was subject to God, the lower powers to reason, and the body to the soul: and the first subjection was the cause of both the second and third. Through this subjection to reason these lower principles participate more perfectly in eternal law. Cf. *SCG* III.129 which states that it is natural for lower powers to be subject to higher ones.

71. Since in order to act in accord with reason each power must be perfected, every definite natural inclination has a corresponding virtue to perfect it. Thus, Thomas notes: "As the philosopher states in *Ethic.* II., aptitude to virtue is in us by nature, but the fulfillment of virtue is in us through habituation or some other cause. Hence it is evident that virtues perfect us so that we follow in due manner our natural inclinations, which belong to the natural right. Wherefore to every definite natural inclination there corresponds a special virtue" (*ST* II-II.108.2) (Sicut philosophus dicit, in II ethic., aptitudo ad virtutem inest nobis a natura, licet complementum virtutis sit per assuetudinem vel per aliquam aliam causam. Unde patet quod virtutes perficiunt nos ad prosequendum debito modo inclinationes naturales, quae pertinent ad ius naturale. Et ideo ad quamlibet inclinationem naturalem determinatam ordinatur aliqua specialis virtus). Thomas continues by stating that since from the irascible power humans have a natural inclination to prevent evil, there is a special virtue of vengeance (just punishment to prevent future evil) which perfects it. Cf. Jean Porter, "What the Wise Person Knows: Natural Law and Virtue in Aquinas' *Summa Theologiae,*" *Studies in Christian Ethics* 12 (1999): 62–65.

72. Whenever a lower power is moved by a higher power, it participates in the act of the higher power. As seen in chapter 2 above, the participant always becomes like that in which it participates to the extent it participates in it. Thus, the appetites are in conformity with reason to the extent they participate in it. See also *ST* I-II.58.2 where Thomas states, "Hence, just as the appetite is the principle of a human act, insofar as it in some way participates in reason, so does a moral habit have the character of a virtue insofar as it is in conformity with reason" (Unde sicut appetitus est principium humani actus secundum quod participat aliqualiter rationem, ita habitus moralis habet rationem virtutis humanae, inquantum rationi conformatur). Cf. I-II.56.4 where Thomas states that the irascible and concupiscible appetites have virtue as participating in reason where they are principles of acts by obeying reason. See also I-II.61.2.

In reference to the practical intellect, prudence is obtained through many actions. When the intellect forms habits, the active intellect causes a likeness of itself in the passive intellect. For example, when the active intellect abstracts the intelligible species of an object, the intellect is moved from being in potency to the intelligible species to being in act as knowing the intelligible species (*ST* I.79.6). By performing this act of knowing, the habit of understanding or the habit of science (in cases of knowing through discursive reasoning) is acquired by the soul. Once an intellectual habit is acquired, the soul has the capability of considering things, even if it is not at that moment considering them (*ST* I-II.50.4). These habits of understanding and science which deal with universal principles are acquired in a single act (although these habits are only perfected by means of many actions of understanding and science).

Prudence, however, considers both knowledge of universal principles and singular principles since it must apply the universal principle to a particular situation. Although the habit of knowing universal principles can be obtained by a single act, the acquired habit of applying these principles through singular principles can only be caused by many repeated actions due to the uncertainty of the conclusion (*ST* I-II.52.3). Hence, in order to have the virtue of prudence, many like actions must be performed. Thomas notes, "acquired prudence is caused by the exercise of acts, wherefore its acquisition demands experience and time, as said in *II Ethic;* hence it cannot be in the young, neither in habit nor in act."[73] In other words, there are many circumstances to take into consideration when applying a universal principle; only through experience and practice is one able to determine which circumstances are essential in determining the act and which are not. Once the virtue of prudence is acquired, it is perfected by continuing to perform like acts of a greater intensity.

Virtues are also formed in the appetitive powers by becoming like the active power of the intellect as being ordered by reason. In reference to how the appetitive powers are disposed by many acts, Thomas states:

A habit is caused by act because a passive power is moved by an active principle. But in order that some quality be caused in that which is passive, the active principle must entirely overcome the passive. . . . Now it is clear that the active principle which is reason, cannot entirely overcome the appetitive power in one

73. *ST* II-II.47.14.3: prudentia acquisita causatur ex exercitio actuum, unde indiget ad sui generationem experimento et tempore, ut dicitur in II ethic. Unde non potest esse in iuvenibus nec secundum habitum nec secundum actum.

act: because the appetitive power is inclined variously, and to many things; while the active principle judges through reason in a single act what should be willed in regard to various aspects and circumstances. Wherefore the appetitive power is not thereby entirely overcome [by a single act], so as to be inclined like nature to the same thing in the majority of cases; which inclination belongs to the habit of virtue. Therefore a habit of virtue cannot be caused by one act but by many.[74]

In every act in which the appetitive powers are moved by reason, they become more disposed by reason. However, because the appetitive powers are inclined to many things, it takes many like actions before a habit is formed in the appetitive powers conforming them to reason. For example, many just actions must be performed before the habit of justice is acquired by the will.

Because a higher principle causes a like disposition in a lower principle by moving it to act, the lower powers of the soul become like reason through the habits of justice, temperance, and fortitude and practical reason becomes like the eternal law through the habit of prudence.[75] By means of many similar actions, the lower powers of the soul are perfected to participate in the higher powers, and by means of many repeated acts of prudence, the intellect is perfected to participate in the eternal law. Hence, the eternal law is reason by its essence, the intellect primarily participates in this reason as determining the proper act to be performed, and the appetitive powers participate in the eternal law by participating in the reason of the intellect.[76]

---

74. *ST* I-II.51.3: Habitus per actum generatur inquantum potentia passiva movetur ab aliquo principio activo. Ad hoc autem quod aliqua qualitas causatur in passivo, oportet quod activum totaliter vincat passivum. . . . Manifestum est autem quod principium activum quod est ratio, non totaliter potest supervincere appetitivam potentiam in uno actu, eo quod appetitive potentia se habet diversimode et ad multa; iudicatur autem per rationem, in uno actu, aliquid appetendum secundum determinatas rationes et circumstantias. Unde ex hoc non totaliter vincitur appetitiva potentia, ut feratur in idem ut in pluribus, per modum naturae, quod pertinet ad habitum virtutis. Et ideo habitus virtutis non potest causari per unum actum, sed per multos. Thomas continues by noting that, unlike in the appetitive powers, in the possible intellect the passive principle can be overcome by a single self-evident proposition causing an intellectual habit. Cf. *ST* I-II.5.7; II-II.51.1.2; cf. *DV* 11.1.

75. See *ST* I-II.51.2.1 where Thomas says that an agent, inasmuch as it moves through being moved by another, receives something from that which moves it, causing a habit. Because of this principle, participation in God is always accompanied by likeness since when a creature receives a perfection by means of participation it is made like God.

76. See also Fabro, *La nozione . . .*, 292–94. Fabro notes that because the will can be determined in accord with reason, it can participate in reason. Likewise, since the other appetitive powers can be moved by the will in accord with reason, they can also participate in reason, although their participation in reason is less intense than that of the will. Cf. *ST* I.77.7; I-II.56.4; II-II.45.5.1, 53.2.

Humans are naturally inclined to the end of natural happiness. However, because they are not determined to any particular means to this
end and require the perfection of several powers through many actions,
they must have virtues in order fulfill their natural inclination to this end.
These virtues perfect the natural inclination, allowing humans to perform
actions that are in accord with this end. Because the eternal law moves
humans to their end by inclining them to this end, the perfection of the
inclinations by the acquired virtues allows humans to be moved and governed more perfectly by the eternal law. Through prudence God directs
the reason to more perfectly determine the proper means to the end. And
because justice, temperance, and fortitude perfect the appetitive powers
to act in accord with reason, through these virtues God moves the soul
to the good determined by reason. Humans are rational and free instrumental causes. Since God moves instrumental causes in accord with their
modes, human perfection by the acquired virtues causes more perfect
natural participation in eternal law by a principle of motion.

Although the acquired virtues perfect natural participation in eternal
law, they are not able to cause perfect natural participation in eternal
law without the help of grace. Notice, that when Thomas speaks of the
different degrees of participation in eternal law, he divides those participating in eternal law into two groups: the wicked and the good (*ST*
I-II.93.6). The good have both perfect natural participation and perfect
supernatural participation. The reason Thomas only divides the partici-
pants into two groups is because there is no such thing as perfect natural
participation in eternal law apart from the life of grace. Because humans
have fallen nature, they are unable to do the good proportionate to their
nature without grace:

Man's nature can be looked at in two ways: first, in its integrity, as it was in our
first parent before sin; secondly, as it is corrupted in us after the sin of our first
parent. Now in both states human nature needs the help of God as First Mover,
to do or desire any good whatsoever, as stated above. But in the state of integrity,
as regards the sufficiency of the operative power, man by his natural endowments
could desire and do the good proportionate to his nature, such as the good of
acquired virtue; but not surpassing good such as the good of infused virtue. But
in the state of corrupt nature, man even falls short of what he could do by his
nature, so that he is unable to fulfill it by his own natural powers.[77]

77. *ST* I-II.109.2: Natura hominis dupliciter potest considerari, uno modo, in sui integ-
ritate, sicut fuit in primo parente ante peccatum; alio modo, secundum quod est corrupta in
nobis post peccatum primi parentis. Secundum autem utrumque statum, natura humana in-

After affirming that God moves humans to all of their good acts whether in accord with nature or not, Thomas distinguishes between corrupted nature and the original state of integrity. In the original state, humans were able to perfectly do the good of acquired virtue,[78] but in the current corrupted state they are not able to perfectly do the good of nature without healing grace.[79]

Thomas makes a distinction between healing grace and elevating grace. Whereas healing grace perfects humans to perform perfect actions in accord with their natural end, elevating grace perfects humans to perform actions in accord with their divine end (*ST* 109.2). Although healing and elevating grace are infused together, since this section is about perfect natural participation in eternal law, perfection of healing grace is being analyzed apart from the perfection of elevated grace.

Because humans are moved as free instrumental causes, the example of the craftsman moving the cutting tool to instrumentally cause the bench is helpful to understand how healing grace perfects participation in eternal law. A broken cutting tool is like a human in the corrupt state of nature and a mended tool is like a human with healing grace. Although the cutting tool is always moved in accord with the form in the mind of the craftsman, a mended tool can participate in this form much more perfectly than a broken one can, for a broken cutting tool could not shape the wood to match the form of the bench in the mind of craftsman nearly as effectively as a mended one could. The same is true with humans: a human with healing grace can be moved to perform the actions to which humans are naturally ordered and can thus participate in the eternal law much more perfectly than one without healing grace.

Since healing and elevating grace are infused together, in the state

diget auxilio divino ad faciendum vel volendum quodcumque bonum, sicut primo movente, ut dictum est. Sed in statu naturae integrae, quantum ad sufficientiam operativae virtutis, poterat homo per sua naturalia velle et operari bonum suae naturae proportionatum, quale est bonum virtutis acquisitae, non autem bonum superexcedens, quale est bonum virtutis infusae. Sed in statu naturae corruptae etiam deficit homo ab hoc quod secundum suam naturam potest, ut non possit totum huiusmodi bonum implere per sua naturalia.

78. *ST* I-II.109.2. Nonetheless, Thomas affirms that humans were created with a supernatural endowment of grace allowing the reason to be subject to God and the lower power to be subject to virtue (*ST* I.95.1 & 3).

79. Thomas states that although humans cannot perfectly do the good in accord with nature in their corrupted state, they are not completely corrupted and thus can do some particular good (*ST* I-II.109.2). Cf. John Jenkins, *Knowledge and Faith in Thomas Aquinas* (Cambridge: Cambridge University Press, 1997), 150–55, and D. J. Billy, "Grace and Natural Law in the *Super Epistolam ad Romanos*," *Studia Moralia* 26 (1988): 15–37.

of his corrupted nature a human cannot have perfect natural participation in eternal law that is not accompanied by supernatural participation by grace.[80] Nonetheless, this theoretical discussion of the natural powers and virtues is necessary because supernatural perfections do not remove natural perfections but perfect them. Hence, an understanding of human nature, the natural inclinations, and the acquired virtues are necessary to understand grace, the theological virtues, and the infused moral virtues, respectively.[81]

God always directs humans in accord with their nature by means of their natural inclinations to their ultimate end. He directs them by His eternal law, which is the exemplary cause of all human actions. Because all instrumental causes are directed in accord with their form, humans are directed as rational and free instruments by means of their natural inclinations. However, these inclinations must be perfected for humans to be directed perfectly by the eternal law. Hence, the virtues determine the intellect, will, and passions to actions that are in conformity with the end to which they are naturally inclined. To the extent humans acquire these virtues, they are perfected and are more like God who is the cause of these perfections. Just as troops with acquired military skills can be directed to greater actions by their general on account of their greater skills, so also it is fitting that God directs humans to greater actions on account of their acquired virtues.

SUPERNATURAL PARTICIPATION IN
ETERNAL LAW AS GOVERNED BY IT

The eternal law directs humans in accord with their form. Now the form by which humans are directed can be either their essential form (the human soul) or a participated form (*ST* I-II.110.3). The eternal law directs humans to their natural end by means of their essential form, and it directs humans to an end that exceeds their nature by means of habitual grace, which is a participation in divine nature.[82] Grace has the same re-

---

80. Cf. *ST* II-II.9.1 where Thomas states that grace is more perfect than nature and hence does not fail in those things where man can be perfected by nature. Cf. I-II.109.8 where Thomas states that without healing grace reason will eventually falter, and a human will sin mortally.

81. Thomas also first treats natural participation and then he treats supernatural participation. For example, he treats the intellectual and moral virtues before treating the theological virtues (*ST* I-II.57–61) and he treats natural law before divine law (*ST* I-II.94–108).

82. Just as Thomas ordinarily restricts the term "moved by the Holy Spirit" to super-

lation to the supernatural end of humans as nature has to their natural end. Just as the eternal law moves humans to their natural end through their natural inclinations, the eternal law moves humans to their supernatural end through supernatural inclinations that come from participation in divine nature. These supernatural inclinations are the theological virtues.[83] And just as the acquired virtues are essential for the natural inclinations to be fulfilled through operation, the infused cardinal virtues are essential for the supernatural inclinations (theological virtues) to be fulfilled by operation.[84] Hence, analogous to the way that nature causes the natural inclinations, which cause good actions by means of the cardinal virtues, habitual grace causes the theological virtues, which cause supernatural good actions by means of the infused cardinal virtues.[85]

Because grace and the corresponding virtues are analogous to nature and the natural virtues, the way the material will be presented in the section will mirror the way it was presented above (natural form, then in-

---

natural acts, Thomas also restricts the term "participation in the divine nature" to supernatural participation (See *ST* I-II.62.1.1, 110.3, 110.4, 112.1; II-II.19.7; III.3.4.3, 9.2.1, 62,1; *QD de Anima* 7.4, 7.9; *Super ad Titam* 3.1; *Super ad Hebraeos* 2.4). See *ST* I-II.111.1.1 where Thomas notes that sanctifying grace is said to make man pleasing to God, not efficiently but formally. Cf. 111.2.1.

83. Thomas states in *ST* I-II.62.3, "The theological virtues direct man to supernatural happiness in the same way as by the natural inclination man is directed to his connatural end" (Virtutes theologicae hoc modo ordinant hominem ad beatitudinem supernaturalem, sicut per naturalem inclinationem ordinatur homo in finem sibi connaturalem). Cf. II-II.26.6; *De Virtutibus in communi* art. 10 and art. 3.2 where Thomas states that grace is the cause of spiritual *esse*, but virtue is a principle of acting spiritually.

84. Thomas states in *ST* I-II.63.3, "Effects must be proportionate to their causes and principles. Now all virtues, intellectual and moral, that are acquired by our actions, proceed from certain natural principles preexisting in us, as above stated. In place of the natural principles, the theological virtues are bestowed on us by God, whereby we are directed to a supernatural end, as stated above. Hence, there must also correspond to these theological virtues, in due proportion, other habits divinely caused in us that are disposed to the theological virtues in the same way that the moral and intellectual virtues are to the natural principles of virtue" (Opertet effectus esse suis causis et principiis proportionatos. Omnes autem virtutes tam intellectuales quam morales, quae ex nostris actibus acquiruntur, procedunt ex quibusdam naturalibus principiis in nobis praexistentibus, ut supra dictum est. Loco quorum naturalium principiorum, conferuntur nobis a deo virtutes theologicae, quibus ordinamur ad finem supernaturalem, sicut supra dictum est. Unde oportet quod his etiam virtutibus theologicis proportionaliter respondeant alii habitus divinitus causati in nobis, qui sic se habeant ad virtutes theologicas sicut se habent virtutes morales et intellectuales ad principia naturalia virtutum). See also *ST* I-II.110.4 where Thomas states that grace is prior to virtue as the powers of the soul are prior to virtue.

85. Thomas calls the acquired virtues, the infused virtues, the gifts of the Holy Spirit, and habitual grace good habits (*ST* I-II.50.2, 55.2, 62.2, 68.3, 110.2). Consequently, all of these types of habits serve as a medium between the soul (the natural form) and acts to which it is naturally or supernaturally inclined.

clination, and then acquired virtues). In this section, habitual grace will be presented first, followed by the theological virtues (supernatural inclinations), followed by the infused moral virtues and intellectual virtues (specifically infused prudence, justice, temperance, and fortitude). Last of all, the gifts of the Holy Spirit that act as additional habits perfecting the soul even beyond that of the infused virtues will be covered. These supernatural habits increase participation in eternal law by allowing humans to be directed to divine actions ordered to their ultimate end.

Participation in Eternal Law by Grace

Thomas makes a distinction between habitual grace and grace that is the movement of the Holy Spirit directing humans to supernatural acts.[86] In this section, I will treat both types of grace since they are both principles of participation in eternal law. I will first analyze habitual grace, which is the principle of supernatural actions just as nature is the principle of natural actions, and then I will analyze the movement of the Holy Spirit. Finally, since in the section on law in the *Summa Theologiae* grace is the primary aspect of the new law, I will briefly analyze the relevant aspects of the new law.

Thomas firmly maintains that all things act in accord with their nature. Hence, humans perform human actions. Good human actions perfect the person and lead to natural happiness. However, humans are not ordered only to natural happiness, humans are ordered to eternal happiness, which is not attained by merely human actions, but by divine actions (*ST* I-II.109.5). Hence, humans need an additional principle that

---

86. *ST* I-II.110.2. In the *Summa Theologiae,* in treating the essence of grace, Thomas first makes a distinction between created grace and God as grace (110.1). Then Thomas distinguishes between habitual grace and grace as divine help moving humans to act (110.2). Hence, even if humans have the supernatural principle of habitual grace, they still need to be supernaturally moved to act. Both of the latter types of grace can be further divided into operating and cooperating grace (111.2). In reference to habitual grace, Thomas notes that every form, including grace, has a double effect. The first effect of a form is being and the second effect is operation. Thus, habitual grace as perfecting the soul (changing the mode of being of the human) is called operating grace, as the principle of meritorious works which spring from free choice it is called cooperating grace. For a secondary source explaining the distinction between habitual and actual grace and the further distinction of both of these into operative and cooperative, see Bernard Lonergan, *Grace and Freedom,* 21–123. Cf. *DV* 27.2 where Thomas states that to obtain an end, three things must occur: the nature must be proportionate to it, there must be an inclination to it, and there must be a movement to it. Grace makes nature proportionate to the supernatural end, charity perfects the inclination to it, and the other [infused] virtues perfect movement.

allows them to perform actions in accord with eternal happiness. That additional principle is habitual grace. Habitual grace is a participation in divine nature allowing humans to perform actions in accord with divine nature: divine actions.[87] By means of these divine actions humans are able to attain eternal life.

An analogy of fire and water is helpful to explain the role of habitual grace. Fire is hot by essence and capable of performing the action of heating other things. Water, however, is not hot by essence, but only by participation in the heat of the fire. Yet, once water has obtained this heat, it is likewise able to perform the action of heating other things. So although all things act in accord with their nature, water is able to act in accord with the nature of fire because it participates in the heat of the fire. God is divine nature by essence and capable of performing divine actions. Humans, however, can only be divine by participation. Yet, once they do participate in divine nature, they are able to perform divine actions flowing from the supernatural inclinations of faith, hope, and charity. These divine actions are in accord with eternal happiness.

Because grace has the same role as nature in reference to supernatural acts, it is proper to say that grace perfects or re-creates nature (*ST* I-II.109, 110.4; II-II.8.1; III.62.2; *DV* 27.2; *DT* II.3). Because the habit of grace is a participation in divine nature, it makes the soul like divine nature through a certain "regeneration" or "re-creation."[88] Thomas elsewhere explains that grace as a created superadded accident re-creates hu-

---

87. There is a second reason that Thomas calls grace a participation in divine nature: to distinguish the habit of grace from the infused virtues. Whereas the infused virtues, which perfect a particular power of the soul, are said to participate in the corresponding attribute of God (e.g., charity participates in divine love), grace which perfects the essence of the soul is said to participate in divine nature. Thomas states in *ST* I-II.110.4, ". . . grace, as it is prior to virtue, has a subject prior to the powers of the soul, so that it is in the essence of the soul. For as man through his intellective power participates in the divine knowledge through the virtue of faith, and with respect to the power of the will participates in the divine love through the virtue of charity, so also in the nature of the soul does he participate in the divine nature, after the manner of likeness, through a certain regeneration or re-creation" (. . . gratia, sicut est prius virtute, ita habeat subjectum prius potentiis animae, ita scilicet quod sit in essentia animae. Sicut enim per potentiam intellectivam homo participat cognitionem divinam per virtutem fidei; et secundum potentiam voluntatis amorem divinum, per virtutem caritatis; ita etiam per naturam animae participat, secundum quandam similitudinem, naturam divinam, per quandam regenerationem sive recreationem). Cf. *ST* III.62.2.

88. *ST* I-II.110.4: ". . . so also in the nature of the soul does he [man] participate in the divine nature, after the manner of likeness, through a certain regeneration or re-creation" (ita etiam per naturam animae participat, secundum quandam similitudinem, naturam divinam, per quandam regenerationem sive recreationem).

mans by making them new beings. They are not new beings in the sense that their essence is changed but in that they are more like God because they have a new mode of *esse*.[89] In other words, as seen in chapter 2, all acts are a participation in God who is pure act. Now the first participation of a subject is the act of *esse*. However, in addition to this substantial act of *esse*, the subject participates in accidental acts of *esse*. These additional acts do not change the nature of something, but change its mode of being.[90] Thus, in the case of grace, grace as a habit is an accidental act of *esse* changing a human's manner of being by imparting a likeness through participation in divine nature.[91]

Unlike other accidental acts of *esse* that change a human's mode of being in a natural way, grace is a participation in God's nature in a degree beyond the natural potency of human nature. A participant is to that participated in as potency is to act, and hence in every case of natural participation that participated in is limited by the nature of the participant. However, in supernatural participation, habitual grace is the principle of the act allowing humans to exceed their natural limitations in causing meritorious acts.[92] Thomas in arguing that only God can cause grace states:

Nothing can act beyond its species, since the cause must always be more powerful than its effect. Now the gift of grace surpasses every capability of created nature, since it is nothing short of a participation in divine nature, which exceeds every

89. *ST* I-II.110.2.3. Thomas quotes Ephesians 2:10, which states that the faithful are created in Christ in order to do the good works that God has predestined them to do. Thomas further explains this notion of being created in Christ when he speaks of Christ as the head of the Church and hence the source of all grace (*ST* III.8). Humans as created in Christ are moved by Christ by means of Christ giving them "grace or the Holy Spirit" (Dare gratiam aut spiritum sanctum—*ST* III.8.1.1).

90. See *DV* 27.1.3 where Thomas states that God creates natural *esse* in us by means of a formal cause, for form is the principle of *esse*. Likewise, God brings about gratuitous spiritual *esse* in us by means of the form of grace. Cf. *De Virtutibus in communi* 3.2.

91. *ST* I-II.110.2.2. See also *ST* I-II.2.5.3 where Thomas lists being happy (beatum) with living, and understanding as a mode of *esse* by which creatures pursue the likeness of God. Thomas states that some desire God's likeness as to *esse* only, some as to *esse* that is living, and some as "*esse* that is living, understanding, and happy" (esse vivens et intelligens et beatum). In the case of conversion, when a human is first given habitual grace, God prepares the soul for habitual grace by moving the soul to turn toward Himself. This act of turning the subject to God causes the proper disposition for the accidental form of habitual grace (*ST* I-II.109.6, 109.6.3; *Ioan* I.5; cf. *ST* III.66.11). Even when moved by God in a natural way, humans acquire a likeness to God because since God is act, the highest likeness of man to God is act (happiness), where man is most perfectly conformed to God (*ST* I-II.55.2.3).

92. See chapter 2 on how obediential potency allows humans to participate in God in a manner beyond the natural powers of the soul. Cf. *De Virtut* I.10.13; *ST* III.11.1.

other nature. . . . For it is as necessary that God alone should deify, bestowing an association of the divine nature by a participated likeness.[93]

Because all act in accord with their mode, this supernatural superadded form deifies humans by making them like God, which allows them to co-operate with God in causing supernatural acts.[94] Thus, whereas other accidental acts of *esse* would not be said to re-create nature, habitual grace, as causing the natural form of a human to exceed its natural limitations by cooperating with God in causing supernatural acts, is said to re-create human nature.

This participated nature allows humans to perform actions that are proportionate to the end of eternal happiness. Thomas notes that in order for something to reach a particular end, it must be proportionate to that end. Since man's ultimate end exceeds his natural capacity, supernatural divine help must be given.[95] Habitual grace, as causing human nature to be proportionate to its ultimate end, is this supernatural help (*ST* I-II.62.1, 110.3.2). Thus, grace as a participation in divine nature re-creates human nature so that it is proportionate to the ultimate end of eternal happiness, which is achieved by means of the theological virtues.[96]

---

93. *ST* I-II.112.1: Nulla res agere potest ultra suam speciem, quia semper oportet quod potior sit effectu. Donum autem gratiae excedit omnem facultatem naturae creatae, cum nihil aliud sit quam quaedam participatio divinae naturae, quae excedit omnem aliam naturam. . . . Sic enim necesse est quod solus deus deificet, communicando consortium divinae naturae per quandam similitudinis participationem. . . . See also *ST* I.12.5 where Thomas states that a supernatural habit, the light of grace, is necessary for humans to understand God. Thomas than states that by this additional light the blessed are made *"deiformes."* Cf. II-II.85.2 and I.13.10 where Thomas states that whenever someone is called god by participation, the name god denotes a likeness to God. See also April Williams, "Deification in the *Summa Theologiae:* A Structural Interpretation of the Prima Pars," *The Thomist* 61 (1997): 219–55. Williams argues that the notion of grace allows one to speak of deification without falling into pantheism or losing the transcendence of God: for example, we are not God by our nature but by participation.

94. Thomas, while wanting to show that humans act by divine power through grace, is nonetheless careful to add that deification of humans is only by means of a participated likeness and not by an identity of nature. Thomas in *ST* III.2.10 further explains this by stating that human nature can be lifted up to God by grace in two ways: by operation and by personal union. The second of these two ways belongs only to Christ, but the first way takes place in the saints who know and love God. Thus, the saints do not become divine by nature but by operation. Cf. III.4.1.2.

95. *SCG* III.147; *ST* I-II.109.5. See chapter 2 on how grace as a superadded form orders humans to an end beyond human nature.

96. Thomas notes that good is placed in the definition of virtue with reference to its fitness to either essential nature or participated nature (*ST* I-II.110.3.2). The theological virtues are good as being in accord with participated divine nature (I-II.62.1.1).

Because perfected human nature is proportionate to this end, the eternal law can move humans to perform acts in accord with divine nature.

Like all other perfections, the addition of grace increases the capacity of a human as an instrumental cause to be moved in accord with the *ratio* in the mind of God. However, unlike the superadded habits of the acquired virtues which increase the natural ability of a creature to participate in the form bestowed by God, grace does not cause an intensification of a natural power, but is a distinct supernatural principal of action (*SCG* III.53, 147; *ST* I.62.2; I-II.5.5; I-II.5.6). Although it is a distinct principle of action, humans still remain free and rational agents of these supernatural actions since they cooperate with this grace.[97] Thomas notes,

Man must reach his ultimate end by his own operations. Now, each and every thing operates in accord with its own form. Therefore, so that man may be brought to his ultimate end by his own operations, a form must be superadded to him from which his operations receive a certain efficacy in meriting his ultimate end in advance.[98]

Thomas, while showing that a human's meritorious actions are beyond the natural power of humans, nonetheless emphasizes that meritorious actions must be caused by the human agent. Thus, although actions that are caused by grace are beyond the natural powers of a human, nonetheless, these actions are truly human actions since a human is moved by God as a rational and therefore a free instrumental cause.[99]

97. Although grace is an external principle of good actions, nonetheless, to the extent it causes actions that are freely consented to by humans, it is called cooperating grace (*ST* I-II.111.2).

98. *SCG* III.150: Oportet quod homo ad ultimum finem per proprias operationes perveniat. Unumquodque autem operatur secundum propriam formam. Oportet igitur, ad hoc quod homo perducatur in ultimum finem per proprias operationes, quod superaddatur ei aliqua forma, ex qua eius operationes efficaciam aliquam accipiant promerendi ultimum finem. Hence, just as in natural participation God moves humans to their appropriate actions by means of their natural principles of action (their natural form), in supernatural participation God moves humans to meritorious actions by means of the supernatural form of grace. See also *De Virtut* I.10, which states that in reference to the natural good of humans, humans cannot receive forms and perfections beyond their natural potency. However, in reference to the good exceeding human nature, humans attain it by receiving forms and perfections that exceed the capacity of their nature since these perfections have God as their principle.

99. *ST* III.1.3. See also *ST* I.62.7 which states that nature is always preserved in the act of happiness. Thomas explains in the first response, "And the imperfection of nature is not opposed to the perfection of beatitude, but underlies it; as the imperfection of the power underlies the perfection of the form, and it is not the power that is taken away by the form,

Habitual Grace and the Movement by the Holy Spirit

Thomas makes a distinction between habitual grace and grace as the movement of the Holy Spirit (*ST* I-II.110.2). Just as even when human nature is the principle of an action, the human must still be moved by God, so also, when grace is the principle of supernatural actions, the human must be moved by God. However, a change in form causes a change in movement. Hence, this supernatural movement is also a supernatural gift from God, a type of grace. In other words, God gratuitously aids humans in two ways: first by giving them habitual grace, and secondy by moving them to act in accord with this supernatural form:

> ... man is aided by God's gratuitous will in two ways: First, inasmuch as man's soul is moved by God to know or will or act, and in this way the gratuitous effect in man is not a quality, but a movement of the soul; for the act of the mover in the moved is a motion. Secondly, man is helped by God's gratuitous will, inasmuch as a habitual gift is infused by God into the soul.[100]

An example from human governance can be helpful to understand why the movement of the Holy Spirit is also grace. If there are two soldiers, one with training in military strategy and one without, the general could command the soldier with military training to a more complex military action than the one without this training. The command that determines the

---

but the privation which is opposed to the form is taken away" (Imperfectio autem naturae non opponitur perfectioni beatitudinis, sed substernitur ei, sicut imperfectio potentiae substernitur perfectioni formae, et non tollitur potentia per formam, sed tollitur privatio, quae opponitur formae). Thomas goes on to give the example of how the imperfection of natural knowledge is not opposed to the perfection of the knowledge in glory. Since grace and glory belong to the same genus (*ST* II-II.24.3.2), these comments that Thomas makes regarding the superadded form of glory also apply to grace. The imperfection of human nature which causes the need for grace does not mean that the power of human nature is taken away by grace but rather perfected. Hence, it is the human with the form of grace who is fully able to act freely. Thomas states that a human freely acts when acting from a suitable habit that inclines as second nature. Since grace is like an interior habit, it causes us to freely do those things becoming to grace (*ST* I-II.108.1.2; *SCG* III.148). Cf. *ST* I.22.2.4; I-II.21.4.2.

100. *ST* I-II.110.2: ... dupliciter ex gratuita dei voluntate homo adiuvatur. Uno modo, inquantum anima hominis movetur a deo ad aliquid congnoscendum vel volendum vel agendum. Et hoc modo ipse gratuitus effectus in homine non est qualitas, sed motus quidam animae, actus enim moventis in moto est motus. Alio modo adiuvatur homo ex gratuita dei voluntate, secundum quod aliquod habituale donum a deo animae infunditur. Thomas further explains that God not only moves creatures naturally to acts, but also bestows on them certain forms by which they are inclined to their acts so that their acts are easy and natural. Likewise, God not only moves humans to the supernatural acts, but also inclines them to it through the habit of grace so that they may be moved by Him sweetly and promptly to acquire the eternal good.

movement of the soldiers varies with the mode of the soldier. The same is the case with humans and grace. When humans have habitual grace, they are no longer directed to merely natural actions, but are directed to supernatural actions. As with the soldiers, the direction varies with the mode of the human, where in the case of grace the human is directed to supernatural actions. Since in the agent, the exemplary cause determines the efficient cause, when the divine agent directs humans supernaturally, this means that the Holy Spirit supernaturally moves them.[101] This supernatural movement is grace.

Both habitual grace and grace as the movement of the Holy Spirit perfect participation in the eternal law. Habitual grace perfects this participation because it elevates the soul, making it like God so that it is now capable of performing actions in accord with divine nature. The gratuitous movement of the Holy Spirit causes humans to freely perform these supernatural actions.[102] These actions are directed by the eternal

101. Although occasionally Thomas will speak of the Holy Spirit moving humans to natural acts since he appropriates the role of moving humans to act to the Holy Spirit in the *Summa Contra Gentiles* (IV.20), in the *Summa Theologiae* (with the exception of a few passages—e.g., I-II.109.1.1), the normal way Thomas uses the term "moved by the Holy Spirit" is in reference to God gratuitously moving the soul as dwelling in the soul by sanctifying grace. Thomas in explaining how the Holy Spirit is called gift because it can be possessed by a rational creature who can be united to it states in *ST* I.38.1, "Other creatures can be moved by a divine person, not, however, in such a way as to be able to enjoy the divine person, and to use the effect thereof" (Aliae autem creaturae moveri quidem possunt a divina persona; non tamen sic quod in potestate earum sit frui divina persona, et uti effectu eius). Thomas later (I.43.3) explains what it means to enjoy the divine person and use the effect when he states that God is in all things by essence, power, and presence, but above this common mode He can be in the rational nature as the object known is in the knower and the object loved is in the lover by sanctifying grace. "And yet the Holy Spirit is possessed by man, and dwells within him, in the very gift itself of sanctifying grace" (Sed tamen in ipso dono gratiae gratum facientis, spiritus sanctus, habetur, et inhabitat hominem). Thomas then states in the first response that to use and enjoy the Holy Spirit is by sanctifying grace. Hence, when Thomas speaks of the Holy Spirit moving the soul, he is normally referring to gratuitous movement of the Holy Spirit which is the effect of the Holy Spirit as known and loved by sanctifying grace. For example, in *ST* I-II.109.9.2 Thomas notes that the Holy Spirit, with the Father and Son, moves and protects humans beyond the effect of habitual grace. Other passages where Thomas refers to the movement of the Holy Spirit as God gratuitously moving the soul are *ST* I-II.68.1, 68.4, 68.6, 69.2, 70.4, 111.4.4, 114.3; II-II.8.5, 23.2, 24.11, 45.1, 52;1; III.7.5, 66.11.

102. See *ST* I-II.114.3 where Thomas states that a meritorious work may be considered in two ways: as proceeding from free choice and as proceeding from the grace of the Holy Spirit. If the work is considered as regards human free choice, the human does not deserve eternal life. But if the work is considered as regards the grace of the Holy Spirit moving humans to life everlasting, the work does merit eternal life because a human who participates in divine nature is an adopted son and thus has a right to the inheritance. Cf. *Ioan* I.5.

law as being in accord with a supernatural end rather than a natural end. Because humans like all instruments are moved in accord with their rational form, they cognitively participate in this divine direction (Cf. *ST* III.18.1.2).

When it comes to participation of a human as an instrumental cause in the eternal law through grace, there is a dissimilarity to the usual analogy of a cutting tool participating in the exemplar form of the craftsman. The analogy does remain helpful in that if a cutting tool was able to participate in a form that allowed it to be moved to actions exceeding its natural power (perhaps if it was made into a power tool), it could be moved to these greater actions (perhaps faster and more precise cutting). Furthermore, because it could be moved to these greater actions, the craftsman could use it for greater projects (a greater end) and thus in accord with greater exemplars in his mind. Because the cutting tool is moved in accord with a different exemplar, the mode of movement also changes. Analogously, grace allows humans to be moved to a more perfect end, resulting in a more perfect participation in eternal law, which requires a more perfect form of movement. The dissimilarity between this "enhanced" cutting tool and humans perfected by grace is that whereas the cutting tool only becomes like the craftsman inasmuch it shares in the movement of the craftsman,[103] humans through grace become like God not only by their actions sharing in divine movement, but also by their nature sharing in divine nature.[104] Hence, to the extent the human is like God, the actions are divine actions as flowing from a supernatural knowledge of the eternal law and a supernatural love.

The New Law   It is through law that humans are directed and moved to their proper end. Hence, when Thomas speaks of the supernatural movement and direction caused by grace, he refers to grace as the new law. The new law is the divine law given by Christ and is primarily the grace of the Holy Spirit and secondarily a written law. Thomas states,

---

103. Although it could be argued that a computer-guided cutting tool has in a way became like the craftsman, since inasmuch as it guides itself in accord with the directions programmed in by the craftsman, it participates in the practical reason of the craftsman.

104. Normally it would not be proper to say that the cutting tool substantially becomes like the craftsman by improving its accidents (e.g., sharpening it, etc.). Nevertheless, because God is all perfections, any time a perfection is superadded to a creature it becomes like God through natural participation. However, in the case of grace, the human becomes like God through supernatural participation.

Now that which is most powerful in the law of the New Testament, and wherein all its power consists, is the grace of the Holy Spirit, which is given through faith in Christ. Consequently, the new law is chiefly the grace itself of the Holy Spirit which is given to Christ's faithful.[105]

The new law is chiefly the law of grace (rather than a written law) because only the grace of the Holy Spirit elevates human beings causing them to perform acts proportionate to their ultimate end (*ST* I-II.106.2).

Although the new law primarily relates to cognitive participation in eternal law (and as such will be treated in chapter 4), it also perfects the soul to be moved and governed by the eternal law. Just as by human nature, the soul causes human actions by the natural light of reason and the natural love of the will, the soul by the superadded form of grace causes divine actions by the light of grace and the love of charity (*ST* I-II.109.1). Thus, grace as the new law is the rule and measure of supernatural acts and empowers the soul to perform these actions (*ST* I-II.106.1.2). In reference to the new law as the rule and measure of all supernatural actions, Thomas notes that the rule of human action is twofold: human reason and divine law. The acquired virtues are habits ordered by human reason. The theological virtues are ordered by the divine law to actions beyond the limited measure of human reason.[106] In reference to the new law empowering humans to perform supernatural actions, Thomas states that the new law makes man fit to participate in eternal happiness through charity which fulfills the law (*ST* I-II.98.1). In other words, a law containing the moral precepts alone cannot move humans to eternal happiness but only a law that also gives humans the ability to fulfill the precepts. The new law not only indicates what humans are to do, but also gives them the ability to do it (cf. *DV* 27.4).

Because the new law is the cause of charity, which orders all human

---

105. Id autem quod est potissimum in lege novi testamenti, et in quo tota, virtus eius consistit, est gratia spiritus sancti, quae datur per fidem christi. Et ideo principaliter lex nova est ipsa gratia spiritus sancti, quae datur christi fidelibus (*ST* I-II.106.1). Thomas continues in this passage by noting that although the new law is primarily the grace of the Holy Spirit, it is secondarily all those things that dispose us to the grace of the Holy Spirit and pertain to the use of that grace. Because the new law also consists of these elements, the faithful need to be instructed concerning them in word and in writing. Hence, the new law contains written elements. See also *QQ* 4.8.2 where Thomas states that the new law contains precepts of the natural moral law, articles of faith, and the sacraments of grace, wherefore it is called the law of faith and the law of grace.

106. *ST* I-II.63.2; cf. II-II.23.6; *ST* I-II.109.1; See also II-II.8.4.1 where Thomas notes that those with charity are instructed by the Holy Spirit in necessary truths.

actions to God, Thomas calls the new law the law of charity.[107] Thomas explains:

> In the case of all who are moved by a first mover, any one of them is moved more perfectly when he participates more fully in the motion of the prime mover, and in his likeness. Now, God, Who is the giver of divine law, makes all things because of His love. So, he who tends toward God in this way, namely, by loving Him, is most perfectly moved toward Him. Now, every agent intends perfection to the extent that he acts. Therefore, this is the end of all legislation: to make man love God. . . . As a consequence, the new law, as the more perfect, is called the law of love, while the old law as less perfect is the law of fear.[108]

An agent is moved most perfectly by God, when he acts out of love for God, for in doing this he is most like God. Because love for God is the end of all divine legislation, Thomas considers the participation in God's motion and likeness that is a result of being moved by fear in the old law to be less perfect than the participation that results from being moved by the new law of love (*ST* I-II.98.1; cf. 107.1). Because it is through love of God that humans embrace and are brought to their last end (*ST* II-II.27.6), the new law is the immediate cause of their being directed to their last end. Because it is through the new law that the eternal law moves and directs humans to their last end of supernatural happiness, it is the cause of the highest participation by a principle of motion in this life (cf. *ST* I-II.106.4).

Because humans act out of love in being moved to the good by God, and actions done out of love are not by coercion but are freely chosen,[109] the new law is also called the law of liberty.[110] Thomas states that hu-

---

107. *ST* I-II.107.1; See also *Duobis Praeceptis Caritatis* 1 which states that the new law is the law of love, Christ, and his Gospel. It is not a law that coerces but is free since love moves one to freely choose the true good. It gives spiritual forms rather than temporal ones and is sweet rather than heavy. Cf. *Ad Galatas* 4.8.

108. *SCG* III.116: In omnibus autem quae moventur ab aliquo primo movente, tanto aliquid perfectius movetur quanto magis participat de motione primi moventis, et de similitudine ipsius. Deus autem, qui est legis divinae dator, omnia facit propter suum amorem. Qui igitur hoc modo tendit in ipsum, scilicet amando, perfectisssime movetur in ipsum. Omne autem agens intendit perfectionem in eo quod agit. Hic igitur est finis totius legislationis, ut homo deum amet. . . . Inde est etiam quod lex nova, tanquam perfectior, dicitur lex amoris: lex autem vetus, tanquam imperfectior, lex timoris.

109. Thomas states that when the Holy Spirit moves the mind by charity, the charity inclines the will to act freely (*ST* II-II.23.2). See also *ST* II-II.19.4 which states that love and freedom go together since love is to be moved by our inclination.

110. See the *Duobis Praeceptis Caritatis* 1 which states that the new law is the law of love, Christ, and his Gospel. It is not a law that coerces but is free since love moves one to freely choose the true good.

mans act freely when they act on their own accord, and they act on their own accord when they are inclined to act by a habit that is suitable to their nature. "Since then the grace of the Holy Spirit is like an interior habit bestowed on us and inclining us to act aright, it makes us do freely those things that are becoming to grace, and shun what is opposed to it."[111] Because humans are moved in accord with their form, humans participate in the eternal law most perfectly when they freely choose to perform the actions known through the divine law.[112]

Grace perfects participation in eternal law both by elevating human nature and moving human nature to perform actions that are ordered to the end of eternal life. Because the nature of the participant limits its degree of participation in an action, the added form of habitual grace allows humans to exceed their natural limitations by participating supernaturally in the divine actions of knowing and loving. In other words, through grace humans are like God and can perform actions in accord with the divine nature in which they participate. Because this gratuitous form by which humans act is supernatural, the movement of the Holy Spirit must also be supernatural. Since an agent always moves an instrument in accord with the exemplar in his mind, supernatural movement results in supernatural participation in the eternal law as moved and governed by it. When Thomas speaks of grace as moving and directing humans to a particular end, he calls it the new law.

Participation in the Eternal Law by the Infused Virtues

Just as the natural form does not directly cause particular acts, but rather causes acts through its natural inclinations perfected by the acquired virtues, grace also does not directly cause specific acts, but causes acts through its supernatural inclinations (the theological virtues) and the in-

---

111. Quia igitur gratia spiritus sancti est sicut interior habitus nobis infusus inclinans nos ad recte operandum, facit nos libere operari ea quae conveniunt gratiae, et vitare ea quae gratiae repugnant (*ST* I-II.108.1.2).

112. See *Ep. ad Romanos* 2.3 where Thomas notes that there are four grades of dignity in humans in reference to their relation to the law. The highest degree of dignity is in people who are led to the good in accord with the law by themselves. The second highest is in those led by others to the good without force. The third is in those who are led to the good by force and the fourth is in those who refuse to be led to the good. D. J. Billy in "Grace and Natural Law in the *Super Epistolam ad Romanos*," *Studia Moralia* 26 (1988): 29, comments on this passage by noting that those with the highest degree of dignity are those who are led by the new law of the Holy Spirit inscribed in their hearts.

fused cardinal virtues.[113] Thus, having covered the participated nature that causes and orders the infused virtues, this section will cover the infused virtues themselves. It will first analyze the infused virtues in general by showing how they differ from the acquired virtues. Then it will cover the theological virtues, which direct humans to their supernatural end in the same way that the natural inclinations direct humans to their connatural end (Cf. *ST* I-II.62.3). Finally, it will treat the infused cardinal virtues, which are formed by the theological virtue of charity.

Thomas states that habits are specifically distinct both in respect to their nature and in respect to specifically different objects (*ST* I-II.54.2). In reference to the former distinction, a virtue has reference to some preexisting nature, since all things are disposed with reference to what is fitting to nature. Whereas the acquired virtues dispose humans according to human nature, the infused virtues dispose them in accord with divine nature which is participated in through grace (*ST* I-II.110.3). Since the infused virtues dispose humans in accord with divine nature, they dispose humans to actions in accord with their ultimate end of knowing and loving God (*ST* I-II.62.3). Also, since they are in accord with divine nature, they are not acquired by habituation like the acquired virtues, but are infused.[114] Thomas explains:

Therefore, human virtue as ordered to the good which is measured according to the rule of human reason, can be caused from human acts: inasmuch as such acts proceed from reason, under whose power and rule such a good consists. On the other hand, the virtue which directs man to good as measured by the divine law, and not by human reason, cannot be caused by human acts, the principle of which is reason, but is produced in us by the divine operation alone.[115]

---

113. *ST* I-II.110.4.2. See also *ST* III.62.2 where Thomas states, "Grace, considered in itself, perfects the essence of the soul, in so far as it is a certain participated likeness of the divine being. And just as the soul's powers flow from its essence, so from grace there flow certain perfections to the powers of the soul, which perfections are called virtues and gifts, whereby the powers are perfected in relation to their actions" (Gratia, secundum se considerata, perficit essentiam animae, inquantum participat quandam similitudinem divini esse. Et sicut ab essentia animae fluunt eius potentiae, ita a gratia fluunt quaedam perfectiones ad potentias animae, quae dicuntur virtutes et dona, quibus potentiae perficiuntur in ordine ad suos actus). Cf. *ST* I-II.110.3).

114. *ST* I-II.62.1 & 2. Because supernatural happiness to which humans are directed by the infused virtues is beyond human nature, their natural principles which enable them to act well according to their capacity do not suffice. Thus, additional principles must be added by God and these are grace and the infused virtues (*ST* I-II.62.1, 63.4, 110.3).

115. Virtus igitur hominis ordinata ad bonum quod modificatur secundum regulam rationis humanae, potest ex actibus humanis causari, inquantum huiusmodi actus procedunt

Because natural reason is the measure of the acquired virtues, it is able to command acts which through repetition form virtues. However, since natural reason is unable to determine actions that are in accord with grace, the infused virtues cannot proceed from natural reason, but must be infused within us through divine operation (Cf. *ST* 110.3.3). Thus, unlike the acquired virtues, the infused virtues dispose humans in accord with grace (*ST* I-II.110.3), are caused by God alone, and dispose humans to actions that are ordered to their ultimate end of eternal happiness.

However, once these virtues are infused, the soul is perfected by the new law and can cooperate with God in causing actions that are in accord with the elevated nature. These repeated actions, although they do not cause the infused virtues, can increase the infused virtues analogous to the way that repeated acts perfect the acquired virtues (*ST* II-II.24.6).

In reference to the distinction based on specifically different objects, it is necessary to divide those virtues infused into humans into two groups: the theological virtues and the infused moral and intellectual virtues. The formal object of the theological virtues is God Himself who surpasses the knowledge of our reason (*ST* I-II.62.2). Like the theological virtues, the ultimate end of the infused moral and intellectual virtues is also God. However, the proximate end determines the species of a habit, and the proximate end of the infused moral and intellectual virtues is a good defined by divine law (and ordered to the ultimate end through charity).[116] Since the formal object of the acquired virtues is a good as defined by natural human reason, the infused virtues also differ from the acquired virtues in reference to their proximate end (*ST* I-II.63.4). Thomas gives the example of the formal object of temperance in regard to proper eating. The formal object of the acquired virtue of temperance is the mean appointed by reason which is that food should not harm the health of the body nor hinder reason, et cetera; whereas, the formal object of the infused virtue of temperance is based on divine law that requires that humans chastise their body through abstinence in food and drink and the like (*ST* I-II.63.4). Thus, unlike the acquired virtues, the infused virtues

---

a ratione, sub cuius potestate et regula tale bonum consistit. Virtus vero ordinans hominem ad bonum secundum quod modificatur per legem divinam, et non per rationem humanam, non potest causari per actus humanos, quorum principium est ratio, sed causatur solum in nobis per operationem divinam (*ST* I-II.63.2; cf. I-II.63.4; II-II.23.3 & 6).

116. *ST* I-II.63.2. The proximate end of the infused moral virtues is the good in accord with divine law. The ultimate end of the infused virtues is God since they are formed by charity which orders all things to God (*ST* I-II.63.4.1).

are in accord with grace, dispose humans to eternal life, are caused by God alone, and have either God as their end or, in the case of the infused moral virtues, the good as defined by divine law.

The Theological Virtues

The theological virtues are the supernatural inclinations that perfect the natural inclinations of humans so that they can be ordered to their ultimate end. Just as by nature humans are ordered to their connatural end through the natural inclinations of the intellect and will, so also by grace humans are given supernatural inclinations of the intellect and will. Thomas notes:

The theological virtues order man to supernatural happiness in the same way as by the natural inclination man is ordered to his connatural end. Now the latter happens in respect of two things. First in respect of the reason or intellect, insofar as it contains the first universal principles which are known to us by the natural light of the intellect, and which are reason's starting point, both in speculative and in practical matters. Secondly, through the rectitude of the will which tends naturally to the good of reason. But these two fall short of the order of supernatural happiness. . . . Consequently, in respect of both the above things, man needed to receive in addition something superadded to direct him to a supernatural end. First as regards the intellect, certain supernatural principles are added to man, which are received by means of divine light: these are able to be believed, concerning which is faith. Secondly, the will is directed to this end, both as to the movement of intention, which tends to that end as something attainable, and this pertains to hope, and as to a certain spiritual union, whereby the will is, so to speak, transformed into that end, and this comes about through charity.[117]

---

117. *ST* I-II.26.3: Virtutes theologicae hoc modo ordinant hominem ad beatitudinem supernaturalem, sicut per naturalem inclinationem ordinatur homo in finem sibi connaturalem. Hoc autem contingit secundum duo. Primo quidem, secundum rationem vel intellectum, inquantum continet prima principia universalia cognita nobis per naturale lumen intellectus, ex quibus procedit ratio tam in speculandis quam in agendis. Secundo per rectitudinem voluntatis naturaliter tendentis in bonum rationis. Sed haec duo deficiunt ab ordine beatitudinis supernaturalis. . . . Unde oportuit quod quantum ad utrumque, aliquid homini supernaturaliter adderetur, ad ordinandum ipsum in finem supernaturalem. Et primo quidem, quantum ad intellectum, adduntur homini quaedam principia supernaturalia, quae divino lumine capiuntur, et haec sunt credibilia, de quibus est fides. Secundo vero, voluntas ordinatur in illum finem et quantum ad motum intentiones, in ipsum tendentem sicut in id quod est possibile consequi, quod pertinet ad spem, et quantum ad unionem quandam spiritualem, per quam quodammodo transformatur in illum finem, quod fit per caritatem. Cf. I-II.62.1 and also *DV* 22.8 where Thomas states that God gratuitously perfects the will by introducing a new form like grace or virtue into the will. These forms incline the will to something beyond that which it was previously naturally inclined to. This supernatural inclination is imperfect now but perfect in heaven.

The intellect is perfected by receiving revealed first principles that are su-peradded to the natural first principles, and it is also perfected by being given the light of grace to understand the superadded principles. This su-pernatural inclination of the intellect is the theological virtue of faith. The natural inclination of the will to tend toward its connatural end is per-fected by the theological virtues of hope and charity.[118]

These supernatural inclinations allow humans to participate in eternal law at a higher level than merely natural participation because through them humans are disposed to their ultimate end and determined to ac-tions in accord with this end. Faith, hope, and charity will now be treated to show specifically how as supernatural inclinations they dispose humans to their ultimate end, determine them to actions in accord with this end, and perfect the powers of the intellect and will.

Faith   Because faith causes humans to have a certain supernatural knowl-edge of the eternal law, it will be primarily covered in the next chapter on cognitive participation in eternal law. However, inasmuch as it is a habit that causes humans to be moved and governed more perfectly by the eter-nal law, it is proper to cover it in now.

The term faith can refer to either an act or a habit. Faith is the act where the intellect of the believer is determined to one object (the first truth) by the command of the will (*ST* II-II.2.1.3, 4.1). God has revealed certain things about Himself that surpass human reason. Because a hu-man's knowledge of these things does not attain the perfection of clear sight,[119] in order for the intellect to assent to these things, the will must command the intellect to assent.[120] Hence, Thomas notes that two things are necessary for faith: that the things of faith are proposed by God and that a human assents. Grace is necessary for both of these things (*ST* II-II.6.1). In the act of faith, the will is gratuitously moved by God to assent to revealed propositions.

---

118. Thomas explains that the will is naturally moved toward its end due to a certain conformity of it to its end (*ST* I-II.62.3).

119. Thomas notes in *ST* II-II.1.2.3 that the object of heavenly vision will be the first truth seen in itself. Hence the vision will not be by way of a proposition, but by way of sim-ple understanding. However, by faith we do not apprehend the first truth as it is in itself.

120. Thomas states that the intellect assents to a thing in two ways. First, the intellect is moved by its very object to assent when the object is either known by itself (through understanding) or through something else already known (through science). Secondly, the intellect assents to something not through being sufficiently moved to this assent by its proper object, but through an act of the will choosing one thing over another (*ST* II-II.1.4; cf. II-II.2.9.2).

Faith as a habit is the disposition whereby the intellect and will are perfected to assent to revealed propositions. Thomas states, "faith is a habit of the mind, whereby eternal life is begun in us, making the intellect assent to what is nonapparent."[121] As a theological virtue, the habit of faith inclines the intellect to receive supernaturally revealed principles by means of the divine light (*ST* I-II.62.3; II-II.2.3.2). The assent to these supernaturally revealed principles is the beginning of eternal life. Thomas explains that unlike irrational creatures that participate in divine goodness merely by being *(essendo tantum)*, or even by living and knowing singulars,

. . . the rational nature, inasmuch as it apprehends the universal character of good and being, is immediately ordered to the universal principle of being. Therefore, the perfection of the rational creature consists not only in what belongs to it in respect of its own nature, but also in that which is attributed to it through a certain supernatural participation of divine goodness. Hence it was said above that man's ultimate happiness consists in a supernatural vision of God: to which vision man cannot attain unless he be taught by God. . . . Now man acquires a participation of this by learning, not indeed all at once, but gradually, according to the mode of his nature: and every such learner must believe, in order that he may arrive at perfect knowledge. . . . Hence, in order that a man arrive at the perfect vision of happiness, he must first of all believe God, as a student believes the master who is teaching him.[122]

Because the rational creature is perfected not only by natural participation in the divine goodness, but also by supernatural participation, his ultimate perfection consists in the vision of God.

However, just as in any science, before perfect knowledge is attained, humans are led to this knowledge by means of a teacher, so also in order for there to be perfect knowledge of God, humans must also be led

121. fides est habitus mentis, qua inchoatur vita aeterna in nobis, faciens intellectum assentire non apparentibus (*ST* II-II.4.1).

122. . . . natura autem rationalis, inquantum cognoscit universalem boni et entis rationem, habet immediatum ordinem ad universale essendi principium. Perfectio ergo rationalis creaturae non solum consistit in eo quod ei competit secundum suam naturam, sed etiam in eo quod ei attribuitur ex quadam supernaturali participatione divinae bonitatis. Unde et supra dictum est quod ultima beatitudo hominis consistit in quadam supernaturali dei visione. Ad quam quidem visionem homo pertingere non potest nisi per modum addiscentis a deo doctore, . . . Huius autem disciplinae fit homo particeps non statim, sed successive, secundum modum suae naturae. Omnis autem talis addiscens oportet quod credat, ad hoc quod ad perfectam scientiam perveniat, . . . Unde ad hoc quod homo perveniat ad perfectam visionem beatitudinis praeexigitur quod credat deo tanquam discipulus magistro docenti (*ST* II-II.2.3; cf. I.1.1).

there gradually by the divine teacher. Thus, God prepares humans for the perfect vision of Himself by means of revealing certain divine truths, and as in all cases where one begins to learn a science, one must believe the principles on the authority of the teacher until one is able to understand them for oneself (*ST* I.1.2). Hence, belief in the divinely revealed principles is the necessary first step toward perfect vision of God which is supernatural happiness.[123] Although the habit of faith is not able to cause the action of knowing God as He is, it nonetheless disposes humans to this ultimate end as the beginnings of supernatural knowledge of God.

The virtue of faith perfects the human to be moved and governed by the eternal law by allowing the intellect to apprehend God as the supernatural end. In any human action, the end that is willed must first be apprehended by the intellect because the will is the intellectual appetite. Although through natural reason the intellect comes to a limited knowledge of God, it is only through faith that God is known as the cause of eternal happiness.[124] Once this supernatural end of man is apprehended by the intellect, the will can tend to it through hope and charity.[125] Once this divine end is intended, acts can be determined that are in accord with this end. In other words, faith apprehends the supernatural end to which all supernatural acts are ordered.[126] By apprehending this end, faith when accompanied by charity determines humans to actions that are in accord with this end.

The habit of faith perfects the intellect by inclining humans to know the revealed truth of God as the end to be obtained through the act of happiness (*ST* II-II.5.2.2). Because this knowledge of the end allows humans to act in accord with this end, faith disposes humans to their ultimate end of attaining God. Although actions in accord with this end are not possible unless the will and the passions are also perfected by infused virtues, when faith is accompanied by these virtues, it determines

---

123. Thomas notes in *ST* II-II.4.7 that faith, by its nature, precedes all other virtues. In this passage Thomas is speaking of perfect virtue, that formed by charity, rather than the acquired virtues that can precede faith.

124. *ST* II-II.4.7. See also II-II.2.7 and 2.8 where Thomas notes that the object of faith, God, is that thing through which humans obtain happiness.

125. Thomas notes by quoting Augustine that although faith is in the speculative intellect, it causes good works through charity, just as the speculative intellect becomes practical by extension (*ST* II-II.4.2.3).

126. *ST* II-II.4.5. Thomas explains in II-II.7.2.1 that things that are in the intellect are the principles of those which are in the appetite, insofar as the apprehended good moves the appetite. Cf. I-II.113.4; II-II.3.1.3.

humans to actions in accord with this ultimate end.[127] Because God is able to direct and move a human whose intellect is perfected by faith to actions in accord with this ultimate end, faith causes a more perfect participation in eternal law. Just as God moves and directs humans to their natural end through their natural inclination to know God, God moves and directs humans to their supernatural end through this supernatural inclination to know God as the object of eternal happiness.

Hope Thomas speaks of two types of hope: natural hope, which is a passion of the irascible appetite, and hope that is a theological virtue. The object of the passion of hope is the arduous future good that is difficult to obtain (*ST* I-II.40.2). Because the passions are in the sensitive appetite, this object of natural hope is a sensible good (*ST* II-II.18.1). Thomas both compares and contrasts the theological virtue of hope with this passion. Like the passion of hope, the theological virtue of hope seeks the arduous future good that is difficult to obtain (*ST* II-II.17.1). However, unlike the passion of hope, the object of the theological virtue of hope is not a sensible good, but the divine good that "is an arduous intelligible [good], or rather [a good] which exists beyond the intelligible."[128] More specifically, Thomas states that the primary object of hope is God as the source of eternal life and the source of the help by which eternal life is obtained.[129]

The intellect perfected by faith first apprehends God as the source of eternal happiness and the source of divine assistance by which eternal life is obtained. Then, the will, perfected by the virtue of hope, tends toward this object.[130] Since the movement toward this object exceeds the capacity of human nature, gratuitous hope must be infused by God (*ST* II-II.17.1.2). Thus, through the virtue of hope, the will tends to the dif-

127. Chapter 4 further shows how faith determines actions to the ultimate end.

128. est arduum intelligibile; vel potius supra intellectum existens (*ST* II-II.18.1.1).

129. Thomas notes that the good that humans ought to hope for is the infinite good as proportionate to the power of God who helps humans achieve this good. "And this good is eternal life, which consists in the enjoyment of God Himself. For there cannot be [sit] anything less to be hoped for from Him than Himself, since His goodness, whereby He imparts good things to His creatures, is no less than His essence" (Hoc autem bonum est vita aeterna, quae in fruitione ipsius dei consistit, non enim minus aliquid ab eo sperandum est quam sit ipse, cum non sit minor eius bonitas, per quam bona creaturae communicat, quam eius essentia; *ST* II-II.17.2; cf. 17.4, 7).

130. Thomas notes that the object of hope in one way is eternal happiness, and in another way is the divine assistance necessary to obtain eternal life. In both ways faith is presupposed by which we know the object of eternal happiness and of the divine assistance by which it is obtained (*ST* II-II.17.7).

ficult, but possible to attain, supernatural good of eternal life.[131] Consequently, like the natural passion of hope, the theological virtue seeks the
future arduous good; however, unlike the passion this good is God Himself and can only be obtained by divine help. Thus, the believer hopes in
eternal life, which is difficult to obtain but possible to obtain by means of
divine assistance.[132]

The theological virtue of hope perfects the will to love. Thomas
notes that all movements of the appetite, including hope, flow from love.
Now love can either be perfect or imperfect. Perfect love is that whereby
someone is loved in himself (for his own sake). Imperfect love is that
whereby someone is loved not for his own sake, but for a good to be
obtained from him. The will tends to God as the good apprehended by
faith in both ways, as loving God for His own sake and as loving God
for the attainment of eternal happiness. "The first love of God pertains
to charity, which adheres to God for His own sake; while hope pertains
to the second love, since he that hopes, intends to obtain possession of
something for himself."[133] Because charity loves God as a friend and not
simply for the acquisition of some benefit, it is the more perfect of the
two types of love. Thus, in the order of perfection, charity comes before
hope, but in the order of generation hope precedes charity because humans hoping to be rewarded by God are encouraged to love Him and
obey Him (*ST* II-II.17.8). Thomas explains:

. . . a man loves a thing because he apprehends it as his own good. Now from the
very fact that a man hopes to be able to obtain some good through someone, he
looks on the man in whom he hopes as a good of his own. Hence for the very
reason that a man hopes in someone, he proceeds to love him.[134]

---

131. Faith grasps that it is possible to attain eternal life, because faith grasps that God is
not only capable of making it attainable, but good and merciful enough to actually make it
attainable.

132. See *ST* II-II.17.5.4, which states that hope as a theological virtue regards something arduous to be obtained by another's help.

133. Primus autem amor dei pertinet ad caritatem, quae inhaeret deo secundum seipsum, sed spes pertinet ad secundum amorem, quia ille qui sperat aliquid sibi obtinere intendit (*ST* II-II.17.8). Cf. II-II.17.3, 17.6 and I-II.66.6.2 which states that hope presupposes
concupiscible love, and charity implies the love of friendship. See *ST* I-II.26.4 for the distinction between concupiscible love and love of friendship. See also Aristotle, *Nichomachean
Ethics* (New York: Random House, 1947), book 8.

134. . . . homo aliquid amat, quod apprehendit illud ut bonum suum. Per hoc autem
quod homo ab aliquo sperat se bonum consequi posse, reputat ipsum in quo spem habet,
quoddam bonum suum. Unde ex hoc ipso quod homo sperat de aliquo, procedit ad aman-
dum ipsum (*ST* I-II.62.4).

Hope perfects the will's inclination to tend toward the good of eternal life that is obtained from God and this causes the ultimate perfection of the will loving God through the virtue of charity.

Since, as already seen, hope is an imperfect love (i.e., loving God for something that is received from Him), like all other virtues hope is not a virtue in the fullest sense until it is perfected by charity (*ST* II-II.17.8; cf. *ST* I-II.65.2). Once it is perfected by charity, a believer has living hope in attaining eternal happiness because then he hopes in the assistance of God who is a friend.[135] In other words, when humans need assistance, they have much greater hope in obtaining that assistance from a friend than from someone who is not a friend.[136] Because God is loved as a friend through charity (*ST* II-II.23.1), the believer hopes for the good of eternal life with even greater intensity because he has a greater desire to enjoy God as a friend and has greater confidence in God's assistance.

Hope perfects the will so that it tends to the supernaturally apprehended good of God as attainable through the act of happiness (*ST* I-II.62.3). Because God's power is identical to His goodness and mercy, God could not be more good than by making Himself the end of the rational creature through participation. Thomas states, "For there cannot be *(sit)* anything less to be hoped for from Him than Himself, since His goodness, whereby He imparts good things to His creatures, is no less than His essence."[137] The theological virtue of hope disposes humans to God as end and determines the will to actions in accord with this end. Since the eternal law orders humans to this divine end, the theological virtue of hope allows humans to perform actions in accord with the eternal law. By willing these actions, humans participate more perfectly in the eternal law as moved and governed by it.

Charity Unlike hope, which adheres to God to obtain something, charity adheres to God for His own sake, and hence fully perfects the will (*ST* I-II.66.6.2). This perfect love is called the love of friendship. Since charity is love of friendship for God, I will first analyze love of friend-

---

135. *ST* II-II.17.8.1. Thomas notes that hope is more perfect with charity because we hope chiefly in our friends (II-II.17.8).

136. Thomas notes that a man begins to love someone because he believes that he can obtain a good from him, and from the fact that he loves him, he then hopes all the more in him (*ST* I-II.62.4.3).

137. *ST* II-II.17.2: Non enim minus aliquid ab eo sperandum est quam sit ipse, cum non sit minor eius bonitas, per quam bona creaturae communicat, quam eius essentia.

ship in general, and then I will analyze charity. Someone with the love of friendship seeks the good of the one he loves and this love causes a union between him and the one that he loves (*ST* II-II.23.1). Thomas explains how this union comes into being by noting that the union between lover and beloved is twofold. There is the union of affection and there is real union.[138]

The union of affection is where the lover considers the beloved to be his other self. Hence, he wills the good of the beloved just as he wills his own good.[139] Thomas states:

So thus, to the extent that the things which belong to a friend the lover judges to be his own, the lover seems to be in the beloved as made the same as the lover. But conversely to the extent that he wills and acts for his friend as for himself, as regarding his friend as the same as himself, in this manner, the beloved is in the lover.[140]

The two have a union of affections because they share all that they have and act for each other's sake. The needs, goals, sorrows, and intentions of the beloved become the needs, goals, sorrows, and intentions of the lover.[141] This love of affection results in real union,[142] because, whereas the operation of the intellect is completed by the thing understood be-

138. The term "affection" is translated from the Latin *affectus*. Thomas uses this term here to mean a union of inclinations or intentions. The connotation of this passage is that friends are united in their intentions or plans that they hold in common. What one friend seeks, so also the other seeks and likewise what one suffers so also the other suffers. The two friends participate in each other's acts and also participate in what happens to each other. See, for example, *ST* III.2.6 where Thomas explains this term: ". . . the unity of affection, inasmuch as the will of the man was always in agreement with the will of the Word of God" (. . . unitatem affectus inquantum scilicet voluntas illius hominis est semper conformis voluntati Verbi Dei). See also Roy Deferrari, *A Lexicon of St. Thomas Aquinas* (Washington, D.C.: The Catholic University of America Press, 1948), 1125. The meaning of this term is far stronger then the typical English use of the word *affection,* which tends to signify an emotional attraction.

139. *ST* I-II.28.1. Thomas continues by noting that love is the efficient cause of real union and the formal cause of union of affection inasmuch as love is this union or bond. Cf. I-II.25.2.2 and 26.2.2.

140. Ut sic, inquantum quae sunt amici aestimat sua, amans videatur esse in amato, quasi idem factus amato. Inquantum autem e converso vult et agit propter amicum sicut propter seipsum, quasi reputans amicum idem sibi, sic amatum est in amante. Thomas continues by noting that there is a third way in which friends mutually indwell in that friends return love for love and both desire and do good things for one another (*ST* I-II.28.2).

141. See *ST* II-II.30.2 where Thomas notes that the lover through the union of affections feels the other's sorrows as if they were his own.

142. Thomas notes that union has a threefold relation to love. Substantial union (likeness) causes love. Union of affection is essentially love. And real union is the effect of love (*ST* I-II.28.1.2).

ing in the intellect, the operation of the will is completed by its resting in the thing loved (Cf. *ST* II-II.23.6.1). Hence, lovers seek to delight in the presence of each other by living together, speaking together, and being united in all like things (*ST* I-II.28.1.2). In other words, because the lover seeks the good of the beloved as his own good, a true spiritual unity results between the two.

In reference to the relation between humans and God, humans through charity have the love of friendship for God. Thomas notes, "Charity not only signifies the love of God, but also a certain friendship with Him; and this implies, over and above love, a certain added mutual act of returning of love along with mutual communion as said in *Ethic.* viii."[143] Hence someone with the virtue of charity loves God for His own sake and therefore has a union of affections causing mutual communion (*ST* I-II.66.6; II-II.23.6).

Although it would not be appropriate to say that someone with charity shares in the needs, goals, sufferings, and intentions of God (as can be said in reference to love of friendship between humans), it is appropriate to say that humans with charity have a union of affection with God as sharing each other's intentions and acting for each others sake.[144] In other words, the end intended by God (the divine goodness) becomes the end intended by humans with charity. Because God's end for them is now their end, they now seek to make all of their actions in accord with God's *ratio* ordering them to the ultimate end. Since God's *ratio* ordering humans to His end is the eternal law, to say that humans share in God's intentions is another way of saying that humans participate in eternal law since they seek to fulfill the plans of their divine friend. This union of affections results in the real union of mutual indwelling, for

143. Caritas non solum significat amorem dei, sed etiam amicitiam quandam ad ipsum; quae quidem super amorem addit mutuam redamationem cum quadam mutua communicatione, ut dicitur in *VIII ethic.* (*ST* I-II.65.5). Cf. *ST* II-II.24.2.2 for how God can be loved as He is in Himself through charity. Thomas notes that God is supremely knowable and loveable in essence, but humans cannot naturally know or love God as He is in Himself. However, through charity humans can love God in this way (even though they cannot know God as He is in Himself through faith).

144. See *ST* II-II.17.6.3 where Thomas notes that charity unites our affections to God. Cf. I-II.109.3; II-II.24.2 See also Waddel, *Primacy,* 63–75. Waddel states that charity is friendship with God and friendship is a special kind of love that includes seeking the good of the friend over our own good. In reference to God, this means seeking His interests in the world. He continues by noting that charity as love of friendship causes humans to lose themselves and take on the likeness of God. This causes humans to love what God loves. Later (90–94) Waddel notes that as we grow in virtues, we become more dependent upon God and we perfect ourselves by being dependent upon God's love.

although God is already in all creatures by essence, power, and presence, He can be in the rational creature in a special way as the object known is in the knower and the object loved is in the lover.[145]

This special mode of God dwelling in us is especially attributed to the Holy Spirit, who as the uncreated love proceeding from the Father and the Son, is considered the source of charity (*SCG* IV.21). Since charity is caused by the Holy Spirit, and an effect always participates in its cause, it is appropriate to say that charity is a participation in the Holy Spirit.[146] Thomas states:

Therefore charity can be in us neither naturally, nor through acquisition by the natural powers, but by the infusion of the Holy Spirit, Who is the love of the Father and the Son, and the participation of Whom in us is created charity, as stated above.[147]

The theological virtue of charity is a supernatural participation in the Holy Spirit who is uncreated charity. Just as the sky is filled with light by participation in the sun, which is essentially light, the human is filled with charity by participating in the Holy Spirit, who is essentially charity. And as the air becomes like the sun through this participation, the human becomes like God through this participation in charity.[148] Thomas

145. *ST* I.43.3; II-II.24.2. See also *ST* III.1.1 where Thomas states that it belongs to the essence of goodness to communicate itself. Since God is the highest good, he communicates Himself in the highest manner by joining creatures to himself. Cf. *ST* II-II.24.11 which states that the Holy Spirit dwells in us by charity and moves the soul to love God, and also see *SCG* IV.18: The Holy Spirit (as God) dwells in a mind by His substance and makes men good by participation in Himself. Elsewhere Thomas notes that all three members of the Trinity dwell in us, and we dwell in God since God loves us (*SCG* IV.21).

146. See Mary Ann Fatula, "The Holy Spirit and Human Actualization through Love: The Contributions of Aquinas," *Theology Digest* 32, no. 3 (1985): 219–22. Fatula notes that charity is a created participation in the Holy Spirit. She also notes that charity actualizes us as human persons and enlarges our *esse*.

147. *ST* II-II.24.2: Unde caritas non potest neque naturaliter nobis inesse, neque per vires naturales est acquisita, sed per infusionem spiritus sancti, qui est amor patris et filii, cuius participatio in nobis est ipsa caritas creata, sicut supra dictum est.

148. There is a twofold relationship between likeness and charity. On the one hand, likeness causes charity and, on the other hand, as seen here, likeness follows charity since an effect is always like its cause. Likeness causes charity because likeness is a necessary condition for love. See *ST* I-II.27.3 where likeness arises when two things have the same quality either actually or potentially. Actual likeness causes love of friendship while potential likeness causes love of concupiscence. In the case of charity, our likeness with God is the participation in eternal happiness that is essentially in God. (*ST* II-II.26.2). When this happiness is potential it causes hope and when it is actual (even if imperfect on earth) we have charity. Cf. I-II.99.2. See also Eberhard Shockenhoff, "The Theological Virtue of Charity," in *The Ethics of Aquinas*, ed. Stephen Pope, 244–56 (Washington, D.C.: Georgetown

affirms this by stating that the Holy Spirit is the love between the Father and Son and we are made like the Holy Spirit in loving God and love with this love (*SCG* IV.21).[149]

Because charity is a participation in the Holy Spirit as the love between the Father and the Son, it is helpful to comment on the nature of this love to show how through charity a human participates in it. Thomas explains that in God "to love" can be taken essentially and notionally. When it is taken essentially, it means that the Father, the Son, and the Holy Spirit love each other by their essence:[150]

But when the term to love is taken in a notional sense, it means nothing else than to spirate [breathe] love; just as to speak is to produce a word, and to flower is to produce flowers. Therefore, just as a tree is said to be flowering by its flowers, so also the Father is said to be speaking Himself and His creatures by the Word or the Son; and the Father and the Son are said to love each other and us, by the Holy Spirit, or by love proceeding.[151]

Thomas continues in the third response by stating that the Father loves not only the Son but also Himself and all creatures by the Holy Spirit. By participating in the Holy Spirit, humans become like God inasmuch as they share in God's love of Himself and His love for all other creatures. Hence, to the extent that humans participate in the love of God by means of charity, they also love all creatures as God loves them.[152] Thomas explains that God in willing his own goodness wills all things

---

University Press, 2002), 246–47, where Schockenhoff notes that friendship denotes a *"communicatio"* between friends: a possession of a common essential form. The common form between humans and God is God's own beatitude in which humans participate. See also Kieran Conley, *A Theology of Wisdom: A Study of St. Thomas* (Dubuque, Iowa: The Priory Press, 1963), 115–16.

149. *SCG* IV.24. The notion of participation in the Holy Sprit by charity and participation in eternal law also come together because the movement of the world by divine government is especially appropriated to the Holy Spirit since divine government orders the world to the divine goodness and all that is ordered to the divine goodness is ordered on account of the divine love (*CP* I.147).

150. Thomas also speaks of charity as a participation in the divine essence of God. Thomas notes that just as goodness and wisdom are the divine essence itself, so also is charity. And, just as humans are said to be good and wise by means of participation in divine goodness and wisdom, so also "the charity whereby formally we love our neighbor is a participation in divine charity" (Caritas qua formaliter diligimus proximum est quaedam participatio divinae caritatis; *ST* II-II.23.2.1).

151. *ST* I.37.2: Secundum vero quod notionaliter sumitur, sic diligere nihil est aliud quam spirare amorem; sicut dicere est producere verbum, et florere est producere flores. Sicut ergo dicitur arbor florens floribus, ita dicitur pater dicens verbo vel filio, se et creaturam, et pater et filius dicuntur diligentes spiritu sancto, vel amore procedente, et se et nos.

152. God does not love all things equally since He wills a greater good to some things

apart from Himself (*ST* I.19.2.2). Since all things are willed by God on account of the divine goodness, humans in loving the divine goodness also love all things: both inasmuch as they receive their goodness by participating in the divine goodness and as ordered to the divine goodness. Thomas affirms this by noting that there is an order to charity where humans are called to have greater love for things with greater participation in God's goodness and lesser love for things with a lesser participation.[153]

Now among things to be loved, Thomas, following Christ's commandment to love our neighbor, especially emphasizes the necessity of loving our neighbor. Thomas states, "Hence it is clear that it is specifically the same act whereby we love God and whereby we love our neighbor. Consequently, the habit of charity extends not only to love of God, but also to love of neighbor."[154] Humans are therefore required to love their neighbor both on account of their substantial goodness and because they are ordered to the end of attaining God. In other words, because charity causes a unity of affections with God, the human with charity seeks that all humans attain the ultimate end on account of their love of God. Thus, the virtue of charity makes humans like God inasmuch as they participate in God's love for Himself, and through this love, they love all others to the appropriate degree.[155]

Because charity attains God Himself, it is the greatest of the virtues. Thomas notes that the theological virtues are greater than the acquired virtues as having God as their object. However, among the theological

---

than to others (*ST* I.20.3 & 4). Likewise, humans in participating in God's love do not love all things equally but have greater love for things that participate in God's goodness more perfectly. In this way participation in the love of God corresponds to how there are different degrees of participation in God's being and thus likewise in His goodness. Cf. *ST* II-II.23.1.2 where Thomas states that not only do we love our friends but also all who belong to our friends. In this way we love even our enemies who belong to God. Cf. *ST* I.19.2.2 and I.20.2.

153. *ST* II-II.26. The quantity of charity is determined not only by its object (the degree of participation in the goodness of God by the apprehended good) but also by the lover. Hence, since a human is nearer to himself than to his neighbor, he loves himself more than his neighbor, even if his neighbor is closer to God than he is (*ST* II-II.26.4). However, in heaven a human will love a neighbor who is closer to God more than himself (II-II.26.13).

154. Unde manifestum est quod idem specie actus est quo diligitur deus, et quo diligitur proximus. Et propter hoc habitus caritatis non solum se extendit ad dilectionem dei, sed etiam ad dilectionem proximi (*ST* II-II.25.1). Thomas also emphasizes that one must also love oneself and one's body out of charity (25.4 & 5).

155. See *ST* I-II.27.4 where Thomas notes that humans love other things through love of God, but know God through knowledge of other things.

virtues charity is the greatest because it approaches nearer to its object (God) than do faith and hope. Faith and hope by their nature imply a certain separation from their object, "but the love of charity is of that which is already possessed: since the beloved is, in a manner, in the lover, and again, the lover is drawn by affection to union with the beloved."[156]

Thomas further explains how charity is greater than faith by noting that although it is better to know things below humans than to love them, it is better to love things above humans than to know them (*ST* I-II.66.6.1). In other words, although it is better to know the material world than to love it, it is better to love God than to know Him. The reason for this is that something is in something else according to the mode of the one that it is in. In reference to the intellect, because the operation of the intellect consists in the thing understood being in the intellectual subject, that which is known is always known according to the mode of the knower. However, because the will rests in its object, the lover rests in the thing loved. Hence, it is better to know things below humans than to love them, because the thing as known is greater in the soul than it is in itself, while the thing as loved draws the soul to its inferior state of being. But for things above humans, it is better to love them than to know them because through love humans are drawn beyond themselves and into the object loved. Thus, charity, as uniting us to God, is the most excellent of the virtues (*ST* II-II.23.6.1, 66.6.1).

Because charity unites us to God who is end of all human actions, it is also the form of the virtues.[157] In morals, the form of an act is primarily taken from the end. Since charity orders humans to their ultimate end, it is considered to be the form of all the other virtues. Thomas notes:

In morals the form of an act is learned chiefly from the end. The reason of this is that the principle of moral acts is the will, whose object and, in like manner, form are the end. Now the form of an act always follows from a form of the agent. Consequently, in morals, that which gives an act its order to the end, must needs give the act its form also. Now it is evident, in accordance with what has been said, that it is charity which directs the acts of all other virtues to the last end, and which, consequently, also gives the form to all other acts of virtue.[158]

156. Sed amor caritatis est de eo quod iam habetur, est enim amatum quodammodo in amante, et etiam amans per affectum trahitur ad unionem amati (*ST* I-II.66.6; cf. II-II.23.6).

157. Cf. *ST* II-II.27.6 which states, "Now, the end of all human actions and affections is the love of God, whereby principally we attain to our last end" (Finis autem omnium actionum humanarum et affectionum est dei dilectio, per quam maxime attingimus ultimum finem).

158. In moralibus forma actus attenditur principaliter ex parte finis, cuius ratio est quia

Charity by ordering all acts to God fashions all acts of the other virtues into acts of love of God for His own sake. In other words, out of love for God, humans with charity perform acts of the other virtues. Because these actions are performed on account of the humans' love for God, charity is the formal cause of these actions.[159] Thomas gives the example of fortitude formed by charity, "for if someone performs an act of fortitude for the love of God, that act is materially an act of fortitude but formally an act of charity."[160] Because a virtue is considered good if it causes actions ordered to the proper end of a creature and the ultimate end of humans is attaining God, only virtues ordered to the ultimate end by charity are perfect virtues.[161] Thus, charity allows every action to be an act of love of God and hence allows the actions of all virtues to be ordered to eternal happiness.

Since it is through charity that humans reach their supernatural end, they seek to grow in charity.[162] Although the initial habit of charity is

principium moralium actuum est voluntas, cuius obiectum et quasi forma est finis. Semper autem forma actus consequitur formam agentis. Unde oportet quod in moralibus id quod dat actui ordinem ad finem, det ei et formam. Manifestum est autem secundum praedicta quod per caritatem ordinantur actus omnium aliarum virtutum ad ultimum finem. Et secundum hoc ipsa dat formam actibus omnium aliarum virtutum (*ST* II-II.23.8). Cf. I-II.65.2.

159. *ST* II-II.23.8.1 & 3. Thomas in 23.8.3 states that charity is called the mother of the other virtues because by ordering them to the last end it causes good acts through them. See also *ST* I-II.114.4 where Thomas notes that charity as having the last end as its object moves the other virtues to act, because the habit to which the end pertains always commands the habits to which the means pertain. Cf. I-II.9.1; II-II.3.1.3; II-II.23.7. Further insights into why charity orders all acts to their ultimate end can be determined by what has already been said. First, because charity causes a unity of affection between humans and God, all charitable acts are done for God. Secondly, God wills all things on account of His goodness (*ST* I.20.1.3). Hence, to the extent they participate in divine love, humans also will all things on account of God's goodness.

160. . . . si enim aliquis actum fortitudinis exerceat propter dei amorem, actus quidem ille materialiter est fortitudinis, formaliter vero caritatis (I-II.13.1). Cf. *ST* I-II.65.4.1 and III *Sent* 27.2.4C.5 which state that all virtues have a form by participation of an inferior power in a superior power. Hence, an act of temperance can be said to be formed by prudence, charity, and grace. See also M. R. Brennan, *The Intellectual Virtues According to the Philosophy of St. Thomas* (Washington, D.C.: The Catholic University of America Press, 1941), 108–9, who notes that certain virtues are the form of other virtues because in Thomas's ordered universe the perfection of higher virtues overflows to lower ones.

161. Thomas notes that a virtue can be ordered to a true particular good apart from charity and can thus be called a true virtue, but it is not a perfect virtue unless it is ordered by charity (*ST* II-II.23.7).

162. Like all attributes in which a subject can participate, charity can also increase. Thomas notes that charity can increase by means of the subject participating of it more and by the subject being more perfectly moved to its act (*ST* II-II.24.5). For example, Thomas

by infusion alone, once possessed, charity, like other habits, can be increased by like acts of a proper intensity. The acquired virtues increase through like actions because a higher principle (the intellect) causes a like disposition in a lower principle by directing it to act in accord with reason.[163] In the case of charity, the soul is perfected by habitual grace and charity is infused. This infusion allows the soul to be directed by the eternal law through the movement of the Holy Spirit (the higher principle) to freely cause actions in accord with divine nature.[164] Since lower principles become like higher principles when they are directed to act by the higher principle, the soul becomes more like God with each additional charitable action. Hence, although charity is an infused virtue, it can be increased with additional acts of charity. Thomas affirms this truth by saying:

> . . . each act of charity disposes to an increase of charity, insofar as one act of charity makes man more ready to act again according to charity, and this readiness increasing, man breaks out into an act of more fervent love, by which he strives to advance in charity, and then charity is increased in act.[165]

Because charity is a participation in the infinite power of the Holy Spirit, the amount that it can increase is unlimited (*ST* II-II.25.7). Since being united to God by charity is the end to which all humans are ordained, the human with charity seeks to increase his charity by performing charitable acts and striving to grow in charity.

Charity is the most important of the supernatural inclinations that come from the participation of the soul in divine nature through habitual grace. As love of friendship with God, it inclines humans to share in God's actions and intentions and unites humans to God. Since a union of affections with God necessitates love of all others, charity also inclines humans to love all others out of their love God. These inclinations are fulfilled by performing human actions ordered to God by charity by

---

speaks of three degrees of subjects with charity: those just beginning, those progressing in virtue, and those who are perfect (*ST* II-II.24.9).

163. *ST* I-II.51.3; *ST* I-II.5.7; II-II.51.1.2; cf. *DV* 11.1.

164. See *ST* I-II.111.2 on how humans freely cooperate with God in performing actions ordered to the ultimate end.

165. . . . quilibet actus caritatis disponit ad caritatis augmentum, inquantum ex uno actu caritatis homo redditur promptior iterum ad agendum secundum caritatem; et, habilitate crescente, homo prorumpit in actum ferventiorem dilectionis, quo conetur ad caritatis profectum; et tunc caritas augetur in actu (II-II.24.6; Cf. I-II.92.1.1). Keep in mind, because charity has an infinite effect of uniting the soul to God, it must be caused by God alone (*ST* II-II.23.2.3).

means of the infused cardinal virtues (*ST* I-II.19.10; cf. I-II.109.3.1). Charity especially perfects participation in eternal law as governed by it, since
it causes humans to share in God's actions and intentions, and to share in
God's intentions is to participate in eternal law. Further analysis of charity
will show more specifically how charity perfects participation in eternal
law.

The Holy Spirit moves and directs humans as instrumental causes in
accord with their form by means of their natural inclinations. When human nature is perfected by grace, the intellect and the will are supernaturally inclined to freely act in accord with their ultimate end. Through
these supernatural inclinations of the theological virtues, the Holy Spirit
is able to move and direct humans to freely choose actions more in accord with the *ratio* in the mind of God. Analogous to the way that the
natural inclinations are perfected by the acquired virtues to perform human actions more in accord with eternal law, the theological virtues also
perfect the natural inclinations to cause human actions that are more
in accord with the eternal law. Specifically, charity perfects the will to
perform human actions out of love of God as a friend. Since the will is
perfected it can be moved and directed to supernatural actions by the
eternal law.

More specifically, charity perfects participation in eternal law because
when someone loves another as a friend, a union of affection results.
Since a union of affection implies a sharing in the actions and desires of
another, the human with charity seeks to share in God's plan *(ratio)* by
which God governs the universe. Now this plan is the eternal law that orders all creation to its end. Thus, the human with charity yearns to fulfill
God's plan by performing actions ordered to the end of eternal happiness
and helping to move others to these acts.[166] In other words, although all
people are moved by eternal law and thus participate in it, humans with
charity are more perfectly moved because charity by its essence causes
them to supernaturally yearn to share in God's plan.[167] Through charity

166. Thomas notes that there are two ways a creature becomes like God's goodness as
ordered by divine governance. First, since God is good, the creature becomes good in being. Second, because God is the cause of goodness in others, the creature moves others to
the good (*ST* I.103.4).

167. Thomas states that substantial union is the cause of love, the union of affection
is essentially love, and real union is a result of love (*ST* I-II.28.1.2). Hence, in the case of
loving God, the substantial union of eternal happiness causes charity. The habitual inclination to supernaturally participate in eternal law is charity, and the result of this union is real
union with God.

humans love the eternal law; they will it to the extent that they know it, and become one with it by supernaturally acting in accord with it. Just as a human subject who loves his governor as a friend makes the governor's end his end and will follow the command of the governor to achieve this end, so also a human with charity follows the eternal law.

Charity increases participation in eternal law because it causes the human to fulfill God's plan. As a human increases in charity, his inclination to act in conformity with the divine will increases, allowing his acts to be more perfectly formed by the Holy Spirit. Thus, Thomas states, "no virtue has so great an inclination to its act as does charity, nor does any virtue perform its act with such pleasure."[168]

Although the natural inclinations do not perfect participation in eternal law but simply cause this participation, the theological virtues, which are analogous to the natural inclinations, perfect participation in eternal law by causing a completely different type of participation: supernatural participation. Although they are analogous to the natural inclinations, they are also virtues, and hence like the acquired virtues they also determine humans to particular types of actions and perfect the intellect and the will to perform actions ordered to the ultimate end of happiness. Specifically, faith, hope, and charity determine humans to actions that are in accord with a supernatural end. This end is known through faith, desired through hope, and charity causes actions to be ordered to this end. Once the intellect perfected by faith knows God as the source of eternal happiness, the will perfected by hope loves God on account of this good that it can receive. This imperfect love of hope becomes the perfect love of charity, since on account of hope in the reward, humans begin to love God as a friend (*ST* II-II.17.8). However, once God is loved as a friend, humans seek to know God even more, since a union of affections is dependent upon knowledge of God and his eternal law. Hence, charity perfects faith, which causes humans to have a greater knowledge of eternal law through the divine law. Likewise, since a union of affections results in real union, humans with charity seek the reward of being united with God for all eternity with greater earnestness since friends seek to be together. Hence, charity also perfects hope.

---

168. . . . nulla virtus habet tantam inclinationem ad suum actum sicut caritas, nec aliqua ita delectabiliter operatur (*ST* II-II.23.2; Cf. I-II.109.3.1). See also I-II.109.3.3 where Thomas states that charity is the supreme of all loves in respect to intensity, motive, and mode.

The Infused Cardinal Virtues

Just as the natural inclinations cause good actions by means of the acquired virtues, the theological virtues likewise cause good actions by means of the infused cardinal virtues (*ST* I-II.63.3). Through charity, humans are able to order their actions to their ultimate end. However, these actions must still be ordered to a proximate end that is in accord with the ultimate end (*ST* I-II.65.3). Thomas argues:

> Consequently, in order for a human to work well in things referred to the end, he needs not only a virtue disposing him well to the end, but also those virtues which dispose him well to whatever is referred to the end: for the virtue which regards the end is the chief and moving principle in respect of those things that are referred to the end. Therefore it is necessary to have the moral virtues together with charity.[169]

The agent must be well disposed not only to the end, but also to the particular goods that are ordered to this end. Charity inclines the human to the ultimate end, while the infused intellectual and moral virtues incline the human to those acts that are ordered to the end.

These virtues must also be infused into the human because effects must be proportionate to their principles. Since these virtues cause supernatural acts, they must be infused by God.[170] These infused virtues include any virtue that can be ordered to the ultimate end of God by charity. In particular they refer to the cardinal virtues, which work together in the performance of any perfect act (*ST* I-II.58.4 & 5, 65.1; cf. 61.3). Thus, charity works through the infused cardinal virtues in order to cause acts proportionate to eternal happiness.

The infused cardinal virtues differ in species from the acquired virtues because whereas the acquired virtues are in accord with natural human reason, the infused virtues are in accord with the divine law (*ST* I-II.63.4). Aquinas notes:

169. *ST* I-II.65.3.1: Unde oportet ad hoc quod homo bene operetur in his quae sunt ad finem, quod non solum habeat virtutem qua bene se habeat circa finem, sed etiam virtutes quibus bene se habeat circa ea quae sunt ad finem, nam virtus quae est circa finem, se habet ut principalis et motiva respectu earum quae sunt ad finem. Et ideo cum caritate necesse est etiam habere alias virtutes morales. Cf. *De Virtutibus in communi* art. 12.

170. *ST* I-II.63.3. The infused moral and intellectual virtues have the same relation to the theological virtues as the moral and intellectual virtues have to the natural inclinations. Just as the natural inclinations cause good acts by means of the acquired virtues, so also the supernatural inclinations of the theological virtues cause good acts by means of the infused moral and intellectual virtues.

the Philosopher says (*Polit.* iii.3) that citizens have diverse virtues according as they are well directed to diverse forms of government. In the same way, too, those infused moral virtues, whereby men behave well in respect of their being fellow-citizens with the saints and of the household of God [Eph 2:19], differ from the acquired virtues, whereby man behaves well in respect of human affairs.[171]

Whereas the acquired virtues are directed by law in the realm of human affairs (the natural and the human law), the infused cardinal virtues are directed by the divine law. Because the divine law is the highest participation in the eternal law, the infused cardinal virtues perfect human participation in the eternal law as moved and governed by it.

To better understand how the infused virtues perfect this participation in the eternal law, knowledge of a distinction that Thomas makes between formal and material conformity with God's will is helpful (*ST* I-II.19.10). In order to explain the moral goodness or evil of a human act, Thomas makes a distinction between the form of the act (the interior act) and the matter of the act (the exterior act).[172] Thomas states:

Now in a voluntary action, there is found to be a twofold action: namely, the interior action of the will and the exterior action. Each of these actions has its own object. Properly speaking, the end is the object of the interior voluntary act: whereas that which the exterior act is concerned with is its object. . . . Now that which is on the part of the will is formal in regard to that which is on the part of the external action: because the will uses the members to act as instruments; and exterior actions do not even have the character of morality except to the extent they are voluntary. Consequently, the species of a human act is considered formally with regard to the end, but materially with regard to the object of the external action.[173]

171. *ST* I-II.63.4: dicit philosophus, in III polit., quod diversae sunt virtutes civium, secundum quod bene se habent ad diversas politias. Et per hunc etiam modum differunt specie virtutes morales infusae, per quas homines bene se habent in ordine ad hoc quod sint cives sanctorum et domestici dei; et aliae virtutes acquisitae, secundum quas homo se bene habet in ordine ad res humanas.

172. This distinction is made in *ST* I-II.18 and then 19 analyzes the interior act and 20 analyzes the exterior act.

173. *ST* I-II.18.6: In actu autem voluntario invenitur duplex actus, scilicet actus interior voluntatis, et actus exterior, et uterque horum actuum habet suum obiectum. Finis autem proprie est obiectum interioris actus voluntarii, id autem circa quod est actio exterior, est obiectum eius. . . . Ita autem quod est ex parte voluntatis, se habet ut formale ad id quod est ex parte exterioris actus, quia voluntas utitur membris ad agendum, sicut instrumentis; neque actus exteriores habent rationem moralitatis, nisi inquantum sunt voluntarii. Et ideo actus humani species formaliter consideratur secundum finem, materialiter autem secundum obiectum exterioris actus.

The interior action is that which takes place within the soul; it is that which a person is rationally choosing to do. The external action is that which the will moves the body to perform. Analogous to the way a substantial form gives form to matter, the interior act of the soul gives form to the "matter" of the exterior act. And just as there is only one individual composed of form and matter, there is only one human action composed of an interior and exterior act.

Although these actions are parts of a single human action, this distinction is helpful because sometimes the object of the interior action does not correspond to the object of the exterior action. Thomas gives the example of taking from others in order to give alms (*ST* I-II.18.7). In the case of involuntary ignorance,[174] someone might choose to acquire the money to give alms by stealing from others. Because this person has involuntary ignorance, he actually believes that the chosen action of stealing is in conformity with the end of helping the poor and is hence a good action. He thus believes that he is doing a good thing by stealing to help the poor. In this case, the interior object is good,[175] but the exterior object is evil. Thomas explains,

> The object of the exterior object can stand in a twofold relation to the end of the will: first, as being of itself ordered thereto; thus to fight well is of itself ordered to victory; secondly, as being ordered thereto accidentally; thus to take what belongs to another is ordered accidentally to the giving of alms.[176]

Because the action of taking from another is only accidentally ordered to the giving of alms and not essentially ordered to it, the material object of the act is evil, even though the formal object is good.[177]

---

174. Thomas distinguishes between involuntary ignorance and voluntary ignorance. Involuntary ignorance excuses the will of evil when the person performs an evil exterior action while voluntary ignorance does not excuse it from evil (*ST* I-II.19.6, 20.4; cf. 19.5).

175. Although closely related, this distinction between the objects of the interior and the exterior act is not the same as the distinction between what is intended and what is chosen. Both intention and choice take place within the interior act. Hence, in this example of stealing to help the poor, the intellect involuntarily errs either in its understanding of the law or in its application of the law. Either way it presents what it has wrongly determined to be a good to the will and the will chooses it. Cf. *ST* I-II.19.7 where Thomas notes that because the reason proposes something to the will as either good or evil based on its apprehension of it, the will is dependent upon the reason in its choice.

176. *ST* I-II.18.7: obiectum exterioris actus dupliciter potest se habere ad finem voluntatis, uno modo, sicut per se ordinatum ad ipsum, sicut bene pugnare per se ordinatur ad victoriam; alio modo, per accidens, sicut accipere rem alienam per accidens ordinatur ad dandum eleemosynam.

177. However, since all parts of an act must be good for it to be called good, the act in itself is still evil.

Just as the intellect must be in conformity with eternal law in order for it to determine the proper actions (*ST* I-II.19.4), the will must be in conformity with the divine will in order to choose the proper actions. This action of stealing to give alms is formally in conformity with the divine will since the object of the interior action is good, but it is not materially in conformity with the divine will.[178]

Because the will is only able to act upon what the reason proposes, and the reason can be involuntarily mistaken, in order to be good, humans are only required to perform actions that are formally in conformity with the divine will and not materially (*ST* I-II.19.10). In other words, humans must always do what they think is God's will, even if it is not actually God's will. Nonetheless, it is more perfect that someone's will is both materially and formally in conformity with the divine will.[179] Since the eternal law directs humans to every action they perform, when a human will is materially in conformity with the eternal law, the human action participates more perfectly in the eternal law.

The cardinal virtues, both acquired and infused, allow the will to not only be in formal conformity with the divine will, but also in material conformity. I will briefly show how the acquired virtues cause material conformity before going on to the task at hand: showing how the infused cardinal virtues perfect participation in eternal law. The natural inclinations automatically cause a certain formal conformity between the divine will and the human will because humans are naturally inclined to will the good and God wills His own goodness.[180] However, the will

178. Most of the time that the human will is not materially in conformity with the divine will but is formally in conformity with it, the objects of the interior and the exterior actions are not this extreme. Usually it is a case where the object of both the interior and the exterior are good, only the exterior action is not what God wills for the human to do at that time. For example, suppose someone chooses to get married out of love for God when God's will is for him to be a priest. Although getting married is a good action, this action would not be the highest mode of participation in the eternal law for him.

179. See *ST* I-II.20.4 where Thomas states that something is not perfect unless it reaches its end. He continues by stating, "Wherefore the will is not perfect, unless it be such that, given the opportunity, it realizes the operation. But if this proves impossible, as long as the will is perfect, so as to realize the operation if it could; the lack of perfection derived from the external action is simply involuntary" (Unde non est perfecta voluntas, nisi sit talis quae, opportunitate data, operetur. Si vero possibilitas desit, voluntate existente perfecta, ut operaretur si posset; defectus perfectionis quae est ex actu exteriori, est simpliciter involuntarium).

180. *ST* I-II.19.10. See also Fabro, *La nozione*, 291–92. Fabro notes that the appetite is naturally right in respect to the ultimate end, for all desire happiness. However, in respect to the particular end the appetite must be determined by reason, so that the will participates in reason and is rational by participation.

is only able to perfect formal conformity through justice and acquire a natural material conformity to the divine will by means of the other acquired virtues. The acquired virtues perfect the intellect and appetite to determine and choose a particular good that is essentially ordered to natural happiness. In other words, by the acquired virtues humans can attain a certain material conformity with the divine will inasmuch as their acts are truly ordered to God whom they are naturally inclined to know and love.

In reference to the infused virtues, the will has supernatural formal conformity to the divine will by means of the virtue of charity (*ST* I-II.19.10; II-II.44.6). As the form of the virtues, charity by its essence causes humans to formally order all of their actions to God. In other words, humans with charity always do what they think is ordered to the end of obtaining God. Nonetheless, although by charity humans love God as He is, faith does not allow them to know God as He is.[181] Thus, humans do not perfectly know the eternal law and human reason may be wrong as to the relation of a particular good to the universal good, thereby causing the material action to be only accidentally ordered to the ultimate end.[182] In order to ensure that the actions are not only formally in conformity with the divine will, but also materially in conformity, the infused cardinal virtues and the gifts of the Holy Spirit are necessary.[183]

Just as the natural inclinations cause acts that are materially in conformity with the natural law by means of the acquired virtues, so also

181. Although on earth knowledge of God's will is always imperfect, in heaven the light of glory allows humans to not only formally will the good that God wills, but also to materially will it. See *ST* I-II.19.10.1; cf. I.62.8.1. Greater knowledge of eternal law perfects charity, so that the will can be in material conformity with the divine will. This is why Thomas places wisdom as the gift of the Holy Spirit that perfects charity. See the next chapter for a fuller explanation. Cf. *ST* II-II.25.7 where Thomas notes that the quantity of charity in glory is incomparable to charity now because it follows the open vision of God. However, keep in mind that the one with greater charity will see God more perfectly because he will receive a greater participation of the light of glory due to greater desire to see God (*ST* I.12.6).

182. Cf. *De Virtutibus in communi* art. 12.12 where Thomas states that just as in speculative matters there are principles and conclusion, in actions there are ends and means. Perfect knowledge for man requires also knowledge of conclusions. Likewise in actions there must be other virtues beyond the theological virtues ordering humans to the proper means. Since all the powers of the soul are involved in causing an action, not only must the intellect be perfected but also the appetitive powers, since rectitude in the appetitive powers is necessary for the intellect to work correctly (cf. *ST* I-II.58.5).

183. The human on earth is only bound to formal conformity with the divine will which is a result of charity (*ST* I-II.19.10). Nonetheless, because charity is a union of affection, the human with charity will also seek material conformity with the divine will and hence more perfect knowledge of the eternal law.

charity is able to cause acts that are supernaturally in material conformity with the divine law by means of the infused cardinal virtues. The infused cardinal virtues ensure that the particular end chosen is in conformity with the universal good intended by charity. Specifically, infused prudence, like acquired prudence, perfects the intellect to find the proper means to the end. However, unlike acquired prudence, infused prudence takes counsel and judges in accord with the divine law and not simply with the natural law.[184] By judging in accord with the divine law that orders humans to every particular action, infused prudence ensures that the action chosen is always essentially ordered to the ultimate end and not only accidentally.

Since the appetitive powers are good to the extent that they participate in reason, the infused moral virtues also increase material conformity by perfecting the appetitive powers to participate in reason. Infused justice perfects the will by inclining it to particular actions of giving God and neighbor their due that are in accord with the ultimate end. However, unlike acquired justice, it inclines the will to God and neighbor as loved through charity.[185] Finally, like acquired temperance and fortitude, which conform the passions to reason, infused temperance and fortitude also conform the passions to reason, only to divine reason as known through the divine law. Thus, through the infused virtues there is a certain material conformity between the human and divine will over and above the formal conformity caused by charity (*ST* II-II.44.6).

The perfection of these powers allows the Holy Spirit to direct and move the soul to freely choose particular goods in conformity with the eternal law as well as to direct the soul to the universal good as loved by charity. Specifically, once a good end is intended out of charity, infused prudence commands an act that is in conformity with divine law as known through revelation.[186] Just as acquired prudence cannot exist without the moral virtues, infused prudence cannot exist without the infused moral virtues that perfect the appetite to tend to the end and means determined by the intellect (*ST* I-II.58.5, 63.3; II-II.23.2). Conse-

---

184. Cf. II-II.52.2. See chapter 4 for an extended treatment of infused prudence, including information on why prudence and faith are the only infused intellectual virtues.

185. See Waddel, *Primacy*, 122. Waddel states that the nearer we are to God in goodness (through charity), the more we come to understand what God sees a virtue to be. For example, justice infused by charity moves toward forgiveness and generosity beyond that of acquired justice. Cf. Waddel, *Primacy*, 127–29.

186. See chapter 4 for how supernatural cognitive participation in eternal law allows human actions to not only be ordered to the divine good formally, but also materially.

quently, to the extent that humans have the infused virtues, the reason is able to supernaturally participate in the eternal law in determining a particular action as ordered to the ultimate end and the appetite is also able to supernaturally participate in the eternal law through this reason.[187]

The Gifts of the Holy Spirit

Not only are the infused cardinal virtues necessary so that all particular actions are essentially ordained to the ultimate end, the gifts of the Holy Spirit are also necessary. These gifts perfect the soul to participate even more perfectly than by the infused virtues alone. Although it would seem that since the infused cardinal virtues perfect the human soul to be in material conformity with the divine will there would be no need for further perfections, Thomas explains that in the case of supernatural actions further perfections are necessary. He states that the intellect is perfected by God in two ways: by the natural light of reason and by a supernatural light (the theological virtues). Although the supernatural light is a greater perfection, the natural light is possessed in a more perfect manner because it is connatural to us. When something possesses a form perfectly, it can be moved by God to act by its own power. However, because the supernatural light is possessed imperfectly, humans cannot perform acts in accord with it by their own power. Hence, the additional movement of the Holy Spirit is necessary.[188] However, in order to be moved by this additional movement, humans must be made proportionate to this movement by means of a habitual disposition whereby they are disposed to be easily and promptly moved, because the more perfect the mover, the more perfect must be the disposition of the one moved:

Consequently, man needs yet higher perfections, whereby he may be disposed to that to which he is divinely moved. These perfections are called gifts, not only because they are infused by God, but also because in accord with them a human is disposed so as to be rendered easily moveable by Divine inspiration . . .[189]

187. See Jenkins, 159. Jenkins notes that just as the acquired virtues allow one to follow the light of reason, the infused virtues allow reason to follow the higher light of grace. He then notes that a higher nature directs a lower nature by participation. Thus, the passions participate in reason which participates in God through grace.

188. (*ST* I-II.68.2). Recall from the section on grace above that not only is habitual grace necessary to perfect the form of the human agent, God must also supernaturally move humans. This movement is the movement of the Holy Spirit.

189. *ST* I-II.68.1: Oportet igitur inesse homini altiores perfections, secundum quas sit dispositus ad hoc quod divinitus moveatur. Et istae perfectiones vocantur dona, non solum

Gifts are superadded habits that perfect humans so that they can be easily and promptly moved by the Holy Spirit to perform acts in accord with the end of eternal happiness.[190]

The gifts of the Holy Spirit aid the theological virtues by perfecting the powers of the soul to be moved by the Holy Spirit. Thomas compares the role of the gifts to that of the moral virtues in aiding the intellectual virtues. He states, "the gifts are habits perfecting man so that he is ready to follow the impulse of the Holy Spirit, even as the moral virtues perfect the appetitive powers so that they obey the reason."[191] Just as the moral virtues perfect the appetitive powers to be directed and moved easily and promptly by the intellect, the gifts of the Holy Spirit perfect all of the powers of the soul to be directed and moved easily and promptly by the Holy Spirit (*ST* I-II.68.3). By making the soul more amenable to the promptings of the Holy Spirit, the gifts are ordained to the perfection of the theological virtues which cause actions that are ordered to the ultimate end.[192]

The gifts of the Holy Spirit perfect participation in eternal law because they perfect the powers of the soul so that a human can be more

---

quia infunduntur a deo; sed quia secundum ea homo disponitur ut efficiatur prompte mobilis ab inspiratione divina. . . . A variety of scholars following John of St. Thomas, *The Gifts of the Holy Spirit* (New York: Sheed & Ward, 1951), 33–36, explain that although the infused virtues are supernatural in origin, they are subject to human reason, which even when perfected by faith and infused prudence, is still subject to ignorance and error. Hence, the gifts of the Holy Spirit are necessary so that humans can be moved directly by the Holy Spirit. For as Dominic Hughes and Mark Egan in their introduction to the text by John of St. Thomas state, only God can fully know how to attain the end of knowing and loving Him. Only the Holy Spirit knows all the pathways and obstacles. Hence the gifts are given to dispose humans to immediate direction by the Holy Spirit (16). See also Fabro, *La Nozione . . .* , 305–6; Jordan Aumann, "Mystical Experience, the Infused Virtues and the Gifts," *Angelicum* 58 (1981): 38–39; Yves Congar, *I Believe in the Holy Spirit*, vol. 2 (New York: Seabury, 1983), 135–36; and Pinckaers, *Morality*, 88.

190. *ST* I-II.68.3; cf. *SCG* IV.21. See John of St. Thomas, *The Gifts . . .* , 28. John notes that the gifts of the Holy Spirit are interior dispositions making man free and unimpeded in operation. Since it is necessary that the movement of the Holy Spirit does not move the will by violence but by actuating its inclination, the gifts of the Holy Spirit must be habits inherent in the soul.

191. *ST* I-II.68.4: dona sunt quidam habitus perficientes hominem ad hoc quod prompte sequatur instinctum spiritus sancti, sicut virtutes morales perficiunt vires appetitivas ad obediendum rationi.

192. *ST* II-II.9.1.3. Cf. *ST* I.68.8: "Wherefore as the intellectual virtues are more excellent than the moral virtues and regulate them, so the theological virtues are more excellent than the gifts of the Holy Spirit and regulate them" (Unde sicut virtutes intellectuales praeferuntur virtutibus moralibus, et regulant eas; ita virtutes theologicae praeferuntur donis spiritus sancti et regulant ea).

easily and promptly directed in accord with the eternal law by the Holy Spirit. The key point is that because of the limitations of human nature (even when perfected by grace), humans need to be directed by God in an even more perfect way.[193] God always knows in every situation which action conforms most perfectly to the eternal law and has the power to cause the action. Hence, through the gifts of the Holy Spirit humans are able to participate in this divine knowledge and power in the highest possible mode. This participation causes them to have the most perfect freedom that can be obtained on earth since they are now free to perform actions that are most in conformity with their ultimate end.[194]

Since all the powers of the soul must be perfected to perform a good act, Thomas places a gift (or gifts) in every power of the soul. Thomas notes that the gifts of understanding, knowledge, wisdom, and counsel perfect the intellect; while piety, fortitude, and fear of the Lord perfect the appetitive powers.[195] Thus, just as the infused intellectual virtues perfect the reason to know which acts to perform to be in material conformity with eternal law, the gifts perfect the intellect beyond the power of human reason to know more perfectly which acts are well ordered to the ultimate end.[196] And just as the infused moral virtues perfect the appetitive powers of the soul to follow the guidance of reason, so also the gifts perfect these powers to follow the reason perfected by the gifts. Thus, the gifts perfect humans to be directed and moved by the Holy Spirit to perform acts that are ordered to the ultimate act of happiness and ultimately the works of the gifts (along with the virtues) cause humans to perform supernatural actions of happiness even here on earth.[197] Thus, the gifts act as additional forms perfecting the ability of humans to be directed by the Holy Spirit and hence perfect participation in eternal law.[198]

193. Thomas notes that these gifts are perfections that are directly infused by God over and above the infused virtues (*ST* I-II.68.1).

194. See Sherwin, *By Knowledge and By Love*, 165–66. Cf. *Super Romanos* 8.3.

195. *ST* I-II.68.4. This list in I-II.68.4 will be altered slightly in presentation of the gifts in the *Secunda Secundae*. There, Thomas places a gift with each virtue to aid the corresponding power in following the prompting of the Holy Spirit. Understanding and knowledge aid the virtue of faith. Fear of the Lord aids hope. Wisdom aids charity. Counsel aids prudence. Piety aids justice. Fortitude aids fortitude. No corresponding gift is placed with temperance.

196. I-II.68.3; cf. 68.5.1; II-II.8.4.1. The gift of wisdom that perfects charity especially increases material conformity with the divine will by allowing the intellect to judge the action to be in accord with the eternal law. See chapter four on specifically how the gifts of understanding, knowledge, wisdom, and counsel perfect the intellect.

197. *ST* I-II.69.2. This question on the beatitudes (69) immediately follows the question on the gifts because the gifts lead to acts of happiness.

198. See Rolando Arjonillo, "Sanctity, Divine Filiation, Sequela Christi, and Virtue in

CONCLUSION

The notion of participation allows Thomas to explain how all actions can be caused by the eternal law and yet some actions are more in conformity with it than are others. All human actions participate in the eternal law inasmuch as the natural inclinations cause human actions ordered to their natural end. However, a greater participation results when the natural inclinations are perfected by the acquired virtues, allowing humans to more easily and promptly perform actions that are in accord with their supernatural end.

The notion of participation is especially essential in explaining how humans can perform supernatural actions. This notion explains (without violating the principle that all things act in accord with their mode) how humans can perform these actions because their nature participates in divine nature through grace. Through grace humans are able to participate in the eternal law in a manner beyond that of their natural potency.

Just as the eternal law directs humans to their natural end by means of the natural inclinations, the eternal law moves humans with grace to their supernatural end through the theological virtues. The theological virtue of faith allows humans to apprehend God as the source and end of eternal happiness and charity allows humans to love God as He is. This love causes the other virtues to be ordered to God and hence cause a formal conformity between the human will and the divine will. In addition to this formal conformity, the infused moral and intellectual virtues cause a material conformity with the divine will and the gifts of the Holy Spirit perfect this material conformity. Humans most perfectly participate in the eternal law when their actions are both formally and materially in conformity with the divine will since these actions are most perfectly ordered to their ultimate end of eternal happiness.

Fundamental Moral Theology. Apropos of a Recent Book, *Scelti in cristo per essere santi*," *Annales Theologici* 14 (2000): 519 and 531. Arjonillo states that perfect participation in eternal law takes place in a Christian when a person through the virtues and the gifts of the Holy Spirit is able to individualize and realize in every situation the way of relating himself with God, himself, and others. Cf. E. Colom and A. Rodriguez-Luno, *Scelti in Cristo per Essere Santi* (Rome: Apollinare Studi, 1999), 241.

CHAPTER 4

Cognitive Participation

ALL CREATURES ARE DIRECTED by God to their particular actions, but what is distinct about humans is that they also freely direct themselves due to their ability to understand and reason.[1] Unlike irrational creatures that are solely directed by another to an end, humans are masters of their own actions as knowing the end and freely directing themselves to it (*ST* I-II.1.2). Thomas refers to these self-directed actions as human actions because they are proper to man as man: freely chosen by the will which is determined by reason (*ST* I-II.1 & 2). In contrast to human actions, Thomas refers to actions that are not rationally chosen as acts of a human (*ST* I-II.1 & 2). For example, humans do not rationally choose to sleepwalk or to digest their food. Many creatures besides humans can perform these latter types of actions, but only humans can perform human actions.[2] Only by means of these acts that are rationally chosen do humans grow in maturity and perfection as human beings.

This ability of humans to rationally direct themselves to an end, at

---

1. *ST* I.76.1, 77.3; *ST* I.75.5 and I-II.1.1 and 2. Thomas makes a distinction between the ability to know individuals and the ability to know universals. Whereas all things with the ability to sense things can know individuals, only the intellectual soul knows a thing in its nature absolutely (*ST* I.75.5).

2. For Thomas, rationality defines an act as human. However, today, many people think that individuality first and foremost defines a human agent. Thus, Thomas makes no sense to them since they hold that since everything they do is their own action, everything they do is a human act.

first glance, can appear to make humans autonomous in the sense that they are independent from God.[3] However, rationality does not make humans independent from God, but rather allows humans to rationally participate in divine direction. Human reason, like all created realities, is what it is because of its relation to its divine cause. Because all effects participate in their cause, human reason has a divine foundation: it exists by participation in God's own knowledge and grows by greater participation in this knowledge. It is only because humans participate in God's knowledge that they are able to direct themselves as human agents.[4]

The eternal law is God's knowledge that directs creation to its proper end. Hence, when humans rationally direct themselves to their end, their reason participates in the eternal law, not just as moved and directed like all other creatures but as directing themselves and others through a certain knowledge of the eternal law.[5] In other words, owing to the fact that humans are rational, humans participate in the eternal law in a specific manner in addition to the more universal form of participation common to all creatures. Thomas refers to this specific manner of participation as cognitive participation (*ST* I-II.93.5 & 6).

Cognitive participation in the eternal law has many similarities to participation as moved and governed. A few of these similarities are: First, every human action participates in the eternal law in both ways (as moved and governed and cognitively). If an action is human, it must be rational, and therefore in every human action humans are not only directed by the eternal law but also have a certain knowledge of it (Cf. *ST* I.115.4.2).

3. See Chapter Five for a description of a type of autonomy held by many people today that is in contrast to the notion of participation in eternal law.

4. Cf. *ST* I.103.5.3 where Thomas notes that rational creatures govern themselves by their intellect and will. Both of these powers must be further governed and perfected by the divine intellect and will. Cf. II-II.52.2.

5. *SCG* III.113; *ST* I.103.5.2; I-II.93.5 & 6; II-II.47.12; *Ioan* I.3. The adjective "certain," which modifies knowledge, shows that although the knowledge is actual knowledge of the eternal law, it is limited and incomplete (*ST* I-II.93.2). Cf. I-II.91.2 where Thomas notes that something is ruled and measured as participating in the rule and measure. Since all are subject to divine providence and are thus ruled and measured by eternal law, all things participate in eternal law. However, rational creatures are subject to divine providence in a most excellent way as participating in it by being provident for themselves and others. This participation whereby the natural reason discerns what is good and what is evil is the natural law, which is an imprint of the divine light. Thomas elsewhere explains that humans are able to rule themselves because flowing from their natural inclination to know things are many intelligible forms within the intellect. Since some inclination follows every form, rational creatures have, in addition to their natural inclination to seek the good apprehended by reason, a variety of rational inclinations allowing them to choose freely a variety of possible actions (*ST* I.47.1, 80.1, 83.1).

Second, in both modes there are different degrees of perfection of participation. In both modes sin reduces the degree of participation while natural virtue increases the degree of participation. And, over and above this natural perfection in both modes, there is a supernatural participation. Thomas notes:

Both modes [of participation in eternal law], however, are imperfect and to a certain extent destroyed in the wicked, because in them the natural inclination to virtue is corrupted by vicious habits, and, moreover, the natural knowledge of good is darkened by passions and habits of sin. But in the good both modes [of participation] are found more perfect, because in them, besides the natural knowledge of good, there is the superadded knowledge of faith and wisdom; and above the natural inclination to the good, there is the superadded interior movement of grace and virtue.[6]

Cognitive participation mirrors participation by a principle of motion in that for both kinds all humans participate in the eternal law, and also for both the wicked participate imperfectly while the good are perfected both naturally and supernaturally. In the case of cognitive participation, the natural perfection is from the natural knowledge of the good and the supernatural participation is by faith and the Holy Spirit's gift of wisdom.[7]

---

6. *ST* I-II.93.6: Uterque tamen modus imperfectus quidem est, et quodammodo corruptus, in malis; in quibus et inclinatio naturalis ad virtutem depravatur per habitum vitiosum; et iterum ipsa naturalis cognitio boni in eis obtenebratur per passiones et habitus peccatorum. In bonis autem uterque modus invenitur perfectior, quia et supra cognitionem naturalem boni, superadditur eis cognitio fidei et sapientiae; et supra naturalem inclinationem ad bonum, superadditur eis interius motivum gratiae et virtutis.

7. A parallel passage shows that Thomas is here (*ST* I-II.93.6) referring to infused wisdom and not to natural wisdom. Thomas in his commentary on Boethius' *DT* 1.2 explains that because humans only know things abstracted from sensible things and God is disproportionate to His effects (created forms), humans cannot know God's essence. However, Thomas then tells his readers three ways that knowledge of God on earth can be increased: by knowing better his effectiveness in producing things, by knowing more noble effects (they have a greater likeness to God), and by knowing that he is more unlike His effects than like them. However, Thomas then notes that over and above these natural ways of knowing God, "the human mind is greatly assisted when its natural light is strengthened by a new illumination: namely, the light of *faith* and that of the *gifts of wisdom* and understanding, by which the mind is elevated above itself in contemplation, inasmuch as it knows God to be above anything which it naturally apprehends" (maxime iuvatur mens humana, cum lumen eius naturale nova illustratione confortatur; sicut est lumen fidei et doni sapientiae et intellectus, per quod mens in contemplatione supra se elevari dicitur, in quantum cognoscit deum esse supra omne id, quod naturaliter comprehendit). I added the emphasis in the English translation to show the parallel of this passage to *ST* I-II.93.6. Cf. *ST* II-II.113.4.2 and II-II.19.7.

Third, in both modes of participation humans are ordered to their proper end. Since the eternal law directs all creation to its end, by cognitively participating in the eternal law humans are able to direct themselves in accord with divine wisdom. The more perfect this form of participation, the closer humans are to their ultimate end.

Cognitive participation is distinct from participation as moved and governed because in this mode of participation humans have genuine (although limited) knowledge of the eternal law. Cognitive participation and the particular ways that it is increased is the subject of this chapter. I will follow a format similar to chapter three by beginning with the participation of the intellect's natural act of knowing in eternal law, and then I will show how the acquired intellectual virtues perfect it, and finally I will show how faith and the gifts of the Holy Spirit supernaturally perfect cognitive participation.

THE INTELLECTUAL ACT AS COGNITIVELY PARTICIPATING IN ETERNAL LAW

Thomas notes that all knowledge is a participation in the divine intellect (*ST* I.12.11.3; I-II.110.4). He states, "For every knowledge of truth radiates from and participates in the eternal law, which is the unchangeable truth."[8] To understand how human knowledge participates in divine knowledge, it is necessary to briefly analyze the divine intellect. Unlike in humans where there is a difference between the act of understanding, the object understood, and the intelligible species by which the object is understood, in God all three of these are identical. Thomas notes:

Since His essence itself is also His intelligible species, it necessarily follows that His act of understanding must be His essence and His *esse*. Thus it follows from all the foregoing that in God, intellect, the object understood, the intelligible species, and His act of understanding are entirely one and the same.[9]

Analogously to how a created intellect understands a thing by means of an intelligible species, God as the act of understanding understands Him-

8. *ST* I-II.93.2: Omnis enim cognitio veritatis est quaedam irradiatio et participatio legis aeternae, quae est veritas incommutabilis. . . .

9. *ST* I.14.4: Unde, cum ipsa sua essentia sit etiam species intelligibilis, ut dictum est, ex necessitate sequitur quod ipsum eius intelligere sit eius essentia et eius esse. Et sic patet ex omnibus praemissis quod in deo intellectus, et id quod intelligitur, et species intelligibilis, et ipsum intelligere, sunt omnino unum et idem. Cf. *ST* I.14.2 which states that since the intelligible species itself is the divine intellect, God understands Himself through Himself.

self by means of Himself. God is essentially the intellectual power, the object understood, and the act of understanding.

Thomas in the next article (12.5) concludes that because God's *esse* is His act of understanding, then He must understand Himself perfectly and that His perfect self-understanding includes a perfect understanding of all that He causes (as well as what He could cause). Thus, God knows all other things by knowing Himself inasmuch as all His effects are in His essence in an intelligible mode, since all things are in something according to the mode of that in which it is in.

Humans likewise have an act of understanding, an object that they understand, and the power to understand. However, humans have all of these things by participation in the divine intellect; whereas God is them essentially (*ST* I.105.3).

HUMAN PARTICIPATION IN DIVINE KNOWLEDGE

When humans understand, God is the both the first efficient and first exemplary cause of the act of human understanding. He is the efficient cause because He gives humans the intellectual power to understand (the light of reason) and He is the exemplary cause because He gives humans the intelligible forms by which they understand (*ST* I.105.3). Since all effects participate in their cause, the human act of understanding participates in the divine intellect in both of these ways (*ST* I.14.8.3, 84.5). In reference to divine efficient causality, the light (power) of the human intellect participates in God who is the divine light (the intellectual power) of His own act (*ST* I.89.1). In reference to divine exemplary causality, the intelligible species through which humans understand participate in God who is the object of His own act of understanding (*ST* I.84.5). Since God causes the act of human understanding by bestowing the participated light and forms, the act of human understanding as a whole can be said to participate in God who is both understanding and truth essentially.

Regarding the human power of understanding participating in the divine light (the efficient cause), Thomas argues that above the active intellect of man there must be a superior intellect because what is by participation, moveable, and imperfect requires something that is essential, immovable, and perfect as its cause. The human soul is not essentially intellect, it reaches truth by movement, and it is imperfect. Thus, the soul's ability to understand is derived from that which is intellectual essentially, is immovable, and is perfect: the divine intellect. Thomas then gives an analogy in which the active intellect is compared to the light that lights the sky and God is compared to the sun (*ST* I.79.4; *SC* 10). The sun is the first and universal cause of the light in the sky and the sky participates in this light since it is not light by its essence (for without the sun it would be dark). Likewise, the soul is not intellectual light by its essence but only by participation in the divine light. Light is a fitting analogy to the intellect since the active intellect makes visible to the mind things that were before invisible. Just as the light by which we are able to see things through our eyes comes from the sun, the light by which our mind sees things comes from God. Thomas states:

We are said to see all things in God and to judge all things in respect to Him, because by the participation of His light, we know and judge all things; for the light of natural reason itself is a participation of the divine light; as likewise we are said to see and judge of sensible things in the sun, that is, by the sun's light.[10]

Regarding the intellect participating in God as the object of divine understanding which includes all intelligible forms (the exemplary cause), Thomas states, "The intelligible species which are participated by our intellect are reduced as to their first cause, to a first principle which is by its essence intelligible: God. But they proceed from that principle by means of the forms of sensible and material things, from which we gather knowledge. . . ."[11] In other words, the divine ideas within God are the exemplary cause of all created beings. These created beings that can be known by the human intellect are then the secondary cause of the intellectual forms within the human mind. However, the first cause

---

10. *ST* I.12.11.3: omnia dicimur in deo videre, et secundum ipsum de omnibus iudicare, inquantum per participationem sui luminis omnia cognoscimus et diiudicamus, nam et ipsum lumen naturale rationis participatio quaedam est divini luminis; sicut etiam omnia sensibilia dicimus videre et iudicare in sole, idest per lumen solis. Cf. *SCG* III.53, 58; *ST* I.89.1, I-II.91.2, III.9.2.1, III.10.4; *LC* 9; *QD De Anima* 5.6.

11. *ST* I.84.4.1: Species intelligibiles quas participat noster intellectus, reducuntur sicut in primam causam in aliquod principium per suam essentiam intelligibile, scilicet in deum. Sed ab illo principio procedunt mediantibus formis rerum sensibilium et materialium, a quibus scientiam colligimus. . . . Cf. *ST* I.14.8.3, 84.5; I-II.3.6; *DT* I.1. By noting that participation in the divine mind takes place through knowledge of sensory objects, Thomas avoids an Augustinian understanding of divine illumination, yet at the same time is influenced by Augustine. See E. Gilson, *The Philosophy of St. Thomas Aquinas,* trans. E. Bullough (New York: Barnes & Noble, 1993), 242–50, for a description of how St. Thomas borrows from both Aristotle and St. Augustine to state that the intellectual soul knows all things by participation in the divine light which contains the eternal essences of all things. Yet this participation takes place by means of sensible things from which the intellect abstracts their intelligible species.

of these intelligible forms remains God.[12] Consequently, every act of the intellect participates in God because God moves the intellect to understand by giving it the principles of understanding: the intellectual power and the intelligible species.[13]

THE ANALYSIS OF AN INTELLECTUAL ACT

When God moves the intellect to understand something by giving it the power and impressing the intellectual form, He acts as the primary cause whereas the human intellect acts as the instrumental cause. Because an instrumental cause always acts in accord with its form, the human intellect is moved by God according to its proper form.[14] Unlike God who understands all things immediately by knowing Himself, the human intellect because of its weakness must abstract intellectual forms from phantasms, judge things, and use discursive reasoning in order to know things more perfectly (*SCG* I.57 and 58; *ST* I.58.4). Consequently, several steps within an intellectual act are necessary for the intellect to be perfected (*ST* I.58.3). Thus, in order to understand how God moves the human intellect as an instrumental cause to knowledge of truth, it is necessary to become at least briefly acquainted with the anatomy of a human intellectual act.

However, because the speculative intellect is moved in a different manner than the practical intellect, before I begin the analysis of the intellectual act, it is necessary to look at the distinction Thomas makes between the practical intellect and the speculative intellect. Thomas notes

12. In reference to intelligible species, the intellect is perfected to the extent that it knows things since the ultimate perfection of the intellect is the act of knowing something else (*ST* I.87.3). Yet, since the intellect becomes formally what it understands (*ST* I.14.2; I.84.6), how could knowledge of things lower than us perfect us? Thomas answers that humans are not perfected by lower forms except that they participate by a certain likeness to that which is above the human intellect, namely, that which is intelligible by essence (I-II.3.6).

13. *ST* I.105.3: "Therefore God so moves the created intellect, inasmuch as He gives it the intellectual power, whether natural, or superadded; and impresses on the created intellect the intelligible species . . ." (igitur deus movet intellectum creatum, inquantum dat ei virtutem ad intelligendum, vel naturalem vel superadditam; et inquantum imprimit ei species intelligibiles . . .).

14. See *DT* I.1 where Thomas explains the necessity of divine activity in the human act of knowing by stating that God gives each thing its proper form and powers by which it can perform its proper operation. However, in addition to this, God directs and moves the powers of all things to their proper operation through His providence, for the created world acts as an instrument of divine governance.

that whereas the things apprehended by the practical intellect are directed toward operation, the things apprehended by the speculative intellect are directed toward consideration of truth.[15] Because the end of speculative knowledge is different from that of practical knowledge, the means of acquiring it also vary. For this reason, although both ways participate in God's act of understanding, the mode of participation varies. For example, Thomas states:

Human reason cannot have a full participation of the dictate of the divine reason, but according to its own mode and imperfectly. Consequently, as on the part of the speculative reason, by a natural participation of divine wisdom, there is in us the knowledge of certain general principles, but not proper knowledge of each single truth, such as that contained in the divine wisdom; so too, on the part of the practical reason, man has a natural participation in the eternal law, according to certain general principles, but not as regards the particular determinations of individual cases, which are, however contained in the eternal law.[16]

Despite the fact that in God His wisdom and law are identical, Thomas nonetheless makes a distinction between the two because it is more fitting to say that human speculative reason participates in God's wisdom (here signifying God's speculative knowledge of all things), while human practical reason participates in God's eternal law (here signifying God's practical knowledge causing creation to be moved to its proper end).[17]

---

15. *ST* I.79.11. Elsewhere Thomas notes that knowledge can be called speculative in three ways: First, as regards the things known which are not ordered to operation by the knower such as a human's knowledge about divine things. Second, as regards the manner of knowing such as a builder considers what a house is in general and not as ordered to the operation of building a house. Third, as regards the end, for the practical intellect is ordered to the end of operation and the speculative intellect to the consideration of the truth. Thus, knowledge that is speculative by reason of the thing known in itself is merely speculative. But that which is speculative in the other two ways is partly speculative and partly practical (*ST* I.14.16).

16. *ST* 93.1.1: Ratio humana non potest participare ad plenum dictamen rationis divinae, sed suo modo et imperfecte. Et ideo sicut ex parte rationis speculativae, per naturalem participationem divinae sapientiae, inest nobis cognitio quorundam communium principiorum, non autem cuiuslibet veritatis propria cognitio, sicut in divina sapientia continetur; ita etiam ex parte rationis practicae naturaliter homo participat legem aeternam secundum quaedam communia principia, non autem secundum particulares directiones singulorum, quae tamen in aeterna lege continentur.

17. See *ST* I.14.16 where Thomas notes that inasmuch as God knows Himself, He has only speculative knowledge, since knowledge of Himself cannot be ordered to operation. However, in reference to those things that He makes, God has both speculative and practical knowledge. He has speculative knowledge as knowing his works in themselves, and He has practical knowledge since as governor and creator his knowledge is ordered to the end of operation. Cf. *ST* I.4.

Thus, whereas the speculative intellect participates in God's wisdom to know truth in itself, the practical intellect participates in eternal law in order to know its proper act.[18]

Because the practical intellect is more properly said to participate in God's knowledge as eternal law, in *ST* I-II.93.6 Thomas is primarily talking about the practical intellect's cognitive participation in eternal law.[19] Nonetheless, I will first briefly treat the acts of the speculative intellect for four reasons: first, because the speculative intellect also cognitively participates in eternal law;[20] second, because in describing the acts of the practical intellect, Thomas very often compares it to the acts of the speculative intellect; third, because speculative knowledge is made practical by extension; and fourth because knowledge of the virtues of the speculative intellect serve as the background for the knowledge of the gifts of the Holy Spirit with the same names as these virtues: understanding *(intellectus)*, science *(scientia)*, and wisdom *(sapientia)*. After briefly treating the anatomy of the act of the speculative intellect, I will show how the act of the practical intellect is related to it and in doing this show the role of the natural law in giving the principles from which practical reason derives its conclusions.

18. Recall in chapter 2 the distinction made between the divine ideas and the eternal law. Both are the exemplary cause of created beings. However, the divine exemplars of substances are called ideas, while the divine exemplar of actions is called the eternal law. Since the practical intellect is ordered to action, it is especially said to participate in the eternal law.

19. Further evidence that Thomas is primarily speaking of the practical intellect is that the context of this passage is within the question of whether all human affairs (res) are subject to the eternal law. Now the eternal law moves creatures to act (93.1) and it is the practical intellect which is ordered to the end of operation (I.79.11; cf. I-II.94.2 and 4 and 100.1 on how laws act as principles in the practical intellect). Furthermore, Thomas speaks of the "natural knowledge of good" (naturalis cognitio boni). The practical intellect's object is the good directed to operation under the aspect of truth (ita obiectum intellectus practici est bonum ordinabile ad opus, sub ratione veri). Hence, it is the practical intellect that has natural knowledge of the good because a human act is always for an apprehended good. Although faith primarily perfects the speculative intellect, it also perfects the practical intellect because the object of faith (the First Truth) is also the end of all our actions and desires, and faith is thus practical by extension (II-II.4.4.3). Likewise, wisdom as a gift of the Holy Spirit also directs human acts by divine rules and is hence practical as well as speculative.

20. Thomas notes that all truths participate in the eternal law (*ST* I-II.93.2; cf. *DV* 1.2). Although acts of the speculative intellect are not ordered to operation, they are nonetheless acts and are thus measured by the eternal law. Knowing truth for its own sake is a participation in the eternal contemplation of God which is the end to which the eternal law orders humans.

The Three Acts of the Speculative Intellect

The perfect act of the intellect is the act of having complete knowledge of something (*ST* I.85.3). The intellect has complete knowledge of something when it contains a perfect likeness of the object known (*ST* I.12.9; *DV* 8.5). In other words, there can be different degrees of understanding. Even children have a rudimentary understanding of a triangle. However, their understanding would not likely include the property that every triangle is half of a square. A more perfect understanding would certainly include this. In order to achieve complete knowledge of something, the intellect must usually perform three actions.[21] The intellect must first abstract intelligible forms from sensible phantasms, then join and divide these forms in order to form propositions, and finally move from these propositions to conclusions through discursive reasoning (cf. *DV* 9.1.8). Thus, following Aristotle, Thomas believes that there are three acts to the intellect: simple apprehension (abstraction of intelligible forms from sensible forms), judgment (joining and dividing forms), and discursive reasoning.[22] I will briefly discuss each of these three steps.

The First Act: Simple Apprehension

The intellect by nature seeks to understand the essence of things by means of their intelligible forms. However, because the soul is united to a body, the intellect can only understand things by turning to sensible phantasms from which the quiddity, nature, or essence of a thing is abstracted.[23] In other words, the light of the intellect abstracts the form of a thing so that it is present in the mind. It is present in an intelligible mode, because

21. In his commentary on the *Posterior Analytics*, Thomas notes that there are four questions that we ask about things: whether it is so (quia), why it is so (propter quid), whether it is (si est), and what is it (quid est). In order to have scientific knowledge of something, we must be able to answer all of these questions and to answer all of these questions a demonstration is required, which requires that propositions be formed to demonstrate from (*PA* II.1).

22. Aristotle, *Posterior analytics*, II.1. See Thomas's *Commentary* on this passage (book II, lecture 1) as well as the prologue to the commentary and also *ST* I-II.90.1.2. For a detailed description of each of the acts of the intellect, see Robert Schmidt, *The Domain of Logic According to Saint Thomas Aquinas* (The Hague, The Netherlands: Martinus Nijhoff, 1966). See also Gilson, *The Philosophy of St. Thomas*, chapters 12–13, for a more metaphysical description of how the intellect knows things. Cf. Mark Johnson, "God's Knowledge in Our Frail Mind," *Angelicum* 76 (1999): 33–37.

23. *ST* I.84.7. Thomas continues by noting that by knowledge of these sensible beings the intellect is able to rise by reasoning to the knowledge of invisible things. Cf. I.58.3. See Schmidt, 177–201, for a detailed analysis of the first act of the mind.

all things are received according to the mode of the receiver.[24] Although these intelligible species of things are within the mind, Thomas insists that what is understood is not the intelligible species, but rather the intelligible species is that by which the mind understands the essence of things outside of it (*SCG* II.94). This intelligible species differs from the sense knowledge that it was abstracted from because sense knowledge is of a particular thing, but the intelligible species is universal.[25] For example, a particular stone is known through sense knowledge, but the intellectual soul knows a stone absolutely by knowing its essence (*ST* I.75.5). Inasmuch as the mind has the power to abstract intelligible forms from sense phantasms, it participates in the divine light (*ST* I.12.2). Inasmuch as it contains intelligible forms within it, it participates in the exemplar forms in the divine mind.

The Second Act: Judgment (Composition and Separation)

Although the first act of apprehension gives knowledge of something, this knowledge is imperfect and confused. The reason that it is imperfect is because due to the weakness of the human mind that which is in reality singular, diversified, and distinct is apprehended as universal and common.[26] Hence, the intellect must combine and separate the intellectual forms derived from simple apprehension in order to determine what forms are in reality together and what forms are not.[27] This act of

24. Because that received is according to the mode of the receiver, that received in the intellect must be immaterial (*ST* I.75.5). Hence, the agent intellect must abstract the form from the matter, making it intelligible (I.85.1). Cf. I.76, I.76.2, which notes that the phantasm is not the form of the possible intellect, rather the intelligible species abstracted from the phantasms is the form. Thomas elsewhere (II-II.173.2) explains that when there is a representation of something in the mind (an intelligible form), there is first a representation of the thing in the senses, then in the imagination, and finally by the power of the active intellect deriving the species from phantasms there is a representation of the thing in the passive intellect.

25. See *ST* I.84.1 where Thomas notes that the soul knows bodies by a knowledge that is immaterial, universal, and necessary. Cf. I.57.2, which states that universals and immaterial things are apprehended by the intellect, and singular and material things are apprehended by the senses.

26. *ST* I.14.6; 58.4 85.3; see especially *SCG* I.58 where Thomas notes that there would be no need to compose and divide (judge) if by apprehending the essence of a thing we grasped what belonged in it and what did not. See also *PA* II.2 where Thomas notes the definition of a thing does not include knowledge of what is *per se* in a thing, much less of those things that are *per accidens* in a thing.

27. Thomas notes that to understand is to penetrate into the essence of a thing, since the object of the intellect is what a thing is. However, there are many different kinds of things that are hidden within. For example, under accidents are hidden the substantial reality, under

combining and separating is called judgment. Thomas explains that matter and form, subject and accident, et cetera are apprehended as being separate. The intellect through judgment combines them by predicating one of the other. He gives the example of the intellect combining the form humanity with the individual Socrates in order to form the enunciation "Socrates is a man."[28] Thus, the intellect constructs an intelligible whole out of the separated data of simple apprehension.[29] In the case of separation, the intellect separates forms apprehended together that are actually separate in reality.[30]

After the intellect judges something, it is able to direct its attention to both the subject and the predicate together and thus understand the whole proposition as one (*SCG* I.55). By the means of the light of the intellect humans are able to put together and separate intellectual forms to understand things as they are in reality.

The most basic propositions that are understood are called first principles. These self-evident principles are known immediately (without any discursive reasoning).[31] Thomas explains that these principles are known immediately by the intellect once it knows the quiddity of things. He continues by noting that the intellect cannot be deceived in reference to these first principles (*DV* I.12). In other words, inasmuch as humans understand the intellectual forms that are combined or separated in these principles, the intellect immediately and without error forms these principles. Because these first principles are applied to the species that are drawn from sense knowledge, they act as the foundation for all speculative and practical knowledge. Thomas further explains:

Now although different things are known and believed to be true by different people, certain things are true on which all men agree, such as the first principles of understanding, both speculative and practical, according as an image of di-

---

words lies their meaning, under effects, their causes, etc. All of these things require the light of understanding to see and the stronger the light of understanding, the deeper it can penetrate into things (*ST* II-II.8.1). Cf. *PA* II.1.

28. *Metaph* IV.11 (1898). Cf. *SCG* I.36; *DV* I.3; *ST* I.3.4.2.

29. See Schmidt, *The Domain of Logic,* 202–12.

30. Cf. *Metaph* IV.11 (1896). For example, toddlers will sometimes mistake raw peeled potatoes for peeled apple slices. However, after tasting the potato, they know that a potato is not an apple. Even though the child may not yet know the words for apple and potato, he is able to separate the intellectual form of potato from that of apple and is able to understand that a potato is not an apple.

31. *SCG* I.61. Cf. *ST* I.58.3 where Thomas states that things immediately grasped (without discursive reasoning) are said to be understood, hence understanding is the habit of first principles.

vine truth is reflected universally in the minds of all men. Therefore, insofar as any mind knows anything whatever with certitude, the object is intuited in these principles, by means of which judgment is made concerning all things. Once the mind resolves things back to these principles, it is said to see all things in the divine truth, or in the eternal reasons, and is said to judge all things according to them.[32]

Because the intellect participates in the divine light it has the power to immediately understand first principles. By applying these principles to other intellectual forms, the intellect judges something with certitude, where the certitude comes from the participation of the intellect in the divine intellect.

Because after the intellect judges something, it not only knows something but knows it as it is in reality, it is only after the act of judgment that knowledge can be called true.[33] Thomas explains:

... Truth is defined by the conformity of the intellect and thing; wherefore, to know this conformity is to know truth. . . . And the intellect can know its own conformity with the intelligible thing; yet it does not apprehend it by knowing of a thing "what a thing is." When, however, it judges that a thing corresponds to the form which it apprehends about that thing, then it first knows and expresses truth. This it does by composing and dividing.[34]

The knowledge of the first act (what a thing is) is not called truth in its proper sense, but rather truth is the correspondence of the intellect with

---

32. *SCG* III.47.7: Quamvis autem diversa a diversis cognoscuntur et creduntur vera, tamen quaedam sunt vera in quibus omnes homines concordant, sicut sunt prima principia intellectus tam speculativi quam practici: secundum quod universaliter in mentibus omnium divinae veritatis quasi quaedam imago resultat. Inquantum ergo quaelibet mens quicquid per certitudinem cognoscit, in his principiis intuetur, secundum quae de omnibus iudicatur, facta resolutione in ipsa, dicitur omnia in divina veritate vel in rationibus aeternis videre, et secundum eas de omnibus iudicare. Cf. *ST* I.79.12. In the last sentence, when Thomas says that all things are judged according to first principles, he is referring to how the mind returns by way of analysis to first principles (I.79.8).

33. *DV* I.3: Thomas states that truth is primarily in the intellect joining and separating. For in the intellect's forming of definitions of things, the intellect merely has a likeness of a thing existing outside the soul, but when the intellect begins to judge, it says something is this or is not this.

34. *ST* I.16.2: . . . per conformitatem intellectus et rei veritas definitur; unde conformitatem istam cognoscere potest, est cognoscere veritatem. . . . Intellectus autem conformitatem sui ad rem intelligibilem cognoscere potest, sed tamen non apprehendit eam secundum quod cognoscit de aliquo quod quid est, sed quando judicat rem ita se habere sicut est forma quam de re apprehendit, tunc primo cognoscit et dicit verum. Et hoc facit componendo et divendo. . . .

reality that results from composing and dividing.[35] For example, the concept rational animal cannot be judged true or false until it is combined
with the concept of Socrates. Since a proper act of judgment yields truth,
Thomas states that the object of the intellect is the universal truth (*ST*
I-II.2.8; cf. *SCG* I.61). In other words, the natural inclination of the intellect is not only to apprehend what something is, but also to know it as
it truly is in reality.[36]

Thomas elsewhere makes a distinction between primary and secondary senses of truth (*DV* I.1). Something is said to be true in the primary
sense when the united and separated forms in the intellect correspond to
how they are united and separated in reality. In a secondary sense things
can be said to be true as proceeding from the intellect either as an act or
as an artifact.[37] For example, an act can be said to be true to the extent
it corresponds to its form in the reason. In reference to God as divine
artist, things are said to be true in the secondary sense as depending and
conforming to God's *ratio* which made them (*ST* I.16.1; cf. *SCG* I.60).
Thus, the divine intellect is the measure of things which are the measure
of the human intellect.[38] By understanding created things through judgment the intelligible forms in the human intellect participate in the exemplars in the divine intellect. Consequently, to the extent that humans
have the intellectual power to understand a proposition, their intellect
participates in the divine light, and to the extent the proposition corresponds to reality, their intellect participates in the divine ideas.

35. *ST* I.16.2; *SCG* I.59. The knowledge from simple apprehension can be called truth
by analogy (*DV* I.1).

36. Although this natural inclination cannot be frustrated in simple apprehension, it
can be frustrated in cases of judgment since the intellect can judge wrongly. Thomas explains that the intellect is always true in reference to the first act of the mind: knowing what
a thing is. Because just as the senses are not deceived in knowing their proper sensible objects, the intellect cannot be deceived in knowing its proper object: the essence of a thing.
It can, however, be deceived in reference to its accidental object which is known by judging
and discursive reasoning (*SCG* I.58; 61; *ST* I.85.6; *DV* I.12). In other words, although the
intellect cannot be deceived in abstracting the intelligible form from phantasms, it can be
deceived in composing a proposition based on apprehended forms and in drawing conclusions from these propositions.

37. This sense of truth is particularly important in morals both because the truth of all
laws comes from their conformity to the eternal law and because actions are said to be true
as being in conformity with human reason that is in conformity with the eternal law.

38. *SCG* I.61; *ST* I-II.93.1.3. Cf. *ST* I.14.8.3 where Thomas notes that natural things
stand midway between God's knowledge and our knowledge, for we receive our knowledge
from natural things which God's knowledge causes.

The Third Act: Discursive Reasoning

Once an intellectual truth is understood, the human mind is able to advance from one thing understood to another, in order to further know intelligible truth.[39] This movement from principles to conclusions is called reasoning. Like judgment, the acquisition of intelligible truth by moving from one truth to another is necessary because of the weakness of the human intellect (*ST* I.79.8). Because not everything which can be attributed to something can be known by immediate understanding alone, the mind must reason to conclusions by means of a middle term.[40] In other words, in the joining and separating of the quiddities of different things, on some occasions the mind is able to immediately join and separate them as in the case of first principles. However, normally a middle term is needed in order to join or separate two particular things due to the weakness of the intellect (*ST* I.58.4). This use of a middle term to join or separate particular things is discursive reasoning. An example of this process can be seen in using an argument to separate the terms "spider" and "insect" by use of the middle term "eight legs": All spiders have eight legs. No insects have eight legs. Therefore, no spiders are insects. The terms spider and insects are separated via the middle term eight legs. Thus, the mind is able to separate the terms spiders and insects in order to have a fuller understanding of reality, since in reality spiders are not insects. The mind judges the truth of the proposition spiders are not insects by means of discursive reasoning.[41] That which is known through reasoning from first principles is called science or knowledge *(scientia)*.[42]

Although some things can be known by immediate understanding, because of the weakness of the human intellect, it reaches its full perfection by knowing conclusions judged to be true by means of premises.[43] Hence, when Thomas speaks of judgment, he uses the term to refer to both the composition and the division of concepts immediately and the composition and division of concepts by means of a middle term.[44] In

---

39. *ST* I.79.8; *Expositio libri Peryermenias* I.1.

40. See Schmidt, *The Domain of Logic*, 242. In Thomas, see *ST* I.58.3 and 4, 85.5; II-II.49.5.2; *SCG* I.57.

41. Unlike in simple apprehension, in this process of drawing conclusions from first principles, the intellect can (and often does) err (*SCG* I.61).

42. *ST* II-II.47.6.

43. *ST* I.58.3 & 4, 79.8; cf. I.12.9. Cf. John Jenkins, *Knowledge and Faith in Thomas Aquinas* (Cambridge: Cambridge University Press, 1997), 95–102.

44. *ST* II-II.53.4; cf. I.79.8. See Daniel Westberg, *Right Practical Reason* (Oxford:

other words, judgment, which causes understanding, both proceeds and follows discursive reasoning (*PA* II.1). Thomas affirms this by stating that reasoning begins with understanding and ends with it.[45] Immediate understanding takes place without the use of reasoning, and mediate understanding takes place via a middle term.[46]

Recall that every human act of understanding participates in divine understanding by receiving both the intellectual power and the intelligible species. When humans participate in the divine intellect in glory, the intellectual power they receive will be sufficient to allow them to immediately know things by knowing the essence of God. However, on earth, both of these modes of participation are less perfect. The intellectual power must join and separate intellectual forms and discursively reason in order to acquire knowledge, and humans are not able to know things by immediate understanding of the divine essence, but rather they know things by means of abstraction and discursive reasoning (cf. *DV* 11.1.13). Because this participation in divine knowledge is indirect, not all things are known with certainty and truth is often mixed with error. Nonetheless, inasmuch as humans know anything at all they participate in divine knowledge.

The Moral Acts of the Practical Intellect as Compared to the Speculative

Whereas the acts of the speculative intellect are ordered to the consideration of truth, the acts of the practical intellect are directed toward operation. Because eternal law orders humans to operation, Thomas is especially talking about the participation of the practical intellect in eternal law when he speaks of cognitive participation.[47] However, Thomas

---

Clarendon Press, 1984), 64–66. Westberg states that for Thomas judgment sometimes immediately follows perception, and sometimes it is the conclusion of a reasoning process. For a list of Thomistic texts in reference to both ways Thomas uses the term judgment; see B. Garceau, *Judicium* (Montreal: Institut d'études médiévales, 1968), 265–78. See also J. Owens, "Judgment and Truth in Aquinas," *Medieval Studies* 32 (1970): 138–58.

45. *ST* II-II.8.1.2. Because reasoning is ordered to understanding, Thomas notes that although reasoning is essential for human knowledge, the act of understanding is the highest action within humans (*SCG* I.57).

46. All cognition takes place through the assimilation of the knower and the known. This assimilation can take place in two ways: either immediately or through a middle term (*DV* 8.5). Unlike humans, God and the angels know things immediately (*SCG* I.57).

47. Although art is also an act of the practical intellect that participates in eternal law, because I am primarily concerned with the participation of moral acts in eternal law, I will not examine art as an act.

feels that the role of the speculative intellect is easier to understand than that of the practical intellect, for when speaking of the practical intellect, Thomas nearly always compares it to the speculative intellect. For example, Thomas argues that just as each of the three acts of the speculative intellect produce a particular effect, so also there are various corresponding effects produced by the practical intellect:

> With regard to the speculative reason, in the first place there is definition; secondly, a proposition; thirdly, a syllogism or argument. And since also the practical reason makes use of a certain syllogism in respect of the operation to be done . . . it is possible to find something in the practical intellect that is related to operations just as in the speculative intellect, the proposition is related to conclusions. Such universal propositions of the practical intellect that are ordered to actions have the nature of law.[48]

Just as in the speculative intellect conclusions are formed by means of propositions, in the practical intellect the conclusion (the act to be chosen by the will) is determined by means of universal propositions (laws). Hence, just as Thomas explains practical reason by comparing and contrasting it to speculative reason, I will also explain the acts of the practical intellect by comparing and contrasting it to the speculative intellect.

The First Act of the Practical Intellect: Simple Apprehension

In reference to the act of apprehension, the only difference between the speculative intellect and the practical intellect is that the speculative intellect orders that apprehended to the consideration of truth, while the practical intellect directs it to operation (*ST* I.79.II; cf. I-II.68.4). Just as what is apprehended by the speculative intellect can be used to form speculative syllogisms, so also what is apprehended by the practical intellect can be used to form practical syllogisms. Thomas notes that the choice of the thing to be done is the conclusion of the practical syllogism (*ST* I.86.1.2). These syllogisms begin with apprehended forms just like

---

48. *ST* I-II.90.1.2: Quod quidem in speculativa ratione primo quidem est definitio; secundo, enunciatio; tertio vero, syllogismus vel argumentatio. Et quia ratio etiam practica utitur quodam syllogismo in operabilibus . . . . est invenire aliquid in ratione practica quod ita se habeat ad operationes, sicut se habet propositio in ratione speculativa ad conclusiones. Et huiusmodi propositiones universales rationis practicae ordinatae ad actiones, habent rationem legis. The end of the first act of the speculative intellect (simple apprehension) is a definition. The end of the second act (judgment) is a proposition, and the end of the third act (discursive reasoning) is the syllogism or argument. In this context, Thomas is explaining that in the practical intellect, laws take the place of propositions and hence are the foundation of practical syllogisms. Cf. I-II.68.4.

they do in the speculative intellect. For example, just as the intelligible species of spider, insect, and eight legs must be known to come to the conclusion that a spider is not an insect, so also the intelligible species of obey, government, and the speed limit laws must be known in order to come to the practical conclusion that a citizen should drive the posted speed limit. As can be seen by the example of the intelligible species of government, these apprehended forms can be directed to either consideration of truth or to a particular action. Hence, it is no surprise that Thomas often states that truths and habits proper to the speculative intellect are practical by extension (e.g., *ST* I.1.4, II-II.4.2.3).

The Second Act of the Practical Intellect: Joining and Separating (Judgment)

Like judgment in the speculative intellect, the practical intellect's act of judgment joins and separates intellectual forms into propositions. In the practical reason, there are two types of propositions: universal (laws) and singular propositions through which the law is applied to a particular context.[49] Thomas explains:

Now it is to be observed that the reason directs human acts in accordance with two kinds of knowing, a universal and a particular kind. For in conferring about things to be done, it makes use of a sort of syllogism, the conclusion of which is a judgment or choice or operation. Actions, after all, are concerned with singulars. Thus, the conclusion of an operative syllogism is singular. Now a singular proposition is derived from a universal only by way of another singular proposition, as a man is prohibited the act of parricide because he knows a father ought not be killed and knows that this man is his father.[50]

In a practical syllogism a singular conclusion (judgment,[51] choice, or operation) is derived from a universal proposition (law) by means of a sin-

49. *ST* I-II.90.1.2; II-II.49.2. I am using the term law to refer to any dictate of practical reason that orders humans to their proper good (or at least to their perceived good).

50. *ST* I-II.76.1: Considerandum est autem quod ratio secundum duplicem scientiam est humanorum actuum directiva, scilicet secundum scientiam universalem, et particularem. Conferens enim de agendis, utitur quodam syllogismo, cuius conclusio est iudicium seu electio vel operatio. Actiones autem in singularibus sunt. Unde conclusio syllogismi operativi est singularis. Singularis autem propositio non concluditur ex universali nisi mediante aliqua propositione singulari, sicut homo prohibetur ab actu parricidii per hoc quod scit patrem non esse occidendum, et per hoc quod scit hunc esse patrem. Cf. *ST* II-II.49.2; cf. *ST* I.86.1.2.

51. In this quotation from Thomas, the term judgment is not used to represent immediate understanding, but the understanding that comes after reasoning. Just as in the speculative intellect judgment applies both to the combining and separating of intellectual forms

gular proposition. Thomas gives an example of a universal proposition (law), A father ought not be killed, and a singular premise, This man is his father. From these propositions the conclusion to not kill his father can be derived.[52]

Because two types of propositions are formed by the practical intellect (laws and singular propositions), the intellect immediately understands these two types of propositions in two different ways. Thomas notes that the intellect in one way understands universals and in another way understands contingent practical matters. The first type of understanding applies to both speculative and practical principles; the second refers to the right estimate of some particular end (*ST* II-II.49.2.1 & 3). Both types of immediate understanding are necessary for practical reasoning (cf. *ST* I-II.76.1; cf. *ST* I-II.58.4), since without both types of propositions, no action can be determined. Thus, I will speak briefly about the understanding of both universal and singular propositions, beginning with the universal.

Just as in the speculative sciences, the first principles are known through a natural habit of understanding, so also the practical intellect knows the first universal principles of practical reason (laws) through a natural habit called *synderesis*. Thomas states:

Just as there is a certain natural habit of the human soul whereby it knows the principles of speculative science, which we call the understanding of the principles, so too in the soul there is a certain natural habit of the first principles of actions, which are the universal principles of natural law.[53]

From the natural habit of *synderesis* come the first principles of practical reasoning from which humans can rationally move to other principles (laws) and ultimately to particular actions.

---

into propositions and the combining and separating of these propositions through discursive reasoning, so also in the practical intellect judgment also refers to the act of the intellect determining the correct action to be done through practical reason (cf. *ST* I-II.57.6).

52. For a detailed analysis of Thomas's use of the practical syllogism, see Kevin Flannery, *Acts amid Precepts* (Washington, D.C.: The Catholic University of America Press, 2001), chapters 1–4. Flannery argues that Thomas believes that lower principles (laws) can be deduced from higher ones and particular actions can also be derived from laws (71–72). See also Ralph McInerny, *St. Thomas Aquinas* (South Bend: University of Notre Dame Press, 1977), 70–74.

53. *DV* 16:1: Sicut igitus humanae animae est quidam habitus naturalis quo principia speculativarum scientiarum cognoscit, quem vocamus intellectum principiorum; ita etiam in ea est quidam habitus naturalis primorum principiorum operabilium, quae sunt universalia principia iuris naturalis; qui quidem habitus ad synderesim pertinet. Cf. *ST* I.79.12; I-II.94.1.2; II-II.47.6.2.

In order to explain these first principles of practical reason, Thomas compares them to the first principles of speculative reason. He notes that just as it is self-evident that the same thing cannot be affirmed and denied at the same time, so also it is self-evident that good is to be done and pursued and evil is to be avoided (*ST* I-II.94.2; cf. 100.1). This universal proposition is the first principle of the natural law and all other propositions of natural law are based upon it. Thomas continues by noting that all things to which humans are naturally inclined are naturally apprehended by the reason as good and are thus to be pursued (*ST* I-II.94.2). He then gives a list of other principles of natural law that flow from the natural inclinations that a human has inasmuch as his act of being includes living and understanding.[54] These principles, which are known by the natural habit of *synderesis*, as well as all other principles that are discovered through experience, learning, and natural discursive reasoning, are the natural law.[55] Because an enormous number of principles can be derived from these first principles, Thomas can speak of many different precepts that make up the natural law, including the moral precepts of the old law such as God should be worshipped (*ST* I-II.99.3.2) and all the commandments dealing with one's neighbor (*ST* I-II.100.1).

The knowledge that the precepts of the natural law hold the same

54. *ST* I-II.94.2; cf. I-II.10.1. See chapter 2 on the different degrees of being based on the different degrees of participation in God.

55. In addition to self-evident knowledge of natural law, Thomas speaks of three other ways of coming to knowledge of it. First, through experience. The idea is that through life experiences humans will identify that certain actions cause humans to achieve their end and certain actions do not. Secondly through learning, as when taught by others who know them. And third through discursive reasoning. See *ST* II-II.47.15 where Thomas states that primary principles of both the speculative and the practical intellect are naturally known (apart from the movement of reason). However, secondary principles are not given by nature, "but are through discovery from experience or through learning" (sed per inventionem secundum viam experimenti, vel per disciplinam). See also *ST* I-II.94.6 where Thomas states, "there belong to natural law, first, certain most general precepts, that are known to all; and secondly, certain secondary and more detailed precepts, which are, as it were, conclusions following closely from first principles" (ad legem naturalem pertinent primo quidem quaedam praecepta communissima, quae sunt omnibus nota, quaedam autem secundaria praecepta magis propria, quae sunt quasi conclusiones propinquae principiis). In *ST* I-II.58.5 Thomas notes that humans obtain the universal principles of action by means of natural understanding and practical science (scientiam practicam). In *ST* I-II.99.2.2 Thomas notes that secondary principles were revealed since the ability of humans to draw these conclusions from the universal propositions of natural law had gone astray. Cf. R. A. Armstrong, *Primary and Secondary Precepts in Thomistic Natural Teaching* (The Hague: Martinus Nijhoff, 1966), and Rhonheimer, *Natural Law and Practical Reason*, 257–87, for a detailed look at how natural law includes both precepts known by simple understanding and precepts derived from them by natural reason.

place in practical reasoning as do the precepts in the speculative reason illuminates the way humans come to know natural law, as well as its use in moral reasoning. Humans discover natural law just as they do propositions in speculative sciences. They first apprehend intellectual forms such as good, evil, pursue, avoid, and so on from phantasms.[56] They then combine and separate these forms into universal propositions such as: Humans should pursue good and avoid evil. By apprehending the rich intelligibility of how humans are naturally inclined to their proper ends, a variety of universal propositions can be formed.[57] From these universal propositions the practical reason is able to derive secondary propositions.[58] Some of these propositions are known by all with very little consideration; others are only known by the wise who are able to understand the various circumstances involved.[59] Once these moral propositions are determined they can be applied via the practical syllogism through an act of prudence similar to the way universal propositions in the speculative intellect yield speculative conclusions via discursive reasoning. Thus, all moral laws and virtuous actions can be deduced back to the universal principles of natural law.[60]

Just as the propositions of speculative knowledge all participate in eternal law, so also the universal propositions of practical knowledge (the precepts of the natural law) participate in the eternal law.[61] Thomas states

56. Thomas notes that all things that are judged can ultimately be reduced to what comes from the senses (*DV* 12.3.2; Cf. *ST* I.84.1, I.85.1, I-II.93.2).

57. See chapters 2 and 3 on how humans are inclined to acts that fulfill their nature by the eternal law.

58. See *ST* I-II.94.6 where Thomas states, "there belong to natural law, first, certain most general precepts, that are known to all; and secondly, certain secondary and more detailed precepts, which are, as it were, conclusions following closely from first principles" (ad legem naturalem pertinent primo quidem quaedam praecepta communissima, quae sunt omnibus nota, quaedam autem secundaria praecepta magis propria, quae sunt quasi conclusiones propinquae principiis).

59. *ST* I-II.100.1: Thomas speaks of some moral precepts of the law of nature that can be known to everyone (such as honor your father and mother, you shall not kill, . . . steal), some precepts that are only known to the wise (such as honor the aged man), and some that are only known by divine instruction (such as you shall not take the Lord's name in vain). Cf. *ST* I-II.100.11, 100.3. Just as in the speculative intellect humans can err in the process of judgment and discursive reasoning, so also in the practical intellect humans can err in these two acts. Hence, God has divinely revealed moral precepts that can be obtained by natural reason (*ST* I-II.100.11).

60. Thomas states that since the natural law includes all to which humans are inclined according to nature, and that the natural form of humans is the rational soul, humans are naturally inclined to act in accord with reason, which is to act according to virtue. *ST* I-II.94.3; cf. I.18.3; I-II.18.5, 55.4.2, 93.1.2, 100.1; II-II.47.6.

61. *SCG* III.47.7; *DV* 11.1 and 3; *ST* I-II.91.3.1. See also Rhonheimer, *Natural Law and*

that all things participate in eternal law as ruled and measured by it, but the rational creature also participates cognitively through the natural law:

Now among all others, the rational creature is subject to divine providence in a more excellent way, insofar as it participates in providence for itself and for others. Wherefore it has a participation of the eternal reason, through which it has a natural inclination to its proper act and end: and such a participation of the eternal law in the rational creature is called the natural law.[62]

Thomas continues in this passage by stating that the natural light of reason is an imprint of the divine light on the rational creature (*ST* I-II.91.2). Just as the speculative intellect participates in the uncreated light in that both the power of the intellect and the intellectual forms are received from the uncreated light, so also in knowing the precepts of the natural law the mind participates in both ways as well.[63]

It participates in the first way by receiving the natural light of understanding. It participates in the second way because the exemplars in God's mind are the cause of the natural inclinations of the rational creature.[64] The human intellect apprehends these inclinations as corresponding to their proper ends and then forms the propositions of natural law. In other words, just as an architect contains the form for the house within his mind, so also God contains the *rationes* of all things within His intellect, including the ends and natural inclinations of humans.[65] By means

---

Practical Reason, chapters 5 and 6, for an analysis of how both the precepts of the natural law which are known by immediate understanding and those known by natural discursive reason both participate in eternal law.

62. *ST* I-II.91.2: Inter caetera autem rationalis creatura excellentiori quodam modo divinae providentiae subiacet, inquantum et ipsa fit providentiae particeps sibi ipis et aliis. Unde et in ipsa participatur ratio aeterna, per quam habet naturalem inclinationem ad debitum actum et finem. Et talis participatio legis aeternae in rationali creatura lex naturalis dicitur. Cf. *DV* 11.1 and 3.

63. *ST* I.84.5: "For the intellectual light within us is nothing else than a participated likeness of the uncreated light, in which are contained the eternal rationes" (Ipsum enim lumen intellectualle quod est in nobis, nihil est aliud quam quedam participata similituda luminis increati in quo continentur rationes aeternae). Thomas will then quote Psalm 4:6–7 as the biblical authority behind this understanding. This is the same verse given in I-II.91.2 in describing the participation of natural law in eternal law. Cf. *ST* I.15, I.79.4, 93.4; I-II.19.4, 91.2; *QQ* 8.2.2; *DSC* 10; *Ad Rom* I.6; *Ioan* I.5 (where Thomas distinguishes this Psalm (4:6–7) which is the authority for natural participation, from Isaiah 60:1, which is the authority for participation by the light of grace).

64. See *ST* I-II.93.5 where Thomas states that God as divine governor imprints on human nature the principles of its proper actions. Cf. *ST* I-II.93.3.

65. *ST* I.15.2; 16.1. Whereas a human concept is only true as being in conformity with things, God's reason is the measure of things, since each thing has truth in it as representing the divine intellect.

of the natural light of reason, humans are able to abstract from phantasms these intelligible forms of the ends and inclinations of human nature. They can then combine and separate these forms into propositions that are a reflection of the eternal law.[66] Thomas states that the natural law is an imprint on us of the divine light, albeit not a direct imprint as in the blessed, but an imprint through knowledge of the effects of the eternal law (*ST* I-II.93.2).

A practical syllogism consists of a universal proposition, a singular proposition, and a conclusion. The universal proposition takes the form of the end to be pursued and the conclusion takes the form of the action to be performed as a means to this end (*ST* I-II.13.3, 90.2; II-II.47.6). Because actions are singular matters, a singular proposition is necessary in order to apply a universal proposition to a particular action (*ST* I-II.76.1; II-II.47.3). Hence, in addition to understanding the universal propositions (the law and end), the practical intellect must be able to understand the singular proposition. The singular proposition is caused by the act of understanding the particular situation to which the law is to be applied (*ST* II-II.47.15). For example, the intellect might compose the proposition that "Today is Sunday" in order to apply the law to keep holy the Lord's day. These singular propositions also participate in eternal law inasmuch as the power to understand the proposition as well as the intelligible form comes from God. However, unlike the participation of universal propositions in eternal law, these do not participate by means of the human intellect recognizing natural ends and inclinations but rather by recognizing the particular circumstances (Cf. *ST* I.76.1).

The Third Act of the Practical Intellect: Practical Reasoning

Just as the weakness of the intellect makes discursive reasoning an essential component for acquiring speculative knowledge, the role of the practical intellect makes discursive reasoning even more essential. Thomas explains that practical matters of action "particularly recede from the condition of things intelligible, and so much farther, as they are less certain and fixed. . . . Prudence above all requires that man be an apt reasoner, so that he may rightly apply universals to particulars, which latter are various and uncertain."[67] In other words, because the intellect can-

---

66. Because natural law like all truths are first and foremost contained in the practical reason of God, Thomas states that natural law is primarily in the eternal law and secondarily in the natural code of human reason (*ST* I-II.71.6.4).

67. *ST* II-II.49.5.2: . . . recedunt praecipue ab intelligibilium conditione, et tanto magis

not immediately understand what to do in every situation but must assess particular situations which vary in number and complexity and then choose from a variety of possible actions, moral reasoning is extremely challenging and being a good reasoner is necessary.

In practical reasoning, conclusions are drawn from the practical propositions in much the same way as speculative conclusions are formed.[68] In speculative reasoning, a universal conclusion can be derived from two universal propositions and a particular conclusion can be derived from a universal and particular proposition.[69] Likewise in practical reasoning, in some cases a universal proposition is derived from two universal propositions (moral science),[70] and in other cases a particular action or judgment is derived from a universal and singular proposition (prudence).[71] In the first case, practical reasoning is used to find secondary precepts of natural law or to derive precepts of human law. Although secondary precepts were already covered in the above section on practical judgment, strictly speaking, the forming of secondary precepts is an act of practical reasoning since they are derived by means of a middle term. In the second case, practical reason determines the particular means to achieve an intended end. When this process of finding the means is in accord with nature, it is called an act of prudence (*ST* II-II.47.2 & 7; I-II.58.4).

Thomas further divides the act of reasoning to a particular means into the intellectual actions of counsel and judgment and adds an additional act of the practical intellect: command.[72] To make sure that these acts are

---

quanto minus sunt certa seu determinata. . . . ad prudentiam maxime requiritur quod sit homo bene ratiocinativus, ut posit bene applicare universalia principia ad particularia, quae sunt varia et incerta.

68. See Flannery, 41–49, for more on practical syllogisms. See also Anthony Celena, "Medieval Theories of Practical Reason," in the *Stanford Encyclopedia of Philosophy*, accessed July 21, 2005, available from *http://plato.stanford.edu/entrie/practical-reason-med/*. Celena argues that Thomas combines the Aristotelian notion of practical reason and roots it in the Augustinian notion of eternal law by means of deriving the first principles of practical reason from the inclinations of human nature.

69. An example of a universal conclusion from two universal propositions is: All mammals are animals. All bears are mammals. Therefore, all bears are animals. An example of a particular conclusion from a particular proposition and a universal proposition is: All carnivores eat meat. Some bears are carnivores. Therefore, some bears eat meat.

70. For example: Humans should always avoid evil acts. All acts of murdering one's father are evil. Therefore, humans should never murder their father. Cf. *ST* I-II.58.5 which notes that humans obtain the universal principles of action by means of natural understanding and practical science (*scientiam practicam*).

71. Thomas gives an example of this in *ST* I-II.76.1: One should not kill his father. This man is his father. Therefore, he should not kill this man.

72. See *ST* II-II.57.6: "Now there are three acts of reason in respect to anything done

properly understood, in the process of explaining them I will also place them in their context of the all the actions of the intellect and will that make up a particular action.[73] Because in practical matters the end comes first, the act begins with a universal proposition that takes the form of the end (*ST* I-II.13.3, 90.2; II-II.47.6). Now this end may be the last end (happiness), or it may be an intermediate end ordained to the last end (*ST* I-II.12.2 & 3). In either case a universal proposition (law) is formed and judged to be a true good by the practical intellect (the second act of the practical intellect).[74] Once the end has been judged to be a true good, the will can tend to this end.[75] This act of the will is called intention.

Once an end is intended, the reason is moved by the will to determine the appropriate means to this end.[76] The reason begins by taking counsel *(consilium)*.[77] Thomas states that because actions are concerned with contingent singulars, a correct judgment of them is uncertain. In uncertain things the reason must first institute an inquiry, and this is called taking counsel (*ST* I-II.14.1). This inquiry begins by recalling how a particular end was attained or not attained in previous experiences.[78] Then the inquiry determines the singular premise by understanding the particular situation, which may involve many different circumstances (I-II.14.2; II-II.49.2; *Ethic* III.8). After the singular premise is determined, the practical syllogism is formed and the intellect is able to derive a conclusion that consists of an action that may be performed. If this action cannot

---

by man: the first of these is counsel; the second, judgment; the third command" (Circa agibilia autem humana tres actus rationis inveniuntur, quorum primus est consiliari, secundus iudicare, tertius est praecipere). In this case, judgment is mediate (by means of a demonstration), not immediate, as will be explained below.

73. As seen in chapter 3, Thomas speaks of many steps that compose a single action. For the steps of an action, see *ST* I-II.11–17, especially 17.3.1.

74. Whereas the speculative intellect judges something to be true, the practical intellect must judge something to be a true good or a true end since the object of the will is the universal good that is grasped by the intellect (*ST* I-II.1.2.3; cf. I-II.61.2).

75. *ST* I-II.12.1 and *Ethic* VI.2. See also *SCG* I.72.7 which states that although the proper object of the will is the end, the intellect must first propose this object.

76. Although those ends that are first self-evident principles are determined by nature, an intermediary end is also determined by practical reason (*ST* I-II.14.2; II-II.47.15) and is also chosen by the will (*ST* I-II.13.3). The means to both the ultimate end and intermediary ends are always determined by practical reason (*Ethic* VI.2; *ST* I-II.12.4 & 5; II-II.47.15).

77. If the intellect has already determined the proper means in deliberating for an earlier act of the same species, it does not need to take counsel but can move directly to judgment (*ST* I-II.14.4.1). See Westberg, *Right Practical Reason*, 131.

78. See *ST* II-II.49.1 on the necessity of memory of past experiences to the virtue of prudence.

be immediately performed, the conclusion instead becomes the end of another syllogism and this process continues until an action is found that can be done immediately.[79] For example, a college student who is enrolling in classes may have the end of becoming a doctor. Based on his situation he determines that the best way to become a doctor is to go to medical school. However, to attain this end he must major in biology, and to attain this end he must take certain classes. He eventually concludes that he must take the class human anatomy in order to go to medical school. Because the intellect is moved to determine the means by the will's desire for the end, throughout the entire process the will consents to the conclusions formed by the intellect and continues to move it until a particular action can be consented to (cf. *ST* I-II.15). Once an agent has determined a possible means to be pursued, he should still consult the experiences of others, preferably the wise (*ST* II-II.49.3).

In judgment, the next act of the practical intellect, the agent judges whether or not the means are truly in conformity with the end, just as in speculative matters conclusions are judged to be true by means of conformity to principles.[80] In other words, just as discursive reasoning

79. *Ethic* III.8; cf. *ST* I.57.6.3; II-II.53.4. In his commentary on the *Ethics,* Thomas explains that to take counsel is to inquire in an analytic method. He then gives the example from the speculative sciences: to prove a conclusion by a diagram or a geometrical explanation one must reduce the conclusion into principles until he reaches the first independent principles. The same thing happens in determining the means to an end. The agent first asks how the end will be attained through this means and then again how this means will be attained. This process continues until the first operation to be undertaken is discovered. For what is first in operation is last in the order of discovery. Thomas gives the example of a man intending to carry out a business venture. He first determines that he needs money. He then inquires into how to get the money. Once he finds the means of getting money, no further deliberation is necessary (*Ethics* III.8). A more modern example might be that of trying to checkmate an opponent's king in chess. Checkmating the king is the intention. But to checkmate the king, you must first move your queen and bishop into the proper places. But in order to do that you must remove your opponent's knight who is blocking this move, and the process goes on until a move is found that is ordered to the ultimate end but can be done immediately. Since you are only guessing what your opponent's response will be to your moves, it is very uncertain as to whether or not your choice will cause the intended end.

80. *ST* II-II.53.4, 47.8, 51.2.2; I-II.57.6.3; *Ethics* III.9. Often the intellect determines two or more syllogisms that correspond to a particular situation (have the same minor premise). Thomas gives the example of fornication where one syllogism would be: I must not commit fornication. To lie with this woman is fornication. Therefore, I must not lie with this woman. The other syllogism would be: I would enjoy fornication. To lie with this woman is fornication. I would enjoy this fornication (II *Sent* 24.3.3). In this case the practical intellect must judge by means of the principles whether or not these actions are in conformity with the end of happiness. See Westberg, 38, 204–6.

ends in judgment in the speculative intellect, so also practical reasoning ends in judgment in the practical intellect. The means are judged to be not only in accord with the immediate end but also in accord with higher ends (cf. *ST* II-II.51.3). For example, in any particular situation, a variety of actions could be derived from practical syllogisms, some which are in accord with the ultimate end and some of which are not. The intellect then judges which actions are in accord with both the immediate end and the ultimate end. If there is only one action determined by taking counsel, then the intellect judges as to whether or not this action will attain the end; if there is more than one action, it determines which action attains the end more perfectly. Since the will already desires the end, once the intellect has judged the proper means to this end, the will chooses this means (*ST* I-II.13.3, 17.3.1). Thus, Thomas states that the choice of the particular thing to be done is the conclusion of the practical syllogism.[81]

Although the conclusion has been determined, the act is not yet completed. The reason must still command that the act be performed (*ST* I-II.17). The will then executes the command by causing the act to be performed. Once the act is performed the end is attained. The speculative intellect contemplates the goodness of this end and the will delights (has joy) in its goodness.[82] This contemplation and corresponding delight is an act of imperfect happiness in reference to the acquisition of an intermediate end, and perfect happiness in reference to the attainment of the ultimate end of God.[83]

In chapter 3, a table with eight of the steps of the human act was presented. Now that the acts of the practical intellect have been analyzed, the full twelve-step table can be presented.[84] (See figure 2.)

---

81. *ST* I.86.1.2. Since the act whereby the will tends to the mean determined by the reason is formally an act of the intellect and materially an act of the will (*ST* I-II.13.1), Thomas will call the conclusion of the practical syllogism either an act of judgment, or choice, or an operation (*ST* I-II.76.1).

82. *ST* I-II.11. For Thomas, the difference between happiness and joy is that happiness is primarily in the intellect, whereas joy is in the will, or, in the case of emotional joy, in the sense appetites. Whenever an appetite rests in an object that it loves, there is joy (or delight). Consequently, just as there is sense love, love of the will, and charity, there is the corresponding passion of joy, natural joy of the will, and supernatural joy, respectively.

83. *ST* I-II.3.6 & 7, 66.3.1. In reference to the delight of the will, Thomas notes that true delight of the will only comes from the attainment of the last end. For as long as the ultimate end is not attained, the will still desires more. Nonetheless, the possession of intermediate ends can result in delight in a certain manner (*ST* I-II.11.3), and the intention of the ultimate end (even without attainment) can result in imperfect delight (*ST* I-II.11.4).

84. For the steps of an action, see *ST* I-II.11–17, especially 17.3.1. See also Daniel West-

FIGURE 2. The Twelve Steps of the Human Action

INTELLECT	WILL
1. Apprehension *(apprehensio)* of the good (the first act of the practical intellect that abstracts the intellectual form that the will desires)	2. Desire *(voluntas)* for the good
3. Judgment *(judicium)* of the universal proposition (law or end) (the second act of the practical intellect)	4. Intention *(intentio)*
5. Deliberation *(consilium)* of means (if necessary)	6. Consent *(consensus)* (if necessary)
7. Judgment *(judicium)* of means	8. Choice *(electio)* of means
9. Command *(imperare)* of means	10. Execution *(usus)*
11. Contemplation *(contemplatio)* of the end achieved (an act of the speculative intellect)	12. Delight *(delectatio)* in the end

Although there are many similarities between the practical syllogism and the speculative syllogism, there are also several dissimilarities of which I will mention two. The first dissimilarity is that because the appetitive faculty plays an indispensable part within the act of the practical reason, the rectitude of the appetite can affect the conclusion of the practical syllogism.[85] If either the will or the sense appetites are not properly formed, they can hinder practical reason. If the will does not tend to the proper end, it will not move the reason to begin the practical syllogism. Likewise,

---

berg, *Right Practical,* chapters 8–12, who gives a detailed analysis of the process of the moral act. He explains the structure of *ST* I-II.11–17 by stating that there are three basic parts to an act: intention (including the intellect's act of apprehension: I-II.12), choice (including judgment: I-II.13), and execution (including command: I-II.16–17). Because many actions can be determined without deliberation, deliberation and consent are treated after judgment and choice (I-II.14–15), even though in the moral act they precede them. Michael Sherwin, *By knowledge and by Love,* expands upon the work of Westberg to include *apprehensio* and *simplex voluntas* as the first steps of the intellect and will (84–85). Cessario, *Introduction,* notes that the first four steps and the last two deal with the end, while steps 6–10 deal with the means (119). Other earlier scholars posited twelve steps to a complete human act. See, for example, J. A. Oesterle, *Ethics: The Introduction to Moral Science* (Englewood Cliffs, N.J.: Prentice-Hall, 1958), 85, and Gilson, *The Philosophy of St. Thomas,* chapter 15. Keep in mind that these are the steps in an ideal action that is successfully completed.

85. See McInerny, *St. Thomas Aquinas,* 72–73, for an account of how the failure to apply the universal proposition can be from a lack of a good disposition in the appetitive faculty.

it can also be led by the sense appetites to reject the means determined by the intellect to be in accord with the end.

Every practical syllogism that results in an action applies an end to a particular situation. The understanding of the particular situation comes from concepts that are apprehended from sense knowledge. Whenever there is sense knowledge, either from the bodily senses or the imagination, this knowledge is followed by a sense appetite (*ST* I.80, 81.1; cf. I.78.4, 77.7). Consequently, in every single action of the practical intellect, in addition to the appetite of the will, there is an accompanying sense appetite. In some cases, this sensual desire is for a sensual form that has not been judged to be a true good by the reason, in which case the sense appetites can lead the will to consent to a means not in conformity with reason.[86] In this case because the reason can find many different means to the end, the will may choose a means that is not determined by reason to be in conformity with the natural law (*ST* I-II.75.1). In other cases, the sense appetites can completely blind the reason, causing it to not determine an action at all. Thus, unruly appetites can hinder the practical reason and keep it from coming to the proper conclusion.

A second dissimilarity between practical and speculative reasoning is that whereas the knowledge *(scientia)* from speculative reasoning is certain, practical knowledge decreases in certainty as it moves further from first principles.[87] Thomas states that because the speculative intellect is concerned with necessary things, its proper conclusions contain truth without fail just as the general principles do:

But the practical reason is busied with contingent matters, about which human actions are concerned: and consequently, although there is necessity in the gen-

---

86. *ST* I-II.24.3. Thomas says that these passions are antecedent to reason and can overcome reason by obscuring judgment (Cf. I.95.2; I-II.17.7, 50.3.1). However, if the sensual desire follows the judgment by reason, then the sensual desire assists in the will's execution of reason's command (*ST* I-II.59.2.3). It is in respect to the passion following the command of reason that Aquinas says that prudence determines the mean of the moral virtues (*ST* II-II.47.7).

87. McInerny, *St. Thomas Aquinas,* contrasts abstract principles of moral reasoning with more concrete conclusions. Although the first are quite certain, they are of very little help in extremely complicated situations due to their vagueness. However, the more concrete conclusions, although much more helpful, are less certain because so many qualifications have been built into them (70–71). Jean Porter, "What the Wise Person Knows," *Studies in Christian Ethics* 12 (1999): 65–66, adds to this by noting that although the precepts of the Decalogue cannot be applied with clear and certain knowledge in every case, we nonetheless have substantive moral knowledge of these conclusions, just as humans have "genuine albeit non-certain knowledge of the individual creatures which we encounter in the world around us."

eral principles, the more we descend to matters of detail, the more frequently we encounter defects.[88]

While the majority of the actions in our life can be determined to be right with relative certainty due to their close connection with the principles of natural law, there are some actions that are so contingent that the greatest natural certainty is obtained by learning from the wise (*ST* II-II.49.3; I-II.2.1.1, 100.1 & 3). Furthermore, actions are applied to particular situations that contain a variety of circumstances. Because it can be difficult to consider all of these circumstances, two different humans who start with the same end may come to different conclusions because they consider different circumstances in applying the end.

   Just as the mind participates in the eternal law by knowing the principles for practical reason (the natural law), so also this participation is extended to knowing the conclusions. The intellectual light of the human mind is not strong enough to immediately understand the proper action in every situation; hence it must illuminate the proper action by means of discursive reasoning. This light of natural reason whereby humans are directed to their proper actions is a participation in the divine light (*ST* I-II.86.1, 91.2). Because the *rationes* of all actions are already contained in the divine intellect, when the human intellect judges that a particular action is to be done, the form of this action is a likeness of the eternal law where the degree of participation is in accord with the goodness of the action. Thomas explains, "Now it is from the eternal law, which is the divine reason, that the human reason is the rule of the human will, from which the human will derives its goodness."[89] Unlike the blessed who see the eternal law directly and understand it by means of the light of glory, humans on earth can only see it in its effects and they must increase their knowledge of it through discursive reasoning.[90] Consequently, in order for the mind to cognitively participate in eternal

88. *ST* I-II.94.4: Sed ratio practica negotiatur circa contingentia, in quibus sunt operationes humanae, et ideo, etsi in communibus sit aliqua necessitas, quanto magis ad propria descenditur, tanto magis invenitur defectus. Cf. I-II.91.3.3; II-II.47.2.3.

89. *ST* I-II.19.4: Quod autem ratio humana sit regula voluntatis humanae, ex qua eius bonitas mensuretur, habet ex lege aeterna, quae est ratio divina. See also Rhonheimer, *Natural Law,* who states that the natural light of the intellect possesses in a participative way the certainty and inerrancy of its source (264).

90. *ST* I-II.93.2. Thomas elsewhere states that just as the participation of the speculative intellect in divine wisdom is imperfect, so also is participation of the practical intellect, since it does not perfectly know the determinations of particular cases which are also contained in eternal law (*ST* I-II.91.3.1).

law by knowing the proper action, the mind must first abstract intelligible forms from phantasms. Then these intelligible forms can be combined and separated into propositions from which the mind can judge and command the particular action.

By means of the natural acts of the intellect, the human agent is able to participate in the divine mind, which is the efficient cause of the natural light of the intellect and the exemplary cause of the intellectual forms. In reference to the practical intellect, the eternal law acts as the exemplary cause of both the ends of the act that are immediately understood and the species of the act which are determined through practical reasoning. The divine light acts as the efficient cause of the power to understand and the power of the practical reason to come to moral conclusions.[91] This cognitive participation in the eternal law is unique to humans who are self-governing and allows them to participate more perfectly than irrational creatures.

THE PERFECTION OF THE INTELLECT THROUGH THE ACQUIRED INTELLECTUAL VIRTUES

Because the intellect is in potency to a variety of actions, habits are necessary to perfect its natural inclination to know things as they are (*ST* I-II.50.5 & 6, 56.3.2; *SCG* I.61; cf. *ST* I-II.49.4). Although the intellect does not err in knowing its proper object, which is the quiddity of a material thing, it can err in its acts of composition and division and of discursive reasoning.[92] In other words, the intellect is capable of composing a variety of propositions about something that could be either true or false, and hence it needs good habits to dispose it to always judge and reason correctly in order for its knowledge to be true. Thomas affirms this by noting that the intellect is able to achieve its end of knowing truth by being perfected by the intellectual virtues (*Ethic* VI.3). He continues by noting that five virtues are needed to do this: understanding,

91. Thomas notes that we know and judge all things by participation in divine light (*ST* I.12.11.3). Cf. I.105.3.

92. *ST* I.85.6; *SCG* III.108.4. Thomas compares the intellect to the senses which do not err in reference to their proper object, but can err in reference to accidental objects (e.g., sight does not err in reference to sensing color unless there is a defect in the organ, but can err in reference to judging size or distance as in the case of judging the sun to be only a foot in diameter, etc.). In addition to knowledge of its proper object, the intellect does not err in knowing first principles unless it does not understand the intellectual species at all (*ST* I.85.6).

science (also called knowledge), wisdom, prudence, and art. Of these virtues, the first three (understanding, science, and wisdom) perfect the speculative intellect and the last two (prudence and art) perfect the practical intellect.

Among these five virtues it is easiest to see how prudence perfects cognitive participation in the eternal law, because it perfects the practical intellect to cause actions that are in accord with the ultimate end to which the eternal law orders humans. However, the other four virtues also perfect participation in the eternal law because they perfect the intellect to act, even if the actions are those of making rather than doing (art) or knowing truth for its own sake rather than for operation (the virtues of the speculative intellect). Because the eternal law orders all creatures to perform actions in accord with their mode, humans are also ordered to make things and especially to understand things.

Furthermore, the ultimate end of humans is the highest act of the highest power: understanding God. When humans understand things on earth, they already begin to participate in the ultimate end to which they are ordered by the eternal law.[93] Thomas notes that although the acts of the practical intellect are closer to the ultimate end by way of preparation or merit, the acts of the speculative intellect are closer by way of similarity.[94] Hence, the virtues of the speculative intellect cause greater cognitive participation in the eternal law by perfecting it to perform its own proper action to which the eternal law orders it.

In addition to perfecting the intellect to know things for their own sake and to make things, the virtues of the speculative intellect and art perfect participation in the eternal law because they confer on the intellect an aptness to perform good actions in the practical realm.[95] In other words, these virtues are practical by extension because the intellectual perfections they cause can be ordered to good moral actions (cf. *ST* I.1.4;

93. Thomas notes that in the speculative virtues we have a beginning of that happiness which consists in the contemplation of truth (*ST* I-II.57.1.2,66.3.1; cf. I-II.3.6 & 7).

94. *De Virtutibus in communi* 7.4. The acts of the speculative intellect are at the very heart of cognitive participation in the eternal law because humans are not only called to be self-directing moral agents but to also be contemplatives.

95. Thomas makes a distinction between virtues that give humans an aptness to perform good actions and virtues that make a human good absolutely (*ST* I-II.56.3). Because the end is the proper object of the will, it is by rectitude of the will that someone is good absolutely speaking (*ST* I.5.4.3). Thus, although all virtues perfect humans, only those virtues that include an act of the will make humans good absolutely. Among the intellectual virtues only prudence and faith include an act of the will. All the other intellectual virtues can be used for evil actions, but prudence and living faith can only be used for good actions (*ST* I-II.57.1).

II-II.4.2.3). Because the only difference between speculative knowledge and practical knowledge is that the latter is ordered to operation, speculative knowledge can become practical if it is used in determining the proper action to be performed.[96] Hence, any intellectual perfections in the speculative intellect can be made practical by extension. In other words, although knowledge of the soul is speculative, it becomes practical when it used to determine universal propositions about how one should act. For example, the speculative premise that humans are rational by nature becomes the practical premise that humans must act in accord with reason (*ST* I-II.18.5, 54.3).

Because the speculative virtues and art can be ordered to good human actions, they can perfect cognitive participation in the eternal law by giving humans the ability to have more perfect knowledge of the end to which they are ordered and how to direct themselves and others to this end. This additional knowledge results in more perfect alignment of the intellect with the ordering of the eternal law, bringing humans to their perfection through rational operation. However, in causing an aptness to do good actions, these virtues and art only increase participation in the eternal law if they are accompanied by a good will, or else they can also be used for evil. Nonetheless, to the extent they are accompanied by a good will they do perfect cognitive participation in the eternal law.

The speculative intellectual virtues and art perfect cognitive participation in the eternal law by perfecting humans to perform the acts of contemplating truth and making things. Humans participate in the eternal law by contemplation because this act prefigures the end to which humans are ordered. They participate in the eternal law through art because the act of making something orders creation and hence participates in God's eternal ordering of it. These virtues also are practical by extension and perfect the ability of humans to perform moral actions that are ordered to the ultimate end. Hence, this section on perfection of participation in eternal law by virtue will cover all of the virtues of the speculative intellect followed by the virtues of the practical intellect.

The First Virtue of the Speculative Intellect: Understanding

The first virtue needed to obtain speculative knowledge is the virtue of understanding *(intellectus)*. Thomas uses the term *intellectus* to desig-

---

96. See *DV* 2.8 which states that practical knowledge follows speculative, since it is made practical by applying it to work. Cf. *ST* I-II.57.1.2.

nate the intellective power, the act of understanding and the habit of understanding.[97] All three of these uses are related since the act of understanding is the proper act of the intellect and the habit of understanding perfects the intellect to perform this act (*ST* I-II.51.2). As seen above, the act of understanding refers to both the act of simple apprehension and to the act of forming propositions by composing and dividing these intelligible species (*DV* 14.1). The intellect needs the virtue of understanding to perfect its act of understanding since it is not able to completely know a thing without this virtue. Thomas notes that to understand is to penetrate into the essence of a thing, since the object of the intellect is what a thing is. However, there are many different kinds of things that are hidden within a thing. For example, under accidents are hidden the substantial reality, under words lie their meaning, under effects lie their causes, and so on. All of these things require the light of understanding to penetrate to the underlying reality, and the stronger the light of understanding, the deeper it can penetrate into things and their principles (*ST* II-II.8.1). The virtue of understanding perfects the natural light of the intellect to penetrate deeper into things by giving it the ability to properly complete simple apprehension by composing and dividing the proper intellectual species.[98]

The intellect perfected by understanding is able to understand a variety of hidden attributes in a single proposition without recourse to discursive reasoning.[99] Because practical reasoning presupposes these propositions, understanding precedes the other intellectual virtues. Thomas notes that before any other intellectual virtue, the intellect must have the virtue of understanding to perfect the intellect's act of understanding the principles of demonstration. This perfection of the intellect is necessary since science is founded upon demonstrative reason proceeding from principles to conclusions (*Ethic* VI.5, n.1175–76; cf. *DT* II.2.7).

97. See M. R. Brennan, *The Intellectual Virtues According to the Philosophy of St. Thomas* (Washington, D.C.: The Catholic University of America Press, 1941), 17. On page 18 she gives a list of the important Thomistic texts which speak of understanding. Cf. *ST* I.79.10; *Ethic* VI.5.

98. *ST* I.58.4; I-II.57.2; II-II.15.1. See also Gilson, *Christian Philosophy,* 262, who states that truth can either be known immediately or through reasoning. Understanding is a permanent disposition of the intellect, aiding it with its knowledge of immediately evident truths or principles.

99. *SCG* I.57.2, 55.2. Cf. *DT* VI.1.3 where Thomas states that in understanding, a whole multitude of truths are seen in the first unified and simple truth. See also *ST* I.89.1 which states that since the soul understands by participation in divine light, the closer to God, the greater the comprehension by fewer ideas.

Among the types of principles that are understood, Thomas especially emphasizes the role of the virtue of understanding in forming first principles (*ST* I.58.3). Thomas states that understanding is a habit whereby a human by the power of the light of the active intellect naturally knows indemonstrable principles (*Ethic* VI.5, n. 1179). Because all humans have this habit by nature, inasmuch as humans grasp the meaning of the terms of the first principles, they understand them.[100] These natural principles of knowledge allow the agent intellect to further understand things through discursive reasoning.[101] Hence, these principles act as a foundation for all knowledge since the intellect does not err in the case of first principles.[102]

Through the virtue of understanding the intellect is perfected to participate more perfectly in the eternal law. This habit aids the natural light of the intellect to perform its proper action: to know things as they are in reality. This knowledge is a participation in the divine exemplars and prefigures the act of contemplating the divine essence. Furthermore, this knowledge can also be ordered to good human actions (cf. *ST* II-II.8.3). Greater understanding of things (including human nature) allows humans to use them more in accord with the way God created them to be used and hence to more perfectly achieve their end and direct other humans to their end.

Science (Sometimes Called Knowledge)   Because of the weakness of the human intellect, humans by nature obtain greater knowledge of the truth by discursive movement from principles to conclusions, rather than knowing it immediately by understanding, as the angels do.[103] Just as the in-

---

100. Thomas gives the example of the terms whole and part. He states that once the intellectual soul has grasped what is a whole and what is a part, it immediately perceives that every whole is larger than its part (*ST* I-II.51.1). Thomas goes on to state that although all humans have this habit by nature, owing to the individual disposition, some are more apt to understand things well than others.

101. Although the habit of understanding is in the possible intellect (*ST* I-II.50.4.1), it increases the ability of the natural light of the intellect to know things. Cf. *DV* 11.1 & 3 where Thomas states that self-evident principles serve the agent intellect like tools serve a craftsman (Cf. *ST* I.79.5.3). See also II-II.8.1.2 which states that reasoning begins with understanding and ends with it.

102. *SCG* I.61. However, Thomas then states that the intellect does on occasion err in the conclusions derived from these principles.

103. *SCG* I.57.2; *ST* I.58.4, 79.8; *PA* 3. In this life humans come to knowledge of truth by means of both understanding and reasoning; however, in the next life, humans will come to knowledge of truth by immediately understanding the divine essence by the power of the participated light of glory (cf. *ST* II-II.180.3 &4). See also *DT* II.2 which states that the

tellect needs the habit of understanding to perfect it in reference to understanding principles, so also the intellect needs a habit to perfect it in determining conclusions from these principles (*Ethic* VI.3). This habit is the virtue of science, which causes greater understanding of the being of a thing by perfecting the intellect to correctly predicate its proper attributes by means of a middle term. In other words, by the habit of science the natural light of the intellect is perfected to penetrate deeper into the being of a thing by a demonstration, which results in a greater understanding of the thing.

Both the virtues of understanding and science are necessary for sound arguments. Understanding ensures that the propositions are true and science ensures that the argument proceeding from these propositions is valid. Together these virtues allow humans to know something completely and with certitude.[104] Thus, the virtue of science perfects the intellect to easily and promptly move from true propositions to true conclusions (*SCG* II.73; I-II.50.4).

Because discursive reasoning begins with understanding and is ordered to understanding, the virtue of science is likewise ordered to the virtue of understanding. Hence, the way that the virtue of science perfects participation in eternal law only differs in degree but not mode from the way that the virtue of understanding perfects participation. Science results in a greater understanding, which means that the intellect is perfected to more perfectly participate in the eternal law in performing its proper action of knowing things as they are in reality.[105] Likewise, this greater understanding can be ordered to good human actions. For example, the virtue of science can be used by the practical intellect to derive further principles from the first principles of practical reasoning.[106]

---

essence of science is that a knowledge of things unknown is derived from things that are known.

104. *PA* I.1–4; *Ethic* VI.3; I *Sent* 3.2; *DV* 12.1.2. That which is known through science is not like an opinion that the will assents to. If the connection between first principles (to which the intellect necessarily assents) and the conclusion is recognized by the intellect, then the intellect necessarily assents to the conclusion (*ST* I.82.2).

105. See *ST* II-II.108.7 which notes that all men naturally desire to know, so consequently they delight in the knowledge of truth. This delight increases with the habits of science and wisdom because they cause contemplation to be without difficulty. Cf. II-II.108.3.

106. Cf. *ST* I-II.100.11. Keep in mind that this derivation of principles is not the same as prudence since things known by science are universal and necessary, while things known by prudence are contingent and singular. The virtue of science increases cognitive participation in eternal law by causing further laws that act as the major premise of the practical syllogism.

Wisdom The intellect by discursive reasoning tends toward conclusions that are last in the order of discovery. If the conclusions are last in a given genus, then the virtue that allows the intellect to reason to them is science. However, if the conclusions are last in reference to all human knowledge, then the virtue that perfects the intellect to reason to them is wisdom.[107] When wisdom considers what is last in the order of human knowledge, it is considering what is first in the order of nature and causality, and all things are judged according to their first causes. Hence, although wisdom is also a science, it is unlike any other science in that wisdom judges both the principles and the conclusions of all other sciences (*ST* I.1.6; I-II.57.2.1; *Ethic* VI.5 and 6, n.1180–87).

To help explain the virtue of wisdom, Thomas (following Aristotle) uses the example of the architect (*Metaph* I.1, n. 28, 35, 50; *SCG* II.24; *ST* I.1.6). The architect knows the end for which the building is to be built. Because the architect knows the end, he can order all parts of the building to fulfill this end. For example, if the building is intended to function as an airplane assembly plant, all the parts of the building will be composed to meet this function (e.g., large open spaces, large doors, many safety features, etc.). If a particular aspect of the building was not ordered to this end, the architect would judge it as being improper.

God as the first cause is the wise architect who orders the universe to Himself as its proper end (*SCG* I.94; II.24). The wise human knows God as end and therefore also this order.[108] Consequently, as the architect judges the features of the building, the wise human judges and directs all other sciences (including moral reasoning) by his knowledge of this end and order.[109] Because wisdom judges the principles and conclusions of all other sciences, it is the most perfect of the intellectual virtues (*ST* I-II.57.2.2, 66.5).

---

107. *ST* I-II.57.2. Elsewhere Thomas makes a distinction between the higher reason that knows eternal things and the lower reason that knows temporal things. Although both belong to the same power of reason, wisdom perfects the higher reason and science perfects the lower reason (*ST* I.79.9; II-II.45.3). See also Gilson, *Christian Philosophy . . .* , 262, who states that because science considers many different objects of human knowledge, there can be many different sciences in the human mind. However, because wisdom bears on last causes and the most universal object, there can be but one object of knowledge and therefore one wisdom.

108. See Brennan, *The Intellectual Virtues,* 46, and Gregory Reichberg, "Intellect Virtues (Ia IIae qq. 57–58)," in *Ethics of Aquinas,* 136–38. Cf. *Ethic* I.1, n. 1, which states that there is a twofold order of things: the order of the various parts of a whole to each other, and the order of all parts to the end. The second is of greatest importance since it is the cause of the first.

109. *SCG* I.50; *ST* I.1.6, 79.9; cf. *ST* I.12.8.

Because wisdom perfects the highest power of the soul to contemplate the highest being, it results in the most perfect natural act of the intellect on earth. This contemplation is a participation in the happiness of knowing God as He is. Thomas notes that wisdom is the greatest of the intellectual virtues because of the greatness of its object (*ST* I-II.66.5). Since this object is the universal truth, which is the object of perfect happiness, perfect wisdom would result in perfect happiness. Thomas states:

If indeed the consideration of wisdom were perfect in respect of its object, there would be perfect happiness in the act of wisdom. But because the act of wisdom in this life is imperfect in respect of its principal object, which is God, it follows that the act of wisdom is a beginning or participation of future happiness.[110]

Because wisdom considers the universal truth itself to which the eternal law orders humans, wisdom results in a great perfection of participation in eternal law.

Furthermore, wisdom is practical by extension as ordering humans to their proper end. Because wisdom considers the last end, and the end is the cause of all human actions, wisdom especially gives humans an aptness to do good actions by giving them the ability to judge whether or not their actions are in accord with the ultimate end. Wisdom judges the principles and conclusions of moral science and even prudence, for although prudence is not a true science, it is a virtue concerning discursive reasoning and hence judged by wisdom (*ST* I-II.66.5.1; II-II.19.7). When wisdom is accompanied by a good will, the wise human is able to determine whether or not the principles and conclusions of his actions are truly ordered to the ultimate end.[111] Since the order of things is based upon their relation to the end, a greater knowledge of the end gives a human an aptness to more perfectly order his actions (*ST* I-II.6.2). Since the eternal law is the divine wisdom that orders things to their end, the virtue of human wisdom gives humans a much greater capacity to cognitively participate in eternal law.

The Virtues of the Practical Intellect
The virtues perfecting the practical intellect are art and prudence. Because art is concerned with making something and not performing a

---

110. *ST* I-II.66.5.2: si quidem esset perfecta consideratio sapientiae respectu sui obiecti, esset perfecta felicitas in actu sapientiae. Sed quia actus sapientiae in hac vita est imperfectus respectu principalis obiecti, quod est deus; ideo actus sapientiae est quaedam inchoatio seu participatio futurae felicitatis. Cf. *SCG* I.1.2.

111. Thomas states that wisdom considers not only God, but also the direction of human conduct to God (*ST* II-II.19, 7; cf. 45.2).

moral action, it only perfects participation in eternal law in a manner
similar to the way the speculative virtues perfect participation. Hence, I
will only analyze the virtue of art in reference to it increasing the capacity of a human to perform good actions. Prudence, on the other hand, is
moved by the will to determine actions that are in accord with ultimate
end, and thus it makes humans good simply speaking. However, because
prudence proceeds from principles that are habitually understood, before treating prudence I will briefly treat the virtue perfecting practical
understanding followed by an analysis of prudence.

Art   Art is the habit of right reasoning about works to be made (*ST*
I-II.57.3). When artists make something, they must first have an exemplar of the artwork in their reason. Consequently, the virtue of art perfects the intellect to form good exemplars of a work to be made. Because
the goodness of this crafted work is the end of the virtue of art, art is
not dependent upon a good will, which has the ultimate end of happiness as its end. Therefore, like the speculative virtues, it results only in
an aptness to do good. Thomas gives the example of the craftsman who
performs his work faithfully when the virtue of art is accompanied with
justice (*ST* I-II.57.3). Inasmuch as this art enables a good will to achieve
results that are otherwise unattainable, it increases cognitive participation in eternal law.[112]

Humans participate in the eternal law not only by governing themselves but also by governing other things and other humans (Cf. *ST*
I.103.6). Art has a particular role in this form of participation. The artist
makes things on account of an end or good they serve. For example, the
builder makes a house to serve as shelter. In the act of making something, an artist orders things to a particular end and if the work is done
with a good will then it is ordered to the common good of all. For example, a house may be built for shelter so that its occupants are able to
perform actions of knowing and loving God and others. Inasmuch as the
artist causes lower goods to be used for the good of humans, the artist
participates in divine governance.

Practical Understanding (Synderesis)   Just as the speculative reason begins with propositions, so also the practical reason begins with propo-

---

112. See also Brennan, *The Intellectual Virtues,* 53–65, on art. Brennan makes the point
that the virtues of art and the desire to produce beautiful things are a likeness to God, the
Creator (65).

sitions (*ST* I-II.90.1.2, 58.4). Consequently, the habit of understanding must also perfect the practical intellect to properly form propositions by means of apprehension and judgment. In the practical intellect two types of propositions are understood: laws (universal propositions) and singular propositions. These two types act as the major and minor premises of the practical syllogism, respectively.[113]

In reference to laws that are naturally understood, the habit of understanding in the practical intellect is called *synderesis* (*ST* I.79.12; II-II.47.6.1; *DV* 16.1–17.2). This habit allows the practical intellect to know without discursive reasoning the first principles of practical reason: the first principles of natural law (*ST* I-II.94.1). In other words, the human with *synderesis* is able to combine and separate the apprehended intellectual species in order to form propositions that are immediately grasped with certainty.[114] For example, the intellectual species "good" and "to be done and pursued" are combined into the proposition "good is to be done and pursued" (*ST* I-II.94.2). From these propositions the practical reason is able to derive further propositions that serve as secondary precepts of natural law.[115] However, in order to derive these further propositions, the practical intellect needs the virtue of science. These propositions that are derived are universal and hence are not derived by means of prudence which in finding the means to an end produces an individual conclusion.[116]

The habits of *synderesis* and moral science allow humans to know the natural law. This knowledge of the natural law is a participation in the eternal law (*ST* I-II.91.2). By means of this knowledge humans are able to direct themselves to their proper end in accord with the eternal law. Hence, the habits of *synderesis* and moral science are essential components to cognitive participation in the eternal law.[117]

113. See *Ethic* VI.9, n. 1247, which states that one type of understanding deals with unchangeables and another deals with the particular or minor proposition in practical reasoning. The latter is an understanding of the sensible and singular. Cf. *ST* I-II.76.1.

114. Although some of these propositions are self-evident in relation to all people, some are only known by the wise who have a more perfect habit of understanding (*ST* I-II.94.2).

115. *ST* I.79.12 and II-II.47.15. Cf. Rhonheimer, *Natural Law and Practical Reason*, 257–87.

116. Although derived laws have more certitude than do prudential actions (*ST* II-II.49.5.2), Thomas states that human laws cannot have the inerrancy that belongs to the demonstrated conclusions of the sciences (*ST* I-II.91.3.3).

117. Cf. *ST* I-II.91.3.1 where Thomas notes, "as on the part of the speculative reason, by a natural participation in divine wisdom, there is in us the knowledge of certain general principles, . . . so too, on the part of the practical reason, man has a natural participation of the eternal law, according to certain general principles . . ." (sicut ex parte rationis speculativae, per naturalem participationem divinae sapientiae, inest nobis cognitio quorundam

Unlike the habit of *synderesis,* which allows humans to understand
universal principles, there is also a habit of understanding that allows
humans to understand singular principles.[118] A law must be applied to a
particular situation to determine the proper action to be performed (*ST*
II-II.47.3). The virtue of understanding also perfects the mind to combine and separate intellectual forms in order to have a true understanding of the particular situation. For example, although the law states that
one should return a borrowed sword, if the lender is a madman, then the
sword ought not to be returned (*ST* II-II.120.1). In order for prudence
to determine whether or not to return the sword, it must not only know
the law, but also the particular situation to see whether or not the law
applies here. In this case the understanding of the particular situation
would include that the sword is borrowed, that the man is mad, and any
other circumstances that might effect the application of the law (e.g., he
is currently angry with his wife). Because there can be an infinite number of different situations, a virtue of understanding must perfect the
intellect to understand the singular proposition within the practical syllogism.

Without the knowledge of the singular proposition, the moral law
could not be applied to a particular situation. The eternal law orders
humans to perform actions in order to reach the ultimate end. Humans
perform these actions in particular situations. Hence, the eternal law not
only contains the exemplars for the universal premises of human action
but also the singular premises (for God's knowledge includes both singulars and universals). Consequently, when the virtue of understanding
perfects the intellect to understand the singular premise, it also perfects
participation in the eternal law.

Prudence   Although the end of a human action is known by understanding and moral science, the means of obtaining this end are manifold and
contingent. Hence, the intellect needs the virtue of prudence to perfect
it to perform the proper means to the end (*ST* I-II.57.4 & 5; I-II.58.4.1;
II-II.47.6). Once the universal proposition (the end) is intended, the in-

---

communium principiorum . . . ita etiam ex parte rationis practicae naturaliter homo participat legem aeternam secundum quaedam communia principia).

118. *ST* II-II.47.15; cf. 47.3. In II-II.49.2.1 Thomas distinguishes between two types of
understanding from which prudence proceeds: the habit of understanding in reference to
universals and the habit of understanding in reference to singular and contingent practical
matters. He calls the latter the understanding that is a part of prudence.

tellect takes counsel, judges, and commands the means that is chosen to reach this end. All three of these actions must be perfected in order to reach the end. Hence, under the virtue of prudence are the virtues of *euboulia, synesis,* and *gnome*.[119] *Euboulia* perfects the act of taking counsel, and *synesis* and *gnome* perfect the act of judgment (*ST* I-II.57.6; *Ethic* VI.7–9). Prudence itself perfects the act of command (*ST* II-II.47.8).

Euboulia, which is derived from the Greek words *eu* ('good') and *boule* ('counsel') is the virtue that perfects the practical reason to properly find the best means to the intended end. It corresponds in many ways to the speculative virtue of science. Just as science perfects the speculative intellect to move from principles to conclusions, *euboulia* perfects the practical intellect to move from the universal propositions (the end) to a particular action (*ST* II-II.49.5, 51.1.1, 53.4). Thomas explains that an ideal act of counsel includes the following five steps: "memory of the past, understanding of the present, shrewdness in considering the future outcome, reasoning which compares one thing to another, and docility in accepting the opinions of others."[120] Hence in taking counsel, one begins with the universal premise (the end) that is already understood. Then one considers relevant past experiences. After this one understands the current situation by forming the singular premise (Cf. *ST* II-II.49.2). Because the shrewd person has an aptness to discover the middle term (*ST* II-II.49.4), the next step is to determine whether or not the major (universal) and minor (singular) premises have two identical terms that allows a conclusion to be derived from them. If they do have a common term, then one next uses reason to derive the proper conclusion from the syllogism.[121] If the conclusion is not yet an action that can be done in the present, then the conclusion is made into the major premise of another syllogism and the process begins again until an action is derived that can be done immediately.[122] Since prudence is concerned with par-

---

119. Cf. John Naus, S.J., *The Nature of the Practical Intellect According to St. Thomas Aquinas* (Rome: Libreria Editrice Dell'Università Gregoriana, 1959), 131–35.

120. *ST* II-II.53.3: memoria praeteritorum, intelligentia praesentium, solertia in considerandis futuris eventibus, ratiocinatio conferens unum alteri, docilitas, per quam aliquis acquiescit sententiis maiorum. Cf. *ST* II-II.48.1.

121. *ST* II-II.49.5. If they do not have an identical middle term or a conclusion cannot be logically drawn from the premises, then the means cannot be chosen because it is not proportional to the end (cf. *ST* II-II.64.7).

122. *Ethic* III.8 and *ST* I-II.14.2. For example, if a student intends the end of graduating from college, he might use a practical syllogism to then determine that he must pass Introduction to Theology to reach this end. However, in order to pass this class, he must pass the first test, and in order to pass the first test he must study. Studying is finally an action

ticular matters which are of an infinite variety, no human can consider them all sufficiently. Thus, the last step is to seek the advice of the wise (*ST* II-II.49.3).

In all cases of discursive reason, a virtue is needed so that the intellect is disposed to move promptly and correctly from premises to conclusions. Since the practical intellect considers singular matters of action of which there can be an uncountable number of things to consider, it especially needs a virtue to perfect it to properly determine the proper means to the end (*ST* II-II.49.5.2). The virtue of *euboulia* perfects the intellect to perform this action.

Just as speculative reason ends in understanding through judgment,[123] so also the practical reason ends with understanding through the act of judgment.[124] Thomas in explaining a vice against practical judgment states, "just as research belongs to the reason, so judgment belongs to the intellect. Wherefore also in speculative matters a demonstrative science is said to judge, insofar as through the analysis of first principles of understanding, it judges the truth of the research."[125] He continues by noting that likewise the act of not judging rightly the research of the practical reason through contempt or neglect belongs to the vice of thoughtlessness (*ST* II-II.53.4). In other words, just as in the speculative sciences, a full understanding of a conclusion is not obtained until the intellect sees the connection between the conclusion and the principles it is derived from, so also in practical matters an act is not understood to be in conformity with its end until the intellect understands through judgment the connection between the principles and the conclusion.

If the principles by which this action is judged are lower principles (the proximate end/law), then the virtue perfecting the intellect to judge

---

he can do immediately. Although in some circumstances it may be necessary to move all the way from the ultimate end of eternal happiness to a particular action through a whole string of syllogisms, usually in our actions we have already determined intermediate ends. Hence, counsel begins with these intermediate ends. In fact, for many of our actions we do not need to deliberate at all since the proper action is already evident without an inquiry (see *ST* I-II.14.4.1–2).

123. See *ST* I.79.12 on how reason both begins and ends with understanding.

124. *ST* I-II.76.1, 93.2.3; *ST* II-II.51.3.2. See also *ST* II-II.51.2.2 where Thomas states that whereas the end of counsel is the discovery of the thing to be done, the end of judgment is the certainty of the practical conclusion.

125. *ST* II-II.53.4: Sicut autem inquisitio pertinet ad rationem, ita iudicium pertinet ad intellectum, unde et in speculativis demonstrativa scientia dicitur iudicativa, inquantum per resolutionem in prima principia intelligibilia de veritate inquisitorum diiudicatur. Cf. *ST* II-II.51.4.2.

is *synesis*. If the action is judged by higher principles (the ultimate end or principles that are closer to it), then the virtue perfecting the intellect to judge is *gnome*. Thomas states:

Cognitive habits differ according to higher and lower principles: thus in speculative matters wisdom considers higher principles than science does, and consequently is distinguished from it; and so must it be also in practical matters. Now it is evident that what is beside the order of a lower principle is sometimes reducible to the order of a higher principle. . . . Now it happens sometimes that something has to be done which is not covered by the common rules of actions, for instance in the case of the enemy of one's country, when it would be wrong to give him back his deposit, or in similar cases. Hence, it is necessary to judge of such matters according to higher principles than the common rules, according to which *synesis* judges: and corresponding to such higher principles it is necessary to have a higher virtue of judgment, which is called *gnome*.[126]

Most of the time, the end (law) that we intend can be directly applied to a particular situation. To use Thomas's example, under normal conditions one must pay back a deposit. The virtue of *synesis* perfects the intellect to judge correctly in these normal conditions. However, in extraordinary conditions, the law that normally applies may not apply, such as when one should not give back the deposit because doing so would not be proportionate to the greater end of allegiance to one's country.[127]

---

126. *ST* II-II.51.3: Habitus cognoscitivi distinguuntur secundum altiora vel inferiora principia, sicut sapientia in speculativis altiora principia considerat quam scientia, et ideo ab ea distinguitur. Et ita etiam oportet esse in activis. Manifestum est autem quod illa quae sunt praeter ordinem inferioris principii sive causae reducuntur quandoque in ordinem altioris principii. . . . Contingit autem quandoque aliquid esse faciendum praeter communes regulas agendorum, puta cum impugnatori patriae non est depositum reddendum, vel aliquid aliud huiusmodi. Et ideo oportet de huiusmodi iudicare secundum aliqua altiora principia quam sint regulae communes, secundum quas iudicat synesis. Et secundum illa altiora principia exigitur altior virtus iudicativa, quae vocatur gnome. Cf. *ST* II-II.51.3 and *Ethic* VI.8 and 9.

127. In other words, under normal circumstances, the end of repaying a deposit is an end that, if not ordered to allegiance to one's country, is at least not contradictory to this higher end. Since the proximate end determines the species of the act (*ST* I-II.18.6), only when an extraordinary condition exists making an act not in conformity with a higher end would one not judge the act through the normal proximate end. In other words, normally the species of the proper act would be repaying the deposit. But due to the extraordinary conditions, the species of the proper act now becomes serving one's country and the deposit is not repaid. This is explained in *ST* I-II.18.10 which states that what is a circumstance (outside the species of the act) in one situation may determine the object of the act in another situation. Usually the relation between the owners of a deposit and the state is a circumstance that would not change the object of the proper act (repaying the deposit), but if the owners are enemies of the state then the object of the proper act is changed. Cf.

This judging of an action by means of higher principles is the practical extension of the virtue of wisdom. The wise know the ultimate end and judge in accord with this end. In morals the end takes of the form of the universal principle and to judge by higher principles is to judge something as being in accord with the ultimate end.[128]

The final act of the practical intellect, command, is perfected by prudence itself. Command is the act of the reason ordering the will to pursue the means that was chosen. Thomas states that there are three important parts of prudence that accompany the act of command: foresight, circumspection, and caution (*ST* II-II.48.1). Foresight, literally *providentia*, is necessary so that the action is properly ordered to a future end (*ST* II-II.49.6). Acts must be properly ordered in the present in order to achieve a particular end in the future. The human with foresight "foresees" the end and orders the acts in the present to be in accord with it. Circumspection is the act of considering the relevant circumstances. Since practical matters contain many combinations of circumstances, circumspection is necessary lest an act that is suitable to the end in itself be made evil because of a particular combination of circumstances.[129] Caution is the act of making sure that the action chosen is truly good since in contingent matters often evil is intermixed with good. A prudent human is cautious not to perform an act that has avoidable evil effects intermingled with the good effects (*ST* II-II.49.8). The virtue of prudence in general perfects the intellect to take good counsel, judge correctly, and command well; specifically it perfects the intellect to command with foresight, circumspection, and caution.

Of all the acquired intellectual virtues, prudence especially perfects

---

ST I-II.94.4; 100.1. Gnome perfects the intellect to judge in extraordinary cases. There is a corresponding virtue that perfects the will to follow this judgment: *epikeia* (*ST* II-II.120; cf. Naus, *The Nature of the Practical Intellect*, 134).

128. *ST* II-II.45.1. See also *ST* II-II.19.7 which states that wisdom considers not only God, but also the direction of human conduct to God. Cf. *ST* I-II.66.5.1, 100.1.

129. *ST* II-II.49.7. Normally a circumstance is outside of the object of an act and does not change the object but only increases or decreases the goodness of an act. However, in certain cases what is normally a circumstance can become the principle condition of the object and thus specify the action (*ST* I-II.18.10.2). Thomas gives the example of stealing from a holy place. In most cases, the place that something is stolen from is a circumstance and does not change the species of the act. For example the species of the acts of stealing from a store and stealing from a bank is identical. However, due to the fact that damaging a holy place is more repugnant to reason than is stealing, the species of the act is changed to sacrilege (*ST* I-II.18.10).

participation in the eternal law. The eternal law is the command of the divine governor that directs all things to its proper end. Because prudence perfects humans to govern themselves and others by determining the action which is in accord with their proper end and commanding it, through prudence humans are made like the divine governor and participate in His divine command. Prudence perfects cognitive participation in eternal law both by increasing the intellect's participation in the divine light and the conformity between the intellectual forms of the actions within the human mind and the exemplars of these actions in the divine mind. In reference to increasing the perfection in the divine light, by means of *euboulia, synesis,* and *gnome* the natural light of the intellect is perfected to determine the proper act. This perfection of the natural light leads to acts that are more perfectly ordered to the ultimate end. Since the eternal law orders humans to their ultimate end, inasmuch as humans command actions that are more in accord with their ultimate end, there is a greater likeness between their practical knowledge and the eternal law.

Because humans are rational, they participate in the eternal law not only as governed by it, but also as knowing something of the *ratio* of the divine governor. However, because humans do not immediately understand the eternal law, they come to participate in knowledge of the eternal law through the acts of the intellect: simple apprehension, judgment, and discursive reasoning (cf. *DT* I.1.4). In order to increase this participated knowledge, the speculative intellectual virtues and art give humans the ability to contemplate truth and make things and give them a greater aptness to perform good works because they are practical by extension. *Synderesis* and moral science give humans the ability to know the natural laws which act as the ends of practical syllogism, and prudence perfects the intellect to reason to the proper conclusion, judge it, and command it. By perfecting the intellect to act in accord with the ultimate end, these virtues increase participated knowledge in the eternal law. Hence, through the acquired intellectual virtues natural cognitive participation in the eternal law is perfected.

Although the natural knowledge of the good is perfected by the acquired virtues, perfect natural knowledge of the good requires grace. Thomas notes that before original sin, humans were able to do the good proportionate to their nature. However, after original sin, humans are not able to reach their natural perfection even by means of the acquired virtues.[130] Because grace does not destroy the good of nature but rather perfects it,[131] when God infuses grace into humans, they are given both healing grace which heals the corrupted nature and elevating grace which allows them to perform supernatural actions (*ST* I-II.109.3,5,9). Hence, in order for humans to have natural knowledge of the good which is proportionate to the potency of human nature, they must have grace.

Grace perfects this natural knowledge in two ways. First, it heals the natural light of the intellect so that the mind can determine the proper action to be performed and avoid sin (cf. *ST* I-II.109.8; I.106.1.2; *SCG* III.160.1). Thomas notes that in the state of original justice, the reason was perfected by God and was subject to Him. However, due to original sin (and actual sin) reason is subject to ignorance and obscured especially in practical matters (*ST* I-II.85.3). Hence, grace is necessary to heal the intellect's ability to understand propositions and reason from these propositions. Secondly, God reveals universal propositions that can be naturally derived.[132] For example, Thomas notes that the old law is given to perfect the knowledge of the natural law which had been obscured on account of the proliferation of sin (*ST* I-II.98.6). Because the moral precepts of the old law are contained in the new law of grace, grace through divine revelation supplies additional natural law precepts. Hence, in reference to the natural law, grace both perfects the intellect's ability to understand by natural means and leads the intellect by means of revelation.[133] Since healing and elevating grace are infused together, in the world of corrupted nature there is no such thing as perfect natural participation in eternal law that is not accompanied by supernatural participation by grace.

130. *ST* I-II.109.2. Thomas states that although humans cannot perfectly do the good in accord with nature in their corrupted state, they are not completely corrupted and thus can do some particular good.

131. Cf. *ST* II-II.9.1 where Thomas states that grace is more perfect than nature and hence does not fail in those things where man can be perfected by nature. See also *DT* II.3 which states that grace perfects nature in such a way that it does not destroy nature but perfects it. Thus, the light of faith does not destroy the natural light of cognition but perfects it.

132. See *ST* I-II.99.2.2 which states that divine law aids the soul not only in things in which human reason is insufficient, but also in areas where human reason is impeded. In other words, when the divinely revealed truth could be known by natural reason, but for various possible reasons (e.g., sloth, lack of intelligence, lack of time to contemplate, . . .) the reason is impeded from coming to this knowledge on its own. Cf. *ST* II-II.2.4.

133. See D. J. Billy, "Grace and Natural Law in the *Super Epistolam ad Romanos*," *Studia Moralia* 26 (1988): 15–37. Billy argues that Thomas believes that grace is essential both to have a perfect understanding of natural law and to keep it.

SUPERNATURAL PERFECTION OF COGNITIVE
PARTICIPATION IN ETERNAL LAW

Although healing grace perfects natural cognitive participation in eternal law, in order for humans to reach their end of supernatural happiness, they must also have elevating grace. Because humans act as rational creatures, their reason must be supernaturally perfected in order for them to perform actions that are in accord with their supernatural end.[134] Consequently, Thomas states that in addition to the natural perfection of cognitive participation in eternal law, "there is the added knowledge of faith and wisdom."[135]

This greater mode of cognitive participation varies substantially from natural reason. Whenever there is participation in something, there are degrees of participation in it. However, the difference of degree can be either accidental or substantial (*ST* I.75.7). For example, that one bar is hotter than another by its participation in fire is a case of an accidental difference of degree; but that an angel participates in the *esse* of God in a higher degree than that of a human is a case of a substantial difference of degree (*ST* I.75.5). In reference to cognitive participation, the greater degree of participation between the unperfected intellect and the intellect perfected by the acquired virtues is an accidental difference of degree. However, because faith and wisdom are supernatural principles, they cause a substantially different type of participation.

In explaining how cognitive participation in eternal law is perfected, this section will begin with the virtue of faith, which gives the supernatural principles from which reasoning can proceed. These principles are the foundation for further reasoning in both the speculative and the practical intellect. Then it will show how in the practical intellect these principles are from the divine law and are the major premises of the practical syllogism. Next, it will show how the virtue of infused prudence perfects the practical intellect to determine the proper act based on the supernatural end known through faith. Finally, it will show how the Holy Spirit's gifts of understanding, science, wisdom, and counsel perfect the intellect to further participate in the eternal law.

---

134. *ST* I-II.109.9; I.113.1.1. See also *ST* I-II.100.1 which states that due to the vast number of circumstances that must be considered, in some manners only the wise will judge correctly and in some manners humans cannot judge correctly without the help of divine instruction.

135. *ST* I-II.93.6: *superadditur eis cognitio fidei et sapientiae.* See also *ST* I.12.2 which notes that the intellectual light is participated by nature, grace, and glory. Cf. *ST* I.64.1; I-II.109.1; *DM* 2.4; *SCG* I.5; *Joan* I.4.

Faith

Because the light of grace does not destroy the natural light of the intellect but perfects it, humans in this life also have supernatural knowledge through apprehension, judgment, and reasoning.[136] The virtue of faith supernaturally perfects the intellect to receive divinely revealed principles through apprehension and judgment by means of the light of grace (Cf. *ST* I-II.62.3; II-II.2.3.2). From these principles the intellect can reason to further conclusions (*DT* II.2).

Because the principles of faith cannot be known by the apprehension and judgment of natural things, God gives humans additional physical signs and images that manifest Him.[137] For example, the physical actions and words of Christ reveal God (Cf. *ST* III.1.1). However, even with these additional signs and images the human intellect is not strong enough to know the principles of faith without additional grace. Hence, just as the natural light of the intellect is needed to abstract intelligible forms and combine and separate these forms into propositions that are understood, the superadded light of grace is needed to form a certain understanding of these divinely revealed signs and images. Thomas states:

The knowledge which we have by natural reason contains two things: images derived from the sensible objects, and the natural intelligible light, enabling us to abstract from them intelligible conceptions. Now in both of these, human knowledge is assisted by the revelation of grace.[138]

Just as both intelligible forms and the intellectual light are necessary for all knowledge, in supernatural knowledge additional intelligible forms are revealed that are comprehended by means of the light of grace.

Although faith is a kind of knowledge inasmuch as through it the intellect has a certain conformity to a knowable object, what is known by faith

---

136. See *ST* II-II.96.1. There is an exception to this rule when God directly impresses the intelligible species on the mind, as in the case of those who receive infused science or wisdom. Thomas gives as examples Solomon or the apostles (*ST* II-II.173.2). Thomas notes that this infused knowledge is not given to everyone but only those chosen by the Holy Spirit (II-II.96.1).

137. Since intelligible forms are abstracted from phantasms in the senses and the imagination, in the case of prophecy, God can either reveal Himself through sensible images or by imaginary forms (*ST* II-II.173.2).

138. *ST* I.12.13: Cognitio enim quam per naturalem rationem habemus, duo requirit, scilicet, phantasmata ex sensibilibus accepta, et lumen naturale intelligibile, cuius virtute intelligibiles conceptiones ab eis abstrahimus. Et quantum ad utrumque, iuvatur humana cognitio per revelationem gratiae. Cf. *ST* I.111.1; II-II.173.2.

falls short of the knowledge that belongs to science.[139] In other words, scientific knowledge is either derived from self-evident principles that are immediately understood or from principles that are from higher sciences that are based on self-evident principles. The principles of faith are not self-evident to humans in this life but are only directly seen by God, the angels, and the blessed (*ST* II-II.1.5). Nonetheless, because these principles are directly seen by God, they can be the basis of a science (e.g., theology) in the same way that principles established by a higher science are the basis of a lower science (*ST* I.1.2). In other words, just as the science of math establishes the principles of the science of music, so also the knowledge of God establishes the principles of theology. Thomas notes, "Whatever is based on these principles [of faith] is as well proved in the eyes of the faithful, as a conclusion drawn from self-evident principles in the eyes of all."[140]

Just as when children first begin to learn a science they do not necessarily understand the principles but must accept them as being true on the authority of the teacher, so also in the case of the science of God humans must accept the principles of this science as being true on the authority of the divine teacher.[141] The intellect can accept a principle as being true in two ways: One way is by deriving it from self-evident propositions or deriving it from previously demonstrated conclusions. The second way is by the will choosing to assent to the proposition.[142]

---

139. Thomas in *ST* I.12.13.3 notes that the intellect is determined by faith to a knowable object. However, this determination does not proceed from the vision of the believer, but from God. "Thus, as far as faith falls short of vision, it falls short of the knowledge which belongs to science, for science determines the intellect to one object by the vision and understanding of first principles" (Et sic, inquantum deest visio, deficit a ratione cognitionis quae est in scientia, nam scientia determinat intellectum ad unum per visionem et intellectum primorum principiorum).

140. *ST* II-II.1.5.2: Ex his autem principiis ita probatur aliquid apud fideles sicut etiam ex principiis naturaliter notis probatur aliquid apud omnes. Thomas continues by noting that because of this, theology is a science.

141. See *DT* II.2.7 which notes that understanding is always the first principle of any science but not always the proximate principle. The proximate principle is often faith in the teacher, since truths are often accepted on authority from those who already know the superior science. In the case of knowledge of God, the divine intellect both understands and is the first principle, but faith is the proximate principle of this knowledge in us. These principles are given to us that we may ultimately attain to an understanding of those things we believe. Cf. II-II.2.3; *DT* III.1.

142. Thomas states that the intellect assents to a thing in two ways. First, by being moved to assent by its very object which is either known in itself (through understanding) or through something else already known (through science). Second, the intellect assents to something

Since the principles of faith are supernatural and therefore cannot be derived from self-evident propositions, the will must choose to hold these propositions as true on account of the authority of God. Hence, Thomas states that to believe is to think with assent.[143] Thus, along with the supernatural perfection of the intellect by means of additional forms and light, the will must also be perfected by grace to assent to these propositions (*DT* III.1). The virtue of faith perfects both the intellect and the will to hold a divinely revealed proposition with certitude.[144]

Because faith includes an act of the will, it makes humans good simply speaking (like prudence).[145] However, despite the fact it is like prudence as including an act of will, it is primarily in the speculative intellect since its object, God as first truth, cannot be ordered to action (*ST* I.1.4). Nonetheless, like the other speculative virtues, faith is practical by extension (*ST* I.1.4, 64.1; II-II.4.2.3, 7.2.1). Whether faith is in the speculative or the practical intellect, it gives the principles from which all supernatural reasoning proceeds. Thomas states that although God knows Himself by simple intuition, we move discursively from the revealed knowledge of first truths to other truths since this is the mode of human thought. The truths of faith are the first principles of this discursive reasoning about God (*DT* II.2, II-II.8.1.2). Because humans know things and determine the action to be performed by reasoning from principles, faith is the beginning of all supernatural knowledge and actions.[146]

The principles of faith are made practical by extension by means of the new law of grace. Through the articles of faith, the object of the last end, supernatural happiness, is in the intellect. This last end is intended by the will, which is perfected by charity. In order to reach this

---

not through being sufficiently moved to this assent by its proper object, but through an act of the will choosing one thing over another (*ST* II-II.1.4; *DV* 14.1; cf. II-II.2.9.2).

143. Thomas defines thinking in this case as the inquiry that precedes the intellect's understanding of something (knowledge by sight).

144. Thomas notes that the principles of faith are the most certain as founded on divine truth (*ST* II-II.4.8; cf. II-II.4.5).

145. *De Virtut* 7; cf. *ST* II-II.2.9 which states that faith is meritorious because it is from a free will.

146. *ST* I-II.62.3; II-II.4.5. Cf. John Jenkins, *Knowledge and Faith,* 161–62, 189–90. Because all supernatural knowledge and acts begin with faith, Thomas at times calls faith "a habit of the mind by which eternal life begins in us" (fides est habitus mentis, qua inchoatur vita aeterna in nobis—*ST* II-II.4.1; *DV* 14.2; *Hebraeos* 11.1). See also *ST* II-II.4.7 which notes that faith precedes all other true virtues since faith places the object of the last end in the intellect where it must exist before it is in the will. However, other virtues can precede faith accidentally as removing barriers to it.

end, the practical reason must determine actions that are ordered to this end. Because in cases of practical reasoning the end takes the form of a universal proposition (a law), the articles of faith must be made into practical propositions by means of the light of grace.[147] Just as in the case of natural law where knowledge of the end becomes practical by being made into law, so also in the case of the new law, knowledge of the end becomes practical by being made into law. For example, in reference to the natural law, knowledge that humans are inclined to the end of living in society results in a variety of laws that order humans to the end of a flourishing society. Someone with a greater knowledge of how society fulfills human nature can compose more perfect laws. The supernatural perfection of this knowledge (that all are created for the society of union with the Trinity) results in an even greater capacity to determine the proper human actions.[148] These practical propositions along with the natural moral precepts are the propositions of the new law.[149]

The natural moral precepts are included because although faith gives

147. Cf. *QQ* 4.8. Analogous to the way that the wise man by knowing the natural end of humans is able to form principles in conformity with this end, so also someone with faith can form principles that are in conformity with our supernatural end. For example, from the natural knowledge that humans are ordered to the good of knowing about God and living in society, Thomas forms the precepts "to shun ignorance, to avoid offending those among whom one has to live, and other such things" (*ST* I-II.94.2: homo ignorantiam vitet, quod alios non offendat cum quibus debet conversari, et cetera huiusmodi). Likewise from the proposition of faith that the ultimate end of humans is the supernatural vision of God, Thomas forms the precept that humans "must first of all believe God, as a disciple believes the master who is teaching him" (*ST* II-II.2.3). Thomas states, "Hence in order that man arrive at the perfect vision of heavenly happiness, he must first of all believe God, as a disciple believes the master who is teaching him" (Unde ad hoc quod homo perveniat ad perfectam visionem beatitudinis praeexigitur quod credat deo tanquam discipulus magistro docenti). Consequently, although the propositions of faith are primarily speculative, they are also practical by extension and include moral precepts specifically revealed by Christ.

148. Every proposition of the faith teaches us something about the ultimate end or the means to this end. Hence, every proposition of the faith is practical by extension. For example, even knowledge of something like the Assumption of Mary teaches us about the role of the body as ordered to eternal life. This knowledge that the body is meant to be supernaturally perfected and not simply discarded is made practical by extension in precepts such as "the human body must be treated with dignity."

149. Thomas states in *QQ* 4.8: "the new law . . . is composed of the moral precepts of the natural law, the articles of faith, and the sacraments of grace. Wherefore it is called the law of faith and the law of grace on account of its determination of the articles of faith and the efficacy of the sacraments" (lex nova . . . est contenta praeceptis moralibus naturalis legis, et articulis fidei, et sacramentis gratiae: unde et dicitur lex fidei, et lex gratiae, propter determinationem articulorum fidei, et efficaciam sacramentorum). The sacraments of grace are included since they are the means through which grace is caused in humans. Cf. *DM* 2.4; *ST* II-II.56.1.

humans knowledge of a supernatural end, which they are ordered to by the new law, the infused virtues do not negate the inclinations of a power but perfect them. Faith and charity cause the natural inclinations to also be ordered to the ultimate end. Hence, the natural inclinations still remain but are perfected and ordered by the theological virtues, which serve as supernatural inclinations.

Actions are always judged by the principles from which they are derived. The higher the principles by which they are judged, the greater the wisdom that is manifested. By means of the law of grace, humans are able to judge an action as being in conformity with the eternal law not only by judging it through the precepts of natural law but also through the articles of faith (*ST* I-II.100.1, 2; II-II.8.3.3). Because the new law determines actions according to the articles of faith, it is also called the law of faith (*QQ* 4.8).

The virtue of faith gives humans the ability to assent to supernaturally known principles and to have a certain understanding of them through the light of grace. By assenting to these principles, humans increase their cognitive participation in God who is the exemplary cause of all knowledge. Through faith the intellect has additional intelligible forms through which it can know God, causing a greater likeness between it and the divine intellect (*SCG* II.4). Two ways that this substantial increase in participation in the eternal law is manifested is that faith perfects humans to perform their proper act, and faith is practical by extension. Faith perfects humans to know God in a supernatural manner. Because this knowledge is the beginning of the knowledge of God by glory, it is substantially different from natural knowledge.[150] Hence, the eternal law directs humans to know God by faith. Because substantially greater knowledge of the end of humans results in more perfect laws ordering humans to this end, faith as practical by extension substantially perfects participation in the eternal law. These principles can be used to determine and judge actions causing a substantially greater conformity between the practical intellect and the eternal law. This participation in the divine light through grace gives the intellect this ability to have a certain knowledge of the precepts of faith and to apply them to the practical realm.

---

150. Thomas contrasts the relation between grace and glory to the relation between grace and nature. Grace is of the same genus of glory for grace is nothing else than the beginning of glory in us, but nature is not of the same genus as grace (*ST* II-II.24.3.2).

Virtues Which Perfect the Intellect to Reason from the Principles Held by Faith

Just as humans come to more perfect natural knowledge of something by reasoning from principles to conclusions, they also come to more perfect supernatural knowledge of God in this life by reasoning from the principles of faith.[151] Thomas explains that although God knows Himself by simple intuition, humans move discursively from the revealed knowledge of first truths to other truths since this is the mode of human thought. The truths of faith are the first principles of this reasoning process (*DT* II.2; cf. *ST* II-II.8.2). When the reasoning process is ordered to contemplation of God, it must be perfected by the virtues of science and wisdom. When the reasoning process is ordered to supernatural actions, it must be perfected by the infused virtue of prudence.

Humans are able to reason from the propositions of faith by means of their naturally acquired virtues of science and wisdom, and Thomas does not to my knowledge speak of the infused virtues of science and wisdom.[152] (However, he does speak of the Holy Spirit's gifts of science and wisdom which, although they are not virtues in the strict sense, are nonetheless infused habits which perfect the intellect to judge from supernatural principles.)[153] However, Thomas does speak of the infused virtue of prudence, which differs in species from the acquired virtue of prudence. In other words, the virtues of science and wisdom that perfect the intellect to reason from supernaturally known principles do not differ in species from those that perfect the intellect to reason from naturally known principles. However, unlike wisdom and science, because infused prudence includes an act of the will ordered to a supernatural end by charity, the actions it performs are determined in accord with a different standard (divine law vs. natural law), and these actions are ordered to a supernatural end (*ST* I-II.63.4). In other words, acquired and infused prudence have different proper objects and a different end and therefore

---

151. Thomas notes that because human perfection comes from knowing God, it is fitting that humans come to this knowledge both through the acts of understanding and reasoning (*DT* II.1).

152. Cf. Kieran Conley, *A Theology of Wisdom: A Study of St. Thomas* (Dubuque, Iowa: The Priory Press, 1963), 60–138. Conley writes extensively about the distinction between wisdom as moving from the principles of faith and wisdom as a gift of the Holy Spirit.

153. These gifts will be covered below. Because the gifts of science and wisdom give the intellect the ability to know things as God knows things, they are substantially different then the virtues of science and wisdom in that they do not include discursive reasoning.

differ in species.[154] Although the virtues of science and wisdom do not necessarily include an act of the will, they are accompanied by an act of the will when they are made practical by extension.[155]

Although Thomas does not speak of the infused virtues of wisdom and science, Thomas does distinguish between all other sciences and the science proceeding from the principles of faith. Thomas notes that sacred doctrine is a science. He then explains that sciences can either come from principles that are known by the natural light of the intellect or by the light of a higher science. Sacred doctrine is the science where its principles are known by the science of God and the blessed (*ST* I.1.2; cf. *DT* V.4). Likewise, Thomas notes that wisdom proceeding from the principles of faith differs from naturally acquired wisdom. Sacred doctrine is the highest form of wisdom because it treats the highest cause, God, not only as He can be known through creatures, but also as He is known to Himself alone and revealed to others.[156]

Just as these virtues are practical by extension when they perfect the intellect to reason and judge from natural principles, so also they are practical by extension when they reason and judge from supernatural principles. In reference to science, all additional knowledge of God obtained by reasoning increases knowledge of the ultimate end, and all additional knowledge of the relation between humans and God increases the understanding of how to achieve this end (cf. prologue to the *Secunda Pars*). This greater knowledge of the end and how to achieve it results in more perfect laws ordering humans to their ultimate end and hence causes a greater cognitive participation in the eternal law. In reference to wisdom, the wise order all of their actions in accord with the ultimate end (*ST* I.1.6.3). In this case, all actions are judged by them as being in accord with the end that is supernaturally known. Hence, wisdom increases cognitive participation in the eternal law by perfecting the intellect to judge actions in accord with the supernatural end.

The virtues of science and wisdom perfect the intellect to contem-

154. *ST* I-II.64.1.1. See chapter 3, the section on the infused virtues, for more on this distinction.

155. Although there are no infused virtues of science and wisdom, they are counted among the gratuitous graces (*ST* I-II.68.5.1, 111.4; cf. *ST* I.1.6.3). Gratuitous graces are those whereby humans may cooperate with God in leading others to Him (*ST* I-II.111.1). This type of grace is not essential to salvation but is a gift to those who teach the faith to others.

156. *ST* I.1.6; *SCG* II.4.4. See Kieran Conley, *A Theology of Wisdom: A Study of St. Thomas*, 23–104, for the distinction between wisdom as judging by naturally known principles and wisdom as judging by supernaturally known principles.

plate God as known through the principles of faith. Apart from the contemplation of God by means of the gifts of the Holy Spirit, this act of contemplating God is the highest act that can be performed by the intellect in this life, and it is thus the most perfect participation in divine happiness that can be had on earth.[157] It especially makes humans like God because they participate in His act of knowing Himself. Since the eternal law orders humans to happiness, these virtues especially increase participation in the eternal law.

Infused Prudence

Unlike wisdom and science, which are primarily ordered to consideration of the truth, prudence is ordered to a particular action. Since it is ordered to a particular action, it not only proceeds from supernatural principles understood by the intellect but also from the supernatural end intended by the will.[158] Just as in the intellect, all conclusions can be reduced to first principles, so also in the will all proximate ends can be reduced to an ultimate end.[159] In other words, because prudence presupposes the intention of a good end, the ultimate end acts as the principle of prudential action both in that the practical intellect draws universal principles from it (law) and the will tends to it (the good). In the case of infused prudence, the universal principles are the new law known by the light of faith, and the ultimate end is God as known by faith and intended by the will perfected by hope and united by charity.[160] Thus, infused

157. *ST* I-II.66.5.2; cf. 62.3. Thomas notes in *SCG* I.2 that among all human pursuits, the pursuit of wisdom is more perfect, noble, useful, and full of joy. He then explains it is more perfect because through it humans even now participate in true beatitude. It is nobler because it makes humans like God. It is more useful because through it humans arrive at the everlasting kingdom. He does not give a reason as to why it's more joyful.

158. *ST* I-II.58.5. The moral virtues order the soul to this end. This is why prudence cannot exist without the moral virtues but the other intellectual virtues can.

159. Thomas notes that this end acts as a principle of action analogous to the way that the principles of reason are principles of knowledge in the speculative intellect (*ST* I-II.65.2, 65.4.1).

160. See *ST* I-II.62.3: "The theological virtues order man to supernatural happiness in the same way as by the natural inclination man is ordered to his connatural end. Now the latter happens in respect of two things. First in respect of the reason or intellect, insofar as it contains the first universal principles which are known to us by the natural light of the intellect, and which are reason's starting point, both in speculative and in practical matters. Secondly, through the rectitude of the will which tends naturally to the good of reason. But these two fall short of the order of supernatural happiness. . . . Consequently, in respect of both the above things, man needed to receive in addition something superadded to direct him to a supernatural end. First as regards the intellect, certain supernatural principles are added to man, which are received by means of divine light: these are able to be believed, concerning

prudence perfects the reason to seek actions ordered to the supernatural end of knowing and loving God as He is, rather than the natural end of knowing and loving God by His effects as in the case of acquired prudence. In determining these actions, the universal principles from which the intellect reasons to the proper means are from the new law rather than only from the natural law as in the case of acquired prudence.

Because the virtue of faith gives additional principles from which the practical reason can proceed (the new law), and the virtue of charity supernaturally orders the will to God, the actions determined by infused prudence are of a different species than the actions determined by acquired prudence.[161] A further explanation of why infused prudence causes specifically different actions is that since prudence determines the action to be chosen, a different end intended (God as supernaturally known and loved) results in a different action being chosen.[162]

---

which is faith. Secondly, the will is directed to this end, both as to the movement of intention, which tends to that end as something attainable, and this pertains to hope, and as to a certain spiritual union, whereby the will is, so to speak, transformed into that end, and this comes about through charity" (Virtutes theologicae hoc modo ordinant hominem ad beatitudinem supernaturalem, sicut per naturalem inclinationem ordinatur homo in finem sibi connaturalem. Hoc autem contingit secundum duo. Primo quidem, secundum rationem vel intellectum, inquantum continet prima principia universalia cognita nobis per naturale lumen intellectus, ex quibus procedit ratio tam in speculandis quam in agendis. Secundo per rectitudinem voluntatis naturaliter tendentis in bonum rationis. Sed haec duo deficiunt ab ordine beatitudinis supernaturalis. . . . Unde oportuit quod quantum ad utrumque, aliquid homini supernaturaliter adderetur, ad ordinandum ipsum in finem supernaturalem. Et primo quidem, quantum ad intellectum, adduntur homini quaedam principia supernaturalia, quae divino lumine capiuntur, et haec sunt credibilia, de quibus est fides. Secundo vero, voluntas ordinatur in illum finem et quantum ad motum intentiones, in ipsum tendentem sicut in id quod est possibile consequi, quod pertinet ad spem, et quantum ad unionem quandam spiritualem, per quam quodammodo transformatur in illum finem, quod fit per caritatem). Cf. *SCG* III.115 & 116.

161. Because it causes actions that are both of a different species (based on reasoning from the new law) and ordered to a different end, Thomas states that infused prudence is of a different species of virtue than acquired prudence (*ST* I-II.63.4). In one sense, the end of acquired prudence and infused prudence is the same: God. However, although we do not love the intellectual form, but the object as known through the intellectual form, we can only love the object to the extent that it is known. In the case of God, our intellectual form of God that is from faith is of a greater species than the intellectual form of God that is known through natural knowledge. Recall the above distinction between degrees of participation that vary accidentally and degrees of participation that vary specifically. Cf. *ST* II-II.47.14 where Thomas notes that whereas acquired prudence takes experience and time to develop, infused prudence is caused by divine infusion and can be in children at least in regard to those things necessary for salvation. He continues by noting that with practice the virtue increases.

162. Cf. Joseph Pieper, *Prudence,* trans. Richard and Clara Winston (New York: Pan-

Although the proximate end determines the object of an action, any particular proximate end is intended because of its relation to a higher end (*ST* I-II.1.1). In the case of infused prudence, the practical intellect takes counsel from and judges by the ultimate end known and loved through the theological virtues. Since counsel is an inquiry moving from a universal end to a particular action, in cases where the inquiry actually begins with the ultimate end,[163] it must usually reason to many intermediate ends before reaching an action that can be done immediately. For example, a student may come to the conclusion that he will study now because of his love of God, but only after reasoning to the intermediate ends that in his situation love of God requires that his knowledge increase and to increase knowledge he must study. From the proposition that one must study to increase knowledge, the student can conclude to study now. Because the proximate end is ordered to the ultimate end, it is intended as a means of achieving the ultimate end.[164] In other words, just as with two speculative syllogisms, two different major premises yield two different conclusions, so also in the practical intellect syllogisms beginning with divine law yield different conclusions than those beginning with natural law.

An example of how infused prudence results in a specifically different

theon Books, 1959), chapter 4. Pieper notes that although prudence is the form of the moral virtues, charity is the form of it and hence is the ultimate measure of the moral virtues. Later scholars would use the argument from Thomas that a different end causes a different means to argue that there is a distinctively Christian virtue ethic. See, for example, Gilbert Meilander, *The Theory and Practice of Virtue* (South Bend: University of Notre Dame Press, 1984), 29–34; Stanley Hauerwaus and Charles Pinches, *Christian among the Virtues* (South Bend: University of Notre Dame Press, 1997), 101–62; and Cessario, *The Moral Virtues and Theological Ethics*, 110–36.

163. With most good actions, prudence does not begin its inquiry with the ultimate end but rather begins with a proximate end that is ordered to the ultimate end. For example, the intellect does not have to always inquire into how giving alms is ordered to the end of eternal happiness. Based either on counsel from other people or from its own act of inquiry it has already determined that giving alms is ordered to knowing and loving God. Nonetheless, the intellect must always judge as to whether or not the action is in accord with the ultimate end, since in special situations (as determined by the virtue of *gnome*) giving alms may not be ordered to the ultimate end.

164. *ST* I-II.12.3. Elsewhere Thomas notes that although the proximate end gives the species of the action, the ultimate end gives the species inasmuch as the proximate end is ordered to the ultimate end (*De Virtut* 10.9; cf. *ST* I-II.6.2). Keep in mind that because the new law contains the natural law, the external actions will still be in accord with the natural law (*ST* I-II.108.2). However, because these actions are judged by a higher standard, different actions that are in accord with the natural law will be chosen in different situations. Since only those with faith can recognize an act formed by charity (*ST* I-II.62.1), to nonbelievers the external act may still appear to flow from natural principles.

action is seen by analyzing how it determines a different object of temperance.[165] In showing how the object of the infused virtue of temperance varies from the acquired virtue of temperance, Thomas states:

> Now it is evident that the mean that is appointed in such like concupiscences according to the rule of human reason, is seen under a different aspect from the mean which is fixed according to divine rule. For instance, in the consumption of food, the mean fixed by human reason, is that food should not harm the health of the body, nor hinder the use of reason: whereas, according to divine rule, it behooves man to chastise his body and bring it into subjection [1 Cor. 9:27], by abstinence in food, drink and the like. It is therefore evident that infused and acquired temperance differ in species; and the same applies to other virtues.[166]

Because infused prudence begins with the principles of the new law and judges actions as being in accord with them, the action that the concupiscible appetite is ordered to through the infused virtue of temperance is specifically different than that of acquired prudence through acquired temperance.[167] Likewise, since prudence orders all of the appetitive powers, the objects of infused justice and fortitude differ specifically from their acquired counterparts.

The intellect perfected by infused prudence not only begins with the premises of the new law, but also judges by them. After it has reasoned to a particular action by taking counsel from the new law, it judges whether or not the particular action is in accord with the ultimate end (*ST* I-II.100.1; cf. I-II.91.4). Just as judgment after reasoning in the speculative intellect allows the intellect to see the conclusion in the principles, by the light of grace the practical intellect is able to see the particular action in its knowledge of the ultimate end.[168] This is an act of practical wisdom since the wise man orders his actions in accord with the ultimate

---

165. It is the job of prudence to determine the mean of all the moral virtues. In determining the mean, prudence determines both the object and the intensity of the appetite (*ST* I-II.64.3).

166. *ST* I-II.63.4: Manifestum est autem quod alterius rationis est modus qui imponitur in huiusmodi concupiscentiis secundum regulam rationis humanae, et secundum regulam divinam. Puta in sumptione ciborum, ratione humana modus statuitur ut non noceat valetudini corporis, nec impediat rationis actum, secundum autem regulam legis divinae, requiritur quod homo castiget corpus suum, et in servitutem redigat, per abstinentiam cibi et potus, et aliorum huiusmodi. Unde manifestum est quod temperantia infusa et acquisita differunt specie, et eadem ratio est de aliis virtutibus.

167. Prudence orders justice, fortitude, and temperance which participate in reason inasmuch as they are ordered by reason (*ST* I-II.64.3). Cf. Joseph Pieper, *Prudence*, 15–22.

168. *ST* I-II.86.1. This ability to judge by means of the ultimate end is perfected by the gift of wisdom, which will be covered below.

end.[169] The intellect is then aided by the grace of the Holy Spirit to command this action. Thus, through the grace of the Holy Spirit which both gives divine precepts to the intellect and helps the intellect reason from these precepts, humans can judge and command an action by the standards of eternal law rather than natural law.

Inasmuch as infused prudence is from the grace of the Holy Spirit, it is in a certain sense part of the new law. Thomas states that unlike the natural law, which only gives general precepts, the divine law directs also to particular matters.[170] The grace of the Holy Spirit directs humans to particular actions by perfecting the intellect to reason from the ultimate end, perfecting it to judge an action by divine standards, and perfecting it to command the proper action.[171]

In chapter three, a distinction was made between the formal conformity of the human will to God's will and material conformity. Charity, in ordering all actions to the end of God loved as a friend, makes every action formally in conformity with God's will. However, because charity works through the cardinal virtues, these virtues are needed in order to assure that the human will is materially in conformity with God's will. Since infused prudence determines the means of performing the action that is ordered to God by charity, it is the virtue that perfects the intellect to determine the will to actions that are materially in conformity

169. *ST* I.1.6.3. See *ST* II-II.19.7: "For seeing that our life is ordained to the enjoyment of God, and is directed thereto according to a certain participation of the divine nature, which is through grace, wisdom, according to us [theologians], is considered not only as being cognizant of God, as it is with the philosophers, but also as directing human life; since this is directed not only by the human law, but also by the divine law . . . the beginning of wisdom as to its essence consists in the first principles of wisdom, which are the articles of faith" (Quia enim vita nostra ad divinam fruitionem ordinatur et dirigitur secundum quandam participationem divinae naturae, quae est per gratiam; sapientia secundum nos non solum consideratur ut est cognoscitiva dei, sicut apud philosophos; sed etiam ut est directiva humanae vitae, quae non solum dirigitur secundum rationes humanas, sed etiam secundum rationes divinas . . . initium sapientiae secundum eius essentiam sunt prima principia sapientiae, quae sunt articuli fidei).

170. *ST* I-II.91.5.3. Cf. I-II.86.1, 99.4, 108.2.3.

171. Thomas states that the new law not only tells humans what to do, but also helps them accomplish it (*ST* I-II.106.1.2). Since prudence is ordered to the ultimate end by charity, the new law is also called the law of love because it does not make people observe commandments by exterior rewards and punishments but by love of virtue (*ST* I-II.107.1.2). Because through prudence the person determines the best action to the end, the new law is also called the law of liberty both in that it gives humans the ability to freely determine the proper action and allows them to determine it (*ST* I-II.108.1). Cf. Congar, *I Believe in the Holy Spirit*, vol. 2 (New York: Seabury, 1983), 125. Congar states that man is free under the new law, not because he is not subject to divine law, but because his inner dynamism from the Holy Spirit leads him to do what divine law prescribes.

with the divine will. In other words, through infused prudence, humans do not only desire that their actions are supernaturally in accord with the eternal law, but their actions actually are supernaturally in accord with the eternal law. This supernatural conformity occurs because in taking prudential counsel, the intellect begins with principles of the new law which participate in the eternal law at a specifically higher level than do the principles of the natural law (*ST* I-II.63.2). From these principles the intellect with the aid of grace is able to reason to actions materially in accord with the end to which eternal law orders humans. After the act of practical reasoning, the intellect by means of the light of grace is able to judge an action as being in conformity with the principles of the new law. Inasmuch as the intellect judges by the virtue of infused prudence, the action is materially in conformity with the divine will. Finally, the intellect commands the action with the aid of the grace of the Holy Spirit. By causing this specifically higher conformity with the eternal law, humans are able to direct themselves and others to actions that are materially in accord with the supernatural end to which the eternal law directs them.

THE GIFTS OF THE HOLY SPIRIT

Because the Holy Spirit moves humans through the infused virtues to a supernatural end, they need additional perfections beyond these infused virtues to be moved perfectly. Even though Thomas holds that the supernatural light is a far greater principle of human reason than its own natural light, still he teaches that the natural light is possessed in a more perfect manner. When something possesses a nature, form, or virtue perfectly, it can be divinely moved to act by its own power:

But that which has a certain nature, or form, or virtue imperfectly, cannot of itself work, unless it be moved by another. Thus . . . a physician . . . who knows the medical art perfectly, can work by himself; but his pupil who is not yet fully instructed, cannot work by himself, unless he is instructed by his instructor. Accordingly, in matters subject to human reason and ordered to man's connatural end, man is able to work through the judgment of his reason. . . . But in matters ordered to the ultimate supernatural end, to which reason moves according to a certain measure and imperfect form through the theological virtues, the motion of reason does not suffice, unless it receive in addition the impulse and motion of the Holy Spirit.[172]

---

172. *ST* I-II.68.2: Sed id quod imperfecte habet naturam aliquam vel formam aut virtutem, non potest per se operari, nisi ab altero moveatur. Sicut . . . Medicus . . . qui per-

Just as the pupil needs to be directed by the physician, so also humans who are ordered to the ultimate end need to be directed by the Holy Spirit. The natural reason of the pupil may very well suffice in some other art, but will not be sufficient for perfect medical actions until the pupil forms the virtue of medical art, and this takes teaching. Likewise, the theological virtues by causing specifically different actions (divine actions), cause in humans a new "art" of which even reason perfected by the theological virtues is not sufficient for perfect actions. Hence, humans need to be led by the divine tutor who instructs them to direct themselves to perfect actions through the gifts of the Holy Spirit (*ST* I-II.68.1).

The gifts of the Holy Spirit are habits that dispose all of the powers of the soul so that they can be easily and promptly moved by the Holy Spirit.[173] In reference to cognitive participation, the gifts of wisdom, understanding, science, and counsel perfect the intellect.[174] Thomas notes that even endowed with the theological virtues, the reason could not avoid acts of folly, ignorance, rashness, dullness, and the like without the gifts of the Holy Spirit to perfect it.[175] In other words, because the knowledge of God through faith is imperfect and human reasoning from

---

fecte novit artem medicinae, potest per se operari, sed discipulus eius, qui nondum est plene instructus, non potest per se operari, nisi ab eo instruatur. Sic igitur quantum ad ea quae subsunt humanae rationi, in ordine scilicet ad finem connaturalem homini; homo potest operari, per iudicium rationis. . . . Sed in ordine ad finem ultimum supernaturalem, ad quem ratio movet secundum quod est aliqualiter et imperfecte formata per virtutes theologicas; non sufficit ipsa motio rationis, nisi desuper adsit instinctus et motio spiritus sancti. Cf. *ST* III.7.5.

173. *ST* I-II.68.3, 68.4, 68.8, 69.1. See Yves Congar, "Le Saint Esprit dans la théologie Thomiste de l'agir moral," in *Atti Del Congresso Internationale: Tommaso D'Aquino Nel Suo Settimo Centenario*, 9–19 (Naples: Edizioni Domenicane Italiane, 1974), 11–12.

174. In *ST* I-II.68.4 Thomas notes that apprehension of truth occurs in both the practical and the speculative intellect. The gift of understanding perfects the speculative intellect for this apprehension and counsel perfects the practical intellect. Judgment concerning the truth perfects both. Wisdom perfects judgment of the speculative intellect and science perfects judgment in the practical intellect. However, by the time he treats the gifts of the Holy Spirit specifically in the *Secunda Secundae*, his view has developed to where both understanding and knowledge are primarily in the speculative intellect but practical by extension (II-II.8.3 and 9.3). Wisdom as a gift is both speculative and practical (45.3) and counsel is only practical. See especially II-II.8.7 where he states why he rejects his reasoning in I-II.68.4.

175. *ST* I-II.68.2.3. John of St. Thomas notes that even within the supernatural order a distinction can be made between perfect movement and imperfect movement. Faith and reason are imperfect in relation to supernatural mysteries; hence the need for additional dispositions. See *The Gifts of the Holy Spirit* (New York: Sheed & Ward, 1951), 59–60. Cf. Congar, *I Believe in the Holy Spirit*, vol. 2, 135–36.

246 *Cognitive Participation*

these principles is also imperfect, gifts are needed to perfect both the understanding of God and the reasoning from these principles.[176] For example, in reference to the gift of counsel, even by infused prudence we will never be able to consider all of the circumstances in a particular situation because we are too limited. Hence, the need for divine counsel to determine the proper means, and divine judgment (the gift of wisdom) to make sure that the act is in conformity with the eternal law.[177] A prime example of the necessity of the gift of counsel is in cases of fraternal correction. Often humans attempt to help others but instead offend them because of their invincible ignorance of a complex situation. However, with the help of the Holy Spirit who always knows the right action, they can perform the right action even in the most complex situations.

Because Thomas speaks of the gifts of the Holy Spirit directing humans in accord with divine reason rather than human reason (e.g., I-II.68.1, 70.1), one could mistakenly believe that the Holy Spirit moves humans in a way such that the human intellect has little or no active role.[178] Thomas makes sure not to convey this understanding by calling the gifts habits.[179] A habit perfects a power of the soul to perform its own proper action. Although the infused habits elevate the natural power of the soul, they do not destroy this power. Hence, human actions still proceed from the will determined by the intellect (*De Virtut* 1.11). Thomas refutes any understanding of humans being moved solely as passive instruments by saying, "But man is not an instrument of that kind; for he is so acted upon by the Holy Spirit, that he also acts himself insofar as he has free choice."[180] Hence, statements that the gifts direct

---

176. Recall that there are no infused virtues of understanding, science, or wisdom but only gifts to perfect the intellect in moving from the principles of faith.

177. See Dominic Hughes and Mark Egan, "Introduction," in *The Gifts of the Holy Spirit,* by John of St. Thomas, 14–27 (New York: Sheed & Ward, 1951). They state that only God can fully know how to attain the end of knowing and loving Him. Only the Holy Spirit knows all the pathways and obstacles. Hence the gifts are given to dispose humans to immediate direction by the Holy Spirit (16).

178. See, for example, *ST* I-II.68.3, objection 2.

179. Because Thomas calls the gifts habits, he is then faced with the difficult task of explaining how they differ from the infused virtues (see *ST* I-II.68.1 & 3). Cf. Congar, *I Believe in the Holy Spirit,* vol. 2, 134. Congar states that the distinction between the gifts and the virtues is an opinion and not an essential element of the faith. The distinction was first made in 1235 by Phillip the Chancellor.

180. *ST* I-II.68.3.2: Tale autem instrumentum non est homo; sed sic agitur a spiritu sancto, quod etiam agit, inquantum est liberi arbitrii. See also II-II.52.2 where Thomas notes that the gift perfecting prudence is called counsel and not command or judgment since the

humans in accord with divine reason rather than human reason should be understood in a similar sense as the statement that the mean fixed by human reason differs from the mean fixed by divine law.[181] This latter statement does not mean that the human reason (perfected by grace) is not involved in fixing the mean (for this is the role of prudence), but that reason perfected by the infused virtues determines a more perfect mean than that of natural reason.

The intellectual gifts of the Holy Spirit are additional habits that allow humans to overcome the imperfections of the human intellect even when enlightened by faith and informed by charity. These habits perfect humans to direct themselves to perfect actions by means of divine instructions given by the Holy Spirit. In order to better understand their role in cognitive participation, I will now analyze individually the gifts of understanding, science, wisdom, and counsel.

Understanding

Just as all natural knowledge begins with principles that are naturally understood, all supernatural knowledge begins with the principles of faith. However, because the human intellect cannot understand these principles by means of the natural light of understanding, an infused gift of understanding is necessary to perfect it to understand these principles (*ST* II-II.8.1.2). In other words, the gift of understanding has a very similar role in reference to supernatural knowledge as the acquired virtue of understanding has in reference to natural knowledge. Both give the intellect the ability to understand principles. Even with this infused gift, the intellect cannot understand perfectly the principle object of faith, God, but it can understand Him imperfectly and can also understand perfectly many revealed truths that are subordinate to this principle object.[182]

---

counseled mind still moves by itself. Cf. *ST* I-II.68.1 and I-II.111.2. See also Jordan Aumann, "Mystical Experience, the Infused Virtues and the Gifts," *Angelicum* 58 (1981): 38–39.

181. For example, *ST* I-II.63.4; cf. 63.2. In both these statements the distinction is between an interior principle of action and an exterior principle of action (for more on this distinction, see the second part of chapter 2). Human reason is an interior principle of action, while both the divine law and the gifts of the Holy Spirit are exterior principles of action (see *ST* I-II.68.1; 109.1.prologue). Cf. Matthew Cuddeback, *Light and Form in St. Thomas Aquinas's Metaphysics of the Knower* (Ph.D. diss., The Catholic University of America, 1998), 197. Cuddeback notes that inasmuch as an impression of knowledge is from God it is an extrinsic principle.

182. *ST* II-II.8.2. To understand something perfectly is to apprehend the essence of a thing and to understand the proposition about the essence of the thing that is composed

This degree of understanding is sufficient for the speculative intellect to reason from these propositions to conclusions about God and salvation, and for the practical intellect to have a right estimate of the end to which all actions are ordered (II-II.8.5). In reference to the practical intellect, Thomas notes that although the gift of understanding is primarily speculative in nature, inasmuch as the rule of human actions is the eternal law, the gift of understanding extends to human actions (II-II.8.3). In other words, in practical reasoning, the law takes the form of the end from which the particular action is derived. The gift of understanding allows the practical intellect to have a certain understanding of the eternal law from which actions can be derived. In reference to the gift of understanding Thomas states, "Now the eternal law surpasses human reason, so that the knowledge of human actions, as ruled by the eternal law, surpasses the natural light of reason, and requires the supernatural light of the gift of the Holy Spirit."[183]

Because understanding God through the principles of faith is the highest act of the highest power in this life, the gift of understanding results in an especially perfect form of cognitive participation in the eternal law. Likewise, as practical by extension, this gift allows humans to supernaturally understand the universal principles from which actions are derived. By means of this gift, the Holy Spirit gives humans a certain knowledge of the eternal law by which humans can guide themselves.

Science

The natural habit of science perfects the intellect's ability to reason discursively from principles so that it can make a judgment with certainty about what something is. In other words, through discursive reasoning the intellect is able to understand a conclusion known through a middle term. The Holy Spirit's gift of science is like this natural virtue in that it also makes one able to make a judgment from the principles of faith. However, it is unlike this natural virtue in that just as God's science is not through discursive reasoning, the gift of science makes a judgment

---

by the intellect. The human intellect on earth is incapable of having this understanding of God even with the infused gifts. However, it can understand God imperfectly inasmuch as it understands the many propositions revealed by God that manifest the divine essence and the relation of creatures to this essence.

183. In *ST* II-II.8.3.3: Lex autem aeterna excedit naturalem rationem. Et ideo cognitio humanorum actuum secundum quod regulantur a lege aeterna, excedit rationem naturalem, et indiget supernaturali lumine doni spiritus sancti.

without discursive reason since it is a participation in God's science.[184] In other words, the gift allows humans to see the conclusions within the principles of faith without having to reason to it through a middle term. Thomas notes that a greater participation of the intellect in God results in a more simple understanding in the sense that greater knowledge is known by fewer intellectual forms.[185] In other words, by knowing the fundamental truths of the faith, the intellect knows many conclusions as well without recourse to discursive reasoning.

If the judgment made by science is about God, it actually comes from the gift of wisdom. However, if it is about created things that are subordinated to the first object of the faith, it is from science, just as natural judgment of lower things is called science, and natural judgment of divine things is called wisdom (*ST* II-II.9.2). The gift of science is practical inasmuch as right use of created things is necessary for humans to reach eternal happiness (*ST* II-II.9.4). Thus, the gift of science allows humans to properly judge created things based on the divinely revealed propositions of faith. Thomas gives the example of someone rightly judging that making a created good an ultimate end would result in the loss of the true good (*ST* II-II.9.4).

Just as natural moral science allows humans to derive other universal principles from the principles of natural law, the gift of science allows humans to derive further moral laws from revealed principles. However, this greater knowledge is without discursive reasoning and is instead a more immediate participation in the eternal law. Through science, cognitive participation in the eternal law is increased since this gift allows a human to know the proper use of created things by knowing the principles of the divine law.

Counsel

Whereas the gifts of understanding and science apply to the formation of moral precepts (proximate ends), the gift of council applies to the finding of the means to these ends. Thomas explains that due to the fact that

---

184. *ST* II-II.9.1.1. The gift of science anticipates the mode of knowing in heaven where God is seen without use of a middle term. Cf. *ST* I-II.68.6; *DV* 8.5.3.

185. Cf. *ST* I.89.1, which notes that the greater the participation of the intellect in God, the greater the knowledge it has by fewer ideas. For example, someone who has the science of architecture upon understanding a particular type of wood used in a beam already knows all the properties of this type of wood and therefore knows immediately how to use it building. He does not have to reason how to use the wood by means of a middle term. This knowledge is already contained within the idea of the wood.

the practical intellect is unable to grasp all the singular and contingent things that may occur, humans must be directed by God who comprehends all things (*ST* II-II.52.1.1). In other words, in any particular action there are an infinite number of circumstances, of which some are relevant to the action and some are not. Only God knows all of the relevant circumstances in a particular situation.

Just as a human on earth may go to a wise friend for counsel, the gift of counsel allows humans to receive counsel from God (II-II.52.1.1). On earth this wise friend is able to order actions in accord with the ultimate end (cf. *ST* I.1.6.3; I-II.1.7; *Metaph* I.2, n.41). However, over and above the direction of the wise friend is the direction of the divine Son (uncreated Wisdom), who through the Holy Spirit directs the actions of others in accord with the eternal law (cf. *ST* I-II.93.1.2; 108.4.*sed contra*). The Holy Spirit gives this counsel by perfecting the human intellect to reason to the proper means (*ST* II-II.52.2).

God perfects the infused virtue of prudence by giving the gift of counsel so that the practical intellect may take into consideration all the relevant circumstances and reason rightly to the action in accord with the eternal law. Once the reason has determined the proper action, the Holy Spirit can move it to judge in accord with divine law and command it (cf. *ST* II-II.52.2.1). Consequently, just as infused prudence perfected cognitive participation by allowing humans to perform supernatural actions of directing themselves and others to a supernatural end, so also the gift of counsel further perfects this participation by allowing humans to receive advice from wisdom Incarnate by the power of the Holy Spirit. When humans act upon this divine advice and direct themselves and others to their ultimate end, they perfect their supernatural participation in divine government.

Wisdom

Of the gifts of the Holy Spirit, the greatest is the gift of wisdom. Unlike the gift of science, which concerns created things, the gift of wisdom concerns divine things (*ST* II-II.9.2). The person with natural wisdom contemplates the highest cause and in knowing the cause understands the order of all effects to this first cause. To the extent that he knows the cause, he is able to judge its effects. Likewise, the person with the gift of wisdom contemplates God as known supernaturally through faith and judges all in accord with this knowledge (*ST* II-II.45.1). In reference to the speculative intellect, the gift of wisdom allows humans to judge

Cognitive Participation

correctly in reference to divine things and to judge all other knowledge
by its relation to God as cause. In reference to the practical intellect,
through the gift of wisdom humans judge actions in accord with the
eternal law, the first cause of all actions.[186]

Just as in the case of the gift of science where judgment does not
follow discursive reason, with the gift of wisdom the intellect is able to
understand the conclusions without an inquiry of reason. Thomas states
that if right judgment of divine things follows an inquiry of reason, then
it belongs to wisdom as a natural intellectual virtue, but if it is on account of a connaturality with them, it belongs to the gift of wisdom.[187]
A judgment is connatural when it is done as if by a natural inclination.[188]
So in the case of wisdom, unlike through the intellectual virtue of wisdom which perfects the intellect to reason discursively, through the gift
of wisdom one is able to immediately judge divine things.[189] Aquinas in
ST II-II.45.2 compares this type of judgment to the judgment done by
one who possesses the virtue of chastity. Whereas in matters of chastity,
some can judge rightly through inquiry by reason, "but he who has the
habit of chastity judges rightly of such matters by a kind of connaturality."[190] In other words, the man with the habit of chastity has already

186. See *ST* I-II.45.2 where Thomas notes that wisdom denotes a certain rectitude of
judgment according to eternal law. In this context Thomas refers to judgment in accord
with eternal law by both the practical and the speculative intellect. In reference to judging
things by knowledge of their divine cause, see also *ST* I.12.8.

187. *ST* II-II.45.2. Thomas usually uses the term connaturality (connaturalitas) to mean
a natural inclination or affinity of one thing to another (Cf. *ST* I.13.1.3, 23.4; I-II.26.1) or a
union between two things caused by the motion of the appetitive power (*ST* I-II.32.3.3; especially II-II.29.2.2 where Thomas says *connaturalitatem* is the union of natural appetites).
These two meanings are closely related since the appetitive power inclines and unites one
to another. Hence, in the case of judging by a connaturality with divine things, the intellect
is united with the divine things in such a way that its act of judgment takes on a supernatural likeness to divine wisdom. Cf. *SCG* IV.21 and *ST* 45.6.1 which state that by the gift of
wisdom we are somehow made like the divine wisdom. See also Defarrari, *Lexicon*, 209, for
more on Thomas's use of the term *connaturalitas*.

188. *ST* I-II.26.1 & 26.1.3. Cf. Thomas Ryan, "Revisiting Affective Knowledge and
Connaturality in Aquinas," *Theological Studies* 66 (March 2005): 50–55, who defines connaturality as natural fittingness. In other words, an object is connatural to a human if it is
fitting. See also Taki Suto, "Virtue and Knowledge: Connatural Knowledge According to
Thomas Aquinas," *Review of Metaphysics* 58 (September 2004): 65–68.

189. Cf. Jacques Maritain, "On Knowledge through Connaturality," chap. 3 in *The
Range of Reason* (New York: Scribner, 1957), 22.

190. *ST* II-II.45.2: . . . sed per quandam connaturalitatem ad ipsa recte iudicat de eis ille
qui habet habitum castitatis. An example of the connatural judgment that Aquinas is talking
about might be that when faced with the possibility of adultery, a man could reason that adultery is wrong or if the man already possessed the virtue of chastity, he would automatically flee

trained the concupiscible appetite to reject sense goods not in accord with reason, and thus he does not need to deliberate as to the right action, but simply judges it.[191] Likewise in the case of the gift of wisdom, the gift of wisdom disposes humans to a particular judgment about divine things in a way similar to how the virtue of chastity disposes the concupiscible power to a judgment about chaste actions. Just as through the virtue of chastity the concupiscible power participates in reason, and hence allows the agent to judge without taking counsel, so also through the gift of wisdom a human participates in divine wisdom and can judge divine things without discursive reasoning.

Whereas the gift of understanding allows humans to understand the principles of the faith, wisdom allows humans to receive the conclusions (both speculative and practical) from these principles immediately. Just as humans understand the first principles of both speculative and practical reasoning immediately by the natural light of the intellect, so also by means of a supernatural light given through the gift of wisdom humans are able to immediately know conclusions of the faith. This way of knowing, which is natural to God and the angels, becomes connatural to humans through the gift of wisdom.

The soul receives this ability to judge by a connaturality with divine things by its union with God through the virtue of charity.[192] Thomas notes that through charity, the uncreated Wisdom (the Son) is united to us and reveals divine mysteries to us. This revelation is the gift of wisdom.[193] In other words, friends seek to know the desires and intentions

---

from the situation on account of having trained the concupiscible appetite to act reasonably. Cf. *ST* II-II.60.1.2.

191. Thomas affirms this in *ST* I-II.109.9 when he notes that when a man does not have the opportunity to reason to the proper action, he judges in accord with his preexisting end and habits. Thomas states that with the premeditation of reason, a man can do something outside of the order of his habitual disposition, but "when surprised, a man acts according to his preconceived end and preexisting habits" (quia in repentinis homo operatur secundum finem praeconceptum, et secundum habitum praeexistentem). Cf. *ST* II-II.123.9. See chapter 3 for an explanation of how the appetitive powers participate in reason by means of virtues.

192. See chapter 3 on the union caused by charity, especially the notion that charity causes the lover and beloved to share each other's intentions and act for each other's sake. Thomas calls this union of inclinations or intentions a union of affection (affectus—e.g., *ST* III.2.6). Elsewhere Thomas will refer to the gift of wisdom in the practical intellect as affective (affectiva) knowledge because it is caused by the love of God (*ST* I.64.1). Cf. Conley, 114–23. Cf. *SCG* IV.21 on the gifts of the Holy Spirit and charity.

193. *ST* II-II.45.6.2. See also *SCG* IV.21, which states that a friend reveals his secrets to a friend. Thomas continues, "For, since charity unites affections and makes, as it were,

of each other in order to act on behalf of the other. Because they seek to be of one mind and heart with each other, knowledge of the other and the good of the other is connatural to them. Since humans are united to God as His friends, it is fitting that God shares with us His divine wisdom, including the end to which He has ordered us and the means of achieving this end, in order for us to contemplate God and act out of love for Him. Hence, although wisdom is in the intellect, it is caused by charity in that through charity the uncreated Wisdom gives the intellect the ability to participate in divine wisdom in a supernatural way.[194]

Even though wisdom is caused by charity, it perfects charity because it allows humans to love God more perfectly by giving greater knowledge of God and by giving the soul the ability to connaturally judge actions in accord with love of God. The will loves that which is apprehended by the intellect as good. However, it does not love the intellectual form by which the good thing is apprehended, but loves the thing itself. Nonetheless, it can only love the thing to the extent the intellect knows it. In reference to God, the intellect is not able to know His essence in this life. However, because the will loves the thing apprehended and not the intelligible form, even with imperfect knowledge, God can be loved as He is in Himself (*ST* I-II.27.2.2). Even though God is loved as He is in Himself, this love is limited by the imperfect knowledge of the intellect. Wisdom gives greater knowledge of God, allowing the will to love God more perfectly (*ST* I-II.67.6.3).

In the practical intellect, charity causes an action to be ordered to God as a supernatural end. However, the means to this end must still be determined by the intellect. Because of the complexity and contingency of each situation, only God knows the action that is most in accord with

---

one heart of two, one seems not to have dismissed from his heart that which he reveals to a friend. . . . Therefore, since by the Holy Spirit we are established as friends of God, it is fitting that through the Holy Spirit humans are said to receive the revelation of the divine mysteries" (Cum enim amicitia coniungat affectus, et duorum faciat quasi cor unum, non videtur extra cor suum aliquis illud protulisse quod amico revelat . . . Quia igitur per spiritum sanctum amici dei constituimur, convenienter per spiritum sanctum hominibus dicuntur revelari divina mysteria). Cf. *ST* I-II.45.2.

194. *ST* I-II.45.4. Although all three persons of the Trinity cause the gifts of the Holy Spirit, the term wisdom is especially appropriated to the Son who is the Wisdom of the Father (*SCG* IV.21; *ST* I.39.7.2). Hence, when the Son dwells within us by charity, He is said to be the cause of the illumination of the intellect even as the Holy Spirit is said to be the cause of charity (*ST* I.43.5.2). Since the eternal law is the wisdom of God, it is also appropriated to the Son (*ST* I-II.93.1.2). Hence, it is through the indwelling of the Son that humans are given the infused wisdom of the eternal law and other divine things.

the eternal law. The gift of council perfects the intellect to discursively reason correctly, but the gift of wisdom surpasses council by allowing the intellect to know the proper action connaturally. In other words, sometimes humans must make a decision when they do not have all of the relevant information.[195] Wisdom gives them the ability to judge in accord with the eternal law even when they do not know all of the premises, so that their actions are not only formally in conformity with the divine will, but also materially in conformity. Hence, wisdom perfects charity so that humans not only intend ends in accord with the eternal law, but actually judge the means to be in accord with the eternal law.

Because the gift of wisdom gives humans the ability to judge connaturally by means of God's knowledge, it is the highest form of participation in the eternal law. Just as the intellect causes the appetitive powers to participate in reason by causing a good habit in them by commanding repeated acts in accord with reason, so also the Holy Spirit causes humans to participate in the eternal law by causing a good habit (the gift of wisdom) in them (although this gift is infused, not acquired like the moral virtues). And as a good habit causes humans to judge the object of the habit connaturally, so also the gift of wisdom causes humans to judge divine things connaturally.

This gift perfects both the speculative and the practical intellect to know divine things without recourse to discursive reasoning. In reference to the speculative intellect, wisdom causes the most perfect act of the intellect on earth. This act is the contemplation of God, to which every human is ordered, but is especially exemplified by the mystics throughout the tradition of the Church. Because the eternal law orders humans to contemplation of God, the gift of wisdom perfects the intellect for the highest participation in the eternal law. In reference to the practical intellect, wisdom perfects the intellect to judge actions by the eternal law. It is the highest form of the new law since it perfects the intellect to connaturally know the action that is most in conformity with the eternal

---

195. For example, when college students decide upon a major, through counsel they would start at the ultimate end and work back through proximate ends until they could decide on their major. For example, their major should be ordered to their eventual occupation, which should be ordered to their vocational status (i.e., married, single, religious), which should be ordered to the ultimate end. However, since sometimes students do not know what their vocational status will be or even their intended occupation, in these cases the gift of wisdom is necessary on account of the lack of information. God knows the proper major and through wisdom the student can be disposed to connaturally judge in accord with God's reason.

law. Through this perfection of the intellect, humans are able to direct themselves and others most perfectly to the end of eternal happiness.

In order to reach the supernatural end of eternal happiness, humans must be led by the Holy Spirit who knows the ultimate end and how to attain it. Along with the infused virtues, the gifts of the Holy Spirit perfect humans, so that they can be led by the Holy Spirit. Since humans are moved as rational creatures, the gifts are habits that perfect humans to direct themselves at the same time they are being led. Because humans move themselves rationally, they must know and choose the action that they are performing. Inasmuch as they know the action God moves them to, they have a true (but limited) knowledge of the exemplar of this action in God's mind, the eternal law. Hence, the gifts of understanding, knowledge, wisdom, and counsel perfect the intellect so that it supernaturally cognitively participates in the eternal law.

CONCLUSION

Because God directs all things to their proper end by means of the eternal law, to the extent humans rationally determine actions that are ordered to this end, they cognitively participate in the eternal law. Because there can be various degrees of understanding of the end and various degrees of rectitude of practical reason, there can also be various degrees of cognitive participation in the eternal law. Humans who misunderstand the end or reason incorrectly in determining the means to the end participate cognitively in the eternal law at a minimal degree, while those with a more perfect natural understanding of the end and a more perfect reasoning participate in the eternal law at a higher level. Over and above this natural participation, there is supernatural cognitive participation. There is a substantial difference in degree of participation between those who participate only by natural powers and those who participate by the divine light of grace.

Since the eternal law is the wisdom of God directing humans to their ultimate end of happiness, the greater the participation in eternal law the closer they are to happiness. Since God moves all things in accord with their form, the human intellect participates in divine knowledge through apprehension, judgment (understanding), and reasoning. This participation is increased by perfecting the intellect by means of the virtues and gifts. The acquired virtues of understanding, science, and wisdom perfect the speculative intellect to understand and reason properly. Prudence perfects the practical intellect to move from laws to particular actions by means of counsel, judgment, and command.

Because grace perfects nature, the intellect perfected by the light of grace continues to know things through the same three acts. Hence, there is a correlation between the acquired intellectual virtues and the infused intellectual virtues and the gifts of the Holy Spirit. Both perfect the intellect to understand things through the acts of apprehension, judgment, and reasoning. However, the difference is that grace gives the intellect the ability to understand by means of a supernatural light and faith gives supernatural principles from which both the speculative and the practical intellect can reason to conclusions. In the practical intellect the additional virtue of infused prudence is given to allow humans to determine actions in accord with their supernatural end. For both the speculative and practical intellect gifts are given which perfect the intellect to understand, reason, and judge more perfectly. The highest perfection of the intellect is the gift of wisdom whereby a human is able to judge things by a connaturality with divine wisdom.

Because the intellect is perfected, it becomes more like the divine intellect in its ability to understand things, direct itself, and direct others. Inasmuch as these virtues and gifts perfect the light of the intellect, they cause a greater participation in the divine light, the efficient cause of all knowledge. Inasmuch as they cause greater knowledge in the intellect, they cause greater participation in the divine exemplars: the divine ideas and the eternal law.

CHAPTER 5

Application to Contemporary Morality

EVEN CHILDREN ARE ABLE to understand moral precepts and apply them to concrete situations. If children can do this, it should be no surprise that through natural wisdom and the guidance of the Holy Spirit humans in many different cultures and at many different times have been able to know basic moral precepts and apply them to particular situations.[1] In its rudimentary form, this ability to know and apply basic moral truths does not require knowledge of an extensive moral system, but only a capacity to reason and to love the good. Nonetheless, when humans freely choose a moral action, their acts stem from an implicit knowledge of an ultimate end, an implicit recognition of one's current condition, and a reasoning process of how to get from one's current position to that ultimate end (cf. *ST* I-II.1.1–2).

Although many humans have only an implicit knowledge of the ultimate end for which they are acting, they nonetheless often determine the right action to perform. However, these same humans may also determine the wrong action out of ignorance.[2] Because speculative knowledge

---

1. Thomas acknowledges that the first precepts of natural law are known by all inasmuch as they have the capacity to understand the concepts. However, some precepts are only known by the wise and others only with divine aid (*ST* I-II.100.1).

2. This ignorance may be either in reference to determining the particular action, in reference to the necessity to cultivate virtues, or in reference to the nature of the end itself.

is practical by extension, to help humans to overcome this ignorance, it is helpful for them to understand explicitly their nature as a human who is ordered to a particular end and to understand that this end is achieved through actions that are in accord with their human nature (or divine nature in the case of grace). This knowledge about the principles and ends of moral actions gives humans a greater capacity to perform good actions.[3] In other words, to perfect their capacity to perform right human actions, humans should understand a moral system that includes an understanding that right actions are in accord with human nature as ordered to a particular end.[4] Yet even this is incomplete if it does not take into consideration the relation of the human agent to God in the moral action.

Knowledge of God as first efficient, exemplary, and final cause of human actions perfects our understanding of the role of human nature within the act, our understanding of the ultimate end, and our understanding of what actions are in accord with this end.[5] God as first efficient cause

---

3. A good analogy for this is the use of a map. On a map people must always know three things in order to get to where they are going. First, they must know where they are located—hence, maps in public places often state in bold letters, "You are here." Second they must know where they are going—the goal of the trip. Only after knowing these two things can they determine how to get there. This speculative knowledge from the map then becomes practical when it is ordered to the action of moving toward the goal. In some cases, a very simple map will give them the capacity to reach their goal. However, in unfamiliar cities that are not rationally organized, a map of intense detail is often needed to reach the goal. In morals, humans are always trying to get from their current state to their ultimate end through human actions. Knowledge of human nature, happiness, law, the virtues, and so on, all aid them in determining the proper action. In other words, a more detailed map (knowledge of morals) can give humans a greater capacity to do the right action. Sure the Holy Spirit can lead humans to the right action without any of this knowledge (the gift of wisdom), but normally the Holy Spirit leads them through the knowledge that they already have or can obtain through study or inquiry.

4. By learning about the powers of the soul, the virtues, the structure of the human act, and the proper end, humans are given an ability to identify moral faults and weaknesses with greater precision, identify more perfectly the relation between their actions and the end, and determine more precisely which actions to perform to reach the end. Although humans do not have to be moral scholars to be morally good people (especially since the Holy Spirit can lead them to act in accord with divine wisdom), speculative knowledge of moral theology can become practical by extension, and when accompanied by a good will, it can perfect the ability of humans to perform good actions.

5. Pinckaers states that there are three highpoints of Thomistic morality: the concept of happiness, the theological virtues, and the new law; see *Sources of Christian Ethics,* 172: "there are three towering peaks, which almost seem to touch the heavens: our journey in search of happiness, . . . the way of the theological virtues, . . . and the evangelical Law, which is the highpoint of legislation issuing from the wisdom of God. . . ." In reality, what Pinckaers has done is listed the highest form of human participation in each of the three types of divine causality: Human happiness refers to the highest form of participation in God as final cause, for in the act of ultimate happiness humans attain their end. The theological

moves all humans to direct themselves and others in accord with their nature that is made in God's image.[6] God as first exemplary cause directs and guides humans to actions in accord with their natural end. And God as the ultimate final cause is the ultimate end that humans seek through actions ordered to attainment of God. Since an effect participates in its cause, the relation between the human agent and the divine is that of participation, and because the eternal law moves humans to actions in accord with the end, at the foundation of moral theology is the notion of participation in eternal law.

The previous three chapters explained the notion of participation in the eternal law in order to explain the theological relation between the human agent and God. Because speculative knowledge is practical by extension, this knowledge helps to perfect the ability of the human agent to determine the proper moral action. In this conclusion, I intend to apply several implications of the notion of participation in the eternal law to contemporary understandings of morality. In the roughly seven hundred and fifty years since the time of Thomas, the intellectual milieu has changed enormously. Nominalism, the Protestant Reformation, modern science, the Enlightenment, and postmodernism have influenced the understanding that both scholars and others have about what humans are and how they are fulfilled.[7] This change in the understanding of anthropology has resulted in a corresponding change in the understanding of morality. Hence, while some of the questions that Thomas responded to are still commonly asked, today there are new problems that elicit new questions, and new and different answers are being given to the original questions.

In addition to this difference, because Thomas was writing for stu-

---

virtues are the highest participation in God as efficient cause, for they are the highest interior principles of action giving humans the ability to perform divine actions. And the new law is the highest participation in God as exemplary cause.

6. *ST* I-II.prologue. See also *ST* II-II.52.3: "The mover that is moved, moves through being moved. Hence the human mind, from the very fact that it is directed by the Holy Spirit, is enabled to direct itself and others" (movens motum ex hoc quod movetur movet. Unde mens humana ex hoc ipso quod dirigitur a spiritu sancto, fit potens dirigere se et alios).

7. For a few accounts of the intellectual roots of current moral beliefs, see Alasdair MacIntyre, *After Virtue* (Notre Dame: University of Notre Dame Press, 1984); Pinckaers, *Sources of Christian Ethics;* Charles Taylor, *The Sources of the Self* (Cambridge, Mass.: Harvard University Press, 1989); and John Milbank, *Theology and Social Theory* (Oxford: Blackwell, 1990). For a history of moral philosophy that is written with Kant as its focal point, see J. B. Schneewind, *The Invention of Autonomy: A History of Modern Moral Philosophy* (Cambridge: Cambridge University Press, 1998).

dents in a different cultural setting, the methodology, language, and meaning of his key terms is foreign to most people today. Furthermore, there is the problem that in many of his works Thomas writes as if the reader already has working knowledge of the majority of his ideas. A consequence of this is that to properly interpret the work of Thomas, one must also at least be familiar with the breadth of his philosophical and theological ideas as well as the many diverse influences upon his thought.

The foreignness of Thomas's language and methodology coupled with the somewhat naïve optimism on the part of Thomas in regard to the academic preparation of his readers has resulted in many contemporary scholars failing to find the brilliant insights within Thomas's writings either because they are unable to understand what he says, or they do not understand what he is saying in the context of his corpus as a whole. This results in them too quickly dismissing Thomas as being wrong (or at least not relevant) because his concepts are not consistent with their twenty-first century ideas that contain different understandings of anthropology and morality. In contrast, a knowledge of the entire Thomistic system would show its remarkable consistency across metaphysics, epistemology, morality, and theology.

In this chapter I will first address some contemporary scholarship of a few groups whose concepts of morality are inconsistent with the understanding of Thomas or at least ignorant of the insights of Thomas. Second, I will address those who are only familiar with a single area of Thomistic thought but do not understand how it fits into Thomas's theology as a whole. This is sometimes a problem within the realm of moral theology (e.g., someone may be an expert only on natural law or virtue). Because God as eternal law is the single cause of all elements of morality, a study of the notion of human participation in eternal law unites all the diverse elements of Thomistic moral thought.[8] Hence, after addressing a few contemporary issues, I will show how the eternal law unites all the foundational elements of morality.

8. See Cessario, *Introduction to Moral Theology*, 79, who notes that the unity of the eternal law is not compromised by different types of participation in it.

KEY INSIGHTS ABOUT PARTICIPATION IN
ETERNAL LAW FOR CONTEMPORARY MORALISTS

Although there are many insights that flow from the notion of participation in eternal law that are relevant for contemporary morality, I will highlight three of the most important ones. First, I will show how the understanding of the notion of participation in the eternal law corrects the contemporary understanding of human autonomy. In order to safeguard human "freedom," many place the notion of autonomy at the foundation of their moral system. I will show how the notion of participation in the eternal law is a more suitable foundation for morality. Second, I will show how the understanding of the participation of the various types of laws in the eternal law serves as a much better foundation for the moral actions of humans in the political arena than is the more contemporary foundation of political liberalism. Finally, I will show how the understanding of participation in the eternal law and especially supernatural participation by means of the new law of the Holy Spirit helps to guide those who seek to discern God's will. In this conclusion I am only showing how a proper understanding of this notion of participation in eternal law is particularly relevant for contemporary society and am not attempting to systematically present or critique the concepts of autonomy, political liberalism, and the contemporary theology of discernment.

Participation in the Divine Exemplary Cause
and Genuine Human Autonomy.

In *Veritatis Splendor*, Pope John Paul II contrasted genuine human autonomy with a false human autonomy.[9] He considers autonomy to be genuine when humans are the source and subject of their actions, but they are this source and subject because human reason draws its own truth and authority from the eternal law.[10] False autonomy is when the

9. See *Veritatis Splendor* (Boston: Pauline Books and Media, 1993), paragraphs 35–41: AAS 85 (1993). This distinction between genuine autonomy and false autonomy was made earlier in *Gaudium et Spes*, 41: AAS 58 (1966). See also Pope Leo XIII, *Libertas Praestantissimum* (1888): *Leonis XIII P.M. Acta*, VIII, 1889. Leo makes a distinction between a genuine understanding of freedom (basically the understanding of freedom found in St. Thomas) and the secular understanding of freedom of that time. See Pinckaers in *Sources of Christian Morality*, chapters 14–16, for his famous distinction between freedom for excellence and freedom of indifference.

10. *Veritatis Splendor*, 40.

person disregards the participation of human reason in the eternal law and instead "posits a complete sovereignty of reason in the domain of moral norms regarding right ordering of life in this world."[11] With false autonomy, human reason alone is the author of the moral law, and God is not considered the author of this law.[12]

There are many different modern notions of autonomy, and hence John Paul II's description of autonomy can be said to be too generic. However, the point of the encyclical is not to focus on any one particular contemporary scholar but to cause all scholars to ask themselves to what extent in their moral theory is human reason the sole arbiter of the moral law. The autonomous leanings of most contemporary scholarship is not as simplistic as the pope's description, but nonetheless in some form or another it shares in the autonomous assumptions criticized by the pope.[13] Likewise, this section will not focus on any particular autonomous scholar but will instead, following the encyclical, speak of the theory of autonomy in general.

One of the most influential founders of this notion of false autonomy was Immanuel Kant. Kant argues that for an action to be moral it must stem solely from an autonomous will. A will is autonomous when it is a law to itself as independent from all foreign causes.[14] In other words, the will is self-ruling as determining its own laws independent of any natural necessity, external command, external reward, or punishment. If the action stems from natural necessity, external commands, or incentives, it is not autonomous but heteronomous, and therefore not moral.[15] Con-

---

11. *Veritatis Splendor,* 36.

12. Ibid., "In no way could God be considered the Author of this law, except in the sense that human reason exercises its autonomy in setting down laws by virtue of a primordial and total mandate given to man by God."

13. The following scholars may have different understandings of autonomy, but all agree that the notion of autonomy is at the heart of moral theory: J. B. Schneewind, in *The Invention of Autonomy* (Cambridge: Cambridge University Press, 1998); John Rawls, *A Theory of Justice* (Cambridge, Mass.: Harvard University Press, 1971) and *Political Liberalism* (New York: Columbia University Press, 1993); Tom Beauchamp and James Childress, *Principles of Biomedical Ethics* (New York: Oxford University Press, 1994). Schneewind in his work notes, "I planned from the beginning to make Kant the focal point of this study because I thought, as I still do, that his conception of morality as autonomy provides a better place to start working out a contemporary philosophical understanding of morality than anything we can get from other past philosophers" (xiv).

14. See Immanuel Kant, *Grounding for the Metaphysics of Morals,* translated by J. Ellington (Indianapolis: Hackett, 1962), 285–86. See also "What Is Enlightenment?" in *Kant Selections,* ed. and trans. Lewis White Beck (New York: Macmillan, 1998), 462–67.

15. Kant, *Grounding for the Metaphysics,* 285–93. See also Charles Taylor, *Sources of the Self* (Cambridge, Mass.: Harvard University Press, 1989), 364. Taylor states, "Kant explicitly

sequently, Kant makes autonomy the foundation of his moral system.[16]

Advocates of modern autonomy have kept the notion of autonomy, but have stripped away the metaphysical background that accompanied this notion in Kant.[17] Once this metaphysical background was removed, a necessary presupposition of this view of autonomy is that God is always considered to be extrinsic to the creature and a threat to absolute autonomy.[18] In contemporary society, advocates of this view of autonomy believe that any external law (e.g., from God) or preordination from nature (i.e., a natural inclination) inhibits the pure autonomy that they think is necessary for genuine responsibility. They seek to be free to create their own conception of the ends of human nature and create the corresponding laws that move the agent to these ends. Thus, although Kant was actually trying to rescue faith and morality from Hume's critiques, his enduring influence has lead to morality being separated from a universe that is ordered and governed by God.

Because this concept of false autonomy rests on a different metaphysics, epistemology, and understanding of the relation of the human agent to God (if the existence of God is posited) than that of Thomas, a com-

---

insists that morality can't be founded in nature or in anything outside the human rational will. . . . We cannot accept that the cosmic order, or even the order of ends in human 'nature,' should determine our normative purposes. All such views are heteronomous; they involve abdicating our responsibility to generate the law out of ourselves." See also MacIntyre, *After Virtue*, 44–45.

16. Kant, *Grounding for the Metaphysics*, 285–86. Kant derives the categorical imperative from the idea that the will is a law to itself: "The proposition that the will is a law to itself in all its actions, however, only expresses the principle that we should act according to no other maxim than that which can also have itself as a universal law for its object."

17. Lewis White Beck, in his introduction to the works of Kant, states that for Kant metaphysical knowledge is beyond the boundary of what can be known by experience. Metaphysical ideas can serve as postulates of moral reasoning, but they give no knowledge of things as they are in themselves. Kant denies this knowledge of these supersensible realities to make room for faith. Truths of faith cannot be proven, but they must be postulated in order to bring together the natural and the moral realm. Hence, Kant postulates the existence of God, an ordered world, eternal life, and the summum bonem ("the necessary highest end of a morally determine reason and a true object thereof"). See *Kant*, 14–17. The last quote is from Kant's *Critique of Practical Reason*, 307. Cf. Taylor, *Sources of the Self*, 83, 365.

18. Charles Taylor, *Sources of the Self*, 84, quotes Iris Murdoch's description of the modern autonomous man: "How recognizable, how familiar to us is the man so beautifully portrayed in the *Grundlegung*, who confronted even with Christ turns away to consider the judgment of his own conscience and to hear the voice of his own reason. Stripped of the exiguous metaphysical background which Kant was prepared to allow him, this man is with us still, free, independent, lonely, powerful, rational, responsible, brave, the hero of so many novels and books of moral philosophy." See Murdoch, *The Sovereignty of God* (London: Routledge, 1970), 80.

plete refutation of this view is well beyond the scope of this conclusion. However, as John Paul II notes, one of the elements at the heart of the matter is that a proper autonomy participates in the eternal law while a false autonomy either misunderstands, denies, or rejects participation in the eternal law. The understanding of the notion of participation in eternal law from the earlier chapters of this work should help to illuminate John Paul's point.

The notion of participation describes a completely different type of relation between the human agent and God than that understood by modern advocates of autonomy. For them, God is always extrinsic to the human agent in the sense that He is always alien to the human agent,[19] and thus there are only two possibilities: either humans forfeit their causal responsibility by following God's commands, or they remain autonomous and do not follow God's command. The notion of participation posits a completely different type of relation between the human agent and God. This relation is not one where authentic human freedom is attained by independence from God, but one where authentic freedom is attained by sharing in God's power, wisdom, and love. The relation of participation does not set the power, wisdom, and end of the human agent in opposition to that of God, but it allows humans to be free by sharing in the power, wisdom, and end of God (the divine goodness). Hence, participation in the eternal law allows humans to maintain their causal responsibility, while at the same time being led by God.

The eternal law is the first cause of all human actions both by moving and governing humans in accord with their form and by being the cause of the practical truth in the human mind (i.e., cognitive participation). An understanding of both of these types of participation shows that the proper foundation of morality is not false autonomy, but participation in God.

The notion of participation in the eternal law as moved and governed by it allows one to understand that humans are related to God as secondary agents to the primary agent. The notion of false autonomy does not include this understanding. God alone can cause being, but so that humans can be more like God, God causes being in such a way

19. Thomas also speaks of God as an extrinsic cause of human actions by means of His grace and law. However, for Thomas, something is an intrinsic principle of action if it is the principle agent of an act and something is an extrinsic principle if it helps the intrinsic principle by strengthening it or assisting it (cf. *ST* I.117.1 and *ST* I-II.68.1). In other words, grace and law help humans to freely act rather than remove freedom, as modern advocates of false autonomy believe.

that humans when they act are also true causes of being. Since secondary causes always act in accord with their form, God causes them to act as rational and free agents. Hence, humans are free because God's eternal law moves and governs them to act freely.

More specifically, because God's wisdom causes all free human actions, humans are free because the intellect and appetitive powers participate in the eternal law. For Thomas, freedom does not come from a blind movement of the will or sense appetites but comes from the will and sense appetites being determined by human reason to intend and choose acts in accord with the ultimate end of humanity.[20] In other words, humans by necessity desire to be happy; however, their intellect must determine what is the proper ultimate end and also determine which actions are in accord with this end. Without the intellect being able to determine a variety of different ends and actions, the will cannot desire one end or action more than another and is not free. Hence, freedom is bound up in rationality, which derives its light and intellectual forms from the eternal law.

Furthermore, the will is only able to act because it participates in God who is the first efficient, exemplary, and final cause of its actions. As the first efficient cause, God gives the will the power to desire the end and the action ordered to this end. As the final cause, all ends that the will desires are good by participation in the divine goodness. And as exemplary cause, the will participates in the eternal law by means of being ordered to a particular end and action by the intellect. Hence, whereas the contemporary understanding of freedom is a complete independence from God and other extrinsic causes, for Thomas, authentic human freedom is first and foremost caused by the eternal law and only caused by the human through the soul's participation in the eternal law.

Because authentic human freedom is caused by participation in the eternal law, perfection of this participation results in a perfection of human freedom. Imperfect participation of the intellect, will, and passions in the eternal law results in a lack of authentic freedom. If the intellect does not know the character of the ultimate end or which actions are in accord with it, then the human person is not free to intend the end

---

20. Thomas contrasts human actions from those of the animals. Whereas the animals judge which act is to be chosen by instinct, humans are able to reason to a variety of actions that are ordered to their natural end. The ability of the reason to know a variety of means is the cause of free choice (*ST* I.83.1).

or choose the actions.[21] Likewise, if the will does not love the ultimate end, then the person is again not free to intend it, and if the person is influenced by the passions to not choose rationally, there is no authentic freedom.

In reference to the intellect, knowledge of the ultimate end and knowledge of acts in accord with this end exceeds the natural ability of the intellect. Hence, in order to be free to attain this end, divine assistance is needed. By increasing the participation of the reason in the eternal law through the infused virtues of faith and prudence, and the gifts of the Holy Spirit, humans are free to know the proper end and determine the proper means to this end. Human freedom is especially perfected by the gifts of the Holy Spirit which give humans the freedom to know what actions to perform in every situation to maximize the happiness of themselves and all others.

Likewise, because the will intends the end and chooses the means on account of this intention, the agent lacks freedom when the will chooses an apparent good that is not in conformity with the true end. The eternal law orders all things to their proper end. Hence, when the will is directed by the eternal law to its true end, the eternal law is not being restrictive or coercive, but giving the will the freedom to choose what it naturally desires (or supernaturally desires in the case of the infused virtues). The infused virtues and the gifts of the Holy Spirit that perfect the participation of the will in eternal law likewise increase the freedom of the will to attain the infinite good that it desires.[22]

The sense appetites can also influence and even blind the reason and hence also remove authentic human freedom. When humans are blinded by their anger or lust, they completely lose their freedom for the moment, and even when the sense appetites do not completely blind the reason, freedom can be diminished by unruly sense appetites. Hence, the sense appetites must be perfected to participate in the eternal law by participating in the reason of the intellect.[23] The infused virtues and the gifts of the Holy Spirit perfect the sense appetites to not only avoid impeding the operation of the intellect and will, but also to aid them so

21. See *ST* I-II.74.5 where Thomas notes that reason can be the cause of sin either by being ignorant of a truth that it ought to know or by commanding the lower powers inordinately or failing to check them.

22. See Pinckaers, *Sources,* 327–99, for more on this type of freedom, which he calls freedom for excellence.

23. Inasmuch as the sense appetites are ordered by reason, they participate in reason which participates in the eternal law.

that the person is free to act with great passion and enthusiasm. Without these perfections of participation in the eternal law, the human is not free to perform good actions in accord with the ultimate end.

An understanding of the human agent participating in the eternal law as moved and governed by it shows that the ability of the powers of the soul to freely act comes from participation in the eternal law and not from independence from divine command, as many who advocate a false sense of autonomy believe.

Because the eternal law orders humans to their proper ends, when the intellect recognizes this order, it is said to cognitively participate in the eternal law. The understanding of cognitive participation in eternal law illuminates the relation between moral truth and human freedom. Humans have a natural inclination to know the truth. When the intellectual form in the mind corresponds to the thing in reality, the intellect performs the act it is naturally inclined to perform. However, if the intellectual form does not correspond to the thing, the intellect has made an error in either judgment or reasoning. To consider this erroneous intellectual form to be true is not authentic freedom but an imperfection. For example, a child's knowledge that $2 + 2 = 4$ is true and flows from the natural inclination of the intellect. The child is *not* authentically free to hold that $2 + 2 = 5$ because this does not correspond with reality and violates the intellect's natural inclination to know the truth. Hence, although a child may argue that he is simply doing creative math, the teacher will inform him that he has made an error. False intellectual forms are not from the proper functioning of the intellect, but from the weakness of the intellect. They are not freedom but an imperfection.

The same principle applies to moral truth. Because humans are naturally inclined to a particular end by participation in the eternal law as moved and governed, certain actions are ordered to this end and certain actions are not. A moral law is true if it orders humans to their ultimate end and false if it does not. Likewise, the application of the law to a particular situation can be determined to be true or false based on whether or not it is in accord with the order instituted by the eternal law. Because the eternal law inclines humans to their particular end and determines which actions are in accord with this end, when humans know moral truths, they cognitively participate in the eternal law. The eternal law acts as the foundation of all moral truth and all laws and actions are judged by their degree of participation in it. With the notion of false autonomy, humans are free to define their own "ends" and create their own "moral truths." However, this notion of freedom is false because it goes against the moral truth established by the eternal law, which humans have a natural inclination to know and to act upon. The intellects of humans who hold laws that are contradictory to the end to which the eternal law inclines them are in error. Without the knowledge of moral truth, they are not free to intend the end or to choose the action that the will ultimately desires. Hence, they lack the freedom to truly act responsibly.[24]

The notion of false autonomy rests upon the assumptions that creation is not ordered to a particular end, that humans should separate themselves from divine guidance, and that humans should determine their own moral truth. In this view, a human's fulfillment is always going to be limited by his own creativity. In contrast, an understanding of participation in the eternal law allows a moral theology to be built upon completely different principles. It first posits that humans are ordered to a particular end by God. This divine ordering means that certain laws and actions are true and others are false. When humans recognize this divine order and which actions are in accord with it, they participate cognitively in God's knowledge. Because God gives them supernatural assistance to increase their participation in eternal law, in their search for fulfillment they are not limited by their natural potency, but are able to participate in the divine nature. By means of this participation, they are free to perform supernatural actions and free to attain the happiness and union with God and others to which they are inclined. This ability of the soul to freely cause supernatural actions is true autonomy in the sense that John Paul II uses the word.[25] This autonomy is not divorced from the eternal law but is based upon the notion of participation in the eternal law.

The Eternal Law as Guide in the Political Realm

Contemporary politics has been highly influenced by the false notion of autonomy in a variety of ways. One of these ways is that many within the

24. Humans are not authentically free to hold the law that murder is licit for them to perform. If they do hold this view, they either lack the freedom to properly understand the moral law (either because of lack of intellectual virtues or intellectual blindness flowing from vice) or they have a false notion of freedom because humans are not free to hold a false view as true.

25. There is a certain danger in using the term autonomy because it can be easily misunderstood in our culture today. Hence, some prefer to use the term theonomous instead of true autonomy. See *Veritatis Splendor*, 41. Rhonheimer who seeks to refute the notion of

United States believe that religious and philosophical doctrines should be kept completely out of political debate. They feel that when those who participate in the legislative process seek to form laws that reflect their religious background, they are forcing their religious beliefs on others. This view that religious and philosophical beliefs are to be kept completely out of the political arena is one of the key elements of political liberalism.[26] This notion is the foundation of many people's belief of how to act in the political arena.

Even those who believe that religious and philosophical beliefs should guide their actions in the political realm will only find religious and philosophical arguments convincing if these arguments conform to their particular religious beliefs. Since there is a great diversity of religious beliefs in America, for prudential reasons, it may be wise to avoid arguing from religious principles lest the audience be immediately unreceptive. Consequently, although there are many valid criticisms of the current political milieu in the United States, like it or not, Christians often lose their credibility in the political arena when they argue from religious principles. So the question is: How can Christians help to establish laws in accord with the eternal law in contemporary society?

Thankfully, the notion of participation in the eternal law can serve as a more adequate foundation for a political system than that of political liberalism. Because political liberalism assumes that humans are isolated individual agents who must be "free" to choose their own theological and philosophical truths, it does not allow for theological or philosophical arguments in the political arena. In this view, if laws are based on theological or philosophical arguments, then they are not allowing oth-

---

"autonomous morality" nonetheless uses the term "participated autonomy" in speaking of the reason's participation in the providence of God (see *Natural Law and Practical Reason*, chapter 5). For a discussion of the distinction between a Christian understanding of autonomy as theonomy and a secular understanding of autonomy, see Walter Kasper, *Theology and the Church* (New York: Crossroad, 1992).

26. Perhaps the most eloquent spokesperson for the notion of political liberalism is John Rawls. Rawls, in his book *Political Liberalism,* argues that because of the diversity of moral traditions in the United States, all public reason must be divorced from religious and philosophical doctrines (10). Instead, laws should be based on a political conception of justice that comes from the fundamental ideas of democratic society (38–40, 97–99, 127, 138). Citizens within society will recognize this concept of justice as rational, and most will locate this notion of justice within their own religious and philosophical system. Those systems that are not in accord with this notion of justice are considered unreasonable and are condemned (39, 152–53). In this way citizens autonomously choose political values by means of their own practical reason, rather than being forced to follow a philosophical or religious doctrine (138–39).

ers to be "free" to choose their own theological or philosophical truths. Unlike political liberalism, the notion of participation in eternal law begins with the idea that humans are ordered to a particular end, and that laws are necessary for them to reach this end. Because of the weakness of the human intellect, divine guidance is necessary for humans to determine the proper laws and actions to reach this end. Furthermore, because both the natural law and the divine law come from the same source, one can be guided by the divine law while at the same time converse in the political arena with arguments accessible to natural reason.

To develop a genuine sense of autonomy (in contrast to the false sense critiqued above), the powers of the soul need to be moved and directed to their proper end. Without external principles of actions, humans will not develop the virtues that allow them to function both as an earthly and a heavenly society.[27] In other words, humans are ordered by the eternal law to perform a certain type of actions, but without the assistance of God and others they will never develop the proper dispositions to perform these actions. Imagine if parents did not establish the law that their children must share with others. These children would likely not develop the virtue of generosity, and unless some other external force moved them to begin practicing acts of sharing, they would have the vice of selfishness. This vice would both hinder them from achieving the earthly common good and their own eternal good. Human laws are established to move humans to perform actions that are in accord with the end of both the earthly and the heavenly society, and by directing them to perform these actions human laws cause them to acquire virtue (cf. *ST* I-II.95.1).

The understanding of participation in the eternal law illuminates the concept that laws are to help move humans to the end that they are ordered to by the eternal law. In other words, by participation in the eternal law as moved and governed, humans are ordered to a particular end, and only certain types of actions can be done to obtain this end. Whenever humans recognize this order to the end and the conforming right actions, their reason cognitively participates in the eternal law. When they direct themselves and others in accord with this participated knowledge, the ordinance of their reason is human law.

---

27. Cf. *ST* I-II.92.1, 107.2. I am using the word "external" in the sense that Thomas uses the term, not in the sense meant by modern advocates of false autonomy. For Thomas, God is an external principle of action through his laws and grace, even though in both of these ways He strengthens and assists the human agent from within.

Since the eternal law orders humans to their proper end, which includes ordering them as a society, the greater the participation of human laws in the eternal law, the more perfectly a society will be ordered (cf. *ST* I-II.93.3.2). However, since the eternal law cannot be known directly, but only through the natural and divine law, human laws are derived from the eternal law by means of the natural and divine law (*ST* I-II.95.2 & 3). Consequently, inasmuch as a human law is in accord with natural reason, it is in accord with the eternal law (*ST* I-II.93.3.2). Thus, Christians can enter into the political debate using arguments based solely on natural reason, and because these arguments are based on natural reason, humans in other traditions have the capacity to understand them. For example, in order to argue that murder is wrong it is not necessary to quote the Decalogue.

However, to say that Christians can argue by means of natural reason only partially solves the problem. Natural reason is subject to error and ignorance both on account of its fallenness (vice and susceptibility to be blinded by the passions) and on account of its natural weakness. Because we recognize the weakness of the human intellect, it is necessary to judge the precepts of our reason by the divine law.[28] The notion of participation in the eternal law explains why humans can judge natural reason by divinely revealed reason. The eternal law is the source of both natural and divine law; however, divine law participates in the eternal law more perfectly.

One way of judging the precepts by means of the divine law is to determine whether or not they are in conformity with the moral law of the Old Testament. For example, although the precepts of the Decalogue can be known by natural reason alone (*ST* I-II.98.6), many would not come to knowledge of the commandment against adultery without the help of divine revelation.[29]

The Christian must not only judge natural reason by the old law but

---

28. See *ST* I-II.99.2.2 which states that divine law aids the soul not only in things in which human reason is insufficient, but also in areas where human reason is impeded—in other words, when the divinely revealed truth could be known by natural reason, but for various possible reasons (e.g., sloth, lack of intelligence, lack of time to contemplate, etc.) reason is impeded from coming to this knowledge on its own. Cf. *ST* II-II.2.4.

29. For some this ignorance is caused by intellectual weakness or lack of time to come to the proper conclusion. For others passions or vices (e.g., lust) blind them. However, many in our society do not come to a natural knowledge that adultery and the corresponding sexual sins are wrong because the opposite view has been so deeply ingrained within them by contemporary culture that they rarely even question its rectitude.

also by the new law. Since the new law has two elements (spiritual and written), natural reason must be judged by its conformity with both elements. The primary element of the new law is the grace of the Holy Spirit. This grace perfects the mind to reason correctly from natural principles and perfects the will to love the proper laws and actions. It also gives supernatural principles (held by faith) and a supernatural light to understand and reason from these principles (the Holy Spirit's gifts of understanding, science, wisdom, and counsel). Furthermore, the Holy Spirit moves the will to desire the proper laws and actions, even when the human does not have all the counsel needed to make a good decision.[30] Because the assistance of the Holy Spirit allows humans to judge by means of God's wisdom (the eternal law), and God always knows the correct laws for the correct circumstances, the new law of grace allows humans to most perfectly direct society to both its earthly and its eternal end.[31]

The secondary element of the new law is the written law. Because humans can be mistaken as to whether or not the Holy Spirit is guiding them, they must always make sure that their intended actions are in conformity with the written laws of the New Testament and the Church.[32] In contemporary society, this means that natural reason must be judged to be in conformity with Church teaching.[33] In judging natural reason

30. Although the law functions primarily through our knowing it, if one loves as one ought, one fulfills the law (cf. Rom 13:8).

31. For a human law to be a good law, it must not only be in accord with the eternal law, it must also be prudent to promulgate it in a particular situation. Not every natural law or divine law can be effectively enforced. For example, although it is against the natural law for mothers to abandon their babies on the steps of a church or another public place, enforcing this natural law by making it illegal to abandon children in a public place often has the undesired effect of children being abandoned in dumpsters or the wilderness. Consequently, it would do more harm than good to enforce laws against mothers abandoning their babies at a place where their children would be safe. Lawmakers with the gift of the Holy Spirit would be able to know which laws to promulgate according to the particular situation.

32. Keep in mind that there are various degrees of ecclesial law. Some ecclesial laws are human laws and potentially subject to error.

33. In all cases of application of a universal Church teaching to a particular situation, circumstances must be taken into consideration (cf. *ST* I-II.94.4). Since other people may take other circumstances into consideration, they may come to a different conclusion even if they begin with the same first principle. Both may be in accord with the principle, but one is more suited to the particular situation than the other (the fault is often not in the reasoning but in the understanding of the minor premise of the practical syllogism). For example, it is a principle of Catholic moral teaching that married couples can only use periodic abstinence to prevent pregnancy when they have a serious reason. However, different people will apply this principle differently even in similar situations because they see different circumstances as

by the new law, inasmuch as the reason is truly directed by the Holy Spirit, it is directed by the eternal law.

The eternal law orders earthly society to a natural end. Knowledge of this order is the natural law. Thus, all precepts necessary to bring society to its natural fulfillment are natural law precepts (cf. *ST* I-II.95.2). Even when humans know them and judge them by means of the divine law, they can still justify them by means of natural reason. Hence, when Christians enter into the moral arena, they can debate in natural law terms even while they are being guided by the new law.[34] For example in the abortion debate, although a citizen is guided by the written law of Church teaching and the guidance of the Holy Spirit, he can argue against abortion from naturally known principles.[35]

There will be some laws known through the divine law that are ordered to the supernatural end of society that Christians will not be able to express in natural law terminology. Although these laws are ordered to the ultimate end of eternal life, they would also help earthly society flourish.[36] However, in the current political situation, in order to convince others to accept these laws, Christians will have to work for the conversion of society.

When the foundation for political morality is political liberalism, laws are determined by natural reason determining what rights an isolated agent can have without harming the rights of others. The goal of these laws is not the unity and fulfillment of society. Furthermore, the wisdom behind these laws is always limited since the human intellect is weakened and influenced by the passions. When the foundation of political morality is participation in the eternal law, the lawmaker recognizes that humans

---

being important. Hence, *Gaudium et Spes* notes that often members of the laity will disagree on what is the best way to implement the gospel into the temporal realm. Neither side can identify their opinion as the teaching of the Church (43).

34. Thankfully, often when the magisterium gives principles that are to guide society, it shows not only their foundation within Scripture and tradition, but also their foundation within natural law.

35. Even this may not be particularly effective if those they are arguing against are people who do not believe that society is ordered to a particular end and that laws are only to protect their "rights." However, because the first principles of natural law are known without demonstration, nearly always at least some commonly held principles can be found at which the reasoning process can begin.

36. An example of this type of law might be one that is derived from the practical application of the propositions of faith concerning participation in the unity of the Trinity. Although this unity found within marriage and the Church is a sign and foretaste of heavenly unity, it also contributes to the flourishing of earthly society beyond the naturally known benefits of marriage and religion as a virtue.

are ordered to a particular end that includes a particular type of society, and human laws are made to move humans to this end. The source of this ordering is the eternal law, which is known through the natural and divine law. Because the natural law is a participation in the eternal law, humans can base their laws on natural reason but yet at the same time be guided by the divine law.

Discernment as Participation in the Eternal Law

In the Church today, the use of the term discernment is very common, especially in reference to discerning a vocation to the religious life.[37] It is also widespread in theology in reference to discerning God's will in general. Although a significant portion of the more recent research on the notion of discerning God's will comes from the Jesuit tradition where discernment is an important aspect of Ignatius's spirituality,[38] there are also many other articles that trace the history of discernment,[39] or simply tell how to discern God's will.[40] Although Aquinas's name does appear within some of these works,[41] in contrast to Ignatius of Loyola who began a whole tradition analyzing the notion of discernment, it would be an exaggeration to say that a tradition of discernment has developed based on the writings of Aquinas. Nonetheless, because to discern God's will is to identify which actions the eternal law moves and directs us to by means of the guidance of the Holy Spirit,[42] to recognize these actions

37. See, for example, Russell Shaw, "What Vocation Shortage?" *America* 190, no. 11 (2004): 10–13.

38. See, for example, Jules Toner, *Discerning God's Will: Ignatius Loyola's Teaching on Christian Decision Making* (St. Louis: Institute of Jesuit Sources, 1991), and *A Commentary on St. Ignatius' Rules for the Discernment of Spirits* (St. Louis: Institute of Jesuit Sources, 1982).

39. See, for example, Joseph T. Lienhard, "Discernment of Spirits in the Early Church," *Theological Studies* 41 (1980): 505–29; Edith Scholl, "The Mother of Virtues: *Discretio*," *Cistercian Studies Quarterly* 36, no. 3 (2001): 389–401; and Diana Billegas, "Discernment in Catherine of Siena," *Theological Studies* 58 (1997): 19–38.

40. See, for example, Ben Johnson, *Discerning God's Will* (Louisville: Westminster/ John Knox Press, 1990).

41. For example, Diana Billegas, "Discernment in Catherine of Siena," speaks of Aquinas's influence on Catherine (19–24), and Francois Dingjan, *Discretio. Les origines patristiques et monastiques de la doctrine sur la prudence chez Thomas d' Aquin* (Assen: Van Gorcum, 1967), who notes that Aquinas speaks of prudence as a rightness of discernment (*discretio*) in *ST* I-II.61.4.

42. Edith Scholl, "The Mother of Virtues: *Discretio*," notes that the Latin root word for discernment, *discernere,* meant "to see deeply in order to separate, distinguish, or discern" (389). The early Church inspired by 1 Corinthians 12, "to another [is given] discernment of

is to cognitively participate in the eternal law. Consequently, both an understanding of the notion of participation in the eternal law as moved and governed and cognitive participation in the eternal law can help humans to more perfectly discern God's will.

Humans do not need explicit knowledge of the notion of participation in eternal law or even an explicit understanding that they are discerning God's will to be guided by the Holy Spirit to a particular action. The most simple of saints by the guidance of the Holy Spirit can perform actions that greatly manifest the wisdom of God. Through their experience and divine instinct, they are able to distinguish which actions are in accord with the eternal law and which actions are not. Nonetheless, because speculative knowledge is practical by extension, an understanding of how humans participate in the eternal law can be helpful in giving humans the ability to discern God's will.

Because the Holy Spirit moves humans as instrumental causes to all of their actions, every action is caused by the Holy Spirit inasmuch as it has *esse* and is an act (cf. *ST* I-II.109.1; *SCG* IV.20). However, just as in all cases of instrumental causality where a defect in the instrument results in the action not perfectly conforming to the exemplar in the mind of the agent, so also in the case of the Holy Spirit moving humans to actions, often humans fail to perform the good action to which they are moved.[43] An analogy can be made between humans as instrumental causes and a piano as an instrumental cause. Both the musician and the piano are the cause of the music that is played. The musician plays based upon the exemplar which is in his mind (or is illustrated by signs within a music book). Even if the musician is accomplished and can play perfectly in accord with the exemplar, a bad piano will make bad music. Hence, only the music that comes from a good piano is a perfect likeness of its exemplar. Likewise, with the Holy Spirit and a human, humans are moved by the Holy Spirit to freely perform good actions that are a likeness of the eternal law. However, on account of the imperfection of the powers of

---

spirits," made a distinction between knowing the inspiration of the Holy Spirit and the inspiration of other spirits (either demonic or one's own). Hence, to discern God's will is to come to know God's will by separating it from one's own will or the will of an evil spirit.

43. Inasmuch as an act is good, both God and the human is the cause of the goodness: God as the first cause and the human as the second cause. Inasmuch as an action is evil (i.e., lacking the goodness of a perfect action), the human alone is the cause (*ST* I.49.2.2; I-II.79.2; *DP* 1.6.5; 3.6.20). Cf. *ST* I.49.3.4: "No being is called evil by participation, but by privation of participation" (nullum ens dicitur malum per participationem, sed per privationem participationis).

the soul, humans can perform actions that are not a perfect likeness of the eternal law and are deficient. Thus, to discern the movement of the Holy Spirit is to separate the defects in participation in eternal law caused by the human alone from the perfections in the participation caused by both God as first cause and the human as a secondary cause.

Although the Holy Spirit moves humans to good natural actions, primarily the term "movement of the Holy Spirit" refers to when the Holy Spirit moves humans to supernatural actions. Just as when humans are moved to actions in accord with human nature, the Holy Spirit remains the primary cause of the supernatural action. The human remains the secondary cause; however, the principle of this movement is not human nature, but the superadded form of grace that is a participation in divine nature. Grace makes humans more like God in that it allows them to overcome the limits of their natural potency and be moved to divine actions. Consequently, to discern the movement of the Holy Spirit is to separate the impulse of the Holy Spirit moving humans to supernatural actions from actions that are either deficient or only naturally good. These supernatural actions conform to the eternal law in a way that exceeds natural conformity.

Although humans with grace are moved by the Holy Spirit to all of their supernatural actions, because they still have the effects of fallen nature, they can be fooled into believing that their own false desires and reasoning are from the Holy Spirit. It is not immediately obvious which actions are supernaturally in accord with the eternal law. In order to discern this conformity, the powers of the soul must be perfected by the new law of grace that allows them to participate in divine wisdom. Since the new law has both a written and a spiritual element, both of these help to guide the soul in the discernment process. First, the human must make sure that the action is in accord with the written law. If an action is not in accord with the truths of divine revelation as manifested by Scripture and Church teaching, then it is not from the Holy Spirit, for the Holy Spirit will never move an individual in a way that violates the laws ordering all of humanity to its ultimate end.

Since the Holy Spirit is moving humans as individuals to particular actions, of which many possible options can be in conformity with the written law, humans will need additional insight beyond the written law to discern the movement of the Holy Spirit. Because speculative knowledge is practical by extension, a speculative understanding of how the

Holy Spirit moves humans in general can help humans to more perfectly interpret the guidance of the Holy Spirit in their lives.

The Holy Spirit moves humans as an instrumental cause, and in all cases of instrumental causality the instrument is moved in accord with its form. In this case, the form is human nature transformed by grace. However, since grace perfects but does not replace the powers of the soul, the Holy Spirit moves humans to supernatural actions by moving the different powers of the soul so that humans rationally and freely perform the proper action. Hence, in order to discern the movement of the Holy Spirit, it is necessary to see how each power is moved.

The Holy Spirit moves the intellect to determine the proper action. Through faith and the gifts of understanding, science, counsel, and wisdom, the intellect is given the ability to know with supernatural clarity and certainty what to do in a particular situation. Since the intellect orders the other powers of the soul, when discerning the proper action, humans must first and foremost follow their intellect. Since the Holy Spirit moves the intellect in accord with its mode, the intellect that is perfected by faith and the gifts of the Holy Spirit can be moved to actions that participate more perfectly in eternal law. Hence, once humans understand the way that they Holy Spirit moves the intellect, they are able to recognize that the actions and habits that supernaturally perfect the intellect's ability to participate in the eternal law are the same actions and habits that aid them in discerning the role of the Holy Spirit. The Holy Spirit guides the intellect to determine the best action in a particular situation by causing it to be guided by the faith (including the written law), to understand the proper end, to take counsel, to judge rightly, and to command the right action.[44] Although holy people do this all the time without any explicit knowledge of participation in the eternal law, knowledge of this notion of participation can help humans to perfect their ability to discern and allow them to have greater confidence that they are following the Holy Spirit.

The Holy Spirit not only moves the intellect to know the proper end and action, the Holy Spirit also moves the will to intend this end and choose this action. Charity perfects the will to love the ultimate end and to choose a particular action on account of the action being ordered to the ultimate end. When taking counsel, often the reason proposes more

---

44. The art of discerning how the Holy Spirit moves the intellect can be perfected by contemplating past actions.

than one action that is ordered to the ultimate end. In this case, the Holy Spirit moves the will to love one action more than another. This is the Holy Spirit's gift of wisdom, causing the will to choose a particular action even if the intellect is not strong enough to determine that this action most conforms with the eternal law.[45]

However, if the intellect judges that the action is not in accord with the ultimate end or the written law, then the desire of the will is not from the Holy Spirit. For example, imagine that someone is attempting to discern what job to take. She has three offers. One would require immoral activities and two would serve the common good in different ways. If the will desired the immoral job, then this desire can be discerned to not be from the Holy Spirit since the intellect would judge that this job is not in accord with the eternal law.[46] However, if the intellect was uncertain which of the other two jobs would be more in conformity with the eternal law on account of being unable to consider all of the possible pertinent information, the Holy Spirit could move the will to love one option over the other. If the will is perfected by charity and the gifts of

45. The will is able to do this because of its union with the divine nature through charity. Because of this union it is able to love things connaturally as led by the Holy Spirit. Thomas explains that connatural wisdom is where humans judge divine things based on an inclination infused by the Holy Spirit (*ST* I.1.6, 64.1, 68.4.5; II-II.45.2, 97.2.2). Aquinas in *ST* II-II.45.2 compares this type of judgment to the judgment done by one who possesses the virtue of chastity. Whereas in matters of chastity, some can judge rightly through inquiry by reason, ". . . but he who has the habit of chastity judges rightly of such matters by a kind of connaturality" (. . . sed per quandam connaturalitatem ad ipsa recte iudicat de eis ille qui habet habitum castitatis). Although Aquinas does not give a concrete example here, I have composed an example to help explain the difference between the two types of judgment. In a situation where one is confronted with a pornographic image, one with the science of morals could reason to the conclusion that he should not look at this image. However, one with the habit of chastity would immediately look away on account of having trained the appetites to act reasonably. Likewise, the will of the person with the gift of wisdom is inclined to the right action on account of "being trained" by the wisdom of God. This connatural knowledge takes the place of the intellectual act of taking counsel, where in this case, the counsel is directly from Christ through the Holy Spirit. Because judgment follows counsel, even when the Holy Spirit guides the will, the intellect still judges whether or not the action is in accord with the ultimate end (*ST* II-II.45.2). Two recent articles on this topic are by Thomas Ryan, "Revisiting Affective Knowledge and Connaturality in Aquinas," *Theological Studies* 66 (March 2005): 49–68, and Taki Suto, "Virtue and Knowledge: Connatural Knowledge According to Thomas Aquinas," *Review of Metaphysics* 58 (September 2004): 61–79.

46. Even in cases where the Holy Spirit guides the will because the human intellect is not strong enough to determine the proper action through counsel, the intellect must still judge this action as being in accord with the written law to ensure that the action is truly from the Holy Spirit (*ST* I-II.106.1; II-II.45.2).

the Holy Spirit, then the Holy Spirit will move it to the proper action but never against right reason.

Understanding how the Holy Spirit moves humans can help them to more accurately discern because they understand that if out of charity for God they desire a good action that is then judged by the intellect to be in accord with the ultimate end, then they can determine with reasonable certainty that they are being guided by the Holy Spirit.

Finally, the Holy Spirit moves the passions to desire the sense goods in a proper manner. Just as the Apostles were filled with zeal for the Lord after receiving the Holy Spirit, the Holy Spirit moves the passions to desire the proper actions. The gifts of the Holy Spirit that perfect the passions allow the Holy Spirit to move them in greater conformity with the eternal law. Because the passions are so unruly due to the effects of original sin and vice, in discerning the role of the Holy Spirit one should be especially cautious about following one's passions. Nonetheless, if they are in accord with the right reason of the intellect and the love of the will, then there can be reasonable certainty that the Holy Spirit is moving them.[47]

When speaking of discerning the role of the Holy Spirit, the long explanation and the usual examples given can cause people to believe that the Holy Spirit only moves certain humans to life-changing decisions on rare occasions. However, this is opposite of the view of Aquinas. Aquinas notes that all people with charity are perfected by the gifts of the Holy Spirit to be moved to all of their actions in accord with the ultimate end (*ST* I-II.68.2–8). The Holy Spirit guides the intellect, will, and passions in accord with their own natural powers, causing them to be principles of

---

47. There has been a trend in contemporary spirituality and moral theology to speak of a holistic approach. An approach is holistic if the moral rectitude of an action is not only determined by the intellect but also by the will and the passions. See, for example, Michael Allsopp, "Moral Decision Making: Changing Models in Twentieth-Century Catholic Thought," *Irish Theological Quarterly* 69 (2004): 117–37. Allsopp argues that in contrast to the majority of moral theologians in the 1950s and 1960s who emphasized the role of reason and logic in making moral decisions, contemporary moral theologians are more apt to emphasize emotion, intuition, and the creativity of the imagination (117–18). See also Lawrence P. Herrera, "The Tradition of Ignatius of Loyola: A Holistic Spirituality," *Journal of Individual Psychology* 56 (2000): 305–13. Although there are some definite differences between Allsopp's moral theory and that of Aquinas, in the sense that the Holy Spirit perfects and moves all of the powers of the soul, Aquinas's moral theory could be considered to be quite holistic. It is essential to keep in mind that for Thomas the appetitive powers participate in the eternal law by participating in reason. In other words, it might be the case that one's passions desire the proper good, but it is only because they participate in reason, and thus they should never be followed if they go against reason.

all of their actions. When the Holy Spirit moves the powers in this way, it gives the intellect "reasons" and the appetitive powers "motives" by which they actually know and love. Consequently, all those with charity are being moved by the Holy Spirit on a daily basis, and being aware of how the Holy Spirit moves them can help them to be more open to the Holy Spirit guiding their intellect and moving their appetitive powers. Everyday decisions like playing with one's children out of love for God can be just as inspired by the Holy Spirit as once-in-a-lifetime decisions such as deciding to get married or to join a monastery.

Many humans perform good actions without knowledge of the powers of the soul and their proper ends. Nonetheless, knowledge of these powers and their ends can be very helpful for a person seeking virtue. The same goes for the guidance of the Holy Spirit. Many humans are guided by the Holy Spirit to good actions all the time even if they are not aware of it. Nonetheless, specifically understanding how the Holy Spirit moves the various powers of the soul can be very helpful for them to reach perfection. This knowledge of how the Holy Spirit moves the various powers can be found by analyzing how a human participates in the eternal law as moved and governed, and this knowledge is a cognitive participation in the eternal law.

The notion of participation in the eternal law acts as a much better foundation for morality than does the modern notion of autonomy. An understanding of participation in the eternal law allows humans to understand how God can act imminently within every human action while these humans are still true causes of their actions. Furthermore, the foundation of the moral law is that humans are ordered to a particular end and when they understand this order and determine that certain actions are in accord with this end, they share in divine knowledge. Hence, human laws can be in accord with human nature and, inasmuch as they come from natural and divine law, they share in the divine authority of the eternal law. Not only do human laws participate in the eternal law, but every human action participates in the eternal law. When humans are more perfectly moved by the Holy Spirit, their participation in the eternal law is increased. An understanding of participation in the eternal law helps humans to more perfectly understand how the Holy Spirit moves them, which allows them to discern this movement more perfectly.

THE ETERNAL LAW AS UNITING THE
FOUNDATIONAL ELEMENTS OF MORALITY

The eternal law functions to give a simple and universal foundation to many diverse elements (principles) that come together in the complex understanding of human action and morality. No single created principle of morality (whether it be reason, nature, virtue, law, happiness, grace, or the gifts) acts as a proper foundation of Thomas's theological moral theory. All of these principles work together in Thomas's moral theory because they cause different modes of participation in the eternal law. In other words, when the eternal law directs humans to their end, it directs them to their end by means of each of these principles. Each of these principles causes actions in their own particular way as ordered by the eternal law.

Whenever there is an order in things, the relation between the things is caused by the relation of the things to their cause. For example, the universe is ordered both in relation to God and within itself. The relation of different substances to each other is caused by their different degrees of participation in the *esse* of God. Hence, in reference to moral theology, by looking at the relation of each principle to the eternal law, the relation of all these principles to each other within the realm of morality is explained. I will now show how each of these principles is related to the eternal law in order to show their relation to each other within the human action.

Because God creates all things as ordered to a particular end, the eternal law orders human nature to particular types of actions that are in accord with the end of happiness. Furthermore, since the eternal law moves humans to act in accord with their nature, human reason is at the foundation of moral actions. When human reason determines how to act in accord with nature, it forms laws that order humans to happiness. These laws, which are based upon knowledge of participation in the eternal law as moved and governed, are a cognitive participation in the eternal law.[48] Hence, human reason and law are ordered in accord with human nature that is naturally inclined to happiness by the eternal law.

Furthermore, virtue is needed to perfect humans to perform the actions that are in accord with human nature. The eternal law likewise causes virtue by moving humans to repetitively perform good actions. These ac-

---

48. Thomas notes in *ST* I-II.19.4, "Now, it is from the eternal law, the divine reason, that human reason is the rule of the human will, from which the will derives its goodness" (Quod autem ratio humana sit regula voluntatis humanae, ex qua eius bonitas mensuretur, habet ex lege aeterna, quae est ratio divina).

tions are determined to be good by human reason and law which cognitively participate in the eternal law. Once these virtues are acquired, they perfect the intellect so that it can know and apply the law more perfectly, and they perfect the appetitive powers to aid and not blind the intellect. For example, take the domestic law made by parents that children are not allowed to show unjust anger through biting or hitting. If parents did not promulgate this law and enforce this law, their children would not likely acquire the virtue of meekness which allows them to control their anger. Without this virtue, when the children grow up, their anger could blind or diminish their reason, causing them to not reason correctly to the proper law or action. Thus, God acts as the first efficient cause by moving humans to perform good actions repetitively in accord with the laws that are caused by the eternal law as first exemplary cause. Furthermore, all virtues are ordered by the eternal law to happiness (the final cause).

The relation of the natural principles of human action to each other can be summarized in the following way: Human nature contains natural inclinations to act in accord with happiness. The exterior principle of law then directs humans to good human actions (in accord with happiness). Through repetitive good actions, virtues are formed that cause even greater actions (which likewise increase virtue . . .). These same virtues allow humans to make good laws to direct others. Last of all, natural happiness is attained. Virtues are essential to attain natural happiness since they give humans the ability to naturally know and love the good.

Not only is the eternal law the foundation and measure of all the natural moral principles, it is the foundation of all the moral principles that stem from a participation in divine nature (grace). The eternal law orders humans to the supernatural end of eternal happiness. Grace as a participation in divine nature perfects the soul to participate more perfectly in the eternal law both by giving the soul the ability to perform actions in accord with eternal happiness and by directing the intellect and will through the written law of Scripture and the inspiration of the Holy Spirit. Since the infused virtues are caused by grace and act in accord with the divine law, the foundation of the infused virtues is also the eternal law. Furthermore, the gifts of the Holy Spirit also perfect humans to act in accord with the eternal law.

Because grace does not destroy nature but perfects it, Thomas's moral theory is organized so that for each natural principle, there is a supernatural principle that perfects it. Human nature is perfected by grace which is a participation in divine nature. The natural inclinations are perfected by

FIGURE 3. The Relation of Moral Principles[a]

Participation in divine nature: Grace $\rightarrow$	Supernatural inclinations; theological virtues $\rightarrow$	The divine law $\rightarrow$	Divine actions $\rightarrow$	Infused cardinal virtues $\rightarrow$	More perfect divine actions $\rightarrow$	Eternal happiness
Human nature $\rightarrow$	Natural inclinations $\rightarrow$	Human and natural law $\rightarrow$	Good human actions $\rightarrow$	Acquired virtues $\rightarrow$	More perfect human actions $\rightarrow$	Natural happiness

a. On both the natural and the supernatural levels, there is an order of causality moving from nature (or its perfection in grace) to happiness (natural or eternal). However, on the natural level, the earlier elements also normally precede the later ones in time. In other words, humans must be directed and motivated by human law to perform many good human actions before they become virtuous. (Keeping in mind that virtues do not develop in all areas simultaneously, so there will often be some cases where motivation by human law is necessary to perform the good actions.) On the supernatural level, grace, the theological virtues, and the infused cardinal virtues are infused simultaneously in terms of time.

the theological virtues which are divine (supernatural) inclinations. These inclinations cause divine actions as directed by the Holy Spirit (the new law of grace that perfects natural and human law). Because the theological virtues work through the infused cardinal virtues, the infused cardinal virtues perfect the acquired cardinal virtues. From these virtues come supernatural or divine actions which are more perfect than natural human actions. Last of all, eternal happiness is more perfect than natural happiness. (See figure 3.)

However, there is one additional supernatural principle. The supernatural inclinations (faith and charity), although more perfect in themselves than human knowledge and love, are nonetheless possessed less perfectly by humans. In other words, human knowledge and love of God is imperfect and does not cause a strong enough inclination to supernatural actions. Hence, there is the additional principle of the gifts of the Holy Spirit which aid the theological virtues by means of divine inspiration (*ST* I-II.68.1 & 2). Since the gifts are an exterior principle aiding the theological virtues to perform divine actions, they accompany the new law of the Holy Spirit (*ST* I-II.68.1).

The interaction of all of the different notions of happiness, virtue, law, and the gifts is also seen within the human action. Every good human action is ordered to happiness, stems from a law, and is caused by virtue that perfects the powers of the soul. As noted in chapter four, a complete human action has twelve steps. Every human action is done on account of a good that participates in the goodness of the ultimate end. This good is apprehended by the intellect and desired by the will (steps 1 and 2). The good is then combined with (or separated from) other intellectual forms in order to form a proposition that takes the form of an intermediary end that is ordered to the ultimate end. In morals this end takes the form of a law that is known by the intellect and intended by the will (steps 3 and 4).[49] Although it may seem strange to speak of this intended end as a law, it does direct the agent to an end, which is the function of a law. Humans then apply the law by reasoning from the law to the particular action that is chosen by the will (steps 5–8). Once the action has been commanded and performed (steps 9–10), the intellect contemplates the good of the end achieved, and the will delights in it (this contemplation and delight is the act of imperfect happiness in reference to an intermediary end and perfect happiness in reference to the ultimate end) (steps 11–12). (Refer to figure 2 in chapter 4 to see all of these twelve steps.)

As illustrated, a law is intended in order to bring about happiness. Along with these two principles, virtues and gifts are also essential in bringing a good action to completion. Different virtues and gifts of the Holy Spirit perfect all of the steps of the human action, allowing humans to perform good actions. At the natural level, simple apprehension and desiring the good apprehended do not need virtues to perfect them since they are the manifestation of the natural inclinations to know the truth and love the good. However, because grace causes the supernatural inclinations of faith, hope, and charity, on the supernatural level faith perfects the first step of apprehension, and hope and charity perfect the second one of desiring the good.[50]

The intellectual virtues of faith, understanding, *scientia,* and wisdom along with the Holy Spirit's gifts of understanding, *scientia,* and wisdom perfect the intellect to determine the proper law or intermediate end (step 3). If this law is from reason perfected by the acquired virtues, then

49. In every intention the intellect forms a law that directs the will and must be applied by the reason. Sometimes the intellect determines that the desired good is not in accord with the ultimate end and then the law is "avoid this action" (e.g., "avoid fornication"). Sometimes the good is determined to be in accord with the ultimate end and then the law is "perform this action" (e.g., "pursue almsgiving").

50. Just as the natural inclination to know the truth causes the intellect to apprehend intellectual forms that can be formed into propositions, faith as a supernatural inclination perfects the intellect to form concepts that surpass our natural ability of apprehension. These concepts can likewise be formed into propositions. The natural inclination of the will is likewise perfected to desire these supernaturally obtained concepts through hope and charity.

it is the natural law. If this law is from reason perfected by faith and gifts, then it is the divine law. The virtue of prudence and the gifts of wisdom and counsel perfect the intellect to determine and command the means (steps 5, 7, and 9). The speculative intellectual virtues and the gifts of understanding, *scientia,* and wisdom perfect the intellect to contemplate the good attained (step 11). The virtues of justice, hope, charity, and the gift of piety perfect the will to perform all the actions since all the steps are different forms of the act of love (steps 2, 4, 6, 8, 10, and 12).

Since every action is applied to a particular situation that requires sense knowledge to know the situation, and since sense knowledge is always followed by the sense appetites, the sense appetites are also a cause of every action. Hence, they must also be perfected by the virtues of temperance and fortitude and the Holy Spirit's gifts of fear of the Lord and fortitude in order to ensure that the correct law is applied in the proper way. The more perfectly this entire process works, the greater the participation in the eternal law.

As can be seen, the understanding of how all of these elements work together in the human act is very complex. A consequence of this is that many moral theories focus on only one or a few of these elements, leaving their moral theory incomplete. However, by understanding the relation between humans and their ultimate end, the relation between the various different elements of morality is also illuminated. Humans are ordered by the eternal law to an ultimate end to which they are naturally inclined (or supernaturally inclined in the case of the theological virtues). However, to perform acts in accord with this end, all the various types of law, virtues, and gifts are necessary, and each has its proper role as assigned by the eternal law.

CONCLUSION

The notion of participation in the eternal law is one of the ways that Thomas connects his theological anthropology and moral theology given in the *Secunda Pars* of the *Summa Theologiae* with his theology of God and creation given in the *Prima Pars.*[51] In Thomas's understanding of reality, God has created a world full of diverse creatures, each of which is providentially ordered to a proper operation. The notion that

---

51. Furthermore, the notion of participation in the eternal law links the *Prima* and *Secunda* with the *Tertia Pars* since supernatural human participation in the eternal law is caused by Christ who fulfills the law in saving us.

explains the relation between these creatures and God is the notion of participation. Each creature is what it is and does what it does because it participates in God who is the efficient, exemplary, and final cause of its being and operation.

However, when God causes being and operation in a creature, He causes this being and operation in accord with the form of the particular creature. For humans, the first cause of the first act of being (that of the substance) is God, but the second cause is their form, which determines their mode of being. Likewise, the first cause of human operation is also God; however, He moves and directs humans to act in accord with their form as rational and free creatures. Hence, although, on the one hand, by participating in God humans are completely dependent upon God for the operation, on the other hand, humans are fully responsible for their actions as true secondary causes. And, since God has created humans for a particular end, when humans act by participating in God's power and direction, they also cause their own perfection as agents (in other words, they increase their participation in God's goodness).

Because the eternal law orders humans to perform actions that increase their perfection, this notion helps illuminate the relation between human perfection and its divine cause. By studying the two ways that humans participate in the eternal law (as moved and governed and cognitively), a greater understanding of how humans can act more perfectly in accord with their divine end is achieved. The study of participation as moved and governed helps elucidate how the agent can be perfected by good habits (virtue, grace, and gifts) to perform divine actions of faith and charity. The role of God as perfecting and moving the human in every human action is highlighted. The study of cognitive participation shows how the Holy Spirit can guide humans in every action through the intellect and will perfected by the virtues, grace, and gifts.

This understanding of the notion of participation in the eternal law helps to lay the foundation for a proper moral theology, not only because it is true and genuinely theological, but also because it precisely counters the modern tendency to disassociate morality from divine action. Rather than founding a moral system upon the notions of autonomy and independence from God, this moral system is founded upon divine movement and guidance through participation in the wisdom, love, and power of God. Yet this divine movement and guidance does not restrict human freedom, but increases and perfects it, allowing humans to remain true causes of their actions.

BIBLIOGRAPHY

Works by Aquinas

Main Editions of Saint Thomas's Works

The Leonine Edition: *Sanct Thomae Aquinatis doctois angelici Opera omina iussu Leonis XIII.* Rome: Cura et studio fratrum praedicatorum, 1882–(in progress).

Parma: *Sancti Thomae Aquinatis Doctoris angelici ordinis predicatorum Opera omnia ad fidem optimarum editionum accurate recognita.* 25 vols. Parma: Petra Fiaccadori, 1852–1873. Reprint: 25 vols. New York: Musurgia, 1948–1950.

Marietti: *Opuscula philosophica* and *Opuscula theological.* Turin: Marietti Editori, 1950–1965.

Individual Works

Compendium Theologiae. Leonine 42. Parma 16. Marietti, 1954. English translation: *Compendium of Theology.* Translated by C. Vollert. Saint Louis: Saint Louis University Press, 1952.

De Substantiis Separatis. Leonine 40. Parma 16. Marietti, 1954. English translation: *Treatise on Separate Substances.* Translated by F. J. Lescoe. West Hartford, Conn.: St. Joseph's College Press, 1959.

Expositio et Lectura super Epistolas Pauli Apostoli. Leonine 32–35 (in progress). Parma 13. Marietti, 1953. English Translations: *Saint Thomas Aquinas, Commentary on Saint Paul's Epistle to the Galations.* Translated by F. Larcher. Albany: Magi Books, 1966. *Commentary on Saint Paul's Epistle to the Ephesians.* Translated by M. Lamb. Albany: Magi Books, 1969.

Expositio libri Posteriorum Analyticorum. Leonine 1*/2 (Editio altera retractata, 1989; the first edition dates from 1882); Parma 18; Marietti, 1964. English translation: *Thomas Aquinas, Commentary on the Posterior Analytics of Aristotle.* Translated by F. R. Larcher. Albany: Magi Books, 1970.

Exposito libri Boetii de Hebdomadibus. Leonine 50. Parma 17. Marietti, 1954. English translation: *An Exposition of the "On the Hebdomads" of Boethius.* Translated by J. Schultz and E. Synan. Washington, D.C.: The Catholic University of America Press, 2001.

Quaestiones de Quodlibit I–XII. Leonine 25. Parma 9. Marietti, 1956. English translation: *Saint Thomas Aquinas, Quodlibetal Questions 1 and 2.* Translated by S. Edwards. Toronto: Pontifical Institute of Mediaeval Studies, 1983.

Quaestiones disputatae de Anima. Leonine 24.1. Parma 8. Marietti, 1965. English translation: *Saint Thomas Aquinas, Questions on the Soul.* Translated by J. H. Robb. Milwaukee: Marquette University Press, 1984.

Quaestiones disputatae de Malo. Leonine 23. Parma 8. Marietti, 1965. English translation: *Saint Thomas Aquinas, Disputed Questions on Evil.* Translated by J. Oesterle. South Bend: University of Notre Dame Press, 1983.

Quaestiones Disputatae de Potentia Dei. Leonine 21 (in progress). Parma 8. Marietti, 1965. English translation: *On the Power of God.* Translated by the Fathers of the English Dominican Province (London: Burns, Oates, & Washburn, 1932–1934).

Quaestiones Disputatae de Spiritualibus Creaturis. Leonine 24.2. Parma 8. Marietti, 1965. English translation: *On Spiritual Creatures.* Translated by Mary Fitzpatrick and John Wellmuth. Milwaukee: Marquette University Press, 1969.

Quaestiones Disputatae de Veritate. Leonine 22. Parma 9. Marietti, 1964. English translation: *Truth.* Translated by R. Mulligan, J. McGlynn, and R. Schmidt. Chicago: Regnery Press, 1952–1954.

Quaestiones Disputatae de Virtutibus. Leonine 24.2. Parma 8. Marietti, 1965. English translation: *Disputed Questions on Virtue.* Translated by Ralph McInerny. South Bend, Ind.: St. Augustine's Press, 1999.

Scriptum super libros Sententiarum magistri Petri Lombardi. Leonine 17–20 (in progress). Parma 6–7. No complete English translation.

Sentencia libri De anima. Leonine 45.1. Parma 20. Marietti, 1959. English translation: *Aristotle's De Anima with the Commentary of St. Thomas Aquinas.* Translated by K. Foster and S. Humphries. New Haven: Yale University Press, 1951.

Sententia Libri Ethicorum. Leonine 47. Parma 21. Marietti, 1964. English translation: *Commentary on the Nicomachean Ethics.* Translated by C. I. Litzinger. Chicago: Regnery Press, 1964.

Sententia libri Metaphysicae. Leonine 46 (in progress). Parma 20. Marietti, 1950. English translation: *St. Thomas Aquinas, Commentary on the Metaphysics of Aristotle.* Translated by J. P. Rowen. Chicago: Regnery Press, 1964.

Sententia libri Physicae. Leonine 2. Parma 18. Matietti, 1965. English translation: *Thomas de Aquino: Commentary on Aristotle's Physics.* Translated by R. J. Blackwell et al. New Haven: Yale University Press, 1963.

Summa Contra Gentiles. Leonine 13–15. Parma 5. Marietti, 1961, 1967. English translation: *Saint Thomas Aquinas: On the Truth of the Catholic Faith.* Translated by A. Pegis and V. Bourke. South Bend: University of Notre Dame Press, 1975.

Summa Theologiae. Leonine 4–11. Parma 1–4. Marietti, 1963. English translation:

Summa Theologica. Translated by the Fathers of the English Dominican Province. New York: Benzinger Brothers, 1947.

Super Boetium De Trinitate. Leonine 50. Parma 17. Marietti, 1954. English translation: *Saint Thomas Aquinas, The Trinity and the Unicity of the Intellect.* Translated by R. E. Brennan. St. Louis: B. Herder, 1946.

Super Joannem. Leonine 31 (in progress). Parma 10. Marietti, 1952. English translation: *Saint Thomas Aquinas, Commentary on the Gospel of Saint John.* Part 1 (1–7): Translated by J. Weisheipl and R. Larcher. Albany: Magi Books, 1980. Part 2 (8–21): Translated by R. Larcher. Petersham, Mass.: St. Bede's Publications, 1999.

Super Librum de Causes. Leonine 49. Parma 21. Marietti, 1955. English translation: *Commentary on the Book of Causes.* Translated by V. Guagliardo, C. Hess, and R. Taylor. Washington, D.C.: The Catholic University of America Press, 1996.

Super Librum Dionysii De divinis nominibus. Leonine 49 (in progress). Parma 15. Marietti, 1950. No English translation.

Works by Other Authors

Annice, M., C.S.C. "A Historical Sketch of the Theory of Participation." *New Scholasticism* 26 (1952): 54.

Aristotle. *Nichomachean Ethics.* In *Introduction to Aristotle.* Translated by W. D. Ross. New York: Random House, 1947.

Arjonillo, Rolando. "Sanctity, Divine Filiation, Sequela Christi, and Virtue in Fundamental Moral Theology: Apropos of a recent book, *Scelti in cristo per essere santi.*" *Annales Theologici* 14 (2000): 485–534.

Armstrong, R. A. *Primary and Secondary Precepts in Thomistic Natural Teaching.* The Hague: Martinus Nijhoff, 1966.

Aumann, Jordan. "Mystical Experience, the Infused Virtues and the Gifts." *Angelicum* 58 (1981): 33–54.

Berquist, Richard. "Human Dignity and Natural Law." Santa Paula, Calif.: Thomas Aquinas College Lecture Series, 2002.

Blanchette, Olivia. *The Perfection of the Universe According to Aquinas.* University Park: Pennsylvania State University Press, 1992.

Billy, D. J. "Grace and Natural Law in the *Super Epistolam ad Romanos Lectura:* A Study of Thomas' Commentary on Romans 2:14–16." *Studia moralia* 26 (1988): 15–37.

———. "The Theological Foundation of Thomas' Teaching on Law." *Divus Thomas Piacenza* 67–68 (1990–1991): 243–56.

Bourke, Vernon. *Ethics.* New York: Macmillan, 1951.

———. "The Role of Habitus in the Thomistic Metaphysics of Potency and Act." In *Essays in Thomism,* ed. Robert E. Brennan, 103–9. New York: Sheed & Ward, 1942.

Bowlin, John. *Contingency and Fortune in Aquinas's Ethics.* Cambridge: Cambridge University Press, 1999.

Boyd, Craig. "Participation Metaphysics in Aquinas's Theory of Natural Law." *American Catholic Philosophical Quarterly* 79, no. 3 (2005): 431–45.

———. "Participation Metaphysics, The *Imago Dei,* and the Natural Law in Aquinas' Ethics." *The New BlackFriars* 88 (2007): 274–87.

Bradley, Denis. *Aquinas on the Twofold Human Good: Reason and Human Happiness in Aquinas' Moral Science.* Washington, D.C.: The Catholic University of America Press, 1997.

Brennan, M. R. *The Intellectual Virtues According to the Philosophy of St. Thomas.* Washington, D.C.: The Catholic University of America Press, 1941.

Brennan, Robert E. *Thomistic Psychology: A Philosophic Analysis of the Nature of Man.* New York: Macmillan, 1941.

Brown, Oscar. *Natural Rectitude and Divine Law in Aquinas: An Approach to an Integral Interpretation of the Thomistic Doctrine.* Toronto: Pontifical Institute of Mediaeval Studies, 1981.

Cessario, Romanus. *Christian Faith and the Theological Life.* Washington, D.C.: The Catholic University of America Press, 1996.

———. *Introduction to Moral Theology.* Washington, D.C.: The Catholic University of America Press, 2001.

———. "Is Aquinas's *Summa* Only about Grace?" In *Ordo sapientiae et amoris,* ed. C. J. Pinto de Oliveira, 197–209. Fribourg: Editions Universitaires, 1993.

———. *The Moral Virtues and Theological Ethics.* Notre Dame, Ind.: University of Notre Dame Press, 1991.

———. *A Short History of Thomism.* Washington, D.C.: The Catholic University of America Press, 2005.

Clarke, W. Norris. "The Limitation of Act by Potency: Aristotelianism or Neo-Platonism?" *The New Scholasticism* 26 (1952): 167–94.

———. "The Meaning of Participation in St. Thomas." *Proceedings of the American Catholic Philosophical Association* 26 (1952): 147–57.

———. *The One and the Many: A Contemporary Thomistic Metaphysics.* South Bend: University of Notre Dame Press, 2001.

Congar, Y. *I Believe in the Holy Spirit.* Vol. 2. New York: Seabury Press, 1983.

———. "Le Saint Esprit dans la théologie Thomiste de l'agir moral." In *Atti Del Congresso Internationale: Tommaso D'Aquino Nel Suo Settimo Centenario,* 9–19. Naples: Edizioni Domenicane Italiane, 1974.

Conley, Kieran. *A Theology of Wisdom: A Study of St. Thomas.* Dubuque, Iowa: The Priory Press, 1963.

Cuddeback, Matthew. "Light and Form in St. Thomas Aquinas's Metaphysics of the Knower." Ph.D. diss., The Catholic University of America, 1998.

Dauphinais, Michael. "Loving the Lord Your God: The *Imago Dei* in Saint Thomas Aquinas." *The Thomist* 63 (1999): 241–67.

Deferrari, Roy. *A Lexicon of St. Thomas Aquinas.* Washington, D.C.: The Catholic University of America Press, 1948.

De Gandolfi, Maria. "Providencia y Prudencia." *Doctor Communis* 50 (1997): 247–57.

Delhaye, Philippe. "La loi nouvelle comme dynamisme de l'Esprit-Saint." In *Lex et libertas,* ed. L. J. Flanders and K. Hedwig, 265–80. Vatican City: Libreria Editrice Vaticana, 1987.

Dewan, Lawrence. "St. Thomas and the Causality of God's Goodness." *Laval théologique et philosophique* 34 (1978): 291–304.

———. "St. Thomas, Our Natural Lights, and the Moral Order." *Angelicum* 67 (1990): 281–307.

———. "Wisdom as Foundational Ethical Theory in Thomas Aquinas." In *The Bases of Ethics,* ed. William Sweet. Milwaukee: Marquette University Press, 2000.

Di Blasi, Fulvio. *God and the Natural Law: A Rereading of Thomas Aquinas.* Translated by David Thunder. South Bend: St. Augustine's Press, 2006.

Dingjan, Francois. *Discretio. Les origines patristiques et monastiques de la doctrine sur la prudence chez Thomas d' Aquin.* Assen: Van Gorcum, 1967.

Dodds, Michael. "Ultimacy and Intimacy: Aquinas on the Relation between God and the World." In *Ordo sapientiae et amoris,* ed. C. J. Pinto de Oliveira, 211–19. Fribourg: Editions Universitaires, 1993.

Ebacher, Jerome. "Grace and Supernaturalization." *Angelicum* 58 (1981): 21–32.

Elders, Léon. "La nature et l'ordre surnatural sélon saint Thomas d'Aquin." *Nova et vetera* 70 (1995): 18–35.

———. "Le Saint Esprit et la *Lex Nova* dans les commentaires bibliques de saint Thomas d'Aquin." In *Credo in Spiritum Sanctum,* vol. 2, 1195–1205. Vatican City: Libreria Editrice Vaticana, 1983.

Etienne, Jacques. "Loi et grace: Le concept de loi nouvelle dans la *Somme Théologique* de s. Thomas d'Aquin." *Revue thologique de Louvain* 16 (1985): 5–22.

Fabro, Cornelio. "The Intensive Hermeneutics of Thomistic Philosophy: The Notion of Participation." *Review of Metaphysics* 27 (1974): 449–87.

———. *La nozione metafisica di partecipazione secondo S. Tommaso d' Aquino.* Milan: Vita e Pensiero, 1939.

———. *Participation et causalité.* Louvain: Universitaires de Louvain, 1961.

———. "Platonism, Neo-Platonism and Thomism: Convergences and Divergences." *The New Scholasticism* 44 (1970): 69–100.

———. "The Transcendentality of *Ens-Esse* and the Ground to Metaphysics." *International Philosophical Quarterly* 6 (1966): 389–427.

Farrell, Walter. *The Natural Moral Law According to Saint Thomas and Suarez.* Ditchling: St. Dominics Press, 1930.

Fatula, Mary Ann. "The Holy Spirit and Human Actualization through Love: The Contributions of Aquinas." *Theology Digest* 32, no. 3 (1985): 217–24.

Fay, Thomas. "Participation: Transformation or Platonic and Neo-Platonic Thought in the Metaphysics of Thomas Aquinas." *Divus Thomas* 76 (1973): 50–64.

Flannery, Kevin. *Acts Amid Precepts*. Washington, D.C.: The Catholic University of America Press, 2001.

Flippen, Douglas. "On Two Meanings of Good and the Foundation of Ethics in Aristotle and St. Thomas." *Proceedings of the American Catholic Philosophical Asscociation* 58 (1984): 56–64.

Floucat, Yves. "Le sens religieux dans l'amour de la sagesse." In *Studi Tomistici* 44, 9–28. Vatican City: Libreria Editrice Vaticano, 1991.

Froget, Barthélemy. *The Indwelling of the Holy Spirit in the Souls of the Just According to the Teaching of St. Thomas Aquinas*. Baltimore: Carroll Press, 1950.

Gahl, Robert. "From the Virtue of a Fragile Good to a Narrative Account of Natural Law." *International Philosophical Quarterly* 37 (1997): 455–72.

Gallagher, David. "Aquinas on Goodness and Moral Goodness." In *Thomas Aquinas and His Legacy*, ed. David Gallagher, 37–59. Washington, D.C.: The Catholic University of America Press, 1994.

———. "The Will and Its Acts (Ia-IIae, qq. 6–17)." In *The Ethics of Aquinas*, ed. Stephen Pope, 67–89. Washington D.C.: Georgetown University Press, 2002.

Garceau, B. *Judicium*. Montreal: Institut d'études médiévales, 1968.

Geiger, Louis. *La participation dans la philosphie de s. Thomas d'Aquin*. Paris: Librairie Philosophique J. Vrin, 1952.

Gilson, Etienne. *Christian Philosophy of St. Thomas Aquinas*. South Bend: University of Notre Dame Press, 1994.

———. *The Philosophy of St. Thomas Aquinas*. [Authorised translation from the third revised and enlarged edition of "Le thomisme."] Translated by E. Bullough. New York: Barnes & Noble, 1993.

Hall, Pamela. *Narrative and the Natural Law*. South Bend: University of Notre Dame Press, 1993.

Hankey, W. J. "Dionysian Hierarchy in Thomas Aquinas: Tradition and Transformation." In *Denys l'Aréopagite et sa postérité en Orient et en Occident, Actes du Colloque International Paris, 21–24 Septembre 1994*, 405–38. Paris: Institut d'Etudes Augustiniennes, 1997.

Hauerwaus, Stanley, and Charles Pinches. *Christian among the Virtues*. South Bend: University of Notre Dame Press, 1997.

Henle, R. J. *The Treatise on Law: Introduction and Commentary*. South Bend: University of Notre Dame Press, 1993.

Hibbs, Thomas. "Divine Irony and the Natural Law." *International Philosophical Quarterly* 30 (1990): 419–29.

Hittinger, Russell. *First Grace: Rediscovering the Natural Law in a Post-Christian World*. Wilmington, Del.: ISI Books, 2003.

Hoonhout, Michael. "The Systematic Understanding of Divine Providence in the *Summa Theologiae*." Ph.D. diss., Boston College, 1998.

James, Helen John. *The Thomist Spectrum*. New York: Fordham University Press, 1966.

Jenkins, John. *Knowledge and Faith in Thomas Aquinas*. Cambridge: Cambridge University Press, 1991.

John of St. Thomas. *The Gifts of the Holy Spirit*. New York: Sheed & Ward, 1951.

Johnson, Mark F. "God's Knowledge in Our Frail Mind: The Thomistic Model of Theology." *Angelicum* 76 (1999): 25–45.

Jordan, Mark. "The Intelligibility of the World and the Divine Ideas in Aquinas." *Review of Metaphysics* 38 (1984): 17–32.

Kant, Immanuel. *Grounding for the Metaphysics of Morals*. Translated by J. Ellington. Indianapolis: Hackett, 1962.

Kasper, Walter. *Theology and the Church*. New York: Crossroad, 1992.

Kerr, Fergus. *Contemplating Aquinas: On the Varieties of Interpretation*. London: SCM Press, 2003.

Klubertanz, George. "St. Thomas and the Knowledge of the Singular." *The New Scholasticism* 26 (1952): 135–66.

Kossel, Clifford. "Natural Law and Human Law." In *Ethics of Aquinas,* ed. Stephen Pope, 171–93. Washington, D.C.: Georgetown University Press, 2002.

Ladrille, G. "Grace et motion divine chez S. Thomas d'Aquin." *Salesianum* 12 (1950): 37–84.

Lindbeck, George. "Participation and Existence in the Interpretation of St. Thomas Aquinas." *Franciscan Studies* 17 (1957): 1–22, 107–25.

Lisska, Anthony. *Aquinas's Theory of Natural Law*. Oxford: Clarendon Press, 1996.

Lonergan, Bernard. *Grace and Freedom: Operative Grace in the Thought of St. Thomas Aquinas*. New York: Herder & Herder, 1971.

Long, Steven. "Obediential Potency, Human Knowledge, and the Natural Desire for God." *International Philosophical Quarterly* 37 (1997): 45–63.

MacIntrye, Alasdair. *After Virtue*. South Bend: University of Notre Dame Press, 1984.

———. *Three Rival Versions of Moral Inquiry*. South Bend: University of Notre Dame Press, 1990.

Maritain, Jacques. "On Knowledge through Connaturality." In *The Range of Reason*, chapter 3. New York: Scribner, 1957.

McCool, Gerard. *Neo-Thomists*. Milwaukee: Marquette University Press, 1994.

McInerny, Ralph. *Aquinas on Human Action*. Washington, D.C.: The Catholic University of America Press, 1992.

———. *Ethica Thomistica*. Washington, D.C.: The Catholic University of America Press, 1982.

———. *St. Thomas Aquinas*. South Bend: University of Notre Dame Press, 1977.

―――. *The Question of Christian Ethics*. Washington, D.C.: The Catholic University of America Press, 1993.

Meilander, Gilbert. *The Theory and Practice of Virtue*. South Bend: University of Notre Dame Press, 1984.

Melina, Livio. *Sharing in Christ's Virtues*. Translated by William May. Washington, D.C.: The Catholic University of America Press, 2001.

Milbank, John. *Theology and Social Theory*. Oxford: Blackwell Publishers, 1990.

Murphy, William. "Martin Rhonheimer's Natural Law and Practical Reason." *Sapientia* 56 (2001): 517–48.

Naus, John. *The Nature of the Practical Intellect According to St. Thomas Aquinas*. Rome: Libreria Editrice Dell'Università Gregoriana, 1959.

Nelson, Daniel Mark. *The Priority of Prudence*. University Park: University of Pennsylvania Press, 1992.

Oesterle, J. A. *Ethics: The Introduction to Moral Science*. Englewood Cliffs, N.J.: Prentice-Hall, 1958.

O'Meara, Thomas. "Interpreting Thomas Aquinas: The Dominican School." In *The Ethics of Aquinas,* ed. Stephen Pope, 355–73. Washington, D.C.: Georgetown University Press, 2002.

O'Rourke, Fran. "Aquinas and Platonism." In *Contemplating Aquinas: On the Varieties of Interpretation,* ed. Fergus Kerr. London: SCM Press, 2003.

―――. *Pseudo-Dionysius and the Metaphysics of Aquinas*. Leiden: Brill, 1992.

Owens, Joseph. *An Elementary Christian Metaphysics*. Milwaukee: Bruce, 1980.

―――. "Human Destiny in Aquinas." In *Human Destiny: Some Problems for Catholic Philosophy,* ed. Joseph Owens, 31–49. Washington, D.C.: The Catholic University of America Press, 1985.

―――. "Human Reason and the Moral Order in Aquinas." *Studia Moralia* 28 (1990): 155–73.

―――. "Judgment and Truth in Aquinas." *Medieval Studies* 32 (1970): 138–58.

―――. "The Accidental and Essential Character of Being." In *St. Thomas Aquinas on the Existence of God*. Albany: State University of New York Press, 1980.

Paretsky, A. "The Influence of Thomas the Exegete on Thomas the Theologian: The Tract on Law (Ia-IIae, qq. 98–108) as a Test Case." *Angelicum* 71 (1994): 549–77.

Pieper, Joseph. *Prudence*. Translated by Richard and Clara Winston. New York: Pantheon Books, 1959.

Pinckaers, Servais. "La loi évangélique, vie selon l'Esprit, et le sermon sur la montagne." *Nova et Vetera* 60 (1985): 217–28.

―――. *L'Évangile et la morale*. Fribourg: Editions Universitaires, 1989.

―――. "Liberte et preceptes dans la morale de Saint Thomas." In *Lex et libertas,* ed. L. J. Flanders and K. Hedwig, 15–24. Vatican City: Libreria Editrice Vaticana, 1987.

―――. *Morality: The Catholic View*. Translated by Michael Sherwin. South Bend, Ind.: St. Augustine's Press, 2001.

———. *Sources of Christian Ethics*. Translated by T. A. Noble. Washington, D.C.: The Catholic University of America Press, 1995.

———. *The Pinckaers Reader*. Edited by John Berkman and Craig Steven Titus. Washington, D.C.: The Catholic University of America Press, 2005.

———. "The Recovery of the New Law in Moral Theology." *Irish Theological Quarterly* 64 (1999): 3–15.

Porter, Jean. *Natural and Divine Law*. Grand Rapids, Mich.: Eerdmans, 1999.

———. *Nature as Reason: A Thomistic Theory of Natural Law*. Grand Rapids, Mich.: Eerdmans, 2004.

———. "What the Wise Person Knows: Natural Law and Virtue in Aquinas' *Summa Theologiae*." *Studies in Christian Ethics* 12 (1999): 57–69.

Ramos, Alice. "The Divine Ideas and the Intelligibility of Creation: A Way toward Universal Signification in Aquinas." *Doctor Communis* 43 (1990): 250–65.

Reichberg, Gregory. "Intellect Virtues (Ia IIae qq. 57–58)." In *Ethics of Aquinas*, ed. Stephen Pope, 136–38. Washington, D.C.: Georgetown University Press, 2002.

Reilley, James. *Saint Thomas on Law*. Etienne Gilson Series 12. Toronto: Pontifical Institute of Mediaeval Studies, 1990.

Rhonheimer, Martin. *Natural Law and Practical Reason*. Translated by G. Malsbury. New York: Fordham University Press, 2000.

Rodriguez, Pedro. "Spontanéité et caractère légal de la loi nouvelle." In *Lex et libertas*, ed. L. J. Flanders and K. Hedwig, 254–64. Vatican City: Libreria Editrice Vaticana, 1987.

Rogers, Eugene. "Aquinas on Natural Law and the Virtues in a Biblical Context." *Journal of Religious Ethics* 27 (Spring 1999): 29–56.

———. "The Narrative of Natural Law in Aquinas's Commentary on Romans 1." *Theological Studies* 59 (1998): 254–76.

Ryan, Thomas. "Revisiting Affective Knowledge and Connaturality in Aquinas." *Theological Studies* 66 (March 2005): 49–68.

Schmidt, Robert. *The Domain of Logic According to Saint Thomas Aquinas*. The Hague, The Netherlands: Martinus Nijhoff, 1966.

Schockenhoff, Eberhard. *Natural Law and Human Dignity: Universal Ethics in an Historical World*. Translated by Brian McNeil. Washington, D.C.: The Catholic University of America Press, 2003.

Sherwin, Michael. *By Knowledge and by Love: Charity and Knowledge in the Moral Theology of St. Thomas Aquinas*. Washington, D.C.: The Catholic University of America Press, 2005.

Scholl, Edith. "The Mother of Virtues: *Discretio*." *Cistercian Studies Quarterly* 36, no. 3 (2001): 389–401.

Sentis, Laurent. "La lumière dont nous faisons usage: La règal de la raison et la loi divine selon Thomas D'Aquin." *Revue des sciences philosophiques et theologiques* 79 (1995): 49–69.

Shanley, Brian. "Aquinas on God's Causal Knowledge: A Reply to Stump and Kretzmann." *American Catholic Philosophical Quarterly* 72 (1998): 447–57.

———. "Divine Causation and Human Freedom in Aquinas." *American Catholic Philosophical Quarterly* 72 (1998): 98–122.

Steel, Carlos. "Rational by Participation: Aquinas and Ockham on the Subject of the Moral Virtues." *Franciscan Studies* 56 (1998): 359–82.

Stump, Eleonore, and Norman Kretzmann. "Being and Goodness." In *Divine and Human Action,* ed. Thomas Morris, 281–307. Ithaca, N.Y.: Cornell University Press, 1988.

———. "Eternity and God's Knowledge: A Reply to Shanley." *American Catholic Philosophical Quarterly* 72 (1998): 439–45.

Suto, Taki. "Virtue and Knowledge: Connatural Knowledge According to Thomas Aquinas." *Review of Metaphysics* 58 (September 2004): 61–79.

Te Velde, Rudi. *Participation and Substantiality in Thomas Aquinas.* New York: Brill, 1995.

Torrell, Jean Pierre. *Saint Thomas Aquinas: The Person and His Work.* Vol. 1. Translated by Robert Royal. Washington, D.C.: The Catholic University of America Press, 1996.

———. *Saint Thomas Aquinas: Spiritual Master.* Vol. 2. Translated by Robert Royal. Washington, D.C.: The Catholic University of America Press, 2003.

Wadell, Paul. *The Primacy of Love.* New York: Paulist Press, 1992.

———. "The Role of Charity in the Moral Theology of Thomas Aquinas." In *Aquinas and Empowerment,* ed. G. Simon Harak, 134–69. Washington, D.C.: Georgetown University Press, 1996.

Westberg, Daniel. *Right Practical Reason.* Oxford: Clarendon Press, 1984.

Williams, A. N. "Deification in the *Summa Theologiae:* A Structural Interpretation of the Prima Pars." *The Thomist* 61 (1997): 219–55.

Wippel, John. *Metaphysical Thought of Thomas Aquinas: From Finite Being to Uncreated Being.* Washington, D.C.: The Catholic University of America Press, 2000.

———. "Thomas Aquinas and Participation." In *Studies in Medieval Philosophy,* ed. John Wippel, 117–58. Washington, D.C.: The Catholic University of America Press, 1987.

———. *Thomas Aquinas on the Divine Ideas.* Toronto: Pontifical Institute of Mediaeval Studies, 1993.

INDEX

Perfecting Human Actions: St. Thomas Aquinas on Human Participation in Eternal Law was designed and typeset in ITC Galliard with Requiem display type by Kachergis Book Design of Pittsboro, North Carolina. It was printed on 60-pound EB Natural and bound by Edwards Brothers of Lillington, North Carolina.